STANDARD COOKING MEASURES

(approximate)

3 teaspoons (t) equals 1 tablespoon (T)

2 tablespoons equals 1/8 cup (C)

4 tablespoons equals 1/4 cup

5 tablespoons plus 1 teaspoon equals 1/3 cup

16 tablespoons equals 1 cup

1 cup equals 8 ounces (liquid measure)

2 cups equals 1 pint (pt)

4 cups equals 1 quart (qt)

4 quarts equals 1 gallon (gal)

1000 milligrams (mg) equals 1 gram (gm)

28 grams equals 1 ounce (oz.) (weight measure)

16 ounces (weight measure) equals 1 pound (lb)

1 fluid ounce equals 2 tablespoons

Dash or pinch equals less than 1/8 teaspoon

OVEN TEMPERATURES

Degrees Fahrenheit

Very slow oven/250-275

Slow oven/300-325

Moderate oven/350-375

Hot oven/400-425

Very hot oven/450-475

Extremely hot oven/500-525

Recipes given in this book are starred
* when reference is made to them in the text. The recipes are
indexed separately, in the back of the book.

THE LOW FAT, LOW CHOLESTEROL DIET

THE LOW FAT,

Introduction by JOHN W. GOFMAN, Ph.D., M.D.,
Professor of Medical Physics,
University of California, Berkeley

and HARDIN B. JONES, Ph.D.,
Professor of Medical Physics and Physiology,
Assistant Director, Donner Laboratory,
University of California, Berkeley

and THOMAS P. LYON, M.D., F.A.C.C.,
Assistant Clinical Professor of Medicine,
University of California Medical School,
San Francisco

Doubleday & Company, Inc.,

LOW CHOLESTEROL DIET

What to Eat and How to Prepare It

Clara-Beth Young Bond R.D., CONSULTING DIETITIAN, SACRAMENTO

E. Virginia Dobbin R.D., former SENIOR DIETITIAN, E. V. COWELL
MEMORIAL HOSPITAL, UNIVERSITY OF CALIFORNIA, BERKELEY

Helen F. Gofman, M.D., SAN FRANCISCO

Helen C. Jones, HOME ECONOMIST, BERKELEY

Lenore Lyon, HOMEMAKER, SAN JOSE, CALIFORNIA

Garden City, New York

TO

OUR FAMILIES

Contents

Section II

The recipe for items marked with a star (★) may be located
by consulting the Index.

Introduction

TWENTY YEARS AGO the authors of this book decided to make available their experiences with low fat, low cholesterol diets—experiences that were at that time based upon early research findings concerning the causes of coronary heart attacks and atherosclerosis (hardening of the arteries) and the possible prevention and treatment of these diseases by dietary means.

It is most gratifying that thousands of physicians and many tens of thousands of patients have found this book a highly practical and authoritative guide in the preparation of enjoyable foods in a dietary approach to the prevention of heart disease. Even more gratifying is the fact that what was then early research concerning heart disease has now become established medical practice.

Then the evidence was highly suggestive that high blood concentrations of cholesterol (especially in certain forms known as lipoproteins) predisposed people to early development of heart disease; today this is well established and beyond any reasonable doubt. Further, the type of diet described in this book has been demonstrated to be a highly practical, effective, and safe approach to reducing the forms of blood cholesterol implicated in heart disease, and the reduction in cholesterol level can be maintained for as long as the diet is followed. Large scale studies have been under way throughout the world to determine precisely how effective dietary approaches are in reducing the incidence of heart attacks. While these studies are still in progress, most medical authorities feel the evidence and logic are so overwhelmingly in favor of this dietary approach that persons should use the diet now. The consensus of medical opinion is that there is much to be gained and nothing to lose.

In the period intervening since the first edition, one discovery has been made that simplifies the dietary approach and at the same time makes it much more enjoyable. This is the discovery that certain fats, namely, the unsaturated oils of vegetable origin, need *not* be restricted;

thus the diet can be low *saturated* fat, low cholesterol and still achieve the desired results.

The allowance of certain vegetable oils plus the recent availability of certain foods in the market, together, make many new recipes possible and the diet much easier to follow for patients and for entire families. The authors have, in this new edition, brought together all this new information plus the latest knowledge of nutritional requirements in the preparation of this useful guide for the person who is following a low saturated fat, low cholesterol diet in a program aimed at prevention of coronary heart attacks.

JOHN W. GOFMAN, Ph.D., M.D.,
Professor of Medical Physics,
University of California, Berkeley

ELEVATED LEVELS of the blood fats and blood pressure are related to destructive accumulation of excesses of fats together with other substances in the walls of arteries and cause deterioration in other vital tissues. Measurement of the blood levels of cholesterol and neutral fat or of the lipoproteins which carry the blood fats gives an important clue to this tendency and to the possibility of lessening it through dietary corrections. Reduction of such physiological imbalances depends upon the application of natural principles of good hygiene: sound nutrition (adjusted initially to correct previous errors), physical activity, and avoidance of smoking and other abuses so as to keep the body in functional balance. Cardiovascular disease and other degenerative diseases are dramatically less likely to occur with adherence to good hygiene than when the principles of hygiene are violated.

A prime factor in maintaining good hygiene is reduction of the usually high intake of saturated fat and cholesterol through replacement of the animal fats by the relatively unsaturated vegetable oils. Animal fats elevate the blood fat level, and withholding animal fats reduces it. In addition, the more highly unsaturated oils—often referred to as the polyunsaturated oils—seem to have an added beneficial effect on the diet aside from the displacement of saturated fats. Addition of polyunsaturated oils has been found experimentally to cause a lowering of the blood cholesterol. I am pleased that the authors have incorporated these principles in their recipes and menus.

HARDIN B. JONES, Ph.D.
Professor of Medical Physics and Physiology,
Assistant Director, Donner Laboratory,
University of California, Berkeley

FOR MANY YEARS research investigators and clinicians have accumulated a massive volume of data on the causes and prevention of arteriosclerosis (hardening of the arteries) as found in coronary heart disease. From these investigations several factors such as exercise, tensions, smoking, heredity, and diet have emerged as influencing the mortality and morbidity from arteriosclerosis. We have now had over twenty years' clinical experience in testing the effects of a low fat, low cholesterol diet on several thousands of people prone to this disease. Certain conclusions can be drawn. Individuals with high blood cholesterol determinations are more susceptible to early and serious complications of hardening of the arteries, as heart disease and strokes. It therefore follows that the reduction of these elements in the blood would be beneficial. In those countries where the diet is high in animal fats and cholesterol, as in the United States, the incidence of coronary heart disease is proportionately high. Numerous studies have shown that a diet low in saturated fats and cholesterol lowers the blood cholesterol. Our own observations reveal that such a diet, followed carefully, retards the progression of arteriosclerosis (coronary heart disease). Fortunately, it has been found that the substitution of unsaturated vegetable oils for animal fats makes the diet more palatable. Of course, overweight must be avoided, and the indiscriminate use of high calorie foods is forbidden.

With the many acceptable foods now available, the diet is not difficult to follow. In its simplest form, if one takes his daily quota of animal fat and cholesterol in lean meat only, he can easily substitute unsaturated fats and other foods to make a balanced diet with adequate calories, vitamins, and other nutritional requirements. This cookbook provides a variety of menus suitable for anyone on a low saturated fat, low cholesterol diet.

THOMAS P. LYON, M.D., F.A.C.C.,
Assistant Clinical Professor of Medicine,
University of California Medical School,
San Francisco

ACKNOWLEDGMENTS

The calculations in this book are based on figures in United States Department of Agriculture publications:

Composition of Foods, Handbook ⅜8
Bernice K. Watt, Annabel L. Merrill with the assistance of Rebecca Picot, Catherine Adams, Martha Louise Orr, Donald Miller; Agricultural Research Service. 1963.

Nutritive Value of Foods, Home and Garden Bulletin ⅜72. Agricultural Research Service. 1964.

Revised Booklets on Fat-Controlled Meat, Marjorie C. Zukel, Journal of American Dietetic Association, January 1969, Vol. 54, ⅜1.

Composition of Loma Linda Foods, International Nutrition Research Foundation, Loma Linda Foods, Riverside, California.

Additional cholesterol values are based on analyses by Dr. Ruth Okey, Professor Emeritus of Nutritional Science and Biochemistry, University of California, Berkeley.

We gratefully acknowledge the generosity of the following for the use of their material:

Dairy Council of California

American Heart Association and its affiliates

Loma Linda Foods

National Live Stock and Meat Board

Oklahoma Agricultural Experiment Station

Oroweat Baking Company

University of California Agricultural Extension Service

United States Department of Agriculture

United States Department of the Interior (material on fish)

Special thanks also for their assistance to:

Mrs. Kenneth Mirk

Mr. Alexander Grendon

Mrs. Constance Hibbard

Section I

CHAPTER I

About This Book

In 1950, when we began the first edition of this book, a diet low in fat and cholesterol was totally unfamiliar to most people. Our book was the result of research then being carried on at the University of California's Donner Laboratory on the relationship of cholesterol and fats to atherosclerosis (hardening of the arteries). As part of that research, groups of people lived on low fat, low cholesterol meals prepared by the dietary department of Cowell Memorial Hospital, University of California. The dietetic data accumulated by Cowell Hospital and our own experiences in preparing palatable and interesting foods suited to that restricted diet formed the basis of our first edition.

It now seems desirable to revise our book and bring it up to date. Current research indicates that, while saturated fats (mostly of animal origin) and cholesterol must still be carefully restricted, polyunsaturated fats (most of the vegetable fats) can be admitted to the diet in moderate amounts with beneficial effects. This new scientific data has allowed us to make the diet more varied and inviting.

Many physicians are recommending a low saturated fat, low cholesterol diet not only for patients with evident cardiovascular disease but also as a preventive measure for persons believed to be suspectible to these diseases. Anyone who, for whatever reason, must follow a diet low in saturated fats and cholesterol will find this book helpful, stimulating, and encouraging.

What we eat is determined by the food practices of the area in which we live as well as by habits passed on to us from parents and grandparents. With the advent of machinery, we have grown sedentary; yet we eat as though we had acquired hearty appetites from outdoor muscular work. The average person in America seems to prefer those foods which are high in saturated fat and cholesterol. It is not easy to change food habits, for we like the foods to which we are accustomed. Planning and some effort are required to make changes.

To those who are unfamiliar with the principles of this diet, it might seem that omitting butter, egg yolks, whole milk, cream and other foods high in saturated fat from your menus would eliminate the foods upon which you depend for good cooking. We will show you how it is possible to eliminate these foods and still serve attractive, nourishing, and tempting meals to your family without complicating your work in the kitchen. Our menus and recipes offer an adequate and healthful diet for the entire family, so that the homemaker is not confronted with the problem of preparing separate meals for the dieter. The Daily Food Guides have been carefully checked by the dietitians of our group for adequacy of vitamins, minerals, and proteins that today's homemaker knows are important for good health.

For most people, the low saturated fat, low cholesterol diet is a change from accustomed food habits. It controls the consumption of saturated fat and cholesterol by putting a limit on the amount of meat consumed, eliminating other saturated fat foods, and replacing the saturated fats with polyunsaturated fats. Remember, however, that dieting is an individual matter, and it is up to your physician to prescribe which Daily Food Guide you should follow and what change, if any, should be made in it.

The foods necessary for this diet are now widely available on grocery shelves. Care in selection is essential, however. There are many products labeled "low fat." Some are acceptable in this diet, but others are not. In the following chapters we tell you which foods contain cholesterol, saturated fat, and polyunsaturated fat and to what extent, how to choose acceptable foods, how to make substitutions, and how to modify favorite recipes. We tell you what fats to use and how much of them, how to limit the kind and amount of meat while continuing to enjoy your meals and how to read the labels to see which packaged foods are acceptable. We warn you of "bewares" in food buying. We show you many pleasing and dietetically acceptable ways to use oil in preparing food and give you many more useful food facts.

We do not intend this book to be a complete cookbook. It is a compilation of what we have discovered from sifting our trials and errors and pooling our experiences. The Daily Food Guides are suggestions and examples of the low saturated fat, low cholesterol diet and provide a pattern to help you adjust your cooking and eating habits. We believe that you will find this book a guide and reference to assist you in following your doctor's directions and an aid in preparing delicious meals that meet the requirements of a low saturated fat, low cholesterol diet.

CHAPTER II

Fats and Cholesterol

It is believed by a large number of medical authorities that an upset in the body's capacity to handle cholesterol and saturated fats in the normal manner is the cause of atherosclerosis and its serious consequences. Atherosclerosis is a form of arteriosclerosis (hardening of the arteries) in which the arteries become so lined with deposits of cholesterol compounds and fatty materials that the blood flow is restricted. Saturated fats and cholesterol are being formed continually in the body from other food substances as a normal process. Excessive dietary intake of cholesterol and saturated fat is associated with a tendency to increase the blood lipids (fatty substance) and cholesterol.

In planning a diet low in saturated fat and cholesterol, it is of vital importance to know in what foods these substances occur. *Saturated fats* and *cholesterol* are found in varying amounts in all tissues of *animal* origin. In addition, *saturated fats* are also found in *some vegetable fats*.

Cholesterol

Cholesterol, a waxy chemical substance, is an essential structural component of animal tissues. It is formed in the tissues of animals (including humans) even though they eat no saturated fat or cholesterol. It is fat soluble and occurs in varying concentrations in the blood and other tissues of all animals. Plants do not contain cholesterol.

The cholesterol content is high in foods of animal origin, especially in visible fat such as butter, cream, and the fat on meat. It can also be high in foods that are not particularly fatty in appearance, as lobster, liver, kidney, egg yolk, and brain. Egg yolk and brain are especially high in cholesterol. Foods from animal sources vary considerably in the amount of cholesterol they contain, as can be noted in the table in Section III, pages 484–85, where it may be seen that cholesterol is present only in foods from animal sources (meat, fish, poultry, eggs, and dairy products).

Fats

The term *fat* applies to the oils as well as the solid fats. Saturation of a fat is a matter of degree, from completely saturated to highly unsaturated. This depends upon the fat's composition (its fatty acid content). For a more complete discussion, read pages 461–463 in Section III.

In preparing a low saturated fat, low cholesterol diet, our main concern is to use the *polyunsaturated* fats (those containing a high percentage of unsaturated fatty acids) and to reduce the *saturated* fats (those containing a high percentage of saturated fatty acids).

The polyunsaturated fats are used because research indicates they do not tend to raise blood lipids or cholesterol and may lower elevated blood lipids and cholesterol, especially when substituted for a substantial part of the saturated fat in the diet. *Saturated fats are restricted,* as they tend to raise blood lipids and cholesterol. Present research seems to indicate that those fats which are only slightly unsaturated (*monounsaturated*) have little effect in lowering blood lipids and cholesterol. Thus the use of polyunsaturated fat is preferred in this diet. (Olive oil is the most commonly used mono-unsaturated fat. The oils in avocados, olives, and most nuts are principally mono-unsaturates.)

What Are the Saturated Fats? (Restrict These)

All fats of animal origin contain some saturated fats. Most are high in saturated fat, such as the fats in whole milk, cream, cheese, butter, and the visible and invisible fat in meats (including cooking fats, such as lard, suet, bacon drippings, and chicken fat). In addition, *some vegetable fats* contain large amounts of saturated fats. The most common ones are solid vegetable shortenings (hydrogenated vegetable oils*), coconut oil, palm oil, and cocoa butter. (Chocolate is high in cocoa butter.)

What Are the Polyunsaturated Fats? (Use These)

They are usually liquid oils of *vegetable origin.*

Those most commonly used in cooking are: corn, cottonseed, safflower, sesame seed, soybean, and sunflower seed oils. These contain a high percentage of unsaturated fatty acids and a low percentage of saturated fatty acids. Walnut oil and some fish fats are highly polyunsaturated.

* See Section III, page 462.

Fats, and foods containing fats, vary considerably in their degree of saturation, as you can see from the tables in Chapter XXXII, pages 484–90. It is not possible to eliminate saturated fats and cholesterol completely from your diet, as they occur to some extent in many essential foods. In the following chapters we will help you learn how to serve delicious food and nutritious meals restricting the use of saturated fat and high cholesterol foods and using the polyunsaturated fats.

How Much Fat and Cholesterol Is Allowed?

This is an individual matter and depends upon your physician's recommendation.

Our most liberal Daily Food Guide allows: 200 milligrams of cholesterol and 30–35 per cent of the total day's calories in fat, with about twice as much polyunsaturated fat as saturated.

Your physician may recommend a more liberal or restricted diet depending on your needs.†

† See page 24.

CHAPTER III

What Foods to Use (and not to use)

WHAT FOODS to eat (and what not to eat) is a question for those on a low fat, low cholesterol diet. Two generalizations are: *restrict* the foods high in saturated fat or cholesterol; and *use* the polyunsaturated fats, in the amounts prescribed by your physician. (See Chapter IV, page 24, for our Daily Food Guides.)

What are the foods high in saturated fat and cholesterol? What about the polyunsaturated fats? How can I tell what products to choose from all those on the grocery shelf? In this chapter we answer your questions about acceptable foods for a low saturated fat, low cholesterol diet.

The Following Foods (of Animal Origin) Are High in Saturated Fat or Cholesterol and Should Be Excluded from the Diet

1. Meat fats (see Chapter VIII, page 76, on "What You Should Know About Meat") Cooking fat from any animal, such as lard, suet, bacon drippings, and chicken fat
   Meat fat that can be removed (sometimes called "separable fat")
   Meat highly marbled with fat (this means the fat is distributed throughout the meat and thus cannot be trimmed off)
   Fat in the drippings of meat and meat broth
2. Organ meats, such as brain, heart, liver, kidney, sweetbreads, tripe, giblets, and prepared meats, such as sausages, pressed luncheon meats, etc., that contain organ meats
3. Butterfat, which includes butter, cream, whole milk, and any products containing these
4. Egg yolks*

* See Section I, page 11 and Section III, page 454.

5. Fish roe and caviar
6. Preparations that contain any of the above foods, such as many bakery products, packaged mixes, canned and frozen foods. Read the label or ask the maker for the contents of the product.

Lean red meat, fish, and poultry are included in our Daily Food Guides because they contain complete protein. (See Section III, pages 458–59.) They also contain highly saturated fat and cholesterol, but in smaller amounts than the forbidden foods listed above. Their use is restricted in amount to your dietary allowance of saturated fat and cholesterol. This will be discussed in detail in Chapter IV, page 24.

What Do We Mean by "No Butterfat"?

In this diet butterfat is excluded. That means *no* butter and none of the following:

Cream (sweet, sour, powdered, half and half, whipped, etc.)
Whole milk (fresh, canned, and powdered)
Cultured whole-milk buttermilk (fresh and powdered)
Whole milk yogurt
Creamed cottage cheese
Cream cheese
Whole milk cheeses
Commercial products containing any of the above foods, as:
    Ice cream and ice milk
    Ice cream drinks such as sodas and floats
    Certain sherbets
    Malted milk and milk shakes
    Most chocolate milk
    Certain filled milks
    Certain chocolate-drink powders
    Certain milk chocolate
    Certain canned soups
    Certain cake, muffin, pancake, and waffle mixes
    Certain pudding powders
    Certain canned puddings
    Certain canned breads
    Certain bakery items
    Certain diet foods

Milk that has had the cream poured off is not satisfactory for this diet, since only about one half the butterfat can be thus removed.

Skim milk, as purchased from the dairy, *canned evaporated skim milk,* or *powdered skim milk* contains essentially no butterfat and is a valuable part of the low saturated fat, low cholesterol diet. Skim milk that has been fortified only with skim milk solids (powdered skim milk) and vitamins is excellent to use, but avoid fortified milk made with whole or only partially skim milk. Milk labeled as "low fat" is a mixture of whole and skim milk and should not be used. Do not use powdered milk that contains any whole milk—check the label.

"Filled" milks on the market are a combination of skim milk and vegetable oil. Beware of these! Sometimes this oil is coconut or a hydrogenated oil, both highly saturated fats. Nondairy imitation milks should not be used as a milk substitute in this diet. They often contain a saturated vegetable fat—coconut or palm oil.

Buttermilk varies in butterfat content. Some of the cultured buttermilk sold in the United States is made from fresh skim milk and some from part skim and *part whole milk.* Check with your dairy. We found some cultured buttermilk in our area contained about 1.5 per cent butterfat—¾ teaspoon of fat in eight ounces of buttermilk. By various methods butter granules are sometimes added and should be strained out before the buttermilk is used. Churned buttermilk can be negligible in fat after the flecks of butter are strained out. The powdered buttermilk on the market is economical and handy to use in cooking. Do not use it if it contains more than 1 per cent butterfat. Check with the manufacturer. We hope that a powdered, skim milk buttermilk will become available.

Yogurt sold as "low fat" is usually made with fresh *partially* skim milk and may be fortified by the addition of nonfat dry milk. Until commercial skim milk yogurt is readily available, "low fat" yogurt will have to do for those who "eat out." Yogurt is easy to make at home from fresh or powdered skim milk. We have found the yogurt makers for home use which are on the market to be very practical. See page 64. Yogurt can be used in many recipes as a substitute for sour cream.

Cottage cheese curd is made from skim milk and contains essentially no fat or cholesterol. It is available commercially at most dairies and in some markets. (Directions for making a palatable cottage cheese and for use of the cottage cheese curd in interesting dishes will be given later in this book.) If cottage cheese curd is not available, a satisfactory substitute may be obtained by washing the commercial "low fat" cottage cheese to remove the cream.

Cottage cheese consists of curd with added cream or milk and hence varies in butterfat content. Creamed cottage cheese should not be used because of its high butterfat content. "Low fat" cottage cheese contains less cream plus some milk. For home consumption we recommend you wash off the cream and milk and eat only the curd.

Cheese is usually high in butterfat so that most cheeses must be avoided. Cottage cheese curd is one of the exceptions. As we have discussed, it is excellent for use in a low saturated fat, low cholesterol diet. In the form of baker's cheese, it is smooth and moist and can be used in much the same way as cottage cheese which has been smoothed in the blender. Bakers use it, especially in cheesecake, and it is available in some delicatessens. Check to be sure it is made entirely from skim milk.

Other skim milk or whey cheeses just aren't readily available. Some are made in foreign countries, but they vary in fat content and are hard to find in delicatessens here. Some cheeses on the market which are said to be skim milk cheeses are actually made with *part* skim milk and may be high in butterfat. We hope good domestic skim milk and whey cheeses will become more available.

Ice cream is excluded because of its high butterfat content. Ice milk and many commercial sherbets are made with whole milk and are, therefore, not acceptable. They vary in fat content as extra fat may be added, usually the highly saturated fat coconut oil.

At present most of the commercial *imitation* ice creams are made with saturated fat—either coconut oil or hydrogenated vegetable oil. We are hoping a product acceptable for use in this diet will be made commercially. In the meantime, make your own using the recipes we give in the dessert chapter.

There are delicious commercial water ices and fruit juice bars on the market acceptable for use in this diet.

What Do We Mean by "No Egg Yolks"?

This means *no egg yolk in any form,* fresh, frozen or dried— including commercial products in which egg yolks or whole eggs are used, such as:

Ice cream
Certain cake, pancake, and waffle mixes
Certain baked goods
Egg noodles
Certain canned soups
Some salad dressings

Egg whites, fresh,* frozen or powdered, are highly desirable to use, since they contain no fat or cholesterol and are a good source of protein. In addition, they are a great help in preparing foods for this diet —especially breads and desserts. Also, try Special Scrambled Eggs★ or Stuffed Eggs★.† See pages 66–67 for some extra tips on using egg whites.

What Do We Mean by "No Organ Meats"?

Organ meats, including brain, heart, kidney, liver, lung, sweetbreads (both pancreas and thymus), tripe, and giblets, are not to be used. Organ meats are all much higher in cholesterol content than animal muscle meat. Prepared meat products that may contain fairly large amounts of ground organ meats are: liverwurst, sausages, frankfurters, and many pressed luncheon meats. You may be able to find a sausage maker in your area who will make frankfurters on special order out of very lean beef and pork.

Cholesterol is not soluble in water, so meat broths made from organ meats, such as giblets, may be used provided the fat and meat particles are *thoroughly* removed from the broth. Follow the directions on page 135 "How to make giblet broth for gravy."

The Following Vegetable Fats, Because of Their High Saturated Fat Content, Should Be Avoided

1. Coconut oil, including coconut in any form
2. Cocoa butter, including chocolate (because of its high cocoa butter content)
3. Palm oil (used in some bakery goods and nondairy imitation milk and cream)
4. Hydrogenated vegetable fat. This includes the solid vegetable shortenings and many margarines. Read the discussion on pages 14–15.
5. Products containing the above. If the label merely says "vegetable oil," check with the manufacturer to see *what kind* of vegetable oil the product contains. Saturated vegetable fats are found in many commercial food preparations. If you aren't sure of the fat in a food, our advice is not to use it, as there are many acceptable products on the market.

* See "Feed Plants with Egg Yolks," pages 470–71.
† Whenever we refer to one of our own recipes in the text, it is starred. The recipes are indexed.

What Do We Mean by "Avoid Coconut Oil"?

Coconut oil is much higher in saturated fatty acids than any of the other commonly used fats, including animal fats. See the chart, page 490. Do not use coconut oil, coconut meat in any form, or products containing these. Coconut oil has a good keeping quality and thus is often used in fillings and coatings of commercially baked goods and candy or in packaged products. It is sometimes used in ice milk, "filled" milk, and nondairy imitation milk and cream, including pressure-canned dessert toppings. Coconut oil or other saturated fats are often used for commercially fried and roasted products, such as chips, nuts, fish, and potatoes. Do not use these. Even if the manufacturer's label says "vegetable oil," don't assume that it is a polyunsaturated vegetable oil; it may be one of the saturated oils. The only way to tell is to check with the manufacturer to see *what* vegetable oil the product contains.

What Do We Mean by "Avoid Cocoa Butter and Chocolate"?

Cocoa butter is the pure fat extracted from the cacao bean. Except for coconut oil, it is higher in saturated fatty acids than any of the other commonly used fats. Cocoa butter is frequently used in candies and is one of the main ingredients in chocolate. Chocolate and other products containing cocoa butter should not be eaten on this diet. Again, avoid products that merely say "vegetable oil" unless you are sure the oil is polyunsaturated.

Cocoa is chocolate minus some of the cocoa butter and therefore is lower in saturated fat than chocolate. Cocoa is about 4 per cent to 11 per cent or more fat, and chocolate 30 per cent or more. Many commonly used brands of cocoa are comparatively low in saturated fat, while other brands of "breakfast cocoa" are higher. Small amounts of a cocoa *low in fat* would add little saturated fat to the diet and may be acceptable—depending on your daily saturated fat and caloric allowance.

Compare the saturated fat content in two cakes! The first is an average recipe for chocolate cake and frosting found in any cookbook. (Just the ingredients containing saturated fat are listed.) The second is modified, using low fat cocoa, egg whites, polyunsaturated vegetable oil, and skim milk. (The dessert chapter, page 292, gives recipes for delicious cakes modified for this diet.)

Chocolate cake	Sat. Fat (gm)	Choles- terol (mg)	Modified Cake	Sat. Fat (gm)	Choles- terol (mg)
3 squares chocolate	2	0	⅓ cup (1 ounce) cocoa	2	0
½ cup butter	50	281	½ cup vege- table oil	0	0
2 eggs	4	550	Egg whites	0	0
1 cup whole milk	6	27	Skim milk	0	7
Chocolate Frosting			Seven-minute icing		
2 squares chocolate	16	0	Egg whites	0	0
2 tablespoons butter	12	70	Sugar	0	0
1 cup whole milk	6	27			
	118	955		2	7

Not only has the saturated fat dropped by modifying the ingredients, but the cholesterol as well, from 955 milligrams to 7!

What Do We Mean by "Avoid Solid Vegetable Fats"?

Vegetable oils are hardened by a process called "hydrogenation" in which they become more saturated. How saturated the oil becomes depends upon how nearly completely it has been hydrogenated (see pages 462–63). The degree of hardness of a hydrogenated fat is usually some indication of the degree of saturation. The label on products containing hydrogenated fats often says "hydrogenated vegetable oil" or "hardened" vegetable oil. Highly hydrogenated oils and products containing them should be avoided. Since labels do not state the kind and amount of the fatty acid content of a product, it is difficult to tell how fully hydrogenated or saturated or polyunsaturated a product is.

Here are some cautions about products that *may* contain large amounts of hydrogenated vegetable oil:

Vegetable shortenings that are solid are likely to be highly hydro-genated and should not be used. Some newer products available are partially hydrogenated oil—some say "highly unsaturated," but they still are not nearly as unsaturated as the polyunsaturated oils. Since the oils are so satisfactory and beneficial to use, our advice would be not to use the solid vegetable shortenings. Many products contain these. Read the label.

Many margarines contain large amounts of hydrogenated vegetable oil, and they, and products containing them, should not be used.

(There are many brands of acceptable margarines on the market. See the section on "special" margarines, pages 16–17.)

Imitation dairy products, such as imitation cream, imitation sour cream, imitation ice cream, and whips usually contain saturated fats in the form of hydrogenated oil or coconut oil and should not be used.

From the discussion so far in this chapter of fats to avoid, it may seem there are none left to use on a low saturated fat, low cholesterol diet. On the contrary, there are many acceptable fats for this diet and products containing them, with new products appearing on the grocery shelves constantly.

Use Polyunsaturated Fat for This Diet

As we have said before, fats vary in their degree of saturation, and it is to your advantage to use those with the highest percentage of polyunsaturated fatty acids. These are usually *liquid oils* of vegetable origin.* (See the chart on page 490 for the polyunsaturated fatty acid content of oils.)

Use These Oils—They Are Highest in Polyunsaturates

Corn
Cottonseed
Safflower
Sesame seed (not readily available for home use)
Soybean
Sunflower seed (not readily available for home use)
Walnut (most highly polyunsaturated of all the oils but not readily available for home use)

Use the above oils in your cooking and buy the products that contain them. If products contain polyunsaturated oil, the label should state this or say *"liquid* corn (cottonseed, safflower, etc.) oil."

In this book when we say add or use oil, we mean only the polyunsaturated oils.

Sometimes these oils have been partially or completely hydrogenated, making them more saturated and thus more solid. You have already read about this in the section on avoiding solid vegetable fats, page 14. Some salad and cooking oils have been lightly hydrogenated. Some

---

* Coconut oil is an exception and, as discussed earlier in this chapter, *must not* be used on this diet. Even though it is liquid at room temperature, it is *highly* saturated.

are labeled as "specially processed." Unless you know what the process-
ing does to the oil, use the unprocessed polyunsaturated oils.

It is important for you *each day to use all the polyunsaturated fat
recommended in the Daily Food Guides* prescribed by your physician.
The polyunsaturated fat is carefully calculated in our Daily Food
Guides and is an *essential* part of a low saturated fat, low cholesterol
diet.

Polyunsaturated oils can be used in most dishes requiring fat, such
as: in salad dressings, sautéing vegetables, in "cream" sauces, soups,
gravies, potato dishes, baked goods, casserole dishes, pancakes, waffles,
etc. See all of our recipes!

When cooking with oil, *do not overheat* it until it smokes or burns,
as some of the polyunsaturates in the fat are destroyed. Bring up the
heat slowly and watch carefully. Avoid using packaged fried foods
such as potato chips, French fries, and other deep-fried snacks, as
the oil used probably was a saturated one or it has become saturated
by prolonged heating. Also, it is difficult to measure the *amount* of oil
absorbed by the food.

Light tends to reduce the degree of polyunsaturation of oil. Some
brands are marketed in dark-colored bottles. Store oil in a dark place.

Other Oils

Olive oil, peanut oil, and rice oil are low in polyunsaturated fatty
acids (high in monounsaturated fatty acids; see pages 6 and 490) and
cannot take the place of the recommended oils for a low saturated
fat, low cholesterol diet.

Mineral oil is completely indigestible in the body and is not classified
as a food. *Do not use it* as an oil for this diet.

When Is a Margarine "Special"?

"Special" margarines are made in which polyunsaturated oil is substituted during the manufacturing process for some of the hydrogenated
(saturated) vegetable fat found in regular margarines. These are permitted on this diet, depending on your dietary allowance of fat and
calories. *Do not use the regular margarines.* The "special" margarines
are higher in polyunsaturated fats than regular margarines but not as
high as the polyunsaturated oils. (See the fatty acid content of fats and
oils on page 490 in Section III.) We allow some "special" margarine
to be used on this diet where oil is not a satisfactory substitute, as for
a spread on bread. "Special" margarines vary in their polyunsaturated
content depending on the kind and proportion of oil used. We call
the margarines "special" if they contain 25 per cent or more *highly*

unsaturated liquid oil and *no more than* 25 per cent saturated fat. Some "special" margarines on the market contain over 40 per cent highly unsaturated liquid oil. This information is not given on the labels. "Special" margarines list *liquid* corn, cottonseed, safflower, etc., oils as the *first* ingredient and *partially hydrogenated* or *hardened* polyunsaturated oils as additional ingredients. This means there is more liquid polyunsaturated than hydrogenated saturated oil present. *Look at the first ingredient listed as a clue when selecting your margarine!* Most of the "special" margarines are in tubs. Not all tub margarines are acceptable—read the label. At present the ones highest in polyunsaturates and lowest in saturates contain *liquid* corn or safflower oil. You will know the margarine is "special" but not *how* "special."

Until more information is given on labels, your dietitian or local heart association may be able to help you select a margarine with the highest percentage of polyunsaturated fatty acids. New products appear on the market and formulas of existing products change, so it is impractical for us to publish a list of brand names.

"Low calorie" margarines that are on the market contain higher percentages of water and air than the regular or "special" margarines. Thus, they are lower in fat and calories, especially if measured by volume. If you use one of these "special" low calorie margarines, you should use about twice as much by volume as the amount of "special" margarine to get the same amount of fats and oils.

What About Nuts?

Nuts are high in fat and are a fair source of protein. They vary in their saturated fat content and in the ratio of polyunsaturated fat to saturated fat. See the table in Section III, page 487. Most of the commonly used nuts are high in *monounsaturated fat* (see page 6). Coconuts are an exception and, as we have stressed, must not be used for this diet due to their high saturated fat content. Avoid peanuts, cashews and Brazil nuts, as they contain at least twice as much saturated fat as most of the other commonly used nuts.

Almonds, beechnuts, filberts (hazelnuts), hickory nuts, pecans, and pistachio nuts are in the same range of saturated fat as walnuts but are lower in polyunsaturated fat.

We highly recommend the use of *walnuts* in this diet, as we feel that, when there is such a satisfactory nut, it should be used in preference to others. They are the highest by far in polyunsaturated fat of the commonly used nuts and are versatile in cooking.

The use of nuts in this diet will depend upon the kind of nut used and on your fat and calorie allowance. Use them raw, roasted in the shell, or dry roasted, to make sure that no fats or oils have been used during roasting. Avoid regular roasted nuts, which may have been roasted in butter, coconut oil, or other saturated fats. One tablespoon chopped nuts contains approximately one teaspoon oil and fifty calories.

As has been discussed above, peanuts are high in saturated fat. Most of the peanut butters in the market have additional saturated fat because some of the peanut oil has been hydrogenated. Walnut Butter★ is delicious! Since walnuts contain only half as much saturated fat as peanuts and are high in polyunsaturates, we recommend using walnut butter (or butters made from other acceptable nuts) if your calorie and fat allowance permits.

What About Avocados and Olives?

Avocados and olives add fat (2 to 3 per cent is saturated) to the diet without adding any significant amount of polyunsaturated fat. A large percentage of their fat is *monounsaturated*. See pages 6 and 487.

How much avocado or olives you eat depends entirely upon your dietary fat and calorie allowance. Those of you on a diet of 1800 calories or more may substitute 5 or 6 small olives or one ounce (2 tablespoons) of avocado served with ½ tablespoon Basic French Dressing★ for 1 tablespoon of the "special" margarine in your diet.*

What About Commercial Mayonnaise?

The amount of egg yolk in one serving is negligible. Commercial mayonnaise in moderation is allowed when you eat out. For home use we have excellent mayonnaise recipes on pages 241 and 242 using polyunsaturated oil and egg whites. Try some of our other salad dressing recipes!

SUMMARY

In this chapter we have told you what foods to use and what foods should be avoided. In summary, the rules are:

1. From animal sources (meat, eggs, and dairy products). Most foods in this group are high in cholesterol and saturated fat and must not be used.

Use these foods:

Egg white	
Gelatin	These foods contain *no* cholesterol
Clear meat broth	or saturated fat.

---

* The dressing is needed for its polyunsaturated oil content to equal that in the "special" margarine.

Skim milk

Skim milk buttermilk

Skim milk cheese—cottage cheese curd, baker's and other
   true skim milk cheeses, if available

Skim milk yogurt

Small amounts of lean meat are included in this diet because it contains complete protein, but no more than the specified amounts should be used, since it also contains saturated fat and cholesterol.

2. From vegetable sources (all plants). No foods from vegetable sources contain cholesterol. A few such as coconut and coconut oil, cocoa butter including chocolate, palm oil, and hydrogenated vegetable fat are high in saturated fat and must not be used. Some foods, such as avocados, olives, and some nuts, are high in monounsaturated fat and should be restricted. See page 16 concerning olive, peanut, and rice oils.

Use these foods:

Fruits (see page 18 concerning avocados and olives)

Grains and cereals

Sugars

Vegetables

Walnuts (see page 17 concerning these and other nuts)

Use the highly polyunsaturated oils. These have a special place in this diet. See page 15.

Our Daily Food Guides specify how much of the above foods to use, and Chapter VI gives directions for using some of the special suggested foods.

Food charts will assist you in determining what foods are low in cholesterol and saturated fat and what foods are high in polyunsaturated fat.* Use only reliable sources such as the government publications, since we found some of the popular charts on the market contain inaccurate information. Consult the mini chart on page 484 and the other charts and tables in Chapter XXXII. See pages 482–83 for information concerning the government publications.

READ THE LABELS

Since the writing of our first *Low Fat, Low Cholesterol Diet* book in 1950, hundreds of food products have come on the market. Many are acceptable for use on this diet and have helped tremendously in food preparation. Many are not acceptable.

* When consulting the food charts, remember that linoleic acid is *polyunsaturated* and oleic is *monounsaturated.*

As we have said many times before in this chapter, reading the food labels is essential in selecting acceptable products for a low saturated fat, low cholesterol diet. Approach label reading as a challenge! This is what it is with all of the food products now available—fresh, frozen, dried, packaged, and canned. Labels are loaded with information, but the challenge is to interpret the information and to detect what may be missing.

After years of label-reading, we still are in doubt about many products because:

> Some labels do not list the ingredients.
> Some labels list ingredients but do not tell enough about them.
> One may not be familiar with some of the terms used to describe ingredients or processes.

Our advice is: **if in doubt, do not use the food product.**

Before you start reading labels, you have to know what may be used and what may not be used on a low saturated fat, low cholesterol diet. This chapter is a compilation of information we feel would be most helpful to you in selecting foods for this diet. You will probably read and reread it and refer to it from time to time. At first you will just use the products easiest to recognize as acceptable. As you become more familiar with the foods to use and not to use, you will become more skilled at label-reading and will find it fun to venture out and find new products to use.

One of our frustrations in food selection is with the vegetable fats and products containing them because:

Manufacturers do not label vegetable oil products with their actual polyunsaturated and saturated fatty acid content.

Manufacturers do not always state when one of the *highly saturated* vegetable oils is used. The label may merely say "vegetable oil."

Beware of products when the label says:

> "vegetable oil"—it could be highly hydrogenated or one of the highly saturated vegetable oils such as coconut oil.
> "vegetable fat"—it probably is one of the saturated ones.
> "liquid vegetable oil"—it could be coconut oil.
> "specially processed" on a bottle of an otherwise acceptable liquid oil. The process may be hydrogenation. Even if lightly hydrogenated, the unhydrogenated oil is higher in polyunsaturates.
> "highly unsaturated"—this often is said of vegetable shortenings that have in fact almost as much hydrogenated as unhydrogenated

oil. Again, the unhydrogenated oils should be preferred for this diet.

"hardened"

"partially hardened" ⎫ These mean some of the oil has

"hydrogenated" ⎬ been saturated. The label does

"partially hydrogenated" ⎭ not say *how much.*

"lowfat"—what kind and how much? The fat may not be an acceptable one or the content too high for use in this diet.

We have listed the above as examples of the "bewares" in label-reading. *New products appear on the market constantly with new labels and words, and the formulas of existing products change.* It would be almost impossible to make a *complete* list of acceptable foods by brand names. Learn what you are allowed and are not allowed on your diet, then become a good label reader!

Some products that do not have the ingredients adequately labeled as to fat content, or which you are otherwise in doubt about, may actually be acceptable for you to use. We have found the manufacturer often will supply the missing information, or your dietitian may have or be able to get the information you need.

Heart associations, local, state, and national, have excellent materials to help you determine what foods to use and not to use.

MARKETING

After reading (and rereading) this chapter you will be a better informed shopper for a low saturated fat, low cholesterol diet and will consider food purchases in a new light. On your food-shopping trip, you select meats with regard to the amounts of cholesterol and fat they contain. You now notice, as you may never have before, that some tissues of meat are marbled with fat and certain cuts bordered with wide layers of fat. You now look for the lean cuts of meat, such as the leanest center cut of ham; you have your ground meat made from very lean beef or veal in place of ordinary ground meat; you ask for the lower-round corned beef in place of a brisket corned beef, a lean sirloin tip roast or rump beef roast in place of a fat rib roast. You buy more fish and poultry, since you know these to be lower in fat.

At the dairy food counter you limit the purchase of whole milk to that for the children and buy skim milk, skim milk buttermilk, and instant dry nonfat milk for the adults. You appreciate the value of curd cottage cheese and have found many ways to use baker's cheese in food preparation.

You also appreciate the value of the new highly polyunsaturated soft margarines put out in tub containers and bypass the old types of highly hydrogenated margarines. You also bypass vegetable shortenings, lard, and butter but reach for an oil high in polyunsaturates.

From the canned goods shelves you pass up the meat and cream soups and buy those free of animal fat or those from which it can be readily removed. You avoid the sardines packed in olive oil and buy those packed in an acceptable polyunsaturated oil.

At the shelves of convenience foods, such as packaged cake mixes and other handy preparations, you no longer ignore the labels. You buy angel food cake mix instead of other cake mixes. You now thoughtfully read the labels, noting in the list of ingredients egg yolks, whole milk, hydrogenated or hardened fat, etc. You will buy the products that contain polyunsaturated fat or no fat.

If you have been buying frozen precooked TV dinners, you will discontinue this practice since you have no measure of the amount of fat or the identity of the kinds of fat in these meals. Precooked foods from "take-out" stands are likewise unsuitable. You will choose the fruits and vegetables that have been frozen plain and avoid those frozen with butter or in sauces that contain fat.

You read labels and learn not to buy those products you are not sure about. You know that there are suitable substitutes for those products you have to pass up and that, in addition, you can prepare tasty foods for a low saturated fat, low cholesterol diet in your own kitchen.

By wise shopping and proper food preparation, you avoid eating excess saturated fat and cholesterol and you add polyunsaturated fat to your diet. As an example, compare the saturated fat, polyunsaturated fat, and cholesterol in the following supermarket menus.

LUNCH FROM A SUPERMARKET FREEZER

	Protein (grams)	Fat (grams)	Carbo-hydrate (grams)	Sat-urated Fat (grams)	Lin-oleic Acid (grams)	Choles-terol (mg)
Beef stew, a serving containing marbeled beef, 3 ounces, vegetables and gravy—approximately	23	16	3	8		60
Biscuits, made with vegetable shortening—2	6	8	36	2		
Butter, 2 squares		12		5		15
Pumpkin pie, approximately 4 ounce piece	5	12	34	5	1	97
Coffee, 2 cups with 1 tablespoon cream each, (2 tablespoons)	1	4	1	1		9
	35	51	74	21	1	181

Calories, 895

A LOW SATURATED FAT, LOW CHOLESTEROL LUNCH

	Protein (grams)	Fat (grams)	Carbo-hydrate (grams)	Sat-urated Fat (grams)	Lin-oleic Acid (grams)	Choles-terol (mg)
Tomato juice, 1 glass	4		10			
Open-face tuna sandwiches						
Tuna, 2 ounces (drained)	14	3		.6	.2	42
Mayonnaise, 1 tablespoon		14		2	8	
Bread, 2 slices	4		30			
Tossed Greens	1		3			
French Dressing, 1 tablespoon		10		2	6	
Applesauce, ½ cup	1		30			
Skim milk, 1 glass	8		12			7
	32	27	85	4.6	14.2	49

Calories, 711

CHAPTER IV

How to Build an Adequate Diet Low in Cholesterol and Saturated Fat

"IN PLANNING her menus the homemaker's chief concern is to meet her family's nutritional needs with foods they enjoy." This statement is still as true today as it was twenty years ago when we first wrote it in our original *Low Fat, Low Cholesterol Diet*. Today the homemaker still has to exclude butter, cream, whole milk, egg yolk, and organ meats from her menus for anyone on a low saturated fat, low cholesterol diet. Now, however, you can add polyunsaturated oils into the menus and thus make the meals more appetizing. We can give a better answer to the question from our first edition: "How do you plan nutritious menus and still provide pleasing meals?" The new daily food and menu guides in this chapter and in Section III meet the National Research Council's recommended daily allowance for proteins, minerals, and vitamins.* In later chapters we provide interesting, easy-to-follow recipes for delightful foods that are low in cholesterol and saturated fat.

How Much Cholesterol and Total Fat Should I Have in My Diet?

The amount of cholesterol and fat allowed in your diet should be prescribed by your physician. The total cholesterol content of each Daily Food Guide outlined in this chapter is less than 200 milligrams. (Some diets outlined have considerably less.) The Daily Food Guides

---

* Since the study of food and nutrition is an extensive field in itself, it must be noted that this book is presented mainly as a menu-planning and recipe guide to those on a low saturated fat, low cholesterol diet. A nutritional discussion, brief and geared mainly to facts pertinent to the aim of this book, is presented in Chapter XXX.

are planned to provide 30–35 per cent of the total day's calories in fat and to have at least twice as much polyunsaturated fat as saturated.* All numerical values for calorie, fat, cholesterol, and other content of the diets are necessarily approximate but sufficiently accurate for your purposes.

Some individuals may need a more rigid restriction of total fat or cholesterol. Daily Food Guides for such diets are found on page 451 in Section II. On the other hand some physicians may prescribe a more liberal diet. Our Daily Food Guides can easily be liberalized by adding more foods containing cholesterol (see page 454) or additional polyunsaturated fats.

How Many Calories Should I Have in My Diet?

An individual's daily caloric requirement depends on many factors, including size, age, sex, and activity. For this reason each person should consult his physician to determine the approximate calorie prescription needed. In this chapter, two of the Daily Food Guides, Diet I and Diet II, are planned to meet the RDA† caloric requirement for a moderately active 35- to 55-year-old male or female. Other Guides for 1500 calories and 1000 calories are included in this chapter for those who might like to lose a few pounds. Additional low and high calorie Daily Food Guides are outlined in Chapter XXVIII. One should choose the Daily Food Guide to fit your physician's recommendation.

If I Don't Need to Lose or Gain Weight, Which Daily Food Guide Do I Follow?

There are many fortunate people who don't have to "count calories." However, they still must restrict their saturated fat and cholesterol. What should they do? We suggest following these two rules:

For a man:

1. Follow Diet I Daily Food Guide for
   a. Meat, fish, and poultry
      and
   b. Fats and oils
2. Eat any other foods that are acceptable to this low saturated

---

* The 800-calorie diet on page 442 is an exception.
† Recommended Daily Allowances of the National Research Council (see page 472).

fat, low cholesterol diet in normal amounts, but prepare these foods according to the recipes and directions in this book.

For a woman:

1. Follow Diet II Daily Food Guide for
   a. Meat, fish, and poultry
      and
   b. Fats and oils
2. Eat any other foods that are acceptable to this low saturated fat, low cholesterol diet in normal amounts, but prepare these foods according to the recipes and directions in this book. You can adapt the two-week menu suggestions for Diet I (see Chapter V) if you remember to use less oil and one ounce less meat.

How Do I Plan My Menu?

With your Daily Food Guide established, your day's menu should always be planned as a unit. The total amount of food to be eaten, including breakfast, lunch, dinner, and snacks, is stated in your Daily Food Guide. The foods are also categorized into groups in your Daily Food Guide.

For ease in planning menus from physicians' diet orders, the American Dietetic Association arranged most foods into six groups,* meat, milk, vegetables, fruits, breads and cereals, and fats. The foods in each group are similar to each other in their nutritive qualities. For example, in the bread group: 1 serving of whole wheat bread (1 slice) is approximately the same in calorie, vitamin, mineral, protein, fat and carbohydrate content as 1 serving (½ cup) of cooked cereal. The starchy vegetables and grains such as rice are also in the bread group; ½ cup (1 serving) of potatoes has about the same calorie content as 1 slice of bread.

The following examples explain how to use the exchange list. Suppose the Daily Food Guide states "Use 1 serving of the bread and cereal group," and you want potatoes for dinner. The list states that 1 small white potato is the equivalent of 1 serving of the bread and cereal group. On the other hand, suppose you want rice instead of potato. The list states ½ cup of *cooked* rice is equivalent to 1 bread serving. Therefore, you may use either the potato or the rice but not both. In other words, you can exchange one serving of a bread list food—such as sweet potato, corn, bread, crackers, corn bread, biscuits, etc.—for a serving of another food in the bread list group depending on what you want to eat.

* ADA calls its groups "exchange lists."

However, a cup of milk in the milk group cannot be exchanged for a slice of bread in the bread group, for these two foods are not the same in protein, fat, calories, minerals, or vitamins. One must not trade a food for one from a different group unless specifically instructed to do so in the diet.

This arranging of foods into food groups proved very useful in planning reduction diets, restricted sodium diets, and fat-controlled diets. With some modification, a similar grouping of foods is useful in planning low saturated fat, low cholesterol diets. The food groups that we use in the low saturated fat, low cholesterol diet contain only foods allowed on this diet. The foods in each group and the size of a serving for each individual food are listed in Chapter XXXI in Section III. Please try to become familiar with the foods and their different groups; it makes your menu planning easier. This is particularly true if your diet is restricted in calories.

We have done the most difficult part for you in your individual menu planning by outlining in Daily Food Guides just how much of each of the various groups you should include to provide your recommended amount of nutrients and still stay within your physician's prescription for fat, cholesterol, and calories. For example, Diet II Daily Food Guide directs you to eat 6 ounces of cooked meat, fish, or poultry daily. This diet says: The total amount of meat, fish, or poultry in each day's menu must not exceed 6 ounces. Other foods and the amounts to be eaten are stated also.

If the Daily Food Guide is followed carefully, you will not have to worry about having too much saturated fat, not enough polyunsaturated fat, or the prescribed amount of calories in your diet. The right amounts have all been carefully calculated and worked out for you in the Daily Food Guides.

What Is the Oil and Fat Allowance in My Daily Food Guide?

The amount of additional fat or oil in your diet may be confusing to you. As explained in Chapter II, Fats and Cholesterol, many foods have invisible fat such as the fat in very lean beef. We have allowed for this in each Daily Food Guide and know that you will automatically be getting some fat in the foods that you eat. The number of teaspoons or tablespoons of fat and oil recommended in your Daily Food Guide is what you should *add* to your menu. Each different Daily Food Guide states how many teaspoons or tablespoons of oil or fat should be added in the menu for that particular diet. For example, the 1000-Calorie Low Saturated Fat, Low Cholesterol Diet (page 40) states:

"B. FATS AND OILS—Daily

Use: 4 teaspoons of oil (½ teaspoon may be "special" margarine). The oil may be used in cooking, added to food or in salad dressings (see pages 69 and 70)."

This means that 4 teaspoons of acceptable oils and fats should be eaten daily in addition to the fat that is automatically consumed in the other foods listed in this food guide. This is necessary in order to have the proper amount of polyunsaturated fats in the diet.

What Constitutes a Teaspoon of Oil or Fat?

Each of the following, for example, is acceptable as "1 teaspoon of oil":

   1 teaspoon of "special" margarine
   1 teaspoon corn, cottonseed, safflower, soybean, or walnut oil
   1½ teaspoons of commercial French or Italian dressing
   1 teaspoon of mayonnaise
   1 teaspoon of oil salad dressing
   1 tablespoon of chopped walnuts

How Do I Use the Oil and Fat Allowance of My Daily Food Guide?

The way you use your oil allowance in your menu depends on your own tastes and food habits. Because "special" margarine contains more saturated fat than the oils, your Daily Food Guide lists the maximum amount of the fat allowance that should be "special" margarine. When your diet is restricted to 1500 calories or less, you probably will use your fat and oil allowance in "special" margarine, mayonnaise, French dressing, added to vegetables, or in low calorie meat preparation.

An example of how to use the 1000-Calorie Diet's fat and oil allowance (4 teaspoons of oil, of which ½ teaspoon may be "special" margarine) is as follows (see pages 40–41):

½ teaspoon of "special" margarine on toast for breakfast
1 teaspoon oil in 1 tablespoon of Low Fat French Dressing★ at lunch
1½ teaspoons oil on the potato for dinner
1 teaspoon oil in 1 teaspoon Mayonnaise★ at dinner
$\overline{4}$ teaspoons oil

Foods such as "special" desserts, fancy breads, casserole dishes, etc., provide a pleasant way to use your oil allowance but have too many calories for a strict reducing diet.

For those of you who have a Daily Food Guide with 1850 calories or more, there are many different ways to use the fat and oil allowance. The oil allowance may be used by adding it directly to foods for flavor, by using it in fancy breads, cookies, salad dressing, cakes, casseroles, "special" scrambled eggs, or in many other ways suggested in our recipes.

One way to use the fat and oil allowance in Diet I (5⅔ tablespoons or 17 teaspoons of oil, of which 2 tablespoons can be "special" margarine) is as follows (see page 31):

2 teaspoons "special" margarine on breakfast toast
1½ teaspoons oil in Basic Scrambled Eggs★ for breakfast
1½ teaspoons oil in Whole Wheat Muffins★ at breakfast
2 teaspoons oil in mayonnaise on the sandwich at lunch
2 teaspoons oil in the Low Fat French Dressing★ for lunch
2 teaspoons oil in the mayonnaise on salad for dinner
4 teaspoons oil in seasoning for vegetables for dinner
1 teaspoon "special" margarine on bread
1 teaspoon in Easy White Cupcake★
—————
17 teaspoons or 5⅔ tablespoons

You incorporate the fat and oil allowance into your menu just the same way for Diet I as you would for the 1000-Calorie Diet, only you have 17 teaspoons of fat and oil to use in Diet I and only 4 in the 1000-Calorie Diet.

If you are restricting calories, don't get carried away and forget to stay within your physician's recommendation for your total day's caloric intake.

Dieter's Choice

Included in the daily food plans for diets of 1500 calories or more is an allowance of unassigned calories that we call Dieter's Choice. You may choose what foods to eat to use these calories provided you do not increase your fats and cholesterol above your daily allowance. You may want extra bread, a fancy dessert, sugar for your cereal and coffee, or extra servings of fruit and skim milk. If the food you choose contains oils, the oil content becomes part of your daily quota of oils. That means that its caloric equivalent (45 calories for each teaspoon of oil) has already been counted in the calories of that Food Guide and should not be counted a second time. As an example:

In the sample breakfast of Diet I on page 33, Basic Scrambled Eggs★ are used as one item of the Dieter's Choice. One serving of

Basic Scrambled Eggs★ has 150 calories and 1½ teaspoons of vegetable oil. The 1½ teaspoons of oil must be counted as part of your daily quota of oil, so subtract the calories for the oil from the total calories for Basic Scrambled Eggs★ to find the calories to be charged as part of the Dieter's Choice.

Total calories of Basic Scrambled Eggs★   150 calories
Subtract for 1½ teaspoons oil   —68 calories

Calories to be charged against the
Dieter's Choice   82 calories

RECIPES

All recipes are calculated for protein, total fat, saturated fat, linoleic acid, cholesterol, and calorie value for each dieter's serving. These values are approximate and the calories have been rounded off to the nearest 5 calories. Starred recipes that are specified within the recipe, as for example the Meringue★ in Apricot Meringue Pie★, are included in the calculations. Additional items, such as garnishes, toppings, and sauces, that follow the calculations must be counted in addition to values given for the recipe, as the Whipped Topping★ in Crunch Torte★. When variations are shown, changes of ingredient may affect calculated value, and user must take this into consideration, as in Tapioca Pudding★ and the variation Fluffy Tapioca Pudding★.

Diet I

2600-Calorie* Low Saturated Fat, Low Cholesterol Diet

90 grams total fat, including:
  15 grams saturated
  43 grams linoleic
  5⅔ tablespoons (17 teaspoons) fat and oil allowance
170 milligrams cholesterol
100 grams protein

A. MEAT, FISH, AND POULTRY—Daily

Use: 7 ounces of cooked lean meat, fish, or poultry. Limit the servings of beef, lamb, and pork to 4 a week. These servings (after cooking) must be only 3 ounces each, so that the amount of saturated fat is limited.

* Recommended Daily Allowance for a moderately active 5'8" man weighing 154 pounds in the age group of 35–55 years is 2600 calories.

For the other meat meals, use poultry, veal, fish, or meat substitutes. The meat servings can be divided among the day's meals as you desire. For example:

3 ounces of chicken for lunch
4 ounces of veal for dinner
or
3-ounce steak for breakfast
Skim milk cottage cheese and fruit plate for lunch
4 ounces of fish for dinner

Meat substitutes: Protein foods to use in addition to, or in place of, meat are: skim milk cottage cheese, skim milk yogurt, dried peas and beans, walnuts and walnut butter, egg white, vegetable-protein meat substitute (see page 475). Be sure to note that, although protein values are similar to meat, caloric values are not.

NOTE: ¼ cup of skim milk cottage cheese or 2 egg whites may be substituted for 1 ounce of meat, fish, or poultry.

B. FATS AND OILS—Daily

Use: 5⅔ tablespoons or 17 teaspoons (2 tablespoons of this may be "special" margarine). The oil may be used in cooking, added to food, or used in salad dressings (see pages 28 and 69, 70).

NOTE: It is important that all of the prescribed oil allowance be used so that you get enough polyunsaturated fat in your diet.

C. SKIM MILK—SKIM MILK BUTTERMILK—Daily

Use: 3 cups fortified with A and D vitamins, or the equivalent in skim milk powder or evaporated skim milk.

D. VEGETABLES—Daily

Use: 3 or more servings of any low- or medium-calorie fresh, frozen, or canned vegetables or vegetable juices.* Avoid those commercially frozen and canned vegetables to which fat or cream sauce has been added. Be sure to include one or more servings of green leafy or yellow vegetables, one of which should be raw.

NOTE: The high-calorie or starchy vegetables are listed in Group F: Bread, Cereals, Cereal Products, and Starchy Vegetables.

* For caloric values of vegetables, see page 477.

E. FRUITS—Daily

Use: 3 or more servings of any kind of fruit or fruit juice—fresh, frozen, canned, or dried.
Your choice should include:
    1 serving of citrus fruit or citrus fruit juice or 2 servings (1 cup) of tomato juice daily
    1 serving of dried fruit two or three times a week

F. BREAD, CEREALS, CEREAL PRODUCTS, AND STARCHY VEGETABLES—Daily

Use: 9 servings. Your choice may include:
    2 servings of whole grain cereal (1 cup of cooked cereal)
    5 servings of bread, rolls, or additional cereal products
    2 servings of starchy vegetables such as potatoes, corn, or lima beans

G. DIETER'S CHOICE (see list on pages 480–81)—Daily

Use: 300–350 calories in foods you desire. They can be supplied by fruit, vegetables, grain products, nuts, olives, "special" desserts, soups, and sweets. Even though these foods are needed to supply your caloric requirements, try to choose foods that add extra vitamins, minerals, and protein to your diet. Don't choose too many "empty calories" such as in carbonated drinks, sugar, and candy. For your convenience see the list of acceptable foods and their caloric values on pages 480–81. If you choose foods that contain part of your oil allowance, see page 29.

H. MISCELLANEOUS (contain few or no calories)

Use: Servings as desired.
    Soups—clear broth, bouillon, and fat free beef-stock soups
    Beverages—coffee, tea, coffee substitutes (without sugar, milk, or cream)
    Seasonings—salt, pepper, herbs, spices, vinegar, lemon juice, and mustard

Here is a menu that illustrates the application of the Diet I Guide in meal planning:
    17 teaspoons oil and fat allowance*
    300–350 Calories Dieter's Choice†

---

* The number in parentheses is the teaspoons of oil or "special" margarine used in that particular food.
† The food enclosed in brackets is a Dieter's Choice.

BREAKFAST
  1 cup orange juice
  1 cup cooked whole wheat cereal
  [1 serving Basic Scrambled Eggs★]   (1½)
  2 Whole Wheat Muffins★   (1½)
  2 teaspoons "special" margarine   (2)
  [2 teaspoons sugar]
  1 cup skim milk
  Coffee or tea if desired

LUNCH
  Sandwich
    2 slices bread
    3-ounce serving sliced chicken
    2 teaspoons Mayonnaise★   (2)
  ½ cup carrots
  Large tossed green salad with 2 tablespoons Low Fat French Dressing★   (2)
  1 fresh pear sliced or ½ cup canned pears
  1 cup skim milk

DINNER
  3-ounce serving roast beef
  Baked potato with 1 tablespoon Herbed Oil★   (3)
  ½ cup string beans with 1 teaspoon Orange Oil★   (1)
  Large sliced tomato salad with
    ¼ cup cottage cheese
    2 teaspoons Mayonnaise★   (2)
  1 serving stewed dried apricots
  [1 Easy White Cupcake★ with Mocha Icing★]   (1)
  1 slice bread
  1 teaspoon "special" margarine   (1)
  1 cup skim milk
  Coffee or tea if desired

BEDTIME SNACK
  1 apple

Diet II

1850-Calorie* Low Saturated Fat, Low Cholesterol Diet

  61 grams total fat, including:
    11 grams saturated

* The Recommended Daily Allowance for a moderately active 5'3" woman weighing 128 pounds in the 35–55 age group is 1850 calories.

28 grams linoleic
3⅔ tablespoons (11 teaspoons) fat and oil allowance
150 milligrams cholesterol
90 grams protein

A. MEAT, FISH, AND POULTRY—Daily

Use: 6 ounces of cooked lean meat, fish, or poultry. Limit the servings of beef, lamb, and pork to 4 a week. These servings (after cooking) must be only 3 ounces each, so that the amount of saturated fat is limited.

For the other meat meals, use poultry, veal, fish, or meat substitutes. The meat servings can be divided among the day's meals as you desire. For example:

2 ounces of chicken for lunch
4 ounces of veal for dinner
or
3-ounce steak for breakfast
Fruit plate and skim milk for lunch
3 ounces of fish for dinner

Meat substitutes: Protein foods to use in addition to, or in place of, meat are: skim milk cottage cheese, skim milk yogurt, dried peas and beans, walnuts and walnut butter, egg white, vegetable-protein meat substitute (see page 475). Be sure to note that, although protein values are similar to meat, caloric values are not.

NOTE: ¼ cup of skim milk cottage cheese or 2 egg whites may be substituted for 1 ounce of meat, fish, or poultry.

B. FATS AND OILS—Daily

Use: 3⅔ tablespoons or 11 teaspoons (1 tablespoon of this may be "special" margarine). The oil may be used in cooking, added to food, or used in salad dressings (see pages 28–29 and 69–70).

NOTE: It is important that all of the prescribed oil allowance be used so that you get enough polyunsaturated fat in your diet.

C. SKIM MILK—SKIM MILK BUTTERMILK—Daily

Use: 3 cups fortified with A and D vitamins, or the equivalent in skim milk powder or evaporated skim milk.

D. VEGETABLES—Daily

Use: 3 or more servings of any low- or medium-calorie fresh, frozen, or canned vegetables or vegetable juices.* Avoid those commercially frozen and canned vegetables to which fat or cream sauce has been added. Be sure to include one or more servings of green leafy or yellow vegetables, one of which should be raw.

NOTE: The high calorie or starchy vegetables are listed in Group F: Bread, Cereals, Cereal Products, and Starchy Vegetables.

E. FRUITS—Daily

Use: 3 servings of fresh, frozen, or canned fruit or fruit juice without additional sugar, to include: ½ cup of citrus fruit or citrus fruit juice or 1 cup of tomato juice.

F. BREAD, CEREALS, CEREAL PRODUCTS, AND STARCHY VEGETABLES—Daily

Use: 7 servings

NOTE: A possible choice would include:
1 serving of whole grain cereal for breakfast
4 servings of bread, rolls, or additional cereal products
2 servings of starchy vegetables such as potatoes, corn, or lima beans

G. DIETER'S CHOICE (see list on pages 480–81)—Daily

Use: 150 calories in foods you desire. The calories can be supplied by fruit, vegetables, grain products, nuts, olives, "special" desserts, soups, and sweets. Even though these foods are needed to supply your caloric requirements, try to choose foods that add extra vitamins, minerals, and protein to your diet. Don't choose too many "empty" calories such as in carbonated drinks, sugar and candy. For your convenience see the list of acceptable foods and their caloric values on pages 480–81. If you choose foods that contain part of your oil allowance, see page 29.

H. MISCELLANEOUS (contain few or no calories)

Use: Servings as desired
Soups—clear broth, bouillon, and fat free beef-stock soups
Beverages—coffee, tea, coffee substitutes (without sugar, milk, or cream)

* For caloric values of vegetables, see page 477.

Seasonings—salt, pepper, herbs, spices, vinegar, lemon juice, and mustard

Here is a menu that illustrates the application of the Diet II Guide in meal planning:

11 teaspoons oil and fat allowance*
150 Calories Dieter's Choice†

BREAKFAST

½ cup orange juice
½ cup cooked whole wheat cereal
[½ serving Basic Scrambled Eggs★]   (½)*
2 Whole Wheat Muffins   (1½)
1 teaspoon "special" margarine   (1)
[2 teaspoons honey]
[1 teaspoon sugar]
1 cup skim milk
Coffee or tea if desired

LUNCH

Sandwich
  2 slices bread
  3-ounce serving chicken
  2 teaspoons Mayonnaise★   (2)
½ cup carrots
Large tossed green salad with 1 tablespoon Low Fat French
  Dressing★   (1)
1 fresh pear or apple
1 cup skim milk

DINNER

3-ounce serving roast beef
½ small baked potato with 1½ teaspoons Herbed
  Oil★   (1½)
½ cup string beans with ½ teaspoon Orange Oil★   (½)
Large sliced tomato salad with 1 teaspoon Mayonnaise★   (1)
½ cup canned apricots
[1 Oatmeal Cookie★]
1 slice whole wheat bread
1 teaspoon "special" margarine   (1)
1 cup skim milk
Coffee or tea if desired

---

* The number in parentheses is the teaspoons of oil or "special" margarine used in that particular food.
† The food enclosed in brackets is a Dieter's Choice.

Diet III

1500-Calorie Low Saturated Fat, Low Cholesterol Diet*

  47 grams total fat, including:
    9 grams saturated
    20 grams linoleic
    2⅔ tablespoons (8 teaspoons) fat and oil allowance
  140 milligrams cholesterol
  88 grams protein

A. MEAT, FISH, AND POULTRY—Daily

Use: 6 ounces of cooked lean meat, fish, or poultry. Limit the servings of beef, lamb, and pork to 4 a week. These servings (after cooking) must be only 3 ounces each, so that the amount of saturated fat is limited.

For the other meat meals, use poultry, veal, fish, or meat substitutes. The meat servings can be divided among the day's meals as you desire. For example:

  2 ounces of chicken for lunch
  4 ounces of veal for dinner
    or
  3-ounce steak for breakfast
  Fruit plate and skim milk for lunch
  3 ounces of fish for dinner

Meat substitutes: ¼ cup of skim milk cottage cheese, 1 cup of skim milk yogurt, or 2 egg whites may be substituted for 1 ounce of meat, fish, or poultry. If egg whites are substituted, the caloric value is reduced.

B. FATS AND OILS—Daily

Use: 2⅔ tablespoons or 8 teaspoons (1 tablespoon of this may be "special" margarine). The oil may be used in cooking, added to food, or used in salad dressings (see pages 28–29 and 69–70).

NOTE: It is important to use all of the prescribed oil allowance so that you get enough polyunsaturated fat in your diet.

* Please read the general discussion for low-calorie diets in How to Build a Low- or High-Calorie Diet, page 440.

C. SKIM MILK—SKIM MILK BUTTERMILK—Daily

Use: 3 cups fortified with A and D vitamins, or the equivalent in skim milk powder or evaporated skim milk.

D. VEGETABLES—Daily

Use: 3 or more servings to include:
   2 or more servings of low-calorie vegetables,* one serving of which should be raw.
   1 additional serving of vegetable that can be either a low- or medium-calorie vegetable. (One of the vegetables eaten should be either dark green or deep yellow.)

NOTE: High-calorie vegetables are listed in Group F: Bread, Cereals, Cereal Products, and Starchy Vegetables.

E. FRUITS—Daily

Use: 3 servings of fresh, frozen, or canned fruit or fruit juice without additional sugar, to include:
   ½ cup of citrus fruit or citrus fruit juice or 1 cup of tomato juice.

F. BREAD, CEREALS, CEREAL PRODUCTS, AND STARCHY VEGETABLES—Daily

Use: 6 servings
NOTE: A possible choice would include:
   1 serving of whole grain cereal for breakfast
   3 servings of bread, rolls, or additional cereal products
   2 servings of starchy vegetables such as potatoes, corn, or lima beans

G. DIETER'S CHOICE (see list on pages 480–81)—Daily

Use: 50 calories in foods you desire. This can be supplied by another serving of fresh fruit, vegetable, sugar for your cereal and beverages, or by other foods as listed on pages 480–81. If you choose foods that contain part of your oil allowance, see page 29.

* For caloric values of vegetables see page 477.

H. MISCELLANEOUS (Contain few or no calories)

Use: Servings as desired

Soups—clear broth, bouillon, and fat free homemade beef-stock soups

Beverages—coffee, tea, coffee substitutes (without sugar, milk, or cream)

Seasonings—salt, pepper, herbs, spices, vinegar, lemon juice, and mustard

Here is a menu that illustrates the application of the 1500-Calorie Guide in meal planning:

8 teaspoons oil and fat allowance*
50 Calories Dieter's Choice†

BREAKFAST

½ cup orange juice
½ cup cooked whole wheat cereal
1 slice whole wheat toast
1 teaspoon "special" margarine (1)
[1 teaspoon sugar for cereal]
[1 teaspoon jelly]
1 cup skim milk
Coffee or tea if desired

LUNCH

Sandwich
  2 slices bread
  3-ounce serving chicken
  2 teaspoons Mayonnaise★ (2)
½ cup carrots
Large tossed green salad with 1 tablespoon Low Fat French Dressing★ (1)
1 fresh pear sliced or ½ cup water-packed canned pears
1 cup skim milk

* The number in parentheses is the teaspoons of oil or "special" margarine used in that particular food.
† The food enclosed in brackets is a Dieter's Choice.

DINNER

   3-ounce serving roast beef
   ½ small baked potato with 1½ teaspoons Herbed Oil★ (1½)
   ½ cup string beans with ½ teaspoon Orange Oil★ (½)
   Large sliced tomato salad with 1 teaspoon Mayonnaise★ (1)
   1 slice whole wheat bread
   ½ cup water-packed apricots
   1 teaspoon "special" margarine (1)
   [1 teaspoon jelly]
   1 cup skim milk
   Coffee or tea if desired

Diet IV

1000-Calorie Low Saturated Fat, Low Cholesterol Diet*

30–32 grams total fat, including:
   5.5 grams saturated
   11 grams linoleic
   5 teaspoons oil and fat allowance
140 milligrams cholesterol
   70 grams protein

A. MEAT, FISH, AND POULTRY—Daily

Use: 5 ounces of cooked lean meat, fish, or poultry. Limit the servings of beef, lamb, and pork to 4 a week. These servings (after cooking) must be only 3 ounces each, so that the amount of saturated fat is limited.

For the other meat meals, use poultry, veal, fish, or meat substitutes. The meat servings can be divided among the day's meals as you desire. For example:

   3-ounce steak for breakfast
   Vegetable plate and skim milk for lunch
   2 ounces of fish for dinner
      or
   2 ounces of chicken for lunch
   3 ounces of veal for dinner

Meat substitutes: ¼ cup of skim milk cottage cheese, 1 cup of skim milk yogurt, or 2 egg whites may be substituted for 1 ounce of meat, fish, or poultry. If egg whites are substituted, the caloric value is reduced.

* Please read the general discussion for low-calorie diets in How to Build a Low- or High-Calorie Diet, page 440.

B. FATS AND OILS—Daily

Use: 4 teaspoons (½ teaspoon may be "special" margarine). The oil may be used in cooking, added to food or in salad dressings (see pages 28–29 and 69–70).

NOTE: It is important to use all of the prescribed oil allowance so that you get enough polyunsaturated fat in your diet.

C. SKIM MILK—SKIM MILK BUTTERMILK—Daily

Use: 2½ cups fortified with A and D vitamins, or the equivalent in skim milk powder or evaporated skim milk.

D. VEGETABLES—Daily

Use: 3 or more servings to include:
   2 or more servings of low-calorie vegetables,* one serving of which should be raw.
   1 additional serving of vegetable that can be either a low or medium calorie vegetable. (One of the vegetables eaten should be either dark green or deep yellow.)

NOTE: High-calorie vegetables are listed in Group F: Bread, Cereals, Ceral Products, and Starchy Vegetables.

E. FRUITS—Daily

Use: 3 servings of fresh, frozen, or canned fruit or fruit juice without additional sugar, to include:
   ½ cup of citrus fruit or citrus fruit juice or 1 cup of tomato juice.

F. BREAD, CEREALS, CEREAL PRODUCTS, AND STARCHY VEGETABLES—Daily

Use: 3 servings

NOTE: A possible choice would include:
   1 serving of whole grain cereal for breakfast
   1 serving of bread (100 per cent whole wheat is preferred)
   1 serving (½ cup) of potato

G. DIETER'S CHOICE

No additional calories are allowed on the 1000-Calorie Diet other than those supplied by Groups A–F.

* For caloric values of vegetables see page 477.

H. MISCELLANEOUS (contain few or no calories)

> *Use:* Servings as desired
>
> Soups—clear broth, bouillon, and homemade fat free beef-stock soups
>
> Beverages—coffee, tea, coffee substitutes (without sugar, milk, or cream)
>
> Seasonings—salt, pepper, herbs, spices, vinegar, lemon juice, and mustard

Here is a menu that illustrates the application of the 1000-Calorie Guide in meal planning:

> 4 teaspoons fat and oil allowance*
> No Dieter's Choice

BREAKAST

> ½ cup orange juice
> ½ cup cooked whole wheat cereal
> ½ cup skim milk for cereal
> 1 slice whole wheat toast
> ½ teaspoon "special" margarine (½)*
> Coffee or tea if desired

LUNCH

> 2-ounce serving sliced chicken
> ½ cup carrots
> ½ cup asparagus
> Large tossed green salad with 1 tablespoon Low Fat French Dressing★ (1)
> 1 fresh peach sliced or ½ cup water-packed peaches
> 1 cup skim milk

DINNER

> 3-ounce serving roast beef
> ½ small baked potato with 1½ teaspoons Herbed Oil★ (1½)
> ½ cup string beans
> Large sliced tomato salad with 1 teaspoon Mayonnaise★ (1)
> ½ cup water-packed canned apricots
> 1 cup skim milk
> Coffee or tea if desired

* The number in parentheses is the teaspoons of oil or "special" margarine used in that particular food.

CHAPTER V

Two Weeks of Sample Menus for the Low Saturated Fat, Low Cholesterol Diet

THE following menus are to assist you in planning your own low saturated fat, low cholesterol diet. They provide approximately 2600 calories per day and follow the Daily Food Guide for Diet I. These menus are just suggestions on how to use the principles and the recipes in this book. You may make your own variations if you follow the principles set down for your individual Daily Food Guide. We have presented a variety of foods and combinations of foods to show you how versatile this diet can be. Take advantage of that versatility by adjusting the menus to your individual likes and dislikes. For example, you may want to eat three servings of the same vegetable in one day instead of one serving of three different vegetables. Do it! You may want to divide your day's menu into five meals. Do it! If you have a small family, you are apt to have more leftovers and will want to utilize them. By all means, do it!

In making up your own menus or adjusting these menus, remember that the starred foods in the menus can be used only if prepared according to the recipes in this book. One serving of each food is specified unless otherwise indicated. In general, one serving is ½ cup, unless otherwise stated. The menus list the food requirements for one person.

Many times we have found in planning our day's menu that we need to incorporate a teaspoon or more of oil to meet our daily oil and fat allowance. We then arrange to add it to one of the foods already planned for the day. We have found that you can add polyunsaturated oil to almost all foods* with an improvement of flavor. We add oil

* Do not add extra oil to dishes such as cakes where the success of the product depends on using the specified proportions of the ingredients.

to applesauce, fruit salads, vegetables, sauces, meat (add while cooking) and casseroles—all with success. We particularly like to add extra vegetable oil to starchy vegetables. Plain safflower oil on baked potatoes is delicious; Herbed Oil★ is even better.

We have kept most of the recipes in this book low in total fat, so that those of you with smaller oil allowances may use them. We know that it is easier to enrich a recipe by adding oil than to deplete it by taking away oil. Therefore, if you notice that a menu example seems to have more oil than the recipe specifies, it is because we have added extra oil that day to meet our Daily Food Guide's oil requirement. You may need to do the same thing, and we fully expect you to add oil to many of our recipes, but you must be careful to calculate the amount correctly. When you add oil to a recipe, multiply the amount of additional oil needed in *each* serving by the number of servings in the total recipe. If you prefer to add the oil to the individual cooked portion, then add the exact amount needed by the individual.

Please try many food combinations and different recipes. Be creative! Here are our suggestions for two weeks of menus:

WEEK NO. 1

Monday

BREAKFAST
　½ cup orange juice
　1 cup enriched wheat cereal
　1 teaspoon sugar
　2 slices French Toast★ fried in 2 teaspoons oil　　　(2)*
　2 tablespoons maple syrup
　2 teaspoons "special" margarine　　　　　　　　(2)
　1 cup skim milk
　Coffee or tea if desired

LUNCH
　Cream of Mushroom Soup★
　Sandwich
　　2 slices bread
　　2 tablespoons Walnut Butter★　　　　　　　　(4)
　"Special" Cottage Cheese★ and Tomato Salad with
　　2 teaspoons Mayonnaise★　　　　　　　　　(2)
　Apple Whip★
　1 cup skim milk

* The number in parentheses is the teaspoons of oil or "special" margarine in that food item.

DINNER

   Deluxe Broiled Steak★ (3 ounces, cooked)
   Baked potato with 1 tablespoon Herbed Oil★   (3)
   Broccoli★
   Tossed green salad with 1 tablespoon Basic French
     Dressing★   (2)
   Cooked dried apricots
   2 White Bread Rolls★
   2 teaspoons "special" margarine   (2)
   1 cup skim milk
   Coffee or tea if desired

                                            17 *teaspoons*

WEEK NO. 1

Tuesday

BREAKFAST

   ½ cantaloupe
   1 serving cooked whole wheat cereal sprinkled with
     1 tablespoon wheat germ
   1 teaspoon sugar
   2 Baking Powder Biscuits★   (2)*
   2 teaspoons "special" margarine   (2)
   1 cup skim milk
   Coffee or tea if desired

LUNCH

   Spring Soup★
   3-ounce Veal Burger★ between 2 slices of French
    Bread   (2)
    Catsup, mustard, dill pickle, slice of tomato,
    1 teaspoon Mayonnaise★   (1)
   Lettuce wedge with 1 tablespoon Italian Dressing★   (2)
   Fruit cocktail
   1 cup skim milk

* The number in parentheses is the teaspoons of oil or "special" margarine in that particular food item.

DINNER

    Boiled fillet of sole (4 ounces brushed with
       2 teaspoons lemon juice and oil)   (1)
    Oven French Fries★   (1)
    Asparagus with 1⅓ teaspoons Herbed Oil★   (1⅓)
    Molded Cucumber Salad★ with Yogurt Dressing I★
    Pumpkin Pie★   (2⅔)
    2 slices whole wheat bread
    2 teaspoons "special" margarine   (2)
    1 cup skim milk
    Coffee or tea if desired

                                               <u>17</u> *teaspoons*

WEEK NO. 1

Wednesday

BREAKFAST

    ½ grapefruit
    1 cup oatmeal with 2 tablespoons raisins
    1 teaspoon brown sugar
    Basic Scrambled Eggs★   (1½)*
    2 slices whole wheat toast
    2 teaspoons "special" margarine   (2)
    1 cup skim milk

LUNCH

    Vegetable Beef Soup★
    Sandwich
       2 ounces water-packed tuna mixed with
       1 tablespoon Mayonnaise★   (3)
       2 slices bread
       2 teaspoons Mayonnaise★ for bread   (2)
       Lettuce
    Dill pickle
    Melon ball salad with 1 tablespoon Fruit Salad
       Dressing★   (1½)
    Tapioca Pudding★
    1 cup skim milk buttermilk

* The number in parentheses is the teaspoons of oil or "special" margarine in that food item.

DINNER

Roast veal (4 ounces, cooked) with Fat Free Gravy★   (2)*
Mashed Potatoes★   (½)
Seasoned Spinach★ *with 1 teaspoon oil*   (1)
Cabbage and Carrot Salad★ *with Special Fat Free*
    Dressing★
Canned plums
1 Walnut Kiss★   (½)
2 servings Corn Bread★   (1)
2 teaspoons "special" margarine   (2)
2 teaspoons honey
1 cup skim milk
Coffee or tea if desired

                                              ‾‾‾‾‾‾
                                              17 *teaspoons*

WEEK NO. 1

Thursday

BREAKFAST

1 cup tomato juice
¾ cup corn flakes with 1 banana, sliced
1 teaspoon sugar
2 slices Raisin Toast★
2 teaspoons "special" margarine   (2)†
1 cup Hot Cocoa★

LUNCH AT THE RESTAURANT

Bouillon
Broiled lamb chops (2 small—lean meat only)
Baked potato with 1 tablespoon polyunsaturated oil‡   (3)
Peas without butter or sauce
Tossed green salad with 1 tablespoon French dressing   (2)
Flavored gelatin dessert (no whipped cream)
1 large French roll
2 pats "special" margarine§   (2)
1 glass skim milk
Coffee or tea if desired

* 2 teaspoons oil to be added to gravy for each serving.
† The number in parentheses is the teaspoons of oil or "special" margarine in that food item.
‡ Bring your own polyunsaturated oil to the restaurant if necessary, or ask the waiter to bring you some.
§ Ask for a polyunsaturated margarine.

DINNER
   Broiled Chicken★ (4 ounces, cooked) with 2 teaspoons
     oil used in preparation   (2)
   Scalloped Sweet Potatoes and Pineapple★
   String beans with 1 teaspoon Herbed Oil★   (1)
   Coleslaw with 2 tablespoons Cooked Salad Dressing★ (1)
   White Cake★ with 7-Minute Frosting★   (2)
   2 slices raisin bread
   2 teaspoons "special" margarine   (2)
   1 cup skim milk
   Coffee or tea if desired

                          <u>17</u> *teaspoons*

WEEK NO. 1

Friday

BREAKFAST
   ½ cup orange juice
   ½ cup whole wheat cereal sprinkled with 1 tablespoon
     wheat germ
   1 teaspoon brown sugar
   Eggs Baked in Bread Baskets★   (4)*
   1 cup skim milk
   Coffee or tea if desired

LUNCH†
   Quick Onion Soup★
   Sandwich
     2 slices bread
     3 ounces chicken
     Lettuce
     4 teaspoons Mayonnaise★   (4)
   Celery sticks
   Large apple
   1 cup skim milk

* The number in parentheses is the teaspoons of oil or "special" margarine in that food item.
† This could be a box lunch.

DINNER
 Oven-baked salmon (4 ounces) with India Relish★
 Stuffed Potatoes★*   (1½)*
 Sherried Beets★
 Tossed spinach salad with 1 tablespoon Basic French
   Dressing★   (2)
 Canned or fresh cherries
 2 Walnut Kisses★   (1)
 2 Potato Refrigerator Rolls★   (1½)
 2 teaspoons "special" margarine   (2)
 1 cup skim milk
 Coffee or tea if desired

SNACK
 Popcorn★   (1)
                                                       ‾‾‾‾‾‾‾‾‾
                                                       17 teaspoons

WEEK NO. 1

Saturday

BREAKFAST
 ½ grapefruit
 Broiled breakfast steak (3 ounces, cooked)
 Hash brown potatoes fried in 1 tablespoon oil   (3)†
 1 slice whole wheat toast
 1 teaspoon "special" margarine   (1)
 1 cup skim milk
 Coffee or tea if desired

LUNCH
 Meatless Chili★
 Carrot sticks
 "Special" cottage cheese and sliced tomato salad with
   1 tablespoon Blender Mayonnaise★   (2)
 Applesauce with Whipped Topping★
 2 tortillas crisped in 2 teaspoons oil   (2)
 1 cup skim milk

* 5 tablespoons extra oil to be added to total recipe or 1½ teaspoons to individual portion.
† The number in parentheses is the teaspoons of oil or "special" margarine
in that food item.

DINNER
   Veal Scaloppine★ (4 ounces cooked meat)   (1½)*
   Brown Rice★ served with 2 teaspoons oil   (2)
   Vegetables Baked in Foil★ (string beans)   (½)
   Molded Pear Cellophane Salad★ with 1 teaspoon
      Mayonnaise★   (1)
   Basic Ice Cream★ with Butterscotch Sauce★   (3)
   2 slices bread
   2 teaspoons "special" margarine   (2)
   Coffee or tea if desired

                                              <u>17</u> *teaspoons*

BEDTIME SNACK
   1 cup Iced Cocoa★

WEEK NO. 1

Sunday

BREAKFAST
   Orange slices with powdered sugar
   4 Bread Crumb Griddle Cakes★   (4)‡
   2 tablespoons boysenberry syrup
   2 teaspoons "special" margarine   (2)
   1 cup skim milk
   Coffee or tea if desired

DINNER
   Roast beef (3 ounces, cooked) with Fat Free Gravy★
   Mashed Potatoes★   (½)
   Baked Acorn Squash★   (½)
   Endive, chicory, and romaine salad with "special"
     Fat Free Dressing★
   Meringue shell★ with strawberries
   2 Buttermilk Rolls★   (½)
   2 teaspoons "special" margarine   (2)
   1 cup skim milk
   Coffee or tea if desired

* Varies with amount used in browning.
† The number in parentheses is the teaspoons of oil or "special" margarine in that food item.
‡ 2 teaspoons of this oil used for frying the griddle cakes.

SUPPER
  Fish Chowder★
  Chicken Salad★ garnished with   (4½)
    1 Whole Stuffed Egg★   (1)
  2 Buttermilk Rolls★   (½)
  1½ teaspoons "special" margarine   (1½)
  2 pieces Divinity Candy
  1 cup Pineapple Yogurt Drink★

                                         $\overline{17}$ *teaspoons*

WEEK NO. 2

Monday

BREAKFAST
  1 banana, sliced
  ¾ cup oat flakes sprinkled with 1 tablespoon wheat
    germ
  1 teaspoon sugar
  Basic Scrambled Eggs★   (1½)*
  2 slices whole wheat toast
  2 teaspoons "special" margarine   (2)
  1 cup skim milk
  Coffee or tea if desired

LUNCH
  Sandwich
    Roast beef (3 ounces)
    2 slices bread
    1 tablespoon Mayonnaise★   (3)
    Lettuce
    Mustard
  Waldorf Salad★ with Pineapple Dressing★
  2 Walnut Drop Cookies★   (2)
  1 cup skim milk

DINNER
  Tuna Ring★ filled with peas and carrots
  Corn seasoned with 1 teaspoon oil   (1)
  Sliced tomatoes with 1 tablespoon Tart French
    Dressing★   (1¾)

* The number in parentheses is the teaspoons of oil or "special" margarine
in that food item.

Basic Ice Cream★, Chocolate Variety★	(3)
2 Buttermilk Rolls★	(½)
2¼ teaspoons "special" margarine	(2¼)
1 cup skim milk	
Coffee or tea if desired	

$\overline{17}$ teaspoons

WEEK NO. 2

Tuesday

BREAKFAST
½ cup orange juice	
Fortified Cooked Cereal★	
1 teaspoon brown sugar	
½ cup skim milk for cereal	
2 poached egg whites on whole wheat toast with 1 teaspoon "special" margarine	(1)*
1 slice whole wheat toast	
1 teaspoon "special" margarine	(1)
Coffee or tea if desired	

LUNCH AT THE RESTAURANT
Bouillon	
Low fat cottage cheese and fruit plate with	(1)†
2 teaspoons mayonnaise	(2)
2 small French rolls	
2 pats "special" margarine‡	(2)
1 slice unfrosted angel food cake	
1 glass skim milk	
Coffee or tea if desired	

DINNER
Broiled ham (3 ounces, cooked)	
Scalloped Potatoes★	(1)
Baked Zucchini Boats★	(1)§
Lettuce section with 2 tablespoons Curry Dressing★	(4)

* The number in parentheses is the teaspoons of oil or "special" margarine in that food item.
† Estimated fat in restaurant-style cottage cheese.
‡ Ask for a polyunsaturated margarine.
§ ½ teaspoon extra oil to be added to each serving.

Canned or fresh raspberries
1 Date Bar   (⅔)
2 slices rye bread
1⅓ teaspoons "special" margarine   (1⅓)
1 cup skim milk
Iced tea if desired

                                                    $\overline{15}$ *teaspoons*

WEEK NO. 2

Wednesday

BREAKFAST
   1 cup tomato juice
   2 Cracked Wheat Cakes★   (3)*
   1 slice Raisin Toast★
   1 teaspoon "special" margarine   (1)
   1 cup Hot Cocoa★

LUNCH
   Meatless Boston Baked Beans★ served with
     2 teaspoons oil added to each serving   (2)
   2 slices Boston Brown Bread★
   1 tablespoon Walnut Butter★   (2)
   Stuffed Celery★
   Applesauce served with 1 teaspoon oil   (1)
   1 cup skim milk

DINNER
   Chili Chicken★ (6–7 ounces, cooked) with
     2 teaspoons oil added to sauce   (2)
   Oven Browned Potato★   (1)
   Parsleyed Carrots★ with 1 teaspoon Herbed Oil★ (1)
   Italian Lima Bean Salad★   (2)
   Orange Mallow★
   2 warmed tortillas with 2 teaspoons "special"
     margarine   (2)
   1 cup skim milk
   Coffee or tea if desired

                                                    $\overline{17}$ *teaspoons*

* The number in parentheses is the teaspoons of oil or "special" margarine in that food item.

WEEK NO. 2

Thursday

BREAKFAST
  ½ cup grapefruit
  1 cup oatmeal with 2 tablespoons raisins
  1 teaspoon sugar
  2 small sweet rolls*
  2 teaspoons "special" margarine   (2)†
  1 cup skim milk
  Coffee or tea if desired

LUNCH
  Creamed Chicken★ (3 ounces) on rice   (3)
  Tossed green salad with 1 tablespoon Italian
    Dressing★   (2)
  Apple Betty★   (½)
  2 slices French Bread
  2 teaspoons "special" margarine   (2)
  1 cup Mocha Milk★

DINNER
  Rolled Stuffed Flank Steak★ (3 ounces of meat)   (½)
  Lemony Yams★   (2)‡
  Broccoli with 2 tablespoons "Special" Sour Cream★ (1)
  Tomato Aspic Salad★ with 2 teaspoons Mayonnaise★   (2)
  Cooked dried apricots
  1 slice bread
  2 teaspoons "special" margarine   (2)
  1 cup skim milk
  Coffee or tea if desired

                                            ─────────────
                                            17 teaspoons

* Made with White Bread Roll★ recipe.
† The number in parentheses is the teaspoons of oil or "special" margarine
in that food item.
‡ 4 tablespoons extra oil to be added to total recipe.

WEEK NO. 2

Friday

BREAKFAST

½ cup orange juice
Cooked corn meal
3 ounces cooked salmon (canned or fresh) creamed
    with ½ cup Thin White Sauce★ on whole wheat
    toast   (1½)*
1 sweet roll†
1 teaspoon "special" margarine   (1)
1 cup skim milk
Coffee or tea if desired

LUNCH

Lentil Soup★
Sandwich
    3 tablespoons "Special" Cream Cheese★ mixed   (1½)
    with 1 tablespoon chopped walnuts   (1)
    2 slices thin pumpernickel
Cabbage slaw with 1 tablespoon Mayonnaise★   (3)
Lemon Sherbet★
1 cup skim milk

DINNER

Roast leg of lamb (3 ounces, cooked) with Fat Free
    Gravy★   (2)‡
Mashed Potatoes★   (½)
French-cut string beans with 1 teaspoon Orange Oil★   (1)
Seasoned Mushrooms★   (2)
Molded carrot and pineapple salad with 1½ teaspoons
    Mayonnaise★   (1½)
Canned plums
2 slices French bread
2 teaspoons "special" margarine   (2)
1 cup skim milk
Coffee or tea if desired

                                                    $\overline{17}$ teaspoons

* The number in parentheses is the teaspoons of oil or "special" margarine
in that food item.
† Made with Buttermilk Roll★ recipe.
‡ 2 teaspoons oil to be added to gravy for each serving.

WEEK NO. 2

Saturday

BREAKFAST
  Cooked prunes
  Cream of wheat with 1 tablespoon wheat germ
  Basic Scrambled Eggs★   (1½)*
  2 slices toast
  2 teaspoons cinnamon margarine†   (2)
  1 cup skim milk
  Coffee or tea if desired

LUNCH
  1 cup spaghetti with Meat and Tomato Sauce★‡   (3)
  Tossed green salad with 2 tablespoons Yogurt No. II
    Dressing★   (¾)
  1 orange
  2 Molasses Cookies★   (1½)
  1 slice French bread
  1¼ teaspoons "special" margarine   (1¼)
  1 cup skim milk

DINNER AT THE RESTAURANT
  Vegetable juice
  Petit steak (3 ounces)
  Baked potato with 1 tablespoon vegetable oil   (3)
  Peas without butter or sauce
  Asparagus spears with 1 tablespoon French dressing   (2)
  Fruit-flavored gelatin
  2 slices bread
  2 teaspoons "special" margarine§   (2)
  1 cup skim milk
  Coffee or tea if desired

                                                  $\overline{17}$ teaspoons

* The number in parentheses is the teaspoons of oil or "special" margarine
in that food item.
† "Special" margarine mixed with cinnamon.
‡ 2¼ teaspoons extra oil to be added to each serving of sauce. The Meat
and Tomato Sauce★ to be made with veal.
§ Ask for a polyunsaturated margarine.

WEEK NO. 2

Sunday

BREAKFAST
   ½ cup orange juice
   Cottage Cheese Omelet★   (1½)*
   2 slices whole wheat toast
   2 teaspoons "special" margarine   (2)
   1 tablespoon strawberry jam
   1 cup skim milk
   Coffee or tea if desired

DINNER
   Roast turkey (4 ounces)
   Brown Rice★ with 2 teaspoons oil   (2)
   Green Peas and Mushrooms★ with 1 teaspoon Orange
      Oil★   (1)
   Sliced tomato salad with 2 tablespoons Fluffy
      Dressing★   (2)
   Mint Cooler★
   2 White Bread★ rolls
   2 teaspoons "special" margarine   (2)
   Coffee or tea if desired

SUPPER
   Scotch Broth★
   Tuna Salad Bowl★   (2)
   ¼ cup Cheese Dip★ with zucchini wedges as dippers   (1½)
   1 apple cut in wedges
   2 servings matzos crackers (fat free crackers)
   2 teaspoons "special" margarine   (2)
   2 Spice Drop Cookies★   (1)
   1 cup skim milk
                                                    ‾‾‾‾‾‾‾‾‾
                                                    17 teaspoons

* The number in parentheses is the teaspoons of oil or "special" margarine
in that food item.

CHAPTER VI

Special Suggested Foods and Helpful Equipment

SPECIAL SUGGESTED FOODS

ALL of the foods needed for a low saturated fat, low cholesterol diet are available in general food markets. Some of these deserve special consideration because of their value and their use.

SKIM MILK

A primary nutritional component of any diet for young or old has long been known to be *milk*. For this diet, we specify *nonfat milk* or, as we refer to it in this book, *skim milk*. When the butterfat of whole milk is removed in making skim milk, the undesirable saturated fat and most of the cholesterol are removed. The remaining skim milk supplies valuable high quality protein and is an excellent source of other needed nutrients. Skim milk is available in different forms.

FRESH SKIM MILK

Fresh skim milk is available from dairies and is stocked on market shelves. It is desirable to use fresh skim milk that has been fortified with Vitamins A and D.

CANNED EVAPORATED SKIM MILK

Since the first edition of this book, *canned evaporated skim milk* has appeared on the grocers' shelves. It can be used in cooking and is good used as "cream" on cereal, in coffee, with desserts, etc. When chilled it can be whipped to substitute for whipped cream. This should be used immediately after preparation, as it falls on standing. By the use of gelatin, a topping with excellent holding qualities can be made as follows:

Directions for Whipping Evaporated Skim Milk

Put in a small bowl and chill
  ⅓ cup evaporated skim milk
  2 tablespoons skim milk powder (optional)
Combine in a small saucepan
  1 tablespoon cold water
  ½ teaspoon gelatin*
Heat, stirring constantly, until gelatin is *thoroughly* dissolved. Add to the milk. Beat with a rotary or electric beater until stiff. Add
  1 tablespoon sugar, or to taste
  ½ teaspoon vanilla or other flavoring to taste
  1 to 2 teaspoons lemon juice, or to taste (optional)
Makes about 1 cup. **Six servings.**

ONE SERVING
  Oil — 0 teaspoons   **Protein** — 2 grams
  Cholesterol — 1 milligram   **Carboyhdrate** — 4 grams
  Saturated fat — 0 grams   **Calories** — 24
  Linoleic acid — 0 grams

SKIM MILK POWDER

In addition to the liquid form, another form of skim milk is now increasing in popularity. It is *instant dry nonfat milk*, which we refer to

* If you are using a gelatin that needs soaking before using, let it soften in the cold water for a few minutes before heating.
  You may vary the amount of gelatin according to the stiffness of the whip desired.

as *skim milk powder*. Among the many ways to use skim milk powder are:

As a beverage: dissolved in water

In cooking, wherever milk is used: white sauce, cream soups, creamed dishes, puddings, etc.

As a way of enriching some foods: extra amounts may be added in preparing breads, sauces, puddings, ground meat dishes, and other foods.

As a substitute for whipped cream: use as a topping for desserts, as a whip for mousses and frozen desserts, etc. See directions for whipping on pages 61–62).

Directions for Reconstituting Skim Milk Powder

Follow directions given on the package. These differ with different brands; therefore no exact proportions can be given. In general, use approximately

1 part skim milk powder

3 parts, or less, water

We find it easier to mix the powder first with about ¼ of the water and beat or blend until smooth, then add the remaining water.

Directions for Enriching Fresh Skim Milk

Commercially enriched skim milk often has extra skim milk powder added, but we often find some butterfat has also been added as in low fat milk. Check with your dairy and avoid milk containing butterfat.

You can enrich fresh skim milk by adding skim milk powder to taste. We suggest starting with:

1 tablespoon skim milk powder to 1 cup skim milk

Directions for Making "Special" Whole Milk

Follow directions on package for 1 quart of milk. Spin in blender for a full minute or until mixture is homogenized:

2⅓ tablespoons oil*

½ cup skim milk powder

½ cup water

Stop blender and add remaining skim milk powder and water. Spin again to mix. Store in the refrigerator.

* Oils vary in flavor. We find some lend a better flavor than others when used in our "special" milk and "special" cream recipes.

This gives a quart of milk approximately equivalent in fat content to whole milk, but it does not contain the saturated fat and cholesterol of whole milk. 1 glass (8 ounces) contains a little less than 2 teaspoons oil.

Directions for Making "Special" Low Fat Milk

Follow directions for "Special" Whole Milk★ above. Use 1 tablespoon of oil in place of 2⅓ tablespoons.* 1 glass (8 ounces) contains approximately ¾ teaspoon of oil.

Directions for Making "Special" Coffee Cream

Spin in blender for a minute or until mixture is homogenized:

⅔ *cup skim milk powder*	*a drop or two of butter*
1 cup water	*flavoring (optional)*
¼ *cup oil**	

This "cream" is comparable to commercial nondairy powdered cream in taste but contains no coconut oil. See comments on coconut oil, pages 12 and 13. 1 tablespoon of this "cream" contains approximately ½ teaspoon oil.

ONE TABLESPOON

Oil — ½ teaspoon	**Protein** — 1 gram
Cholesterol — 1 milligram	**Carbohydrate** — 1 gram
Saturated fat — negligible	**Calories** — 35
Linoleic acid — 1 gram	

WHIPPED SKIM MILK POWDER

Surprisingly, skim milk powder in concentrated solution can be whipped, and the whipped mixture possesses somewhat the same characteristics as whipped cream. Since it is low in calories and fat and contains only a trace of cholesterol, whipped skim milk powder is excellent to use in this diet. It lets you have strawberry shortcake and other dishes we associate with whipped cream. But this is not its only use. Whipped skim milk powder makes excellent ice cream. Folded into a thick, cornstarch-type cake filling and heaped on angel food cake, it produces a delectable dessert. It can be blended with puréed fresh berries or sieved canned fruit for an excellent mousse. It adapts itself to gelatin mixtures for an icebox cake or Bavarian cream. Whipped and blended with fruit juice, it becomes a refreshing milk shake.

* Oils vary in flavor. We find some lend a better flavor than others when used in our "special" milk and "special" cream recipes.

Directions for Making Whipped Topping I

Put in a bowl
  ⅓ cup water
  *1–2 teaspoons lemon juice (optional, but improves the
    stability and flavor)*
Add
  ⅓ cup skim milk powder
Beat with an electric mixer or rotary beater until stiff. Add
  1 tablespoon sugar, or to taste
  *¼ teaspoon vanilla or flavoring to taste, depending upon its
    use*
Six servings.

ONE SERVING
  Oil — 0 teaspoons
  Cholesterol — 1 milligram
  Saturated fat — negligible
  Linoleic acid — 0 grams
  Protein — 1 gram
  Carbohydrate — 4 grams
  Calories — 20

For a more stable foam, blend the skim milk powder and water
thoroughly with a beater and chill before whipping. The foaming
ability of the powdered skim milk varies owing to unknown factors,
but in general the volume will treble. If the whipped topping has been
kept in the refrigerator, it may be rewhipped even a day or two later.

Directions for Making Whipped Topping II

(The use of gelatin gives this topping excellent holding quality.)
Put in a small bowl and chill
  ¼ cup cold water
  ⅓ cup skim milk powder
Combine in a small saucepan
  1 tablespoon cold water
  *½ teaspoon gelatin**
Heat, stirring constantly, until gelatin is *thoroughly* dissolved. Add
to the milk. Beat with a rotary or electric beater until stiff. Add
  1 tablespoon sugar, or to taste
  ½ teaspoon vanilla or other flavoring to taste
  1 to 2 teaspoons lemon juice, or to taste (optional)
Makes about 1 cup. **Six servings.**

* If you are using a gelatin that needs soaking before using, let it soften in the
cold water for a few minutes before heating.
  You may vary the amount of gelatin according to the stiffness of the whip
desired.

ONE SERVING

Oil — 0 teaspoons
Cholesterol — 1 milligram
Saturated fat — negligible
Linoleic acid — 0 grams

Protein — 2 grams
Carbohydrate — 4 grams
Calories — 25

BUTTERMILK

Whenever strained churned buttermilk is available, no better fat free milk can be found for use as a beverage. The kind of buttermilk more commonly found on market shelves, however, is cultured buttermilk, and its fat content varies. See page 10. Since the buttermilk has certain special health values, we hope that the fat free variety will become the standard kind in order to fit into a low saturated fat, low cholesterol diet.

Directions for Culturing Buttermilk

If available, add buttermilk culture to skim milk. If neither skim milk buttermilk nor culture is available, use fresh buttermilk as a culture. So that foreign bacteria do not develop, start with fresh culture *very frequently*. Add

½ cup fresh buttermilk (strain if butter particles present)

to

3 cups skim milk

Stir until smooth. Let it clabber overnight at room temperature. Place in refrigerator.

Directions for Making "Special" Sour Cream

Spin in blender

1 cup skim milk buttermilk
3 tablespoons oil

ONE TABLESPOON

Oil — ½ teaspoon
Cholesterol — negligible
Saturated fat — negligible
Linoleic acid — 1 gram

Protein — negligible
Carbohydrate — 1 gram
Calories — 25

YOGURT

Commercial yogurt is usually either whole milk or low fat type. If skim milk yogurt is not available, it can be made at home. The easiest and surest way is to use a yogurt culture and an *electric yogurt maker.* You can purchase the culture at a supermarket and the electric yogurt maker at a hardware store. The yogurt maker is an electrically heated container that is controlled at incubation temperature. Follow the simple directions that come with the yogurt maker, first boiling the skim milk, cooling it, adding the culture, and transferring the mixture to the warm yogurt maker, which holds the correct temperature until the incubation period is complete. Refrigerate the product at once.

Directions for Making Skim Milk Yogurt (Without an Electric Yogurt Maker)

Heat to simmering
 1 *pint skim milk*
Cool to lukewarm (about 110° F.) and stir in
 2 *tablespoons yogurt culture (if not available, substitute commercial yogurt)*
Pour into a sterilized jar and cover. Set jar in a pan of lukewarm water. Cover the pan, wrap in towels, and set in warm place until the milk is thickened (from 2 to 4 hours). Check constantly toward the end of the incubation period, as the whey separates from the curd if the incubation period is too long. Chill immediately after the mixture has thickened.

To Make a Thicker Culture

Add ¼ *cup skim milk powder* to the milk in the above recipe.

Yogurt stays fresh in the refrigerator about 4 to 5 days. Save some of your homemade culture to start your next yogurt, or use fresh culture. It is important to use *sterile dishes* and to keep them covered so that foreign bacteria do not develop along with the culture. *Starting with a fresh culture very frequently is imperative.*

When homemade yogurt is beaten, it makes a beverage similar to buttermilk, and you can use it in place of sour cream, buttermilk, or sour milk in baking, salad dressings, and in meat recipes.

COTTAGE CHEESE

Cottage cheese is commercially available in these forms (see pages 11–12):
   creamed cottage cheese
   low fat cottage cheese
   cottage cheese curd (including baker's cheese)
We recommend the use of *cottage cheese curd.*

Directions for Making "Special" Cottage Cheese

Mash or blend
   ½ cup cottage cheese curd
with
   2–3 tablespoons skim milk

ONE HALF CUP

Oil — 0 teaspoons	**Protein** — 19 grams
Cholesterol — 16 milligrams	**Carbohydrate** — 6 grams
Saturated fat — negligible	**Calories** — 100
Linoleic acid — 0 grams	

VARIATIONS:
   2–3 tablespoons Skim Milk Yogurt★
   2–3 tablespoons "Special" Sour Cream★
   2–3 tablespoons "Special" Cream★
   2–3 tablespoons vegetable or fruit juice
   2–3 tablespoons salad dressing (see Chapter XVII)

Baker's cheese is finer grained and more moist than regular curd and is useful in dishes such as cheesecake and in preparing dips and spreads. It can be combined with yogurt, evaporated skim milk, or "Special" Cream★, to make a smoother kind of cottage cheese. One of its particular uses is that of preparing your own "Cream" Cheese★, which can be used as you would use commercial cream cheese.

Directions for Making "Special" Cream Cheese

Spin in blender
   ½ cup baker's cheese   *1 teaspoon oil*
   2 tablespoons "special"   *¼ teaspoon salt*
      margarine
It is necessary to stop and start the blender several times and scrape down the sides in order to have the ingredients well mixed.

Special flavoring can be added to make spreads and dips (see Chapter XXI, Appetizers, Snacks, and Sandwich Spreads).

ONE TABLESPOON

Oil — ½ teaspoon	**Protein** — 2 grams
Cholesterol — 1 milligram	**Carbohydrate** — negligible
Saturated fat — negligible	**Calories** — 35
Linoleic acid — 2 grams	

POWDERED EGG WHITES*

You will find powdered egg whites indispensable for this diet, since they can be used in so many ways, not only as white of egg but also as a substitute for whole eggs in many recipes. They have the same qualities as fresh whites in cooking and there are no yolks to dispose of.

While saturated fat is present and cholesterol is abundant in the yolk of egg, both fat and cholesterol are completely absent in the white. Although the white of egg does not exactly substitute nutritionally for the whole egg, it is an almost perfect form of protein, for it contains the essential amino acids in ideal proportions.

Powdered egg white is inexpensive and easy to use, and we have used it with very satisfactory results. One ounce of powdered egg white is equal to the whites of ten eggs.

Directions for Reconstituting Powdered Egg White

For each egg white combine
  1 *tablespoon powdered egg white*
  2 *tablespoons water, barely lukewarm*
Let stand for several minutes, then stir to dissolve or place in the refrigerator until dissolved. It can be quickly dissolved by spinning in a blender, but the product comes out foamy and takes time to settle. For convenience, keep a supply ready for immediate use in the refrigerator or freeze in small containers in measured amounts. For each egg white needed, measure 2 tablespoons of dissolved white.

To Beat Powdered Egg White

It is not necessary to dissolve the dry egg white first. Simply put the measured powdered egg white and water into a bowl and proceed to beat with a hand beater or an electric beater. It will fluff up and whip quickly.

* Sold commercially as *powdered egg albumen*.

"Substitute Whole Egg" for Use in Cooking*

3 tablespoons reconstituted white
¼ teaspoon lecithin granules (see page 68)
1½ teaspoons oil

Beat lightly with a fork to mix ingredients. Before using for cooking, beat again.

You will find numerous uses for egg white and "substitute whole egg" among recipes in the following chapters. We direct your attention to breakfast "Special" Scrambled Eggs★ and other breakfast "egg" entrees.

In cooking, egg white and "substitute whole egg" serve very well. Where the success of a recipe depends upon egg yolks, however, whites cannot replace them as, for example, in chiffon cake and gold cake.

Directions for Making Hard-cooked Egg Whites

Dissolve
4 tablespoons powdered egg white
in
½ cup water
Add
¼ cup water or skim milk
dash of salt

Pour into a baking dish (or dishes). Place the dish in a pan filled one inch deep with water. Bake in a 325° F. oven until a knife when inserted comes out clean. Do not overcook, as the mixture will become hard. Use sliced or diced on salads, as a garnish, and in sandwich spreads.

Where can I get powdered egg white?
Powdered egg white in small amounts is available at retail stores in some areas. If you do not see it in your market, ask for it. Or inquire from a baker or candymaker's establishment for the name of a producer to whom you can write. In some cities, co-operative stores carry powdered egg albumen.

How to store powdered egg white:
Store powdered egg white tightly covered in a refrigerator or in a freezer. If it is not kept covered, the powder takes up moisture, becomes lumpy, and acquires a strong flavor.

* Not the same as whole egg in food value.

FROZEN EGG WHITES

Frozen egg whites are just as satisfactory to use as powdered egg white, but they are difficult to obtain on the retail market. At present they are frozen in large lots, mostly for bakers and candymakers. After defrosting, the egg white is the same as fresh egg white and can be used in the same way. Use 2 tablespoons for each egg white needed.

LECITHIN GRANULES

Lecithin granules are helpful when using egg whites as a substitute for whole eggs in cooking, since they perform the *emulsifying function* of the egg yolk. It is for this reason that we suggest their use. If you do not see them in your food market, you can obtain them from a drugstore.

BUTTER FLAVORING

Butter flavoring can enrich the taste of certain dishes in which milk is a chief ingredient. It can improve the flavor of white sauces, milk puddings, mousses, whipped skim milk powder, and whipped evaporated skim milk as well as "Special" Cottage Cheese★ and "Special" Cream Cheese★. If this product is not available among the spices and seasonings on the market shelves, you may find it in the gourmet section or in a specialty food store.

Polyunsaturated vegetable oils containing butter flavoring are also useful. We have found it practicable to transfer the contents of a quart of butter-flavored oil to small containers and freeze them. Even though stored in the refrigerator, a quart bottle of oil can become rancid before it is all used.

FLAVORED OILS*

Oils incorporating various flavors provide tasty seasonings for vegetables, meats, sauces, etc. Prepare oils with herbs or seasonings to your liking. Following are directions for making some of our favorites.

* 1 teaspoon of these oils is equal to 1 teaspoon of oil in your diet.

Directions for Making Orange Oil*

Wash the rind of one large, fresh-smelling orange. Use a potato peeler to pare thin slices of the rind and add to them the oil obtained by scraping the outer surface of an orange with a knife edge. Add peelings and scrapings to a half cup of polyunsaturated vegetable oil and heat gently, stirring constantly, as the peelings become limp and the oil takes up the orange color of the peel. Drain the flavored oil into a covered jar and store it in the freezer.

The fresh orange taste will keep indefinitely if the oil is tightly covered and frozen. It will also keep for several weeks in the refrigerator. Small amounts of the orange-flavored oil, when added to vegetables after cooking and just before serving, will enhance their flavor. Large quantities impart a distinct orange flavor, which may also be acceptable, depending on your style of cooking.

Directions for Making Herb Oil*

Heat lightly in a small saucepan until the herb flavors are released

1 cup vegetable oil   ½ clove garlic, crushed
1 teaspoon Italian seasoning   (optional)
1 teaspoon Beau Monde
   seasoning

Remove from heat and strain through a tea strainer into a small bottle or container to store in the refrigerator. Use to season vegetables or meat.

Prepare other flavored oils with herbs or seasonings to your liking.

SOME WAYS TO USE OIL

If occasionally your daily food intake does not meet your Daily Food Guide's recommendation for polyunsaturated oil, here are some quick and pleasing ways of adding it. Oil can *enhance* the flavor of many foods.

Fruits: Stir oil into applesauce or toss with berries or diced fruit.
Juices: Stir into orange juice or any fruit juice, or add some to ginger ale.
Beverages: Blend oil into a "shake" of fruit juice and skim milk powder.

* 1 teaspoon of these oils is equal to 1 teaspoon of oil in your diet.

Cereals: Add oil to a serving of cooked cereal or rice.

Sauces: Add oil to any sauce. Make "maître d'hôtel" sauce with oil, lemon juice, and parsley.

Soups: Add oil to a serving of any soup.

Vegetables and Salads: Use extra oil in a tossed salad or stir into a cooked vegetable.

Puddings: Stir oil into a serving of blanc mange, tapioca pudding, or fruit pudding.

Gelatin: Beat oil into a gelatin dessert or salad when it begins to congeal.

WHEAT GERM

Wheat germ, the little jewel box of the wheat kernel, is rich in the B-complex vitamins and iron that we need in our food every day. It has important value for a less commonly known nutrient, Vitamin E. This vitamin is believed by some authorities to be specifically needed for a diet containing a high proportion of polyunsaturated fatty acids.

Wheat germ is marketed both raw and toasted. The toasted form is necessary in making yeast breads, since the raw form retards the rising process. To toast raw wheat germ, spread it in a pan and heat under the broiler, at a distance of several inches, for a minute or two. Shake frequently and toast lightly. Do not toast to a dark color, since overheating destroys vitamins.

Use wheat germ in:

Yeast bread (add 2 tablespoons, toasted, for each cup of wheat flour)

Cookies, muffins, brown bread, corn bread, pancakes, etc. (approximately 4 tablespoons to ¾ cup flour)

Cereal, rice, macaroni, etc.

Meat dishes

SOYBEAN PRODUCTS

Unlike any other vegetable product, soybeans contain a *complete protein and therefore can substitute for animal protein.* Populations in many parts of the world where very little animal food is available subsist well with soybeans as the foundation of the food supply. Because of the abundant meat, eggs, and milk of the Western world, our food practices have not made use of soybeans. No food, however, is more suitable in a low saturated fat, low cholesterol regimen. Soybeans have three times as much polyunsaturated fatty acids as saturated and are low in total fat. They contain no cholesterol.

Soy flour is available, and it can be added to wheat flour in making certain baked foods, such as muffins and cookies.

Soy grits are a product highly desirable nutritionally and one to be favored as well in recipes. You can use soy grits in:

Ground beef—any proportions; best if well seasoned

Bread—example: Soy Date Bread★

Desserts—examples: Apple Betty★ Date Roll Candy★

Cereal—examples: use as a cereal or add some to other cereals

MEAT SUBSTITUTES
(or vegetable-protein products)

Certain vegetable-protein products made with a base of wheat and soybean protein can provide satisfactory meat substitutes. These are foods that vegetarians rely upon for a large part of their protein requirements. Some of these products are suitable for use in this diet, depending upon whether they contain saturated fat and how much. All are free of cholesterol if the ingredients are all vegetable.

Some commercial varieties look like burgers and steaks, even little sausages, and they resemble meat in texture and in flavor. The vegetable burger can be mixed with ground meat, thereby stretching the meat. This is particularly successful in dishes with Mexican flavoring (taco seasoning) or with Italian seasoning (see our recipes, Chapter XIII). If you do not readily find these products in your food market, ask for them. Read the labels well before buying, to determine whether saturated fat *in any form* is present and whether all other ingredients are acceptable. Many of these vegetable-protein products contain *saturated* vegetable fats and should not be used.

HELPFUL EQUIPMENT

Thermometers

Few gas or electric ovens are manufactured without oven temperature controls. If, however, your oven happens not to have a thermostat, a small *oven thermometer* placed on an oven rack can assist you in controlling heat, which is very important in preparing our recipes.

To save guesswork in roasting meat, poultry, and fish, a *meat thermometer* is a necessity.

A *steak thermometer*, for broiling, is useful in producing steaks that are rare, medium, or well done as desired.

Do You Have the Blender Habit?

Let your blender save you time and work. Here are some job-saving uses for it:

  Mixing or puréeing for soup—example: Gazpacho Soup★
  Beating fruit-milk drinks—example: Strawberry Shake★
  Spreads and dips—example: Cheese Dip★
  Frozen desserts—example: Buttermilk Sherbet★
  Salad dressings—example: Blender Mayonnaise★
  Chopping walnuts—example: Walnut Butter★
  Grating orange and lemon rind—example: Crisp Cookies★
  Liquefying fruits or vegetables—example: purées for omelets or soufflés
  Making bread crumbs
  Grinding coffee
  Making "Special" Cream★, "Special" Sour Cream★, "Special" Cream Cheese★

Teflon

Improved Teflon is now available not only in pots and pans but also in oven racks, broiler racks, and other utensils. Unlike the early Teflon, the improved coating permits the use of ordinary metal stirring spoons and spatulas. Teflon is especially useful in *low fat* cookery and will save you much time in your kitchen chores.

Deep Freezer

Your deep freezer can be a great help as a work and time saver, especially on this diet. Some suggestions are:

  Double the recipes and put half in the deep freezer.
  Freeze dough for rolls, cookies, pies, and pie shells.
  Freeze baked breads, cookies, and cakes. Leave cakes unfrosted when using egg-white frosting, since such frosting does not freeze well.
  Freeze cooked waffles to be dropped into the toaster before serving.
  Freeze bread crumbs and croutons.
  Freeze stews,* meat pies,* soups,* soup stocks, water drained from

---

* Omit potatoes, as they become grainy when frozen. They may be added when serving.

cooking vegetables, bones and scraps for soup stock, fat free meat drippings, etc. Freeze them in portions of the right size to use.

Freeze cooked boned chicken, turkey, and fish to have for salads and "creamed" casserole dishes.

Freeze raw egg whites,* especially reconstituted powdered egg white. Put in individual small containers such as paper cups or flexible cube trays. Cover tightly.

Freeze snack foods and sandwiches.

Freeze cottage cheese curd.

Freeze desserts. (Recipes for mousses, parfaits, sherbets, and "ice creams" are included in the dessert chapter.)

Freeze orange rind, lemon rind, and bell peppers. (These grate easily while still frozen.)

Freeze chopped onions, chopped nuts, chopped parsley, fresh herbs. (These mince easily while frozen.)

* Hard-cooked egg whites do not freeze well.

CHAPTER VII

About Changing Food Habits

CHANGING food habits presents a challenge to the one who plans and prepares the food. This can be a kind of adventure which gives to kitchen work a new zest and a new purpose.

Even though some strides are being made by the food industry in developing foods suited to this diet and educating the public to use them, in the last analysis, changing food habits is personal and comes back to the home. The home food planner who bears the responsibility can try to make meals better than ever before. Though menus be simple, bring extra good flavors and even a touch of candle glamour to your table. Consider eye appeal, if it be only coating a steamed potato with chopped parsley or dusting an oven-baked potato with paprika. Let colorful foods work for you to enhance your fare. Consider contrast—crisp foods served with soft, ice cold with piping hot, spicy or tart with bland. Use flavors artfully.

If you discover the magic of herbs in your kitchen, you will acquire an epicurean's touch. Dried whole leaves of herbs, superior to dried ground ones, retain more of the characteristic fragrance of those plucked from a garden or window box. For the exotic flavors of Italian and Spanish dishes, use orégano, marjoram, sweet basil, and rosemary. For Mexican dishes, use chili powder and orégano, or, better still, use taco flavoring. Let capers complement lamb; use sweet basil in tomato broth; rosemary and marjoram in pot roast and stews; fresh dill in salads. This is only a beginning. Chives, parsley, thyme, savory, tarragon, and many others "do things" to food. As a guide in the use of herbs, follow your favorite herb chart, remembering that with herbs, like perfume, you must be subtle.

Simple meals, garden-fresh vegetables, precision in methods of cooking, thoughtful planning for good nutrition, even diverting the table conversation away from too much talk of diet and dishes and tastes of food—all of these have a part in helping to make mealtime a pleasure and to give a certain quality of satisfaction inherently associated with good food.

CHAPTER VIII

What You
Should Know About Meat

(*Beef, Veal, Lamb, Pork, Fish, and Poultry*)

MEAT is one of the foods containing high quality protein and is a good source of vitamins and minerals. Being an animal product, it also contains cholesterol and saturated fat, but, because it is a complete protein food, some meat is allowed in a low saturated fat, low cholesterol diet. The proper *selection* and *preparation* of meat can be very important factors in lowering your daily intake of cholesterol and saturated fat.

When we refer to meat in this chapter, we mean not only beef, veal, lamb, and pork but also fish and poultry. The last two are indeed preferred, since they are generally lower in saturated fat and cholesterol.

Three essential rules to follow are: eat only the amount of meat allowed on your diet; avoid meats extremely high in cholesterol; eat as little meat fat as possible.

How do you apply these rules? What are the best meats to use? How should meat be prepared? What about gravy? This chapter contains answers to these and other questions you may have about meat.

WHAT MEAT TO EAT

I. *Do not eat meats extremely high in cholesterol,* such as liver, brains, heart, kidney, sweetbreads, tripe, giblets, fish roe, and caviar. Avoid eating meats that might contain any of the above meats, such as ground meat, frankfurters, bologna, liverwurst, or other pressed luncheon meats, unless you have reliable information that they contain very little or no organ meat and are low in saturated fat.

II. *Buy lean meat.* Lean poultry and fish should be your choice of meat for most of your meals, as these are lower in saturated fat and cholesterol than lean beef and other lean red meats. Fish fat is high in polyunsaturates compared to other meat fats.*

Have your ground meat made from trimmed lean meat. Ready-ground meat usually contains fairly large amounts of fat. By careful trimming of meat before grinding, the fat content can be greatly reduced. Explain your needs to your butcher. Unless he has been grinding very lean meat, or unless you are ordering about five pounds or more of ground meat, you should grind your own, as the butcher's grinder will contain meat from the previous grinding. Ask the butcher to separate from your order as much of this meat as possible as it comes out of the grinder. Electric meat grinders for home use do an excellent job, and you can be sure all separable fat is removed by grinding your own meat.

Do not buy prepared ground meat products such as patties and mock chicken legs.

Avoid buying cuts of meat in which large amounts of fat are distributed throughout the meat and cannot be removed, as in some roasts and steaks. This is called "marbling." Fish, poultry, and most veal cuts do not have marbling of fat. Range beef is tougher, but has less marbling of fat than meat from cattle that has been prepared for market in a feed lot.

We used to consider the prime and choice grades of beef, lamb, and veal to be the highest in fat content. However, according to the National Live Stock and Meat Board:

"In today's grading of carcasses the amount of lean is one of the important factors which determines how high a grade a carcass will receive. Thus, a carcass with more lean meat—for example, a large rib eye area—may be graded higher than a more marbled carcass."

Since grade does not indicate fat content, look for and buy the kinds and cuts of meat which, by test, contain the least fat (see chart pages 488–89†) and which appear to have the least marbling and streaking of fat. It is impossible to present lists of cuts that are sure to be lean, as meat varies a great deal in fat content and the types of cuts vary in different parts of the country. Use these lists as a guide, but, since fat content varies even between two meat cuts of the same type, the final criterion in selecting lean meat is the *appearance* of a minimum of fat in the *individual cut.*

III. *Avoid eating the visible fat in meat.* The separable fat should

---

* In most fish the polyunsaturated fatty acids are those other than linoleic acid, so food composition charts giving just the linoleic acid content do not present a true picture of the polyunsaturated fat content of fish.

† Heart Association material and the U. S. Department of Agriculture's *Home and Garden Bulletin No. 72* give additional material on the fat content of various kinds and cuts of meat.

be removed from most cuts of meat before they are cooked. Some separable fat is not removed but must not be eaten. Some fat cannot be removed before cooking—such as the fat streaks that run through meat. Do not eat this fat or *any* visible fat in meat which can be avoided.

Eat only the leanest section of a piece of meat. Just as some cuts of meat (with separable fat removed) are leaner than others, in every cut of beef, lamb, and pork there is a fat-marbled section and a more lean section (see figures below). By eating only the *leanest part,* your animal fat intake is greatly reduced. In a lean heel of round, for example, the lean cooked part contains 5.4 per cent fat and the whole piece (with separable fat removed), 10 per cent. By eating only the lean section, your fat intake would be cut almost in half, as compared to eating the same weight of meat from the whole piece (lean plus marble).

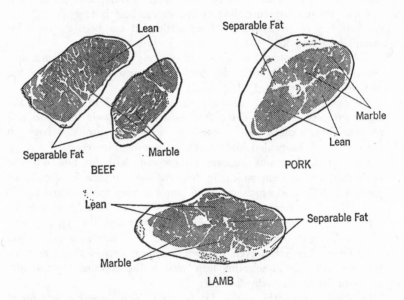

Veal versus Beef

Veal is considered a lean red meat after it is trimmed of separable fat. The advantage of veal, like that of fish and poultry, is that there is no marbling of fat in most cuts. In these meats the entire piece may be eaten, exclusive of the separable fat, which is never allowed on this diet. You do not have to select just the leanest portion of a serving to eat, as you must do with most other meats, since there generally is no leanest part in these meats. If one ate *only* the leanest part of a piece of lean beef, it would be about as lean as veal. This may not be practical, and in addition, unless the lean section of beef is separated from the marbled section before it is served, it is a temptation to eat the entire piece of beef. Veal is slightly higher in cholesterol than beef, but since it is lower in saturated fat, we prefer veal to beef unless the beef is exceptionally lean.

Horsemeat, Venison, and Wild Rabbit

Horsemeat, venison, and wild rabbit are lean meats.

What About Pork?

Lean cuts of pork and ham may be used *occasionally* if, when cooking them, you *carefully* follow the principles of meat cookery for this diet. See the chart, pages 488–89, for some of the leaner cuts of pork and ham. You must remember these figures are for just the *leanest* part of *well-cooked* pork and ham.

Cold cuts or luncheon meats vary in fat content and should be avoided, since some are extremely high in fat.

If you must have a little bacon for flavoring, see Bacon Bits★, page 115.

(There are substitutes for cooked bacon bits on the market, but these should not be used unless acceptable oils are used in their preparation. The vegetable oil used in the brands we found is mainly coconut oil. Also, one should be cautious about the use of smoked flavoring. See page 84.)

What About Shellfish?

Because of their low saturated fat content, limited use of crab, shrimp, and clams is permitted in this diet. However, you must remember they are about twice as high in cholesterol-like substances as lean red meat. Substituting *one half* as much crab, shrimp, or clams for a specified weight of red meats makes your cholesterol intake about the same. On the occasional day when you choose to eat these shellfish, your protein loss will have to be made up in cholesterol-free, high-protein foods such as skim milk, cottage cheese, skim milk yogurt, etc. See the list of equivalents of 1-ounce servings of meat on page 475. *Lobster, scallops, and oysters are extremely high in cholesterol-*

substances and should be avoided. Research results on other shellfish are inconclusive at this time.

Canned and Frozen Meat

Buy only lean canned and frozen meats or those from which the fat can be removed. When using these canned meats, remove the fat from the broth. If the broth has jelled, put the meat and broth in a pan with a small amount of water, cover closely, and steam until the broth has melted. Remove the fat from the broth before using (see page 85). Avoid using meats canned or frozen in thickened broth or frozen crumbed meat (for example, fish sticks) because it is difficult to remove the fat.

HOW MUCH MEAT TO EAT*

The amount of meat you may eat will depend upon the amounts of saturated fat and cholesterol allowed in your diet. The Daily Food Guides we present range from seven ounces of *cooked* lean red meat, fish, or poultry daily down to rigid restrictions.

How to Determine a Serving

Since meat is one of the saturated fat, high cholesterol foods, it is very important that you eat no more than the amounts specified in the diet recommended by your physician. The servings of beef, lamb, pork, and ham will probably be smaller than you are used to eating. The weights we give in these diets are for the cooked meat you actually eat. How much meat you eat at any one meal will depend on how you choose to divide your total daily meat allowance.

Each of our recipes states the *approximate* number of ounces of cooked meat it contains per serving. This varies from 1 ounce in the low meat dishes to 3 ounces in our regular meat recipes. We give servings as *family serving* in our recipes when the meat is cooked before skin or bone are removed, therefore making it difficult to estimate the amount of raw meat to use. A family serving may contain more (or less) than 3 ounces of cooked meat. The calculations, however, are for a *portion* containing 3 ounces of cooked meat. Determine your diet portion after the cooked meat is separated from the skin and bone.

Weigh or measure a serving of meat after it is cooked in all recipes where this is possible. For those recipes in which the meat is mixed

* See Chapter IV, pages 25–26.

with other ingredients and therefore cannot be separated, a serving is determined from the amount of meat used in the total recipe. In these recipes, weigh (or measure) meat carefully *before* adding it to other ingredients.

Scales Are Helpful

It is difficult, even for experts, to estimate accurately a specified serving of meat by weight. We find the use of a *small scale* very helpful in weighing servings. A postal scale, which weighs in ounces, is accurate and inexpensive. A diet scale calibrated in both grams and ounces, with a 1-pound (16 ounces) capacity, is also available. We purchased ours from a stationery store.

When a Scale Is Not Available

If you must determine servings when a scale is not available, here are some examples of approximate weight equivalents of cooked meat which we have found useful:

(Borrow a scale to check your estimated measures occasionally as we found variations; for example, as much as 3 ounces per cup of tuna depending on how solid the tuna was and how firmly it was packed in the measuring cup.)

Approximate Weight Equivalents of Cooked Meat

Approximate 3-ounce servings:
  ½ cup canned tuna or salmon, firmly packed
  ½ cup chicken meat, firmly packed
  Half a breast, or leg and thigh, of 2½–3-pound chicken
  2 slices roast beef or veal, 3 by 3 by ¼ inches
  1 medium loin pork chop, ¾ inch thick
  1 meat patty, 3 inches diameter and ½ inch thick

Other equivalents:
  1 cup flaked tuna or salmon weighs approximately 6 ounces
  1 cup diced chicken or turkey weighs approximately 5 ounces
  1 cup ground raw beef or veal weighs approximately 8 ounces
  (½ pound)

Consider the Trimmings and the Shrinkage

When buying meat, remember some weight will be lost in trimmings (bone, skin, separable fat, and other waste) and some in shrinkage during cooking. Since meat varies a great deal in the trimmings it contains and in the amount it will shrink, the amount of raw meat required for a serving (in ounces) of cooked meat can only be an estimate. This is an especially rough estimate when the meat is to be cooked with bone or skin.

Most of our recipes state the amount of meat required as raw, trimmed weight. This *does not mean the bone and skin have to be removed before the meat is cooked* but means to estimate the amount of raw meat needed for the recipe considering the size of bone and amount of skin, fat, and other trimmings it contains, and to allow for this when buying your meat.

Following is a *rough guide* (especially rough when bone is involved, as the bone content of meat varies such a great deal) for the number of ounces to allow for trimmings and shrinkage when buying raw meat.

Cooked meat	Raw meat without bone (allowance for shrinkage)	Raw meat with bone (allowance for trimmings and shrinkage)
For 3 ounces	buy 4 ounces (¼ pound)	or 5 ounces
For 6 ounces	buy 8 ounces (½ pound)	or 10 ounces
For 12 ounces	buy 16 ounces (1 pound)	or 20 ounces (1¼ pounds)

HOW TO PREPARE MEAT

Although there are many ways of preparing meat, our recipes use those methods which are suited to a low saturated fat, low cholesterol diet and which we have found practical in our own kitchens. If you prefer, you may use other methods, provided they follow the principles of this diet. The foremost principle is: *Cook meat by a method that reduces saturated fat to a minimum.* Therefore, the following rules are advisable:

1. Where possible, cut off excess fat from meat before the meat is cooked. Kitchen shears and a sharp knife are both useful for removing fat.
2. Render as much fat out of meat by long, slow cooking as taste and appearance permit.
3. Do not let meat "sit" in fat during cooking, as some of the fat

that otherwise could be removed is absorbed by the meat. Remove any fat that accumulates in the pan during pan-broiling or browning; place meat on a rack while oven broiling or roasting. We cook meat on pleated foil to keep it out of the fat in certain recipes. A rib-bottomed skillet helps keep meat out of the fat during pan-broiling. (If lean, well-trimmed meat is used, little or no removable fat will accumulate.)

4. Do not baste meat with its own drippings while cooking. Baste with a liquid free of saturated fat, such as fat free drippings saved from previous cooking or broth, wine, or vegetable juices. Do not reuse the liquid to baste the meat.

5. Extra meat fat can be absorbed from some cooked meat by placing the hot meat between two layers of paper toweling and blotting.

6. Remove the fat from meat drippings or broth before they are used. See pages 85 and 135. (If lean, trimmed meat is used, there will be little or no removable fat in the drippings or broth.)

7. Avoid flouring or crumbing meat, since flour and crumbs absorb fat that could otherwise be removed. (Lean fish is an exception. See page 117.)

We find the use of Teflon-coated pans and broiler racks a great help in keeping lean meat from sticking during cooking.

We have outlined in Chapters IX, X, and XI some ways of preparing red meat, fish, and poultry, applying the above principles.

How to Brown Meat

Oil (polyunsaturated) may be used in the browning of meat. (The amount depends on your fat and calorie allowance.) Be sure to keep the temperature *below the smoking point.* When fats are heated above this point, chemical changes occur that cause fats to become more saturated and produce harmful carcinogens.

Since lean meat is used for this diet, the browning of some meats may be difficult without oil. Following are some hints we have found helpful. Wiping the pan with a cloth or an absorbent paper containing polyunsaturated oil or brushing with a lightly oiled pastry brush is often all that is necessary to keep lean meat from sticking. Even without oil, a satisfactory browning may be obtained by careful watching and frequent turning of the meat. No oil is needed (except for lean fish) when a Teflon-coated pan is used. Starting the browning in a small, cold pan with low heat usually requires less oil. We find that oil goes farther if it is brushed on the meat, especially poultry. We like to use the broiler for browning. It does a good job and the meat is kept out of any fat that may accumulate in the lower part of the broiler pan. Remember to keep the temperature below the smoking point of the fat.

Often a better flavor is given to a meat dish if fresh oil is added after the meat has been browned. This is a good way to get additional polyunsaturated fat into your diet if your oil allowance requires it.

Any oil used in browning of meat or added later must be counted as part of your daily fat and calorie intake.

What About Barbecuing and Smoked Flavoring?

Exposure of food to smoke during cooking or the addition of smoked flavoring is not recommended because there seems to be growing evidence that all such smoke contains poisonous substances that increase the risk of cancer and also disturb metabolic functions. The flavors sought in wood smoke are volatile natural substances released by the burning wood; they are not harmful in themselves, but so far these flavors have not been commercially available separated from the tar products of combustion.

The recommended method for broiling or rotisserie cooking is to use ovens having the source of heat above or at the side of the food being cooked. *Unless the food is burned,* this method does not expose the food to smoke. Wood fires used for outdoor cooking always have some smoke from the fire, and even though charcoal fires reduce this tendency, during the cooking process drippings from the food fall upon the coals and are converted to smoke. Cancer-producing compounds have been found in abundance in foods cooked in this manner. Preferably such outdoor cooking methods should use an arrangement in which the meat is not directly above the hot coals. With the fire at one side of the meat being cooked, the meat drippings do not fall on the coals and no smoke is formed to rise onto the meat. The meat is cooked by concentrating the heat against a reflector. Such devices can cook meat faster than the direct fire methods.

WHAT ABOUT GRAVY?

Nicely browned, well-flavored gravy is a tasty addition to any meat or meat-substitute dish. You may use gravy if you make it according to the principles of this diet.

The brown drippings left in the bottom of the pan in which meat is cooked, or the water in which it is cooked, should be used for flavoring gravy, soups, and vegetables. Usually, however, melted fat is contained in the drippings or the cooking water, and this fat should not be eaten. We have measured the fat accumulated in the drippings during the cooking of meat and in the broth of fresh, frozen, and canned meat and have often found the amount amazingly large. This fat would normally be eaten in gravy, stews, or soups but should be removed before the drippings and broth are used in this diet.

How to Remove the Fat from Drippings and Broth

The following three methods have proved satisfactory for fat removal. First, if the drippings are scant, add a little water and bring it to a boil, scraping those drippings which are stuck, as the brown deposits are high in meat flavor.

Chilling method: Suitable for meat that can be cooked in advance, such as Swiss steaks, stews, and pot roasts.
1. Pour the drippings or broth into a metal container with a wide opening.
2. Chill.
3. Remove the fat cake before using.
The above method can be modified for use with roasts by removing some of the drippings before the meat is done. Chill them in a shallow pan in the freezing unit and remove the hardened fat. By this method, the gravy can be made while the meat is finishing cooking. If there is less than one cup of drippings, see ice cube method below.

Quick cold water method: Suitable for any meat, but does not assure as complete a removal of fat as the chilling method.
1. Pour drippings or broth into a metal container with a wide opening.
2. Set the container in cold water. The fat will quickly rise to the top.
3. Spoon off as much fat as possible.
4. Blot off the remaining fat with absorbent paper.

Quick ice cube method: Suitable for less than one cup of drippings.
1. Pour the drippings into a cup.
2. Add ice cubes.
3. Stir and remove the fat as it hardens.

Store in the freezer or refrigerator a stock of any extra meat drippings or broth. These can be used when needed for gravy, soup, sauces, or flavoring. Drippings will keep several days in the refrigerator if the fat cake is left on until the liquid is used and will keep indefinitely frozen. We freeze it in convenient portions in small dishes or a flexible ice cube tray. Store the frozen portions in a covered container.

How to Make Fat Free Gravy

There are several acceptable methods of making gravy. One that has proved satisfactory to us is:

1. Remove the fat from the drippings or broth (see pages 85 and 135).
2. Measure the liquid, adding more water, bouillon broth, skim milk, or vegetable or meat stock, depending on the flavor desired and the amount of gravy needed.
3. Use 1 or 2 tablespoons browned flour (see below) or 1 tablespoon uncooked flour for each ½ cup liquid. Browned flour may be used for the added color and flavor it gives to gravy.
4. Put some of the liquid in a jar, add the flour, cover tightly, and shake until the mixture is smooth.*
5. Pour into a pan, add remaining liquid, and heat, stirring constantly
6. Add seasonings to taste. In addition to salt and pepper, use chopped parsley, chopped celery stalk and leaves, chopped onion, grated horseradish, or any other favorite seasoning. Garlic, orégano, and sweet basil are favorites.
7. Simmer for a few minutes, stirring constantly. If uncooked flour is used, the gravy will need to be cooked longer to avoid the taste of raw flour. Add gravy coloring if desired.
8. If your daily fat allowance permits, add about 1 tablespoonful (or more if desired) of polyunsaturated oil per ½ cup of total liquid in step 4.

To make browned flour, spread flour in a shallow pan and cook, using very low heat and stirring occasionally until lightly browned. Larger quantities, to be stored for later use, may be browned in the oven (300° F., about 15 minutes).

Variations for Gravy

1. If broth or meat drippings are not available, a good gravy can be made by using bouillon cubes, Savorex, or other meat flavorings.
2. Use cooked vegetables, puréed in an electric blender, for part of the liquid in the above recipe. For example, for 2 cups of gravy, cook in a small amount of water until barely tender and blend
   ¼ cup minced onion   *¼ green pepper*
   ½ small stalk celery (about   *¼ small carrot (about*
   ⅓ cup chopped)   *2 tablespoons chopped)*
Measure and add enough strong Savorex broth, bouillon broth, or meat broth to make 2 cups, and follow directions for making fat free gravy.

* For use of extra oil, see step 8. Oil is added in step 4.

Avoid a Last-minute Rush

Waiting until the meat is done to make gravy usually results in cold meat being served or a rush to get the gravy done. Here are some ways to have the gravy ready when the meat has finished cooking:

1. To make gravy for meat cooked with some liquid added, such as Swiss steaks, stews, pot roasts, veal cutlets, and braised chicken:

    Take meat from liquid (referred to as liquid I) when it is almost done.

    Finish cooking meat in small amount of added liquid (referred to as liquid II).

    Remove fat from liquid I by quick method (see page 88).

    If meat is to be served in the gravy, return the meat to the gravy (save liquid II for later use).

    Make gravy.

2. Gravy for oven roasts can be made by removing the drippings before the roast is done. Make the gravy while the roast is finishing cooking (see page 85).

3. Since broiled meats should be served as soon as they are done for fullest enjoyment of their flavor, we recommend making the gravy from drippings stored in the freezer or refrigerator.

GARNISHES AND ACCOMPANIMENTS

When the amount of meat is limited, the way it is served becomes increasingly important. A dash of color or a touch of garnish can turn a plain dish into an attractive and appetizing one. Following are some suggested garnishes and accompaniments for meat.

GARNISHES

Lemon slices or wedges (for fish)

Cooked whole or sliced beets

Carrot tops

Carrot curls or sticks

Celery tops

Celery curls or sticks

Chopped parsley or parsley sprigs

Chopped watercress or watercress sprigs

Radish roses or slices

Pimiento strips

Whole, sliced, or chopped pickles

Paprika

Green pepper rings or strips

Cucumber slices or sticks

Mushroom caps or slices

Fresh onion rings

ACCOMPANIMENTS

Cinnamon apples

Cinnamon pears

Peaches or apricots, broiled with a sprinkling of brown sugar

Spiced peaches, pears, apricots, or prunes

Spiced watermelon rind

Applesauce or steamed apple rings

Pineapple wedges or slices

Broiled bananas

Well-seasoned slice of tomato, either cooked with seasoned crumbs or marinated with herbs

Fat free bread crumb dressings

Relishes, such as chutney, cranberry jelly or sauce, mint jelly or sauce, catsup, or chili

SEASONINGS

The use of herbs, spices, special meat seasonings, wines, and vegetables adds a great deal to meat cookery. Seasoning is an individual matter. For suggestions, take advantage of material published by herb, spice, and wine producers. Packaged mixed seasonings, such as for meat loaf, tacos, chili, stroganoff, enchilada sauce, and meat marinade, are acceptable if they do not contain saturated fats.

OIL CALCULATIONS

Be sure to calculate as part of your daily oil intake just that oil in the portion which you actually eat. Don't, for example, include oil left in the cooking pan or on your plate, or the oil you added to the entire recipe or used to brown all the meat in a recipe. To find how much oil there is in the portion you eat, divide the total amount of oil used in the recipe by the number of portions of that size in the entire recipe.

CHAPTER IX

Beef, Veal, Lamb, and Pork

BECOME familiar with the principles in What You Should Know About Meat, Chapter VIII (page 76), before buying, cooking, or eating beef, veal, lamb, or pork.

COOKING METHODS

There are six specific methods for cooking meat—roasting, broiling, pan-broiling, frying, braising, and cooking in liquid. The method selected depends upon the tenderness of the cut, its size and thickness, personal preference, and the cooking facilities. Frying is not recommended for this diet because: 1) some of the melted meat fat is absorbed by the meat; 2) the cooking oil absorbed by the food cannot be accurately measured.

Usually, tender cuts of meat are best when cooked by dry heat, such as roasting, broiling, and pan-broiling. Less tender cuts of meat are made tender by long, slow cooking in moisture to soften the connective tissue. Less tender cuts may be ground, pounded, scored, cubed, or marinated and then cooked by the same methods as tender cuts.

During cooking, most cuts of meat are made leaner. Fat is cooked out of the meat, as is evident in the bottom of the pan. We think of pork as a fat meat, for example, but by long, slow cooking some cuts are made acceptable for occasional use in this diet.

When cooking cuts of meat which lose appreciable amounts of fat during cooking, it is especially important not to let the meat "sit" in the fat. Oven-broil—do not pan-broil—these cuts. When braising or cooking them in water, it is important to remove the meat from the liquid as soon as the meat is done. Fat will have cooked out into the liquid.

In addition to rendering out some of the fat during cooking, fresh pork must be *well cooked* to kill any trichinosis infection. Use a thermometer when roasting pork to be certain the center of the meat is thoroughly cooked.

Among the accepted methods for the preparation of meat, we have adapted certain ones for use in this diet. Consult the charts on pages 95 and 96 for the method to use and the length of time to cook a specific cut of meat. Cooking time is only approximate, as the quality of meat, its size, shape, and temperature at the start all affect the time required. Use a meat thermometer if you have one, as it is an accurate guide to the degree of doneness of all kinds of roasts, thick steaks, and chops. Insert it so the bulb is in the center of the largest muscle without touching bone or resting in fat or dressing. Thermometers designed just for broiling are now on the market.

As we have said in Chapter VIII, do not allow the fat of meat or any oil used in cooking to become hot enough to *smoke*. This means the temperature is too high for the oil and also for the meat.

HOW TO ROAST

1. Season with salt and pepper.
2. Place the meat, fat side down, on a rack in an open, shallow roasting pan. The rack holds the roast out of the drippings. If meat becomes dry, baste with a liquid free of saturated fat (see page 83), or cover top loosely with aluminum foil, or place a thin cloth moistened with oil over the top. Do not baste with the meat's own drippings.
3. Do not add water. Do not cover with lid. (If these are done, the meat becomes a pot roast, not an oven roast.)
4. Roast in a slow oven (300°–350°) to the desired degree of doneness. See the timetables, pages 95–96, for roasting beef, veal, lamb, and pork. Meat continues to cook for a time after it has been removed from the oven. If it is not going to be served immediately, a roast should be removed from the oven when the thermometer registers 5 to 10 degrees below the desired degree of doneness. Roasts carve more easily if permitted to "set" after cooking.
5. Remove the fat from the drippings before they are used.

How to roast in a very slow oven. Less tender cuts are usually cooked by one of the methods that use added liquid; however, we frequently oven-roast a less tender cut of meat by cooking on a rack for many hours at a very low temperature. We have found this method excellent, as the juices stay in the meat, leaving it deliciously tender. Follow the directions for oven-roasting, using a meat thermometer and having the oven temperature 10 to 20 degrees above the internal temperature the meat will reach when done. Consult the meat chart (page 95) for the temperature for rare, medium, and well-done roasts. Unless you are certain your oven thermostat is accurate, use an oven thermometer and check occasionally during the cooking period to be sure the oven temperature is remaining constant. This method of roasting meat will take two or three times longer than the usual roasting time. We have found the succulence of the meat cooked by this method well worth the extra roasting time. Tender cuts can also be roasted by this method.

HOW TO BROIL

It is not necessary to remove the excess fat before broiling, since the meat does not stand in the melted fat. Do not eat any fat that can be removed.

1. Place the meat on the rack of the broiler pan. (The broiler can be preheated or not, as desired.) If desired, brush a lean meat such as veal with oil before broiling.* The top surface of steaks, chops, or patties 1 to 2 inches thick should be 3 to 5 inches from the heat; those less than 1 inch in thickness about 2 to 3 inches from the heat. See the timetables on pages 96–97.
2. Broil until top surface is brown.
3. Turn and brown the other side.
4. Season and serve at once on a hot platter.
5. Remove the fat from the drippings before they are used.

HOW TO PAN-BROIL

1. Remove separable fat from meat.
2. Place the meat in a heavy frying pan, rib-bottomed skillet or Teflon skillet, or on a griddle. See "How to Brown Meat," page 83. Since searing does not hold in meat juices, a gradual browning is best. Less tender cuts that have been made tender by pounding or scoring are likely to lose juices because so much surface is exposed, so they should be cooked quickly in a hot pan.

* This oil must be calculated into your daily oil allowance. Some authorities do not recommend broiling veal, as it is not considered a tender meat. They recommend long, slow cooking in moisture to soften the connective tissue.

3. Do not add water. Do not cover.

4. Turn occasionally so the meat will cook evenly.

5. Remove fat as it accumulates in the pan. If it is permitted to collect, the meat will absorb some of the fat.

6. Cook until meat is brown on both sides. Do not overcook.

7. Season and serve at once on a hot platter.

8. Remove the fat from the drippings before they are used.

HOW TO BRAISE

1. Cut separable fat from meat. When possible, cook the meat in advance so the liquid can be chilled and the fat more completely removed.

2. Brown meat slowly on all sides in a heavy utensil. See "How to Brown Meat," page 86. If the meat is extremely lean, wipe the pan lightly with vegetable oil. It is not necessary to brown the meat, but browning develops flavor and a pleasing color. Do not flour or crumb meat, as flour and crumbs absorb fat.

3. Season with salt, pepper, herbs, spices, and vegetables as desired.

4. Add a small amount of liquid, such as water, soup stock, or vegetable juice, to less tender cuts.* If the liquid cooks away, a little more may be added.

5. Cover closely and cook at a simmering temperature (not boiling) until tender. This may be done on top of the range or in a slow oven, not above 300° F. See the timetables, page 97, for cooking beef, veal, lamb, and pork.

6. Take the meat out of the liquid and put in a pan, platter, or casserole and keep hot. Remove the fat from the liquid.

7. From the fat free liquid make a sauce or gravy to be poured over the meat or served in a separate bowl, as it is a desirable part of any braised meat dish.

HOW TO COOK IN LIQUID

The main difference between braising and cooking in liquid is that more liquid is added in the latter method. This method is used for cooking some large cuts of meat, such as pot roasts, and for stews.

---

* The addition of lemon juice, tomato juice, or vinegar to the cooking water helps to tenderize meat.

When possible, cook the meat in advance so the liquid can be chilled and the fat more completely removed.

The following directions are for stewing. For a large cut of meat, the only modification is to eliminate step 2 and cook the meat in one large piece.

1. Buy lean meat and cut excess fat from it.
2. Cut meat in uniform pieces, usually 1- to 2-inch cubes. If desired, the meat may be cut into rectangular pieces or long narrow strips.
3. If a brown stew is desired, brown the pieces of meat on all sides in a heavy utensil. See "How to Brown Meat," page 83. If a light-colored stew is preferred, omit browning. Do not crumb or flour the meat, as crumbs and flour absorb fat.
4. Add enough water, vegetable juices, or soup stock to cover the meat.* The liquid may be added hot or cold.
5. Season with salt, pepper, herbs, and spices, as these are important for a good stew.
6. Cover the kettle closely and simmer until meat is tender. Do not boil. (1 to 3 hours will be required, depending upon the meat.) See the timetables, page 98, for cooking beef, veal, lamb, and pork.
7. Add vegetables at the proper time to prevent overcooking them. The vegetables may be left whole, quartered, or cut in small, uniform pieces. Use any suitable vegetables, such as carrots, onions, potatoes, and peas. (Omit this step for pot roasts if you wish.)
8. Remove the meat and vegetables from the liquid, put in a pan or casserole, and keep hot. Remove the fat from the liquid.
9. Make the gravy and serve the gravy, meat, and vegetables together, or remove the meat and vegetables and serve the gravy in a separate bowl. (Gravy is served separately for pot roasts.)
10. If desired, make meat pie from the stew, as a meat pie is merely a stew with a top on it. The top may be made of pastry, mashed potatoes, or cooked cereal. Cook the pie in a hot oven until the top is brown.

PRESSURE-COOKING

Pressure-cooking may be used for cuts of meat which require braising or cooking in water. The meat is cooked to tenderness in approximately one-fourth to one-half the usual time. Follow the directions for your particular pressure cooker.

* See footnote page 92.

ROTISSERIE ROASTING

For rotisserie cooking, follow the directions that come with your rotisserie. Roasts and poultry are easy to cook this way, as are kebobs and meat balls on skewers. We do not recommend rotisserie cooking of meats directly over coals. See page 84.

COOKING FROZEN MEAT

Frozen meat may be either defrosted or left in the frozen state for cooking. *When defrosting before cooking,* you may do it:

In the refrigerator
At room temperature
In water—recommended only if the meat is to be cooked
   in liquid

Defrost the meat in its original wrappings and do not allow it to remain at room temperature after defrosting. Defrosted meat is cooked in the same way as other fresh meat. Refreezing raw meat is not recommended.

TIMETABLE FOR DEFROSTING FROZEN MEAT*

Meat	In Refrigerator	At Room Temperature
Large roast	4 to 7 hours per pound	2 to 3 hours per pound
Small roast	3 to 5 hours per pound	1 to 2 hours per pound
1-inch steak	12 to 14 hours	2 to 4 hours

* National Live Stock and Meat Board, *Lessons on Meat,* 1965.

When cooking meat from the frozen state: Allow extra cooking time. Frozen roasts require about one third to one half more cooking time than defrosted roasts. The additional cooking time needed for frozen steaks and chops varies according to their size and thickness.

Thick frozen chops, steaks, and ground meat patties should be placed farther from the heat when broiling.

When pan-broiling frozen steaks and chops, turn more frequently so the meat will cook through evenly.

TIMETABLE FOR ROASTING*

Cut	Approx. Weight (Pounds)	Oven Temperature Constant	Interior Temperature When Removed from Oven		Approx. Cooking Time Min. per lb.
BEEF					
Standing rib†	6–8	300°–325° F.	140° F.	(rare)	23–25
			160°	(medium)	27–30
			170°	(well)	32–35
	4–6	300°–325°	140°	(rare)	26–32
			160°	(medium)	34–38
			170°	(well)	40–42
Rolled rib	5–7	300°–325°	140°	(rare)	32
			160°	(medium)	38
			170°	(well)	48
Delmonico (rib eye)	4–6	350°	140°	(rare)	18–20
			160°	(medium)	20–22
			170°	(well)	22–24
Tenderloin, whole	4–6	425°	140°	(rare)	45–60 (total)
Tenderloin, half	2–3	425°	140°	(rare)	45–50 (total)
Rolled rump (high quality)	4–6	300°–325°	150°–170°		25–30
Sirloin tip	3½–4	300°–325°	140°–170°		35–40
(high quality)	4–6	300°–325°	140°–170°		30–35
VEAL					
Leg	5–8	300°–325°	170°		25–35
Loin	4–6	300°–325°	170°		30–35
Rib (rack)	3–5	300°–325°	170°		35–40
Rolled shoulder	4–6	300°–325°	170°		40–45
PORK, FRESH					
Loin					
Center	3–5	325°–350°	170°		30–35
Half	5–7	325°–350°	170°		35–40
Blade loin or sirloin	3–4	325°–350°	170°		40–45
Rolled	3–5	325°–350°	170°		35–45
Leg (fresh ham)					
Whole (bone in)	10–14	325°–350°	170°		25–30
Whole (rolled)	7–10	325°–350°	170°		35–40
Half (bone in)	5–7	325°–350°	185°		40–45

Cut	Approx. Weight (Pounds)	Oven Temper- ature Constant	Interior Temperature When Removed from Oven	Approx. Cooking Time Min. per lb.
PORK, SMOKED				
Ham (cook before eating)				
Whole	10–14	300°–325°	160°	18–20
Half	5–7	300°–325°	160°	22–25
Shank or butt portion	3–4	300°–325°	160°	35–40
Ham (fully cooked)‡				
Half	5–7	325°	130°	18–24
LAMB				
Leg	5–8	300°–325°	175°–180°	30–35

* Adapted from National Live Stock and Meat Board, *Lessons on Meat,* 1965.
† Ribs which measure 6 to 7 inches from chine bone to tip of rib.
‡ Allow approximately 15 minutes per pound for heating whole ham to serve hot.

TIMETABLE FOR BROILING*

Cut	Weight or Thickness	Approximate Total Cooking Time	
		Rare	Medium
BEEF	Pounds	Minutes	Minutes
Chuck steak (high quality)—1 inch	1½–2½	24	30
1½ inches	2–4	40	45
Rib steak—1 inch	1–1½	15	20
1½ inches	1½–2	25	30
2 inches	2–2½	35	45
Rib eye steak—1 inch	8–10 ounces	15	20
1½ inches	12–14 ounces	25	30
2 inches	16–20 ounces	35	45
Club steak—1 inch	1–1½	15	20
1½ inches	1½–2	25	30
2 inches	2–2½	35	45
Sirloin steak—1 inch	1½–3	20	25
1½ inches	2¼–4	30	35
2 inches	3–5	40	45
Porterhouse steak—			
1 inch	1¼–2	20	25
1½ inches	2–3	30	35
2 inches	2½–3½	40	45

Cut	Weight or Thickness	Approximate Total Cooking Time	
		Rare	Medium
	Pounds	Minutes	Minutes
Filet Mignon			
1 inch	4–6	15	20
1½ inches	6–8	18	22
Ground beef patties			
1 inch thick by 3 inches	4 ounces	15	25
PORK—SMOKED			
Ham slice—tendered			
½ inch	¾–1	Ham always	10–12
1 inch	1½–2	cooked well done	16–20
Loin chops	¾–1		15–20
PORK—FRESH			
Rib or loin chops	¾–1 inch	Always cooked well done	20–25
LAMB			
Shoulder chops—			
1 inch	5–8 ounces	Lamb chops	12
1½ inches	8–10 ounces	are not usually	18
2 inches	10–16 ounces	served rare	22
Rib chops—1 inch	3–5 ounces		12
1½ inches	4–7 ounces		18
2 inches	6–10 ounces		22
Loin chops—1 inch	4–7 ounces		12
1½ inches	6–10 ounces		18
2 inches	8–14 ounces		22
Ground lamb patties			
1 inch by 3 inches	4 ounces		18

* This timetable is based on broiling at a moderate temperature (350° F.). Rare steaks are broiled to an internal temperature of 140° F.; medium to 160° F.; well done to 170° F. Lamb chops are broiled from 170° F. to 175° F. Ham is cooked to 160° F.

TIMETABLE FOR BRAISING*

Cut	Average Weight or Thickness	Approximate Total Cooking Time
BEEF		
Pot Roast		
arm or blade	3–4 pounds	2½–3½ hours
boneless	3–5 pounds	3–4 hours

Cut	Average Weight or Thickness	Approximate Total Cooking Time
Swiss steak	1½–2½ inches	2–3 hours
Fricassee	2-inch cubes	1½–2½ hours
Beef birds	½ inch (×2×4) inches)	1½–2½ hours
Short ribs	Pieces (2×2×4 inches)	1½–2½ hours
Round steak	¾ inch	1–1½ hours
Stuffed steak	½–¾ inch	1½ hours
PORK		
Chops	¾–1½ inches	45–60 minutes
Tenderloin		
Whole	¾ to 1 pound	45–60 minutes
Fillets	½ inch	30 minutes
Shoulder steaks	¾ inch	45–60 minutes
LAMB		
Neck slices	¾ inch	1 hour
Shanks	¾ to 1 pound each	1–1½ hours
VEAL		
Breast—rolled	2–3 pounds	1½–2½ hours
Veal birds	½ inch (×2×4 inches)	45–60 minutes
Chops	½–¾ inch	45–60 minutes
Steaks or cutlets	½–¾ inch	45–60 minutes
Shoulder chops	½–¾ inch	45–60 minutes
Shoulder cubes	1–2 inches	45–60 minutes

* Adapted from National Live Stock and Meat Board, *Lessons on Meat,* 1965.

TIMETABLE FOR COOKING IN LIQUID*

Cut	Average Weight	Approx. Time Per Pound	Approx. Total Cooking Time
	Pounds	Minutes	Hours
Smoked ham (old style and country cured)			
Large	12–16	20	
Small	10–12	25	
Half	5–8	30	
Smoked ham (tendered)			
Shank or butt half	5–8	20–25	
Fresh or corned beef	4–6	40–50	
Beef for stew			2½–3½
Veal for stew			2–3
Lamb for stew			1½–2

* Adapted from National Live Stock and Meat Board, *Lessons on Meat,* 1965

BEEF, VEAL, LAMB, AND PORK RECIPES

Using the preceding directions for cooking meats and the meat charts, one can prepare a variety of meats for this diet.

For illustrative purposes we have included a few of our favorite meat recipes that have been adapted for use in this diet, indicating in each case the method it illustrates. You can do the same with some of your favorites by following the cooking outlines and meat charts and by keeping in mind the two main cooking principles for this diet:

1. Use only those foods acceptable for this diet.

2. Cook by a method that ensures the consumption of a minimum of saturated fat.

We have found that often all that is necessary to make a recipe acceptable is doing such things as trimming off excess fat, using an acceptable oil in marinating mixtures, substituting yogurt for sour cream, or substituting egg whites for yolks.

More oil than a recipe calls for may be used if it is calculated as part of your daily dietary fat intake. You may wish to use more for the browning of meat or to add extra oil to a meat dish for flavor or texture. Veal, being a lean meat, can use added oil during cooking (up to 1 teaspoon per serving in ground veal dishes*). We have kept the oil to a minimum in most recipes. It is easy for you to add extra oil, depending on your fat and calorie allowance.

The amount of meat as given in our recipes in this chapter is for raw, trimmed weight (trimmed of bone, fat, and other waste). This does not mean the bone has to be removed before cooking, but its weight is taken into account when buying the meat. (See "How to Determine a Serving," pages 80–81.) Each serving contains approximately 3 ounces of *cooked* meat (except a serving of tacos, which contain approximately 2 ounces of cooked meat). See Chapter XII for recipes containing approximately 1 ounce of cooked meat per serving.

Broiling Method

DELUXE BROILED STEAK

Slash at the edges
   1 lean sirloin steak 1½–2 inches thick (1 pound, boned, trimmed weight)

---

* Lean veal may be substituted for very lean beef in many recipes. See discussion on veal, pages 78–79.

Blend

1 tablespoon wine vinegar   ⅛ teaspoon thyme
1 clove garlic (crush well in   ⅛ teaspoon marjoram
  the vinegar, then remove   ½ teaspoon orégano
  if preferred)

Brush onto the steak with a pastry brush. Let the steak stand for 1 hour. Place the steak 3 inches from the flame or heating element of the broiler. When nicely browned on one side, turn and continue broiling until rare, medium, or well done, as desired. Season, garnish with chopped parsley, and serve at once on a warm platter. Remove the fat from the drippings before using. **Four servings.**

ONE SERVING (CONTAINS 3 OUNCES COOKED MEAT)

Oil — 0 teaspoons   **Protein** — 27 grams
Cholesterol — 63 milligrams   **Carbohydrate** — negligible
Saturated Fat — 4 grams   **Calories** — 190
Linoleic acid — negligible

SHISH KEBOBS

Remove separable fat from

lean lamb steaks ¾ inch thick, cut in 1-inch squares (1 pound, trimmed weight)

Soak meat squares for 3 or more hours in a marinade made of

⅓ cup lemon juice   1 bay leaf, crumbled
⅓ cup vinegar   1 tablespoon parsley, chopped
1 onion, minced or grated   ¼ teaspoon pepper
1 clove garlic, minced   1 teaspoon salt

If desired, add

dry red wine to cover

After 3 or more hours drain meat and put it on skewers, alternating

square of meat
thick slice of small, ripe tomato
mushroom cap

Fill skewers until the meat is used up. Broil close to flame, removing every few minutes to roll in marinating sauce. Repeat this until meat is done and all sides are nicely browned. **Four servings.**

ONE SERVING (CONTAINS 3 OUNCES COOKED MEAT)

Oil — 0 teaspoons   **Protein** — 29 grams
Cholesterol — 63 milligams   **Carbohydrate** — 4 grams
Saturated fat — 4 grams   **Calories** — 225
Linoleic acid — 0 grams

Broiling or Pan-broiling Method

TERIYAKE TYPE STEAK FOR TWO

Marinate for 15 to 30 minutes on a plate
½ pound lean steak (beef or veal, boned, trimmed weight)
in a sauce of
    2 tablespoons soy sauce   *a sprinkling of garlic salt*
    1 tablespoon lemon juice   *¼ teaspoon powdered ginger*
    1 teaspoon sugar

Prick the steak repeatedly with a fork to allow the sauce to penetrate. After 10 minutes or so, turn the meat, spoon the marinade over it, and prick that side with the fork. Before broiling, a tenderizer may be sprinkled over the steak. This is desirable if top round of beef is used.

Oven- or pan-broil according to timetable, pages 96–97. **Two servings.**

ONE SERVING (CONTAINS 3 OUNCES COOKED MEAT)
    Oil — 0 teaspoons   **Protein** — 27 grams
    Cholesterol — 63 milligrams   **Carbohydrate** — 3 grams
    Saturated fat — 4 grams   **Calories** — 200
    Linoleic acid — negligible

VEAL PATTIES

Mix together
    1½ pounds lean ground veal   *3 tablespoons skim milk*
    ¼ cup wheat germ   *powder*
    ¼ cup enriched bread crumbs *2 tablespoons chopped onion*

Mix together
    1 egg white, slightly beaten   *2 teaspoons salt*
    ½ cup skim milk   *½ teaspoon pepper*
    2 teaspoons Worcestershire   *2 tablespoons oil*
      sauce

Stir into the meat mixture and form into 6 patties. Oven-broil or pan-broil in a Teflon skillet, or pan-broil in a skillet in
    1–2 tablespoons oil

Turn when browned and cook until meat is done. (May be served with a sauce, if desired, such as Mushroom Sauce★ or Spanish Sauce★—not included in the calculations below.) **Makes six patties.**

ONE SERVING (CONTAINS 3 OUNCES COOKED MEAT)

Oil — 2 teaspoons	**Protein** — 33 grams
Cholesterol — 82 milligrams	**Carbohydrate** — 6 grams
Saturated fat — 4 grams	**Calories** — 300
Linoleic acid — 5 grams	

VEAL BURGERS

Mix together

1 pound lean ground veal	¼ teaspoon pepper
1 tablespoon vegetable oil	½ teaspoon salt
1 tablespoon finely chopped onion	

Form into 4 patties and oven-broil, or pan-broil in a Teflon skillet, or pan-broil in a skillet in

1–2 tablespoons oil

(May be served on 1 or 2 slices of toast or bread, with sliced tomatoes, pickles, mustard, chili sauce, or catsup—not included in calculations below.) **Makes four patties.**

ONE SERVING (CONTAINS 3 OUNCES COOKED MEAT)

Oil — ¾ teaspoon	**Protein** — 30 grams
Cholesterol — 81 milligrams	**Carbohydrate** — negligible
Saturated fat — 3 grams	**Calories** — 210
Linoleic acid — 2 grams	

Roasting Method

MEAT AND POTATO MEAT LOAF FOR TWO

Toss together

½ pound very lean ground beef (or lean veal)	¾ teaspoon salt
2 cups coarsely grated potato	¼ teaspoon pepper
1 teaspoon instant minced onion	¼ teaspoon monosodium glutamate

Shape into a loaf, place on a rack, and bake at 350° F. until done. (If veal is used, you may desire to add 1–2 teaspoons oil—not included in calculations.) **Two servings.**

ONE SERVING (CONTAINS 3 OUNCES COOKED MEAT)

Oil — negligible

Cholesterol — 63 milligrams

Saturated fat — 4 grams

Linoleic acid — negligible

Protein — 30 grams

Carbohydrate — 26 grams

Calories — 305

VEAL MEAT LOAF

Remove crusts, then cube

  3 slices enriched bread

Pour over the bread

  ½ cup beef stock

When it has been absorbed, add

  ½ cup tomato sauce

  1 teaspoon onion powder

  2 teaspoons poultry seasoning

  1 teaspoon Worcestershire sauce

  1½ pounds lean ground veal

  ¼ cup wheat germ

Stir together until well mixed. Form into a loaf and place in a baking pan. Pour over the meat loaf

  ½ cup beef stock

Bake in 325° F. oven for 1½ hours. Serve hot or cold. **Six servings.**

ONE SERVING (CONTAINS 3 OUNCES COOKED MEAT)

Oil — 0 teaspoons

Cholesterol — 81 milligrams

Saturated fat — 2 grams

Linoleic acid — 0 grams

Protein — 32 grams

Carbohydrate — 10 grams

Calories — 230

Cooking in Liquid Method

CORNED BEEF AND CABBAGE

Remove separable fat and place in a deep saucepan

  5 pounds BOTTOM ROUND *corned beef*

  6 peppercorns

Cover with unsalted water and simmer (do not boil) for 4 to 5 hours (50 to 60 minutes per pound). About 1 hour before serving time, take 2 cups of the stock from the saucepan, chill it, and remove the fat.

Cook until tender
  2 pounds thinly sliced cabbage
in
  the 2 cups fat free stock
  2 cups water
Remove the meat from the liquid while still hot so it doesn't absorb the fat from the liquid. Serve the corned beef and cabbage with horseradish or prepared mustard or both.

ONE PORTION CONTAINING 3 OUNCES COOKED MEAT

Oil — 0 teaspoons
Cholesterol — 63 milligrams
Saturated fat — 4 grams
Linoleic acid — negligible

Protein — 28 grams
Carbohydrate — 5 grams
Calories — 215

VEAL STEW AND DUMPLINGS

Remove all separable fat from
  lean veal stew meat (2 pounds trimmed weight)
Brown in a heavy kettle using
  2 tablespoons oil
Add
  3 cups hot water
  salt and pepper
  ½ bay leaf
  sprig of rosemary or ½
  teaspoon dry rosemary
Cover and simmer for 1½ hours. Remove fat (see page 85). Bring to the boiling point, reduce heat and add
  3 medium carrots, quartered and cut into 2-inch lengths
  4 medium potatoes, quartered
Cook for 15 minutes, then add
  1 package frozen peas
  1 green pepper, cut into squares or strips
  1 tablespoon Worcestershire sauce
Thicken gravy with a mixture of
  2 tablespoons flour
  ¼ cup cold water
Add seasonings if desired. Drop Dumplings★ from a teaspoon into the hot stew. Cover and cook 15 minutes. Do not lift cover during cooking. Before serving, sprinkle over stew and dumplings
  2 tablespoons chopped parsley
Eight servings.

ONE SERVING (CONTAINS 3 OUNCES COOKED MEAT)
(DUMPLINGS INCLUDED IN CALCULATIONS)

Oil — ¾ teaspoon

Cholesterol — 82 milligrams

Saturated fat — 2 grams

Linoleic acid — 2 grams

Protein — 38 grams

Carbohydrate — 41 grams

Calories — 410

LAMB PIE WITH MASHED POTATO BORDER

Remove separable fat and cut into 1-inch pieces
lean lamb (1½ pounds trimmed weight)
Put in a heavy pan with a tight-fitting lid and add
water to cover
salt
pepper
Cover pan tightly and simmer until almost tender, about 1½–2 hours.
Add and cook until both meat and vegetables are tender

1 medium onion stuck with
  2 cloves
3 stalks celery, chopped

5 medium carrots, chopped
1 cup peas

Strain the meat and vegetables out of the stock. Remove the fat from
the stock and make gravy (see page 86). (If stock is insufficient, add
more liquid.) Pour the gravy over the meat and vegetables placed in
a casserole. Spoon around the edge of the meat
Mashed Potatoes★
Brown the top of the potatoes under the broiler. Remove from the
broiler and put in the center of the dish
½ cup peas
Six servings.

ONE SERVING (CONTAINS 3 OUNCES COOKED MEAT)
(GRAVY AND POTATOES INCLUDED IN CALCULATIONS)

Oil — ½ teaspoon

Cholesterol — 65 milligrams

Saturated fat — 4 grams

Linoleic acid — 1 gram

Protein — 34 grams

Carbohydrate — 29 grams

Calories — 360

Braising Method

BEEF POT ROAST

Remove separable fat from
   1 lean beef pot roast (3 pounds boned, trimmed weight—buy
       about 4 pounds of meat, depending on bone and fat
       content)
Brown meat on all sides in a heavy pan with a tight-fitting lid, using
   1 teaspoon oil (or more if needed)
Pour off any accumulated fat. Add to the browned meat

2 or 3 medium-size onions,	*2 teaspoons salt*
chopped	*1 teaspoon celery salt*
3 cloves garlic, chopped	*½ teaspoon pepper*
1½ cups claret wine	*sprig of parsley*
2 whole cloves	*pinch of thyme*
2 bouillon cubes	*pinch of rosemary*
2 small bay leaves	*2½ cups canned tomatoes*
1 teaspoon paprika	

Cover pan closely and simmer slowly for 2 to 3 hours, or cook in a
250° F. oven. Stir and turn meat about every half hour. Remove the
fat from the liquid before using. The gravy is good served over steamed
rice (not included in calculations). **Twelve servings.**

ONE SERVING (CONTAINS 3 OUNCES COOKED MEAT)

Oil — 0 teaspoons	**Protein** — 29 grams
Cholesterol — 63 milligrams	**Carbohydrate** — 5 grams
Saturated fat — 4 grams	**Calories** — 215
Linoleic acid — negligible	

ROLLED STUFFED FLANK STEAK

Prepare Bread Stuffing★, using half the recipe (2 cups of crumbs).
Remove separable fat from
   1 lean flank steak (1½ pounds trimmed weight)
Sprinkle with
   salt
   pepper
Spread with
   stuffing

Bring the sides of the steak together, making a long roll, and sew with twine or tie securely. Brush meat and pan with oil, using in all

½ teaspoon (or more) vegetable oil

Brown meat on all sides. Pour off any accumulated fat. Slip a rack under the meat and cover the pan closely. Cook in oven at 250° F. about 2 hours. Remove fat from the drippings and make gravy.

If desired, the steak can be cooked with the following sauce. Combine

¼ cup chili sauce
¼ cup water
½ small onion, sliced, or 2 or 3 scallions

1 cup chopped vegetables, such as celery, green pepper, and carrots

After browning, place meat on rack and spread this sauce over the meat. Cover the pan and cook at 250° F. about 2 hours. Remove any fat from the sauce before serving. Pour the fat free sauce over the top of the meat and garnish as desired. **Six servings.**

ONE SERVING (CONTAINS 3 OUNCES COOKED MEAT)
(SAUCE INCLUDED IN CALCULATIONS)

Oil — negligible
Cholesterol — 63 milligrams
Saturated fat — 4 grams
Linoleic acid — negligible

Protein — 29 grams
Carbohydrate — 14 grams
Calories — 255

BEEF STROGANOFF

Remove separable fat from

lean sirloin steak (2 pounds trimmed weight). Round steak or stew meat may be substituted but will have to be cooked longer.

Cut meat in strips and brown in a pan brushed with

½ teaspoon (or more) oil

Pour off any accumulated fat. Add

1 pound mushrooms, quartered
1 can Italian tomato paste
1 cup nonfat yogurt, slightly beaten

2 small onions (or 1 large), finely chopped

Cover and simmer 30 minutes, adding extra water as needed during cooking. Before serving add

salt to taste

Eight servings.

ONE SERVING (CONTAINS 3 OUNCES COOKED MEAT)

Oil — negligible

Cholesterol — 64 milligrams

Saturated fat — 4 grams

Linoleic acid — negligible

Protein — 31 grams

Carbohydrate — 9 grams

Calories — 250

TACOS

Prepare the following meat sauce. Brown in a covered heavy iron pan

1 *pound very lean ground beef* (*or lean veal*)

Drain off any fat. Add

1 *package taco seasoning mix* (*be sure the brand you buy contains no fat*)

1 *cup water*

Bring to a boil, cover, and simmer 15 to 20 minutes, stirring occasionally. Keep hot. Makes about 2 cups.

Prepare and set aside

1 *onion, chopped*

3 *large tomatoes, cut into small pieces*

½ *head of lettuce, shredded*

Put on a hot griddle wiped with oil (allow ½ teaspoon per serving)

1 Mexican *tortilla, or more depending on size of pan* (*the tortillas can be purchased packaged*)

Turn the tortilla once and cook until soft and warm. On one half of the tortilla put one-sixth of the hot meat sauce. Fold the other half of the tortilla over the sauce and put on a warm platter. Repeat until you have made 6 tacos. Stuff into the filling of each taco one-sixth of the onion, tomato, and lettuce. Garnish with taco sauce—a bottled tomato purée containing spices, vinegar, chilies, onion, and garlic, and no fat. **Makes six tacos.**

ONE TACO (CONTAINS 2 OUNCES COOKED MEAT)

Oil — ½ teaspoon

Cholesterol — 42 milligrams

Saturated fat — 3 grams

Linoleic acid — 1 gram

Protein — 21 grams

Carbohydrate — 19 grams

Calories — 240

TOP O' THE STOVE MEAT LOAF FOR TWO

Crumble onto a plate
½ pound very lean ground beef (or lean veal)
Sprinkle over the meat

1 tablespoon steak sauce or	⅓ teaspoon salt
soy sauce	⅛ teaspoon pepper
2 tablespoons wheat germ	dash of monosodium
dash of garlic salt	glutamate

Toss lightly to mix. Form 2 small loaves 1 by 1 by 5 inches
and place on a rack* in the top pan of a deep double boiler. Cover,
place top pan over water in the lower pan of the double boiler, and
boil rapidly. Cook until meat is done (about 60 to 70 minutes).
Remove fat from drippings (see page 85) and make gravy (see page 86),
not included in calculations. **Two servings.**

ONE SERVING (CONTAINS 3 OUNCES COOKED MEAT)

Oil — 0 teaspoons	**Protein** — 29 grams
Cholesterol — 63 milligrams	**Carbohydrate** — 5 grams
Saturated fat — 4 grams	**Calories** — 215
Linoleic acid — negligible	

VARIATIONS:

Use 2 tablespoons soy sauce or steak sauce.

Add other seasonings to your liking, such as sage, orégano, or
other herbs, dash of celery salt or onion salt.

Serve with one of our meat sauces such as Spanish Sauce★, Mushroom
Sauce★, or Horseradish Sauce★.

If veal is used, you may desire to add 1 to 2 teaspoons oil.

VEAL SCALOPPINE

Remove separable fat from
thin slices lean veal (1½ pounds trimmed weight)
Brown in a pan with a tight-fitting lid, brushing the pan with
½ teaspoon (or more) oil

---

* If you do not have a rack, use aluminum foil. Fold it in half for strength and
then into accordion pleats as in making a fan. Extend it enough to place across
the bottom of the double boiler to hold the meat. The fat and juices will accumulate in the ridges.

Add

1 clove garlic, crushed	1 cup water
1 cup dry white wine	salt and pepper to taste

Cover tightly and simmer three quarters of an hour, or until the veal is very tender. Remove the fat from the liquid before it is used. If desired, after removing fat, add to the gravy (not included in calculations)

lemon juice

chopped parsley

mushrooms (cooked)

Six servings.

ONE SERVING (CONTAINS 3 OUNCES COOKED MEAT)

Oil — negligible	**Protein** — 30 grams
Cholesterol — 81 milligrams	**Carbohydrate** — 2 grams
Saturated fat — 2 grams	**Calories** — 180
Linoleic acid — negligible	

VEAL BIRDS

Remove separable fat from

6 thin slices lean veal cut into 3- to 4-inch strips (1½ pounds trimmed weight)

Combine

1½ cups bread crumbs	½ teaspoon salt
3 tablespoons chopped parsley	¼ teaspoon pepper
3 tablespoons chopped onion	water to moisten slightly

Spread veal with dressing, roll up, and fasten with toothpicks or small skewers. Brown meat on all sides in a pan brushed with

½ teaspoon (or more) oil

Sprinkle with

salt

pepper

Place in a casserole and add

1½ cups boiling water

Cover and bake in a preheated moderate oven (350° F.) 30 minutes, or until veal is tender. Remove the veal birds from the liquid. Remove the fat from the liquid and make gravy (see page 86). Replace the birds in the casserole and pour gravy over them. Return to the oven and cook 30 minutes. **Six servings.**

ONE SERVING (CONTAINS 3 OUNCES COOKED MEAT)
(GRAVY INCLUDED IN CALCULATIONS)

Oil — negligible   **Protein** — 32 grams
Cholesterol — 81 milligrams   **Carbohydrate** — 11 grams
Saturated fat — 2 grams   **Calories** — 235
Linoleic acid — negligible

STUFFED VEAL

Stuff with Apple Dressing★
    veal shoulder roast (2 pounds boned, trimmed weight—buy
      about 2½ pounds of meat depending upon the bone and
      fat content)
Close opening with skewers. Wipe roast with
    2 tablespoons oil
Sprinkle with
    2 teaspoons salt
    ¼ teaspoon pepper
Place on a rack in a heavy Dutch oven. Cover and roast in 300° F. oven
2½ hours. Make gravy, see page 86 (not included in calculations).
Eight servings.

ONE SERVING (CONTAINS 3 OUNCES COOKED MEAT)
(DRESSING INCLUDED IN CALCULATIONS)

Oil — 1 teaspoon   **Protein** — 31 grams
Cholesterol — 83 milligrams   **Carbohydrate** — 6 grams
Saturated fat — 3 grams   **Calories** — 270
Linoleic acid — 3 grams

BRAISED VEAL CUTLETS IN TOMATO SAUCE

Wipe with a damp cloth and remove separable fat from
    2 veal cutlets (round steak) cut 1 inch thick (2 pounds
      boned, trimmed weight)
Mix together for a marinade
    3 tablespoons oil   *1 clove garlic, crushed*
    1 tablespoon vinegar   *1 onion, thinly sliced*
    ½ teaspoon salt   *1 bay leaf*
    ½ teaspoon paprika
Place the cutlets in a baking dish that can be tightly covered. Pour the
marinade over the meat, cover, and let stand several hours. Remove

meat and brown in a Teflon-coated pan or a heavy frying pan. Cut each cutlet into 4 pieces and return to baking dish.
Make a sauce by shaking in a covered jar

> 2 tablespoons flour
> ¼ cup water

Place in a saucepan

> 1½ cups canned puréed tomatoes

Heat, then stir in the flour and water mixture. Stir and cook until thickened. Remove from heat, add the remaining marinade, and stir until smooth. Pour sauce over the cutlets, cover, and bake in a 300° F. oven 1½ hours. **Eight servings.**

ONE SERVING (CONTAINS 3 OUNCES COOKED MEAT)

Oil — 1 teaspoon	**Protein** — 31 grams
Cholesterol — 81 milligrams	**Carbohydrate** — 6 grams
Saturated fat — 3 grams	**Calories** — 245
Linoleic acid — 3 grams	

VEAL AND MUSHROOMS

Remove the separable fat from

> lean veal stew meat (2 pounds trimmed weight) cut in 1-inch cubes

Season with

> 2 teaspoons salt
> ¼ teaspoon pepper

Brown meat in a heavy skillet in

> 2 tablespoons oil

Remove meat, add, and sauté

> ¼ pound fresh mushrooms, sliced, or a 4-ounce can sliced mushrooms

Add and sauté until onion is limp

> 1 onion, chopped
> 1 clove garlic, minced
> 1 cup celery, sliced

Return meat to the pan and add

> 1 green pepper, cut in strips
> 2 cups canned tomatoes
> ½ cup dry red wine

Cover tightly and simmer until meat is tender, about 1½ hours.
Combine

> 2 tablespoons flour
> ¼ cup cold water

Stir into the sauce and cook, stirring constantly until thickened. **Eight servings.**

ONE SERVING (CONTAINS 3 OUNCES COOKED MEAT)
    Oil —— ¾ teaspoon   **Protein** —— 31 grams
    Cholesterol —— 81 milligrams   **Carbohydrate** —— 6 grams
    Saturated fat —— 3 grams   **Calories** —— 240
    Linoleic acid —— 2 grams

SEASONED VEAL

Cut into strips ½ inch wide, removing bones, connective tissue, and any separable fat from
    veal steak (1½ pounds boned, trimmed weight)
Brown the meat in a heavy pan in
    3 tablespoons oil (or less)
Mix together and sprinkle over meat
    1 teaspoon seasoned salt   *½ teaspoon dry thyme,*
    1 small pinch saffron (very   *crushed*
      little gives strong color)   *1 tablespoon instant minced*
    ¼ teaspoon garlic salt   *onion*
    ¼ teaspoon black pepper
Stir meat until well coated with spices. Cover and cook slowly until meat is tender, about 45 minutes. Add a few tablespoons of beef broth or hot water if dry. Add
    2 cups Medium White Sauce★
Serve over rice or eggless noodles (not included in the calculations below). **Six servings.**

ONE SERVING (CONTAINS 3 OUNCES COOKED MEAT)
    Oil —— 1½ teaspoons   **Protein** —— 33 grams
    Cholesterol —— 83 milligrams   **Carbohydrate** —— 6 grams
    Saturated fat —— 3 grams   **Calories** —— 275
    Linoleic acid —— 4 grams

Meat Sauces and Meat Flavoring

MEAT AND TOMATO SAUCE

Brown (using a covered heavy iron pan)
   2 pounds very lean ground beef (or lean ground veal)
Drain off any fat. Grind

1 onion	*½ green pepper, seeded*
1 clove garlic	*¼ pound fresh or*
3 stalks celery	*canned mushrooms*

Sauté in
   2 tablespoons oil
Put through a food mill to remove seeds and pulp, then add to the meat
   1 large can solid pack tomatoes (3½ cups)
Add

1 can tomato paste	*½ cup chopped parsley*
2 sprigs rosemary or 1	*1 tablespoon chopped sweet*
teaspoon dry rosemary	*basil or 1 teaspoon crushed*
1 bay leaf	*dried*
1 sprig fresh thyme or a	*salt to taste*
pinch of dry thyme	*pepper to taste*

Cover and simmer 2 hours. Add
   ½ cup chopped fresh or canned mushrooms
Simmer for a few minutes. May be served on macaroni, spaghetti, or rice (not included in the following calculations). Note that this is a *meat* recipe. When it is used, it must be counted as part of the daily meat allowance. **Eight servings.**

ONE SERVING (CONTAINS 3 OUNCES COOKED MEAT)

Oil — ¾ teaspoon	**Protein** — 23 grams
Cholesterol — 56 milligrams	**Carbohydrate** — 11 grams
Saturated fat — 2 grams	**Calories** — 210
Linoleic acid — 0 grams	

ITALIAN BEEF AND TOMATO SAUCE

Brown in a heavy covered pan
   2 pounds very lean ground beef (or lean ground veal)
Drain off any fat. Chop
   2 medium onions
   2 cloves garlic

Sauté in
   3 tablespoons oil
Add to browned meat, then add

2 cans tomato sauce
1½ cups water
1 teaspoon salt
4-ounce can mushrooms

1½ teaspoons Italian
   Seasoning
pepper to taste

Cover tightly and simmer gently 2 hours. Note that this is a *meat* recipe. When it is used, it must be counted as part of the daily meat allowance. **Eight servings.**

ONE SERVING (CONTAINS 3 OUNCES COOKED MEAT)
Oil — 1 teaspoon
Cholesterol — 54 milligrams
Saturated fat — 2 grams
Linoleic acid — 3 grams
Protein — 22 grams
Carbohydrate — 7 grams
Calories — 195

BACON BITS FOR FLAVORING

Finely chop or grind
   ½ pound bacon (about 10 thin slices)
Place in skillet. Stir constantly and fry out all the fat possible. Drain the crisp meat pieces on absorbent paper toweling while they are still hot. Store in a covered jar in the freezer or refrigerator and use sparingly. Note that this is a *meat* recipe. When some bacon bits are used, they must be counted as part of the daily meat allowance. **Makes ½ cup of bits.**

TOTAL RECIPE
Oil — 0 teaspoons
Cholesterol — 63 milligrams
Saturated fat — 18 grams
Linoleic acid — 6 grams
Protein — 17 grams
Carbohydrate — negligible
Calories — 122

CHAPTER X

Fish

FISH (not including shellfish*) are *excellent* meats to use in this diet because of their low total fat and low saturated fat content. In addition, fish fats contain a higher proportion of poly-unsaturated fatty acids than do the fats of red meat or poultry.† The cholesterol content of most fish is comparable to that of lean red meat. *Use fish often for the meat in your diet.*

Become familiar with the principles in Chapter VIII, "What You Should Know About Meat," before buying, cooking, or eating fish.

Do not use fish liver oils in this diet, as they contain large amounts of cholesterol.

Do not use fish packed in olive oil or other products unacceptable in this diet.

Do not use frozen fish coated with a batter or crumbs unless you are certain the ingredients used are acceptable in this diet.

Fish may be purchased fresh, frozen, or canned; whole, dressed, in steaks, chunks, or fillets. They are baked, broiled, steamed, creamed, jellied, used in chowders, casserole dishes, salads, etc. Canned fish are convenient to use and are especially useful in areas where fresh or frozen fish are not readily available.

There are dozens of varieties of edible fish. All are very acceptable in this diet, as even the so-called "fat" fish‡ are lean in comparison to most red meat. The fat content of fish varies with the variety and with the season of the year. The fat content may be less than 1 per cent for bass, flounder, sole, haddock, halibut, perch, pike, snapper, and fish of the cod family, or as much as 12 to 20 per cent for salmon (Atlantic and Chinook—other varieties are lower in fat), mackerel, lake trout, and eel.§

* See the discussion of shellfish on pages 79–80.
† See footnote on page 77.
‡ Fish containing 5 per cent or more of fat is classified as fat.
§ Also see U. S. Department of Agriculture *Agriculture Handbook* No. 8, 1963, for the fat content of various varieties of fish.

COOKING METHODS

There are only a few basic methods of cooking fish. Any fish may be cooked by any method, but for best results, adjust the method according to the fatness of the fish. Fat fish are best for baking and broiling, as they do not dry out. When lean fish are baked or broiled, it may be necessary to baste them with oil during cooking. Try baking lean fish wrapped in lightly oiled aluminum foil. Lean fish are best for steaming and simmering, since the flesh is firmer.

Variety in fish cookery is obtained mainly by using different fish sauces and seasonings. Some sauces are cooked with the fish; others are heated and poured over the fish just before serving, or are served separately at the table. (For a list of fish sauce recipes, see page 126.) Often fish is served plain with lemon wedges, minced parsley, or tomato slices, etc. See page 122 for suggested garnishes.

Fish does not have the tough connective tissue of meat, and since it is tender, it should be cooked just before serving for *as short a time as possible.* Cook just until the flesh can be easily flaked with a knife or fork.

Our experience has been that very little fat cooks out of lean fish, so it is not necessary to try to remove the fat from the fish drippings or liquid in which the fish is cooked *unless a significant amount* has accumulated. Save any juices or any liquid in which the fish is cooked to use in sauce for the fish or in soup. Since very little removable fat cooks out of *lean* fish, it is the one meat we feel can be crumbed when it is to be broiled or baked. Brush the pan or broiler rack lightly with oil. Fish may be cooked in Teflon pans or on Teflon racks with almost no added oil.

Any oil used during the preparation or cooking of fish that is absorbed by the fish must be calculated as part of your daily calorie and oil intake. We have used a minimum of oil in most recipes. You may wish to add more in such recipes as Fish Loaf★, Tuna Ring★, Bread Stuffing★, etc.

HOW TO BROIL FISH

1. Use fish fillets, steaks, or flat pan-dressed* fish. Use fish 1 inch thick in preference to thinner ones. If frozen, thaw before use.

* Pan-dressed fish—small fish that are ready to cook as purchased.
Dressed fish—fish with scales and entrails removed, and usually the head, tail, and fins are removed.
Drawn fish—fish with entrails removed but still has scales and fins (and often the head).

2. Wash and wipe pan-dressed fish with cloth.
3. Salt on both sides.
4. Do *one* of the following (if the fish is a fat variety, you may omit this step):

Brush with oil.
Brush with equal parts oil and lemon juice.
Dip in skim milk.
Dip in a mixture of 1 egg white and ½ cup skim milk, and then into a mixture of ¼ cup flour and ¾ cup *fine* bread crumbs, corn meal, or rolled corn flakes.
Dip in a sauce, or brush on the sauce and use rest of sauce for basting during broiling (see sauces on page 126).

5. Put the fish on oiled broiler rack, skin side down. Place in a preheated broiler about 3 or 4 inches from the heat. Broil until done (about 10 to 15 minutes). If desired, turn carefully when the fish is almost done and brown on the other side. If necessary, baste with added oil or sauce during broiling to keep the fish moist.
6. Serve sizzling hot on a heated platter with lemon wedges or a sauce.

HOW TO PAN-BROIL FISH

1. Use fish fillets, steaks, or flat pan-dressed fish. If frozen, thaw before use.
2. Wash and wipe pan-dressed fish with cloth.
3. Salt on both sides.
4. Place the fish (skin side up) in a cold pan that has been brushed with vegetable oil.* (No oil is necessary for a fat variety of fish.) Start cooking over low heat and cook until almost done. Turn and finish cooking.
5. Serve sizzling hot on a heated platter with lemon wedges or a sauce.

HOW TO OVEN-BAKE FISH (moderate oven method)

1. Use fillets, steaks, or dressed† fish, fresh or frozen.‡
2. Wash and wipe dressed fish.
3. Salt on both sides.

---

* Fish may be crumbed as in step 4 above in "How to Broil Fish." More oil will be needed in the pan. How much oil you may use in pan-broiling fish depends on your fat and calorie allowance. Be sure to measure oil used.
† See above footnote, page 117.
‡ See "Frozen Fish," page 122.

4. Do *one* of the following:

Brush with oil.
Brush with equal parts oil and lemon juice.
Dip in skim milk.
Dip in a mixture of 1 egg white and ½ cup skim milk, and then into a mixture of ¼ cup flour and ¾ cup *fine* bread crumbs, corn meal, or rolled corn flakes.

5. Place the fish, skin side down, in oiled baking dish.
6. Baste with oil to keep the surface moist if fish is not baked in a sauce or with a topping.
7. Bake in a preheated oven at 350° F. until done. See timetable, page 121, for approximate cooking time.

VARIATIONS:

1. Omit step 4. Pour a sauce over the fish just before baking, such as Spanish or Mushroom Sauce★. See page 126 for other sauces.
2. Omit step 4. Place a well-seasoned stuffing on top of fish fillets or steaks before baking.
3. Baste the fish twice during baking with white or red table wine, or sherry. For a fish of 3 to 4 pounds, use 1 to 2 tablespoons wine for each basting.

HOW TO OVEN-BAKE FISH (hot oven method)

This hot oven method simulates frying. The fish acquires an attractive brown crust. Do not bake large fish, large pieces of fish, or stuffed fish by this method.

1. Use fillets, steaks, or pan-dressed fish. If frozen, thaw before use.
2. Wash and wipe pan-dressed fish with a cloth.
3. Dip the fish in skim milk to which has been added 1 teaspoon salt for each ½ cup skim milk, then dip in finely sifted bread crumbs, corn meal, or rolled corn flakes.
4. Place in oiled baking dish. If possible, use a dish from which the fish may be served at the table. Sprinkle or brush lightly with oil.
5. Bake in a preheated very hot oven (500° F.) until done (about 10 to 15 minutes).
6. Serve immediately, plain or with a sauce.

HOW TO STUFF-BAKE FISH

1. Use a 3- to 5-pound dressed or drawn* fish. If frozen, thaw before use.

2. Remove the scales and fins. Remove the blood line along the backbone if it is present. Bone for easier serving if desired.

3. Rinse the fish quickly with salted cold water. Dry the inner cavity.

4. Salt the cavity of the fish.

5. Stuff the cavity loosely with the stuffing desired. (See pages 283–84 for some suggested stuffings.)

6. Draw the cut portions together, both back and belly side, by use of skewers or heavy toothpicks, lace with string.

7. Place the belly side down on a baking dish that has been lined with an oiled double thickness of aluminum foil. Allow the foil to overlap at both ends of the dish to use as handles to transfer cooked fish to serving platter.

8. Oil the back of a lean fish. It may be necessary to baste the fish during cooking.

9. Bake in a preheated oven at 350° F. until done, approximately 10 minutes per pound for a fish up to 4 pounds. Add 5 minutes for each additional pound.

10. Remove fastenings and serve immediately, plain or with sauce.

. DIRECTIONS FOR STEAMING OR SIMMERING FISH

Steaming and simmering are preferred and easy methods of cooking fish. Steam or simmer fish to be used in casserole dishes, salads, etc.

1. Use fish fillets, steaks, or small dressed fish cut into serving pieces, fresh or frozen.†

2. Salt, using about ¼ teaspoon salt for each pound.

3. To *steam*, place the fish in a colander or in a metal basket with legs. Place in a pot over boiling water, cover pot with a tight lid and steam until tender. (See timetable page 121.) The water may be plain or seasoned with spices, herbs, and wines.

To *simmer*, use one of the following methods:

1. Place the fish in a single layer in a skillet and barely cover with water or a sauce (see below). Cover the skillet and simmer until done. (See timetable page 121.)

2. Line a shallow baking pan with large double sheets of aluminum foil. Arrange fish in baking pan. For 2 pounds of fish, pour 1½ cups of

* See footnote page 117.
† See "Frozen Fish," page 122.

liquid over the fish. This may be seasoned broth, fish stock, a wine mixture, a milk mixture, a tomato sauce, etc. Make a cooking package by bringing the foil up over the fish and sealing with a triple fold. Fold and turn up the ends of the foil to hold in the juice. Cook in a 400° F. oven until done. When the fish is done, gently pour out the liquid to remove the fat‡ and thicken the fat free liquid for a sauce, keeping the fish hot in the foil.

3. Place the fish in a cheesecloth bag. Lower into a small amount of boiling water or fish stock. Add ½ to 1 cup of cold water, cover, and simmer until tender. (See timetable page 121.)

If desired, add seasonings to the water in which fish is simmered, such as spices, herbs, skim milk, skim milk buttermilk, white wine, etc. In methods 1 and 2, the liquid may be a sauce, such as Spanish★, Mushroom★, or the Vermouth★ or Barbecue★ sauce used to broil fish. See page 126. More liquid may need to be added. These make delicious sauces to be served with the fish. Thicken if necessary.

If the fish is simmered in seasoned water, remove the fish and cook the water down, remove the fat and thicken the fat free liquid for a sauce.

TIMETABLE FOR COOKING FISH*

Method of Cooking	Market form	Amount for 6 (pounds)	Cooking Temperature	Approximate† Cooking time (minutes)
Baking, Moderate Oven Method	Dressed	3	350° F.	45–60
	Pan-dressed	3	350° F.	25–30
	Fillets or steaks	2	350° F.	20–25
Baking, Hot Oven Method	Pan-dressed	3	500° F.	15–20
	Fillets or steaks	2	500° F.	10–15
Broiling	Pan-dressed	3		10–16 (turning once)
	Fillets or steaks	2		10–15
Simmering (Poaching)	Fillets or steaks	2	Simmer	5–10
Steaming	Fillets or steaks	1½	Boil	5–10

* Adapted from *Let's Cook Fish!*, Fishery Market Development Series No. 8, U. S. Department of the Interior, Fish and Wildlife Service, Bureau of Commercial Fisheries.
† Cook just until the flesh can be easily flaked with a knife or fork. Cooking time varies according to size of pan, thickness of fish, temperature of fish and sauce at the start of cooking, etc.
‡ See "How to Remove the Fat from Drippings and Broth," page 85. If lean fish is used, very little fat accumulates.

FROZEN FISH

Frozen fish should not be thawed until just before it is to be used. If extra cooking time is allowed, fish (that is not to be breaded or stuffed) may be baked, simmered, or steamed without thawing.

To thaw fish, leave them in their wrappings and use one of the following methods:

1. Thaw in the refrigerator only enough so you can prepare the fish. A 1-pound package takes about 18 hours.
2. Place whole or drawn fish in cold running water for quick thawing. Time varies with size and shape of fish. Packaged fillets and steaks take about 30 minutes.

Do not thaw fish at room temperature or in warm water. Do not refreeze raw fish.

GARNISHES FOR FISH*

GARNISHES	SUGGESTED PREPARATION
Beets	Cooked whole or sliced
Carrots	Tops, sticks, curls, or shredded
Celery	Tops, hearts, sticks, or curls
Chives	Chopped
Cucumbers	Slices or sticks
Dill	Sprigs or chopped
"Special" Deviled Eggs★	Halved or quartered, sprinkled with paprika
Lemons or limes	Slices, twists, or wedges
Lettuce	Leaves or shredded
Mint	Sprigs or chopped
Oranges	Slices, twists, or wedges
Paprika	Sprinkled sparingly
Parsley	Sprigs or chopped
Peppers, green or red	Sticks or rings
Pickles	Whole, sliced or chopped
Radishes	Whole, sliced or roses
Tomatoes	Whole or sliced, broiled or raw
Watercress	Sprigs or chopped

* Adapted from *Let's Cook Fish!*, U. S. Department of the Interior (see reference, page 121).

SAUCES AND RELISHES TO SERVE WITH FISH

Cheesy Sauce★   Relish for Fish★
Cucumber Sauce★   Tartar Sauces I and II★
"Egg" Sauce★   Yogurt Sauce★
Mushroom Sauce★

FISH RECIPES

We have given you the basic methods of cooking fish. By varying
the sauces and seasonings used, you can serve dozens of different, tasty,
and interesting fish dishes. Many of the fish recipes found in cookbooks
are acceptable without change. Others can easily be modified for this
diet. If they call for butter, mayonnaise, sour cream, cheese, etc.,
substitute polyunsaturated oil, "special" mayonnaise, yogurt, or buttermilk, "Special" Sour Cream★ and "special" or other skim milk cheese.

The following recipes for fish illustrate some of the above principles
of fish cookery. Explore other cookbooks* and have fish as your meat
dish often, served in a variety of ways.

The number of servings and the approximate ounces of cooked
meat per serving (2 to 3 ounces) are stated for each recipe in this
chapter. See "How to Determine a Serving," pages 80–81. Refer to
Chapter XII for fish recipes containing 1 to 1½ ounces cooked meat
per serving.

STUFFED BROILED FISH FILLETS

Combine
   2 tablespoons finely chopped onion (or 1½ teaspoons instant
      minced onion)
   ½ cup finely chopped celery
   3 tablespoons water
Cook in covered pan until tender. Add
   2 cups coarse bread crumbs   ½ teaspoon thyme or other
   ½ teaspoon salt   savory seasoning
   pepper   2 tablespoons oil
Mix well, adding liquid to moisten if necessary. Place stuffing on
   1½ pounds fillets (trimmed weight) sprinkled with salt

* See pages 126–27 for suggested fish recipe books.

Roll and fasten with toothpicks. Roll the stuffed fillets in mixture of
  1 egg white
  ¼ cup skim milk
Then roll them in mixture of
  2 tablespoons flour
  ½ cup fine dried bread crumbs
Put the fish on oiled broiler rack and place in preheated broiler. When
almost done on one side, turn carefully. Cook until tender (about
10 minutes). Remove fastenings; garnish and serve immediately. Serve
plain or with a sauce (not included in calculations). **Six servings.**

ONE SERVING (CONTAINS 3 OUNCES COOKED FISH)

Oil — 1 teaspoon	**Protein** — 24 grams
Cholesterol — 63 milligrams	**Carbohydrate** — 18 grams
Saturated fat — 2 grams	**Calories** — 265
Linoleic acid — 3 grams	

CURRIED FISH (simmering method)

Place in a shallow pan
  2-pound dressed fish
Add
  small quantity water
Cover and simmer until tender, about 10 minutes. Drain and save the
liquid. Combine

  1 tablespoon chopped green   ¼ cup chopped celery
  pepper   ½ teaspoon oil
  1 small onion, chopped (or
  1 tablespoon instant
  minced onion soaked in
  2 tablespoons water)

Cook for a few minutes, stirring frequently, until onions are lightly
browned. Shake together in a covered jar
  2 tablespoons flour
  liquid from simmered fish
Pour into a 1-cup measure and add
  skim milk to fill cup
Put mixture into a pan and cook over low heat until thickened, stirring
constantly. Add
  browned vegetables
  ⅛–1 teaspoon curry powder, according to taste
  salt to taste

Remove skin and bones from the cooked fish. Arrange fish on a hot platter. Pour sauce over fish and sprinkle top with 2 tablespoons chopped parsley. **Six family servings.***

ONE PORTION CONTAINING 3 OUNCES COOKED FISH

Oil — 0 teaspoons
Cholesterol — 63 milligrams
Saturated fat — negligible
Linoleic acid — 1 gram

Protein — 22 grams
Carbohydrate — 4 grams
Calories — 145

FISH LOAF

Combine and mix well

2 cups flaked cooked
  fish (12 ounces of meat)
¾ cup cooked or canned
  tomatoes
1½ cups soft bread crumbs
2 egg whites, slightly
  beaten

1 tablespoon minced onion
  (or 1 teaspoon instant
  minced onion)
¼ teaspoon savory seasoning
salt to taste
dash of pepper

Place in a small, oiled loaf pan. Bake at 350° F. until firm (about 45 minutes). Serve plain or with a sauce (not included in calculations). **Four servings.**

ONE SERVING (CONTAINS 3 OUNCES COOKED FISH)

Oil — 0 teaspoons
Cholesterol — 63 milligrams
Saturated fat — 1 gram
Linoleic acid — negligible

Protein — 24 grams
Carbohydrate — 12 grams
Calories — 185

TUNA RING

Mix together

2 cups flaked water-packed tuna (12 ounces of meat)
2–4 tablespoons lemon juice, according to taste

Combine in a separate bowl and add to the tuna

1½ cups skim milk
1 cup bread crumbs
3 egg whites, slightly beaten

Add

salt to taste
pepper

* See page 80 for an explanation of family servings.

Place in an oiled ring mold. Set the mold in a pan of water and bake at 350° F. until firm. **Six servings.**

ONE SERVING (CONTAINS 2 OUNCES COOKED FISH)
>   **Oil** — 0 teaspoons   **Protein** — 21 grams
>   **Cholesterol** — 51 milligrams   **Carbohydrate** — 8 grams
>   **Saturated fat** — 1 gram   **Calories** — 150
>   **Linoleic acid** — negligible

SAUCES FOR FISH COOKERY
(oven broiling and baking methods)

Following the directions for oven-broiling or baking of fish on pages 117–20, use one of the following sauces for marinating fish, basting fish to be broiled, or for pouring over fish for baking:

> Broiled Meat Sauce★
> Tomato Sauce for Fish★
> Fish Sauce★
> Mushroom Sauce★
> Spanish Sauce★
> Vermouth Sauce for Fish★

Send for Some of These

Some books containing fish recipes that we have found very adaptable to this diet are published by the Bureau of Commercial Fisheries. They give excellent recipes and some have beautiful colored illustrations showing the fish dishes with their garnishes and accompaniments. Many of the recipes in these books are usable as is, some can be adapted for use, and others can't be used at all in this diet.

Recipe Publications Available in Full Color

Florida Fish Recipes 49.49/2:1	35 cents
Fancy Catfish 49.49/2:6	25
Seafood Slimmers 49.49/2:7	25
Let's Cook Fish! 49.49/2:8	60
Take a Can of Salmon 49.4:60	25
Fish Recipes from the Great Lakes 49.4:201	25
Top o' the Mornin' with Fish and Shellfish 49.39.15	25

Other Publications Available Not in Color

How to Cook Salmon 49.39:4	20 cents
How to Cook Ocean Perch 49.39:6	20
How to Cook Halibut 49.39:9	20
How to Cook Tuna 49.39:12	20
Heirloom Seafood Recipes 49.49/2:3	20

Mail your order with check or money order (do *not* send stamps), to:

Superintendent of Documents
Government Printing Office
Washington, D.C. 20402

CHAPTER XI

Poultry

LEAN CHICKEN and turkey are *excellent* meats to use in a low saturated fat, low cholesterol diet, since they are low in both. Other poultry, if lean, is also recommended: for example, capon, Cornish hen, and squab. *Choose poultry often as your source of meat for this diet.*

In addition to being a lean meat, poultry is readily available, versatile, and usually economical. Most poultry is available whole, in halves, quarters, serving pieces, frozen, stuffed, canned, etc. It can be served whole or in serving pieces; its meat can be used in soups, salads, stews, sandwiches, casserole dishes, etc. Chicken and other lean poultry can be used interchangeably in most recipes calling for any specific kind of cooked poultry.

Become familiar with the principles in Chapter VIII, "What You Should Know About Meat," before buying, cooking, or eating poultry.

For canned and frozen poultry products, see page 80.

Do not use the commercially frozen stuffed poultry, as saturated fats have usually been used in the dressing.

Do not use poultry that has been injected with added fat.

Do not use the giblets, since they are organ meats and are extremely high in cholesterol. When dressing poultry, be careful to remove the entire oil sac from the tail and to remove all bits of kidney, lung, and other organs that might remain attached to the bird.

The light meat of poultry is leaner than the dark meat. However, the dark meat is still a lean meat.

Do not eat the skin, as the saturated fat content of poultry is highest in, and directly under, the skin layer. Your cooking methods for poultry should be those which will assure a minimum consumption of the skin and fat. Methods of cooking to brown or crisp the skin of poultry are for appearance only, as the skin will not be eaten by those on our diet.

COOKING METHODS

Remove the skin before cooking from poultry pieces to be braised or stewed, if you desire. This can easily be done with a sharp knife. **Do not pan-fry or deep-fat-fry poultry.**

Cook all poultry at a moderate temperature, and do not overcook. Poultry, whether fresh or thawed,* should be cooked as promptly as possible, though it may be refrigerated for 2 or 3 days. Although there are many ways of cooking poultry, following are some methods that we recommend for use in this diet.

HOW TO ROAST WHOLE CHICKEN AND TURKEY

1. Select a young bird and remove excess fat from the inside and along the incision made to remove the internal organs.
2. After the bird has been cleaned, stuffed (not necessary), and trussed,† place it breast down in a roasting rack (a turkey rack is best) in a shallow pan. If a thermometer is used, insert it into the center of the inside thigh muscle, or the thickest part of the breast muscle, or in the center of a boneless turkey roll. Do not have thermometer touching a bone or dressing. (For un-stuffed poultry, season inside of bird if desired.) See pages 282, 284–85 for stuffing recipes.
3. Do not add water. Do not cover. Baste if desired, as the basting fat stays on the skin.
4. Roast until tender. See "Roasting Guide for Poultry," page 130. When done, the joints move easily and the juice running out has no pink color.
5. Remove the fat from the drippings before they are used.

HOW TO ROAST CHICKEN AND TURKEY PIECES

1. Place pieces skin side up on rack in an open pan.
2. The skin may be brushed with oil if a crisp skin is desired for appearance.
3. Do not add water. Do not cover.
4. Follow "Roasting Guide for Poultry," page 130. For chicken pieces, an alternative method is to roast in 400° F. oven, turning once during roasting.

* See pages 133–134 for directions for frozen poultry.
† Neck and breast incisions skewered, wings and legs skewered or tied down.

HOW TO ROAST A BONELESS TURKEY ROAST

1. Place on rack in an open pan.
2. Do not add water. Do not cover.
3. Follow printed directions on the package or insert a thermometer in the center of the roast and follow "Roasting Guide for Poultry," below.

ROASTING GUIDE FOR POULTRY*

Kind	Ready-to-cook weight† (pounds)	Approximate total roasting time at 325° F.‡ (hours)	Internal temperature of poultry when done (degrees F.)
Chickens, whole:			
Broilers, fryers,	1½–2½	1–2	
or roasters	2½–4½	2–3½	
Capons	5–8	2½–3½	
Poultry pieces		varies—turn during roasting	
Ducks	4–6	2–3	
Turkeys			
Whole	6–8	3–3½	180–185 (in thigh)
	8–12	3½–4½	180–185
	12–16	4½–5½	180–185
	16–20	5½–6½	180–185
	20–24	6½–7	180–185
Halves, quarters,	3–8	2½–3	
and pieces	8–12	3–4	
Boneless turkey			
roasts	3–10	3–4	170–175 (in center)

* *Poultry in Family Meals*, U. S. Department of Agriculture, 1967.
† Weight of giblets and neck included for whole poultry.
‡ Cooking time suggested is for stuffed poultry (except for turkey parts and boneless turkey roasts). Unstuffed whole poultry may take slightly less time than shown. Cooking time is only approximate; a meat thermometer should be used to determine doneness of whole turkeys and boneless turkey roasts. Cooking time is based on chilled poultry or poultry that has just been thawed—temperature not above 40° F. *Poultry cooked from the frozen state will take slightly longer.*

Do not partly roast stuffed poultry one day and finish roasting the next day.

The very slow oven method (pages 90–91) is dangerous for use with stuffed poultry, as it can produce food poisoning. Avoid it. Use only the above roasting guide.

HOW TO BROIL CHICKEN AND YOUNG TURKEY

1. Preheat the broiling oven.
2. Use young birds. Clean and cut bird in half or cut into serving pieces. Remove excess fat.
3. Unless you are sure the bird is young and tender, steam it in a little water in a covered pan before broiling for 10 to 15 minutes (depending on size of bird).
4. Brush with oil.
5. Place the bird on the lightly oiled rack of the broiler pan, with the highest part 4 to 5 inches from the heat. Broil until the bird is tender and nicely brown, watching it carefully and turning it frequently.
6. Remove the bird to a hot platter. Sprinkle with salt and pepper and serve immediately.
7. Remove fat from the drippings before using them for gravy.

ROTISSERIE COOKING

Follow the directions that come with your rotisserie. We do not recommend rotisserie cooking of meats directly over coals. See page 84.

HOW TO BRAISE POULTRY

This method is used:

1. For less tender poultry. The added moisture tenderizes the meat and brings out the flavor.
2. To cook tender poultry and boneless turkey roasts faster than roasting.

POULTRY PIECES

1. Preheat the broiling oven.
2. Remove excess fat from pieces (purchased as such or cut from whole bird).
3. Brush with oil.
4. Place the pieces on the lightly oiled rack of the broiler pan, with the tops of the pieces 4 to 5 inches from the heat. Watch carefully and turn the pieces frequently until all are browned.

5. Place in a pan with a tight-fitting lid and season with salt, pepper, and desired herbs.
6. Add a small amount of water.
7. Cover closely and cook in the oven at 325° F. or on the burner at a simmering temperature (not boiling) until tender. Add extra liquid during cooking if needed. Cooking time about 1½ to 2½ hours.
8. Take the poultry out of the liquid and put in a pan or casserole to keep hot in a slow oven (300° F.) while gravy is being made.
9. Remove the fat from the liquid before using. Make a sauce or gravy from the fat free liquid to pour over the meat or serve in a separate bowl.
10. If vegetables are added, add them at the proper time so they will not be overcooked.

WHOLE POULTRY

1. Preheat oven
   young poultry—450° F.
   mature birds—325° F.
2. Season and brush with oil.
3. Place poultry on rack in roaster pan or other heavy pan. Cover tightly.
4. Cook until tender. When done, flesh on the leg is soft and pliable and the joints move easily.
5. If browning is desired for appearance, uncover for the last 30 minutes.
6. Follow steps 8, 9, and 10 of "Poultry Pieces," pages 131–132.

BONELESS TURKEY ROAST

Follow directions on package for braising (if given), or:

1. Preheat oven—400° F.
2. Insert thermometer in center of roast.
3. Place on rack in roaster pan or other heavy pan. Cover tightly.
4. Cook until tender, internal temperature 170° F. (about 1½ hours for 3-pound roast).
5. If browning is desired for appearance, uncover for last 20 minutes.
6. Follow steps 8, 9, and 10 of "Poultry Pieces," pages 131–132.

HOW TO STEW POULTRY

If meat is to be used in a recipe calling for cooked poultry, such as in a salad or creamed dish, cook meat until completely done in step 6 below and omit steps 7 and 8.

If possible, when stewing poultry cook the meat in advance so the chilling method (see page 85) can be used to remove the fat completely from the liquid in step 6.

1. Cut up bird into serving pieces or leave whole.
2. Remove excess fat.
3. Place poultry in a kettle and add enough hot water to cover. A few chopped vegetables may be added to flavor the cooking water, such as a carrot, small onion, and 2 or 3 stalks of celery.
4. Cover the kettle tightly and simmer until meat is tender when pierced with a fork (about 2 hours or more). Do not boil.
5. Add salt and pepper when the bird is about half cooked.
6. When meat is almost done, take it from the liquid. Remove the fat from the liquid.
7. Return the meat to the fat free liquid and complete cooking. If vegetables are to be added, add them at the proper time so they will not be overcooked.
8. When done, make a sauce or gravy from the fat free liquid.

PRESSURE COOKING

Poultry may be braised or stewed in the pressure cooker.

Prepare poultry for braising or stewing as described above. Cook the poultry in the pressure cooker according to the manufacturer's directions. After braising poultry, if crispness is desired for appearance, put poultry under broiler for a few minutes.

FROZEN POULTRY

Frozen poultry is usually thawed before cooking, but it may be cooked without thawing by allowing more cooking time. For commercially frozen poultry, follow directions on the package.

When using a whole frozen bird in this diet, it is best to thaw before roasting so the giblets and excess fat can be removed before cooking.

To thaw before cooking, follow the directions on the package or thaw in the original plastic wrap using one or a combination of the following methods:

1. Thaw at room temperature by placing in a heavy paper bag or wrapping in newspaper.

GUIDE FOR THAWING POULTRY AT ROOM
TEMPERATURE*

Kind	Weight	Approximate time
Very small birds	Less than 4 pounds	4–6 hours
Small birds	8–12 pounds	about 12 hours
Larger birds	20–25 pounds	about 16 hours

Refrigerate or cook bird within 1 to 3 hours after thawing.

2. Thaw in the refrigerator until pliable.

GUIDE FOR THAWING POULTRY IN REFRIGERATOR*

Kind	Weight	Approximate time
Chickens	Less than 4 pounds	12–16 hours
	4 pounds or over	1–1½ days
Ducks	3–5 pounds	1–1½ days
Turkeys	Less than 18 pounds	1–2 days
	18 pounds or over	2–3 days
Pieces of large turkey (half, quarter, half breast)		1–2 days
Cut-up pieces		3–9 hours
Boneless roasts		12–18 hours

3. Cover with cold water and change often to speed thawing.

GUIDE FOR THAWING POULTRY WITH COLD WATER*

Kind	Approximate time
Small chickens	about 1 hour
Large turkeys	about 6–8 hours

It is best to cook thawed poultry as soon as possible, but it can be kept in the refrigerator for 2 to 3 days. *Do not refreeze raw poultry.*

* Adapted from *Meat and Poultry Cooking Know-How,* University of California Agricultural Extension Service, 1968.

HOW TO MAKE GIBLET BROTH FOR GRAVY

High cholesterol meats such as giblets may be used for broth or stock as long as it is well cleared. Since cholesterol is not soluble in water, it will not cook out of the meat into the water.

1. Cover giblets with salted water and simmer until very tender. Strain out meat and season broth to taste. Do not eat this meat, as it is high in cholesterol.
2. Chill the stock, allowing sufficient time for the fat to cake on top. Carefully remove the fat cake. Wipe off any remaining fat from the jelly and the bowl with a damp cloth.
3. Heat the stock just enough to melt it.
4. Measure, and allow 2 egg whites and shells for every quart of stock.
5. Slightly beat the whites and add the shells, crushed into small pieces.
6. Thoroughly stir the whites and crushed shells into the *cool* stock. These must be suspended throughout the liquid before the egg is coagulated by heating.
7. Heat to a rolling boil, stirring constantly. Remove from heat and allow stock to stand in a warm place undisturbed for 20 minutes. The coagulated egg gathers around itself the particles of solid substance in the stock, leaving the clear broth.
8. Strain stock through a strainer lined with 2 layers of cheesecloth.

POULTRY RECIPES

By using the cooking principles outlined above, some of your own poultry recipes can be adapted for use in this diet. Recipes for the roasting and broiling of meat are all rather similar. It is the braising and stewing methods that permit great variety in poultry cookery. The following recipes illustrate use of the above principles in these methods.

The servings as stated in these recipes are for *family servings*. The calculations for each recipe are given for *portions containing 3 ounces* of cooked poultry. See "How to Determine a Serving," pages 80–81. Refer to Chapter XII for poultry recipes containing less than 2 ounces of cooked meat per serving.

Braising Method

"SOUR CREAM" CHICKEN CASSEROLE

Cut into serving pieces and remove visible fat from
  3-pound frying chicken
Place the pieces on the lightly oiled broiler rack. Broil, turning frequently, until brown. Combine

2 medium-size carrots, diced	*1 clove garlic, minced*
2 medium-size onions,	*4 sprigs parsley, chopped*
sliced or chopped	*1 small bay leaf*
1 celery heart (including	
leaves), chopped	

As each piece of chicken is browned, add
  salt
  pepper
and place in a casserole, layering with the vegetable mixture. Pour over this
  1 cup skim milk yogurt
Shake together and pour over the chicken and vegetables
  1 cup consommé or defatted chicken broth
  2 tablespoons flour
Cover and cook in a 350° F. oven 1 hour, or until chicken is falling from the bones. Remove fat from the liquid before using. This dish is good a second day also. **Six family servings.**

ONE PORTION CONTAINING 3 OUNCES COOKED POULTRY

Oil — 0 teaspoons	**Protein** — 28 grams
Cholesterol — 56 milligrams	**Carbohydrate** — 13 grams
Saturated fat — 2 grams	**Calories** — 200
Linoleic acid — 1 gram	

Good served on steamed brown rice. More vegetables may be added to stretch the meat.

CHILI CHICKEN

Cut into pieces and remove visible fat from
  3- to 4-pound lean chicken
Place on lightly oiled broiler rack and broil until all pieces are browned,

watching carefully and turning frequently. As each piece of chicken is browned, add

> *salt*
> *pepper*

and place in pressure cooker. Combine

> *1 large onion, chopped*   *1 tablespoon vinegar*
> *½ cup chili sauce or catsup*   *3 tablespoons water*
> *½ teaspoon paprika*

Pour mixture over the chicken and cook according to directions for your pressure cooker (at medium pressure for about 15 minutes). Let pressure reduce, then remove lid. Remove fat from the liquid before it is used. If a pressure cooker is not available, this dish may be cooked in a covered pan on top of the stove or in the oven (350° F.). It will require about 1 hour cooking time. **Six family servings.**

ONE PORTION CONTAINING 3 OUNCES COOKED POULTRY

Oil — 0 teaspoons   **Protein —** 24 grams
Cholesterol — 54 milligrams   **Carbohydrate —** 7 grams
Saturated fat — 2 grams   **Calories —** 190
Linoleic acid — 1 gram

CHICKEN WITH HERBS

Wash, remove visible fat and skin from

> *2 pounds chicken parts*

Arrange pieces in a baking dish and marinate for an hour in

> *¼ cup oil*   *sprig of rosemary (or 1*
> *½ cup water*   *teaspoon dry)*
> *1 tablespoon wine vinegar*   *salt*
> *1 teaspoon dried orégano*   *pepper*

Add

> *½ cup dry white wine*

Cover tightly and cook in a 350° F. oven for 45 minutes. Remove lid and continue cooking until brown. Remove the fat from the liquid before using. **Four family servings.**

ONE PORTION CONTAINING 3 OUNCES COOKED POULTRY

Oil — 3 teaspoons   **Protein —** 24 grams
Cholesterol — 54 milligrams   **Carbohydrate —** 1 gram
Saturated fat — 4 grams   **Calories —** 280
Linoleic acid — 9 grams

CHICKEN AND ARTICHOKE HEARTS

Cut in half, wash and dry, and remove visible fat from
   3 chicken breasts or 6 legs and second joints
Wipe lightly with oil and sprinkle with
   ½ teaspoon salt
   ½ teaspoon paprika
   ¼ teaspoon pepper
Broil until nicely browned and meat fat has cooked out. Slice in large pieces
   ¼ pound mushrooms
Sauté in
   1 tablespoon oil
Sprinkle over the mushrooms
   2 tablespoons flour
Stir until smooth. Add
   ⅔ cup consommé
   3 tablespoons dry sherry
Cook for 5 minutes, stirring until smooth. Arrange the chicken pieces in a casserole with
   1 15-ounce can artichoke hearts (water-packed), drained
Pour the mushroom sauce over the chicken and artichokes. Cover and bake in 375° F. oven 40 minutes. **Six family servings.**

ONE PORTION CONTAINING 3 OUNCES COOKED POULTRY

Oil — ½ teaspoon	**Protein** — 26 grams
Cholesterol — 54 milligrams	**Carbohydrate** — 7 grams
Saturated fat — 2 grams	**Calories** — 215
Linoleic acid — 2 grams	

SHERRIED TURKEY

Cut into serving pieces or purchase young turkey parts. (Frozen turkey may be used. Defrost thoroughly.) Remove visible fat from
   4- to 5-pound turkey
Brown in a heavy skillet with a tight-fitting lid in
   ⅓ cup oil
Add

3 cups hot water	*1 onion, sliced*
¼ teaspoon pepper	*1 teaspoon salt*
¼ teaspoon nutmeg	*½ cup dry sherry*
½ teaspoon celery salt	

Cover tightly and simmer until the turkey is tender. Take the turkey from the broth and remove the fat from the liquid. Make a sauce by shaking together in a covered jar

1 tablespoon flour
¼ cup water

Add to broth and cook, stirring constantly until thickened. Season to taste. **Eight family servings.**

ONE PORTION CONTAINING 3 OUNCES COOKED POULTRY

Oil —— 3 teaspoons	**Protein** —— 24 grams
Cholesterol —— 54 milligrams	**Carbohydrate** —— 2 grams
Saturated fat —— 3 grams	**Calories** —— 240
Linoleic acid —— 6 grams	

This may be served with enriched rice, brown rice, or cracked wheat.

Stewing Method

CHICKEN CASSEROLE

Cut into pieces and remove visible fat from
3- to 4-pound stewing chicken
Put in kettle and cover with
water
Add

½ cup chopped celery	*salt*
¼ cup sliced carrots	*¼ teaspoon whole*
1 large onion, chopped	*black pepper*
1 bay leaf, crushed	*¼ teaspoon marjoram*

Simmer until tender (about 3 or more hours). Remove the chicken from the stock. Strain the stock and chill. Remove the fat from the chilled stock. Remove the chicken from the bones and cut into bite-size pieces, using only lean chicken. Discard the skin and fat. Make gravy by thickening

2 cups fat free chicken stock
with
2 tablespoons flour
Add

¼ cup chopped pimiento	*¼ teaspoon garlic salt*
½ to 1 cup mushrooms, as	*3 to 6 drops Tabasco*
desired	*salt to taste*
¼ teaspoon monosodium	
glutamate	

Combine the chicken meat with this gravy and
> *1 cup cooked rice*

Put in a casserole, cover with
> *¼ cup bread crumbs*

Bake in a moderate oven (350° F.) 1 hour. Serve with a sauce made by thickening
> *2 cups stock*

with
> *4 tablespoons flour*

Cook, stirring constantly, until smooth and thick. Season with
> *salt to taste*
> *pepper to taste*
> *marjoram to taste*

Six family servings.

ONE PORTION CONTAINING 3 OUNCES COOKED POULTRY

Oil — 0 teaspoons	**Protein** — 30 grams
Cholesterol — 54 milligrams	**Carbohydrate** — 17 grams
Saturated fat — 2 grams	**Calories** — 242
Linoleic acid — 1 gram	

CHAPTER XII

Low Meat Dishes

THE low meat recipes have their meat reduced one half or more from the amount called for in the original recipe in order to decrease their saturated fat and cholesterol content. (Increase the meat if desired, provided your dietary restriction allows the additional meat.)

Whether to use beef or veal in those of the following recipes that offer a choice depends upon the leanness of the beef. See the discussion of ground meat on page 77 and "Veal versus Beef" on pages 78–79. The recipe calculations are made for beef.

We have kept the oil extremely low in the following recipes. You may prefer to add oil if your calorie and oil allowance permits, especially when you use veal in place of beef.

The number of servings and the approximate ounces of cooked meat per serving (1 to 1⅔ ounces) are stated for each recipe in this chapter. See "How to Determine a Serving," pages 80–81.

SPANISH RICE

Brown
    ½ pound very lean ground beef (or lean ground veal)
Pour off any accumulated fat. Add

    1 cup chopped onions   2 teaspoons salt
    1 cup chopped celery   ½ teaspoon pepper
    1 green pepper, chopped   ½ teaspoon chili powder
    3½ cups tomatoes

Mix well. Add
    1 cup uncooked, enriched white or brown rice
Cook in covered pan over high heat until mixture starts to steam.

Turn heat very low and steam 35 minutes without raising the lid. **Six servings.**

ONE SERVING (CONTAINS 1 OUNCE COOKED MEAT)

Oil — 0 teaspoons   **Protein** — 11 grams
Cholesterol — 21 milligrams   **Carbohydrate** — 36 grams
Saturated fat — 1 gram   **Calories** — 215
Linoleic acid — negligible

BEEF WITH VEGETABLES (SUKIYAKI)

Remove all separable fat and cut into small pieces
   *very lean sirloin beef steak, sliced ⅛ inch thick (ask butcher to
      use slicing machine) (½ pound boned, trimmed weight)*
Brown meat in a heavy pan brushed with
   ½ teaspoon oil
Pour off any accumulated fat. Add

1 bunch Swiss chard, chopped   *1 can mushrooms, drained*
1 bunch celery, chopped   *1 cup bean sprouts*
2 bunches green onions,
   chopped

If available, add
   1 cup water chestnuts
   1 cup bamboo shoots
Then add
   3 tablespoons sugar
   ½ cup soy sauce
Cover tightly and steam until vegetables are heated through but still rather crisp. Serve directly from hot skillet. **Six servings.**

ONE SERVING (CONTAINS 1 OUNCE COOKED MEAT)

Oil — 0 teaspoons   **Protein** — 14 grams
Cholesterol — 21 milligrams   **Carbohydrate** — 17 grams
Saturated fat — 1 gram   **Calories** — 155
Linoleic acid — negligible
Serve over steamed rice.

CHILI

Brown
  ½ pound very lean ground beef (or lean ground veal)
Pour off any accumulated fat and add
  salt to taste
Meanwhile, in a large saucepan or Dutch oven combine
  5 cups cooked red kidney   1 tablespoon sugar
  *   beans   ½ to 1 teaspoon chili powder*
  2½ cups canned tomatoes
Add the browned meat to the beans. To the meat skillet add
  ½ teaspoon oil
Brown and add to the beans
  1 large onion, sliced
Simmer slowly 45 minutes to 1 hour. The flavor improves with warming over. **Six servings.**

ONE SERVING (CONTAINS 1 OUNCE COOKED MEAT)
  Oil — 0 teaspoons   **Protein** — 28 grams
  Cholesterol — 21 milligrams   **Carbohydrate** — 42 grams
  Saturated fat — 1 gram   **Calories** — 310
  Linoleic acid — negligible
This is good served with rice.
The meat can be reduced to ¼ pound and still make a well-flavored dish.

ENGLISH BROWN STEW

Remove all separable fat and fibrous tissue from
  lean beef (or veal) stew meat (½ pound trimmed weight)
Cut into ½-inch cubes and brown in a large skillet or Dutch oven.
Pour off any accumulated fat. Add
  2½ cups boiling water   ⅛ teaspoon allspice
  4 tablespoons chopped   1 teaspoon sugar
  *   onions   ½ teaspoon lemon juice*
  ½ clove garlic, chopped   ½ teaspoon Worcestershire
  1½ teaspoons salt   sauce
  ¼ teaspoon pepper   ¼ cup tomato juice
  ¼ teaspoon paprika
Cover and simmer until meat is tender (about 1 hour). Take the meat

from the pan and remove the fat from the liquid. Return the meat to the liquid. Add

1 cup chopped onions   ½ cup diced celery
1 cup sliced carrots   1 cup canned or fresh peas
2 cups cubed potatoes

Cover and cook 30 minutes. Taste and add more salt if necessary. The liquid can be used to prepare a thick gravy if desired—not included in following calculations. **Six servings.**

ONE SERVING (CONTAINS 1 OUNCE COOKED MEAT)

Oil — 0 teaspoons   **Protein** — 13 grams
Cholesterol — 21 milligrams   **Carbohydrate** — 19 grams
Saturated fat — 1 gram   **Calories** — 155
Linoleic acid — negligible

STUFFED GREEN PEPPERS

Wash, cut off the stem end, and scoop out the seeds and membranes from

6 large green peppers

Steam 3 minutes. Drain and fill with a mixture of

½ pound very lean ground   2 tablespoons grated onion
    beef (or lean ground veal)   1 teaspoon salt
2 cups cooked rice   ⅛ teaspoon pepper
½ cup tomatoes

Place in a shallow baking dish. Add a small amount of water to cover the bottom of the dish. Bake in a 350° F. oven 45 minutes. **Six servings.**

ONE SERVING (CONTAINS 1 OUNCE COOKED MEAT)

Oil — 0 teaspoons   **Protein** — 11 grams
Cholesterol — 21 milligrams   **Carbohydrate** — 17 grams
Saturated fat — 1 gram   **Calories** — 135
Linoleic acid — negligible

LASAGNE

Brown in a heavy frying pan that has a tight-fitting lid

½ pound very lean ground beef (or lean ground veal)

Drain off fat. Add to the meat

¾ cup tomato paste   ¼ cup oil
¾ cup water   2 tablespoons spaghetti
½ cup dry red wine   sauce seasonings

Cover and simmer 30 minutes. Mix together and set aside
> 2 *egg whites, slightly beaten*
> 1 *package frozen chopped spinach, thawed*

Have ready to use
> 2 *cups "special" cottage cheese or baker's cheese*

Cook according to the directions on the package
> ½ *pound lasagne*

Drain the lasagne well. In a 7- by 11-inch oiled baking dish, arrange layers of ⅓ of the lasagne, ⅓ of the cheese, ⅓ of the spinach mixture, and ⅓ of the meat sauce. Repeat layers, ending with the sauce. Bake in a 350° F. oven until hot through (about 30 minutes). Serve hot. **Six servings.**

ONE SERVING (CONTAINS 1 OUNCE COOKED MEAT)

Oil — 2 teaspoons	**Protein** — 24 grams
Cholesterol — 26 milligrams	**Carbohydrate** — 38 grams
Saturated fat — 3 grams	**Calories** — 365
Linoleic acid — 5 grams	

SPAGHETTI MEAT SAUCE

Brown and cook in a skillet until done
> ½ *pound very lean ground beef* (*or lean ground veal*)
> *salt*
> *pepper*

Pour off any accumulated fat and put meat into saucepan. Soak together
> 1 *small package* (*½ ounce*) *dried mushrooms*
> 1 *cup hot water*

Brown
> 1 *large onion, finely chopped*

in
> ½ *teaspoon oil*

Add the prepared mushrooms and water and onions to the meat, together with
> 3½ *cups canned tomatoes*
> 1 *cup hot sauce*
> 1 *dried chili pepper*

Cook slowly over low flame 1 hour, stirring occasionally. When done, remove the chili pepper from the sauce. Cook
> 1 *pound spaghetti*

in about
4 quarts boiling salted water
Drain and mix with the sauce. **Eight servings.**

ONE SERVING (CONTAINS 1 OUNCE COOKED MEAT)
Oil — 0 teaspoons   **Protein** — 16 grams
Cholesterol — 16 milligrams   **Carbohydrate** — 51 grams
Saturated fat — 1 gram   **Calories** — 295
Linoleic acid — negligible

INDIA CURRY

Remove all separable fat and fibrous tissue and cut into cubes (about ½ inch)
veal or lamb (½ pound trimmed weight)
Add
water to cover meat   *1 pinch thyme*
3 medium-size onions,   *1 sprig parsley*
*   sliced*
¼ to ½ teaspoon ground
*   black pepper*
Cook until tender. Strain off liquid. Remove fat and use liquid to make gravy with
4 tablespoons flour   *dash cayenne pepper*
½ teaspoon salt   *extra water if needed*
1 to 2 teaspoons curry powder
Combine the gravy and meat with
½ cup chopped celery   *¼ pound mushrooms*
¾ cup chopped carrots   *   (optional)*
1 cup peas
Cook until vegetables are done, adding more water and cayenne pepper if necessary. **Six servings.**

ONE SERVING (CONTAINS 1 OUNCE COOKED MEAT)
Oil — 0 teaspoons   **Protein** — 12 grams
Cholesterol — 21 milligrams   **Carbohydrate** — 13 grams
Saturated fat — 1 gram   **Calories** — 125
Linoleic acid — negligible
Serve over steamed rice and sprinkle over each serving
raw chopped onion
Suggested accompaniments:
India relish
chutney
raisins
India curry is good served with banana salad or broiled bananas.

TUNA CASSEROLE

Cook in boiling salted water until tender
>   2 *cups macaroni broken into small pieces*
>   ½ *teaspoon dried orégano*

When nearly done, add
>   1 *small clove garlic, chopped*
>   1 *small onion, chopped*

Complete cooking and drain, leaving the herbs in the macaroni. Shake together in a covered jar
>   2 *tablespoons flour*
>   *juice from 4-ounce can mushrooms*

Pour into a cup, measure, and add
>   *enough skim milk to make 1 cup of mixture*

Pour in pan and cook until thick, stirring constantly. Add
>   1 *4-ounce can mushrooms, drained*
>   1 *cup flaked water-packed tuna (6 ounces meat)*
>   ½ *cup dry sherry*

Add the macaroni and mix thoroughly. Add salt to taste. Turn into casserole dish and bake, covered, in a moderate oven (350° F.) 30 minutes. Remove cover for last 5 minutes to brown. **Six servings.**

ONE SERVING (CONTAINS 1 OUNCE COOKED MEAT)

Oil — 0 teaspoons	**Protein** — 14 grams
Cholesterol — 21 milligrams	**Carbohydrate** — 33 grams
Saturated fat — negligible	**Calories** — 205
Linoleic acid — negligible	

FISH AND NOODLES

Cook in boiling salted water until noodles are tender
>   1 *cup noodles (made without egg yolk)* (*or spaghetti or macaroni*)
>   3 *tablespoons chopped onion*
>   ⅓ *cup diced celery*

Drain, leaving the vegetables with the noodles. Mix and heat
>   2 *cups canned or raw tomatoes, cut in pieces*
>   ½ *teaspoon salt*
>   *pepper*

Measure
>   1 *cup flaked, water-packed tuna (6 ounces meat)*

Put alternate layers of noodles, fish, and hot tomato mixture into a baking dish. Top with

   ¼ *cup bread crumbs*

Bake in a moderate oven (350° F.) until the mixture is heated through and the bread crumbs are browned (about 20 minutes). **Six servings.**

ONE SERVING (CONTAINS 1 OUNCE COOKED MEAT)

Oil — 0 teaspoons	**Protein** — 10 grams
Cholesterol — 21 milligrams	**Carbohydrate** — 19 grams
Saturated fat — negligible	**Calories** — 130
Linoleic acid — negligible	

VARIATIONS:

Other cooked fish, such as codfish, may be substituted for tuna.

SALMON, RICE, AND TOMATOES

Combine in a large saucepan and bring to a boil

   2 *cups canned tomatoes*   ¼ *cup diced green pepper*
   and juice (or 2½ cups raw   1½ *cups boiling water*
   tomatoes) cut in pieces   *salt to taste*
   ¼ *cup diced onion*   *pepper*

Add

   1 *cup rice, uncooked*

Cover and simmer until the rice is tender (20 to 25 minutes), adding more water if needed. Add

   1 *cup flaked canned or cooked salmon (6 ounces meat)*

Cook 2 or 3 minutes longer to blend the flavors. **Six servings.**

ONE SERVING (CONTAINS 1 OUNCE COOKED MEAT)

Oil — 0 teaspoons	**Protein** — 10 grams
Cholesterol — 21 milligrams	**Carbohydrate** — 32 grams
Saturated fat — negligible	**Calories** — 180
Linoleic acid — negligible	

VARIATIONS:

Other cooked fish, such as cod or water-packed tuna, may be substituted for salmon.

CREAMED TUNA

Shake together in a covered jar
    4 *tablespoons flour*
    1 *cup skim milk*
Pour into a pan and add
    1 *cup skim milk*
Cook until smooth and thick, stirring constantly. Add
    1 *cup flaked water-packed tuna* (6 *ounces meat*)
Mix well and add

salt to taste	*drop of yellow food coloring*
dash pepper	1 *to* 2 *teaspoons lemon juice*
⅛ *teaspoon monosodium*	
glutamate	

Four servings.

ONE SERVING (CONTAINS 1½ OUNCES COOKED MEAT)

Oil — 0 teaspoons	**Protein** — 16 grams
Cholesterol — 35 milligrams	**Carbohydrate** — 11 grams
Saturated fat — negligible	**Calories** — 128
Linoleic acid — negligible	

VARIATIONS:

1. Other cooked fish, such as finnan haddie, may be substituted for tuna.
2. Finely chopped, cooked vegetables may be added to the creamed fish.
Serve on toast, rice, or Curds and Rice★.

CHICKEN PIE

Prepare
    1 *cup boned chicken with fat and skin removed* (5 *ounces*
    meat)
Arrange half of the chicken in bottom of baking dish. Add

1 *cup diced boiled potatoes*	½ *cup cooked, sliced carrots*
1 *large onion, sliced and*	½ *cup cooked, chopped*
steamed in a little water	*celery*

Cover with rest of the chicken. Combine and cook, stirring constantly,
until smooth and thick
    1½ *cups chicken broth from which the fat has been removed*
      (*or* 2 *bouillon cubes dissolved in* 1½ *cups boiling water*)
    3 *tablespoons flour*

Add

¾ teaspoon salt
⅛ teaspoon pepper
¼ teaspoon nutmeg
pinch rosemary
¼ teaspoon cardamom

1 drop oil scraped from
rind of lemon
1 to 2 drops yellow food
coloring

Pour over the chicken mixture. Top with cooked cereal or a thin pastry crust, or use peas in place of potatoes in the casserole and top with mashed potatoes. Bake in a hot oven (475° F.) until golden brown. **Four servings.**

ONE SERVING (CONTAINS 1¼ OUNCES COOKED MEAT)
(CALCULATIONS DO NOT INCLUDE TOPPING)

Oil — 0 teaspoons
Cholesterol — 23 milligrams
Saturated fat — 1 gram
Linoleic acid — negligible

Protein — 14 grams
Carbohydrate — 15 grams
Calories — 145

TURKEY CROQUETTES

Combine and cook, stirring constantly, until smooth and thick
⅔ cup fat free turkey broth
2 tablespoons flour
Combine in a separate bowl

1 cup cooked brown or
enriched white rice
1 cup diced, cooked lean
turkey (or chicken) (5 ounces
meat)
2 teaspoons lemon juice
½ teaspoon salt
few drops onion juice

¼ teaspoon celery salt
1 teaspoon finely chopped
parsley
pepper
¼ teaspoon monosodium
glutamate
1 drop yellow food coloring

Add white sauce to turkey mixture, adding enough to make it as soft as can be handled. Cool; shape into 4 balls. Roll in
¼ cup wheat germ
Brown in 400° F. oven or in the broiler. **Four servings.**

ONE SERVING (CONTAINS 1¼ OUNCES COOKED MEAT)

Oil — 0 teaspoons
Cholesterol — 23 milligrams
Saturated fat — 1 gram
Linoleic acid — 1 gram

Protein — 14 grams
Carbohydrate — 15 grams
Calories — 140

CREAMED CHICKEN

Cook chicken (or turkey) by stewing method, pages 132–33. Save fat free cooking liquid. Remove meat from bone, chill, and cube. Freeze any leftover poultry or cooking liquid for use later. Shake together in a covered jar until smooth

3 tablespoons oil	½ cup fat free chicken
3 tablespoons flour	(or turkey) broth
1 cup skim milk	
2 tablespoons skim milk powder	

Pour into a saucepan and cook over medium heat, stirring constantly, until the sauce thickens. Add

1 cup cooked lean chicken (or turkey) meat, cubed (5 ounces meat)	2 tablespoons chopped pimiento
	1 teaspoon chopped capers
4 ounces canned mushrooms, including juices	½ teaspoon salt

Three servings.

ONE SERVING (CONTAINS 1⅔ OUNCES COOKED MEAT)

Oil — 3 teaspoons	**Protein** — 19 grams
Cholesterol — 33 milligrams	**Carbohydrate** — 12 grams
Saturated fat — 3 grams	**Calories** — 275
Linoleic acid — 9 grams	

This may be served hot over toast or rice. Garnish with paprika.

LOW CALORIE CREAMED CHICKEN

Combine and cook in a pan until vegetables are tender

½ cup chopped celery	¼ cup water
1½ teaspoons chopped onion	
1 tablespoon chopped green pepper	

Shake together in a covered jar and add to the vegetables

2 cups fat free chicken (or turkey) broth
¼ cup flour
⅓ cup skim milk powder

Cook to a smooth sauce, stirring constantly. Add

1 cup diced, cooked lean chicken or turkey (5 ounces meat)	⅛ teaspoon monosodium glutamate
½ teaspoon salt	1 to 2 drops oil scraped from rind of lemon
pepper	1 drop yellow food coloring

Heat the mixture thoroughly and serve. **Four servings.**

ONE SERVING (CONTAINS 1¼ OUNCES COOKED MEAT)

Oil — 0 teaspoons	**Protein** — 15 grams
Cholesterol — 24 milligrams	**Carbohydrate** — 10 grams
Saturated fat — 1 gram	**Calories** — 125
Linoleic acid — negligible	

Serve on rice, Curds and Rice★, or toast.

CURRIED CHICKEN

Combine and cook, stirring constantly, until smooth and thick
    2 cups fat free chicken broth
    4 tablespoons flour
Add

¼ teaspoon salt	½ to 1 cup chopped onion
pepper to taste	⅔ cup chopped celery
1 to 2 teaspoons curry powder, to taste	1 cup chopped carrots
2 cups diced, cooked lean chicken (10 ounces meat)	1 cup peas
	1 drop yellow food coloring

Cook until vegetables are done. Salt to taste. **Six servings.**

ONE SERVING (CONTAINS 1⅔ OUNCES COOKED MEAT)

Oil — 0 teaspoons	**Protein** — 18 grams
Cholesterol — 30 milligrams	**Carbohydrate** — 11 grams
Saturated fat — 1 gram	**Calories** — 145
Linoleic acid — 1 gram	

Serve on flaky boiled rice or Curds and Rice★.

CHICKEN AND PINEAPPLE

Cook over low heat about 5 minutes, stirring occasionally
    1 cup pineapple tidbits
    ½ cup fat free chicken broth

Combine and cook, stirring constantly, until smooth and thick

1 cup fat free chicken broth
4 tablespoons flour

Combine the 2 mixtures with

½ teaspoon salt
1 cup diced, cooked lean
*   chicken (5 ounces meat)*
2 to 3 drops Tabasco

¼ teaspoon monosodium
*   glutamate*
1 to 2 drops yellow food
*   coloring*

Cook a few minutes to blend flavors. **Four servings.**

ONE SERVING (CONTAINS 1¼ OUNCES COOKED MEAT)

Oil — 0 teaspoons
Cholesterol — 23 milligrams
Saturated fat — 1 gram
Linoleic acid — negligible

Protein — 12 grams
Carbohydrate — 18 grams
Calories — 145

Serve on rice, Curds and Rice★, or toast.

CHICKEN TAMALE PIE

Combine

1 cup fat free chicken broth
1 cup yellow corn meal

Line sides and bottom of a casserole with the corn meal paste, saving about ¼ of this mixture for the top. Combine in a separate bowl

⅓ cup fat free chicken broth
½ teaspoon salt
1 teaspoon chili powder
¼ teaspoon cloves
¼ teaspoon garlic salt
¼ cup seedless raisins
1 cup fresh or canned
*   tomatoes*

1 cup tomato sauce
½ cup chopped green pepper
½ cup chopped onion
1 cup diced, cooked lean
*   chicken (5 ounces meat)*

Pour into the lined casserole. Sprinkle and spread the remaining corn meal paste on the top. Bake in a 350° F. oven 1 hour. **Four servings.**

ONE SERVING (CONTAINS 1¼ OUNCES COOKED MEAT)

Oil — 0 teaspoons
Cholesterol — 23 milligrams
Saturated fat — 1 gram
Linoleic acid — 1 gram

Protein — 17 grams
Carbohydrate — 26 grams
Calories — 202

CHAPTER XIII

Low Saturated Fat, Low Cholesterol
Main Dishes that Contain No Meat

THE dishes described in this chapter are very low in saturated fat and extremely low in cholesterol, as they contain no meat. These will be helpful when you have already used your day's meat allowance or plan to use it for the following meals of that day.

Most of these dishes are high in protein and depend for their protein content on the following foods:

Vegetable-protein meat substitutes, such as vegetable-burger and vege-
table-burger steak*
Skim milk cottage cheese
Skim milk and skim milk powder
Beans, peas, and lentils

The use of some of these foods has been discussed in previous chapters. You may be able to modify many of your own recipes by using one or more of the above foods and thus make them acceptable as a no-meat, low saturated fat, low cholesterol dish. Sometimes the products have recipes on the labels which are acceptable or can be modified satis-factorily.

Vegetable-protein meat substitute products are canned, high protein foods. These products vary a great deal in the types of fat and in the amount of fat (and calories) they contain. The ingredients are listed on the label, and in many cases the amounts of protein, fat, carbo-hydrate, and calories in the product are listed. Do not use products containing ingredients high in saturated fat. See the list of "bewares"

---

* Some of the vegetable-protein meat substitute products (see page 71) made by Loma Linda Foods, Battle Creek Food Company, and Worthington Foods, Inc., are acceptable in this diet. You may find other acceptable brands and products in your area. New brands continue to come on the market.

in label-reading, page 20. Whether you use a product high in acceptable fats depends on your fat and calorie allowance.

Our recipes are calculated on the basis of vegetable-protein products with not more than 5 per cent fat. We refer to these products in our recipes as "vegetable-burger" (when a ground "meat" is required) and "vegetable-burger steak" (when a "steak" or "chop" is required). Vegetable-burger may be sliced and used as vegetable-burger steaks. The steaks and chops vary in size according to the brand; therefore in our recipes weight in ounces is given for vegetable-burger steak.

Try using some of the acceptable prepared seasonings with the high protein, no-meat foods. See page 88.

The oil has been kept to a minimum in the following recipes. You may prefer to add more and may do so, depending on your calorie and oil allowance.

MEATLESS INDIAN CURRY

Simmer 5 minutes

2 cups vegetable-burger
3 onions, sliced
¼ teaspoon pepper

3 dashes thyme
1 sprig parsley, chopped
1 cup water

Strain off liquor and save. Shake together in a covered jar

½ cup cold water
4 tablespoons flour

Pour into deep skillet or Dutch oven and heat until thickened, stirring constantly. Add

1 to 2 teaspoons curry powder
½ teaspoon salt
⅛ teaspoon pepper

liquor from cooking
  vegetable-burger and onions

Stir until smooth, then add

vegetable-burger and onions
1 cup chopped carrots
1 cup chopped celery

1 cup peas
mushrooms if desired

Cook 1 hour, adding more liquid if necessary. **Six servings.**

ONE SERVING

Oil — 0 teaspoons
Cholesterol — 0 milligrams
Saturated fat — negligible
Linoleic acid — 1 gram

Protein — 17 grams
Carbohydrate — 17 grams
Calories — 155

Serve over steamed brown rice. Accompany with India relish, chutney, raisins, or chilled banana halves.

EGG FOO YUNG

Combine
½ cup chopped green onions   *1 cup bean sprouts*
¼ cup sliced water chestnuts   *½ cup vegetable-burger*
    (sliced celery hearts may
    be used instead)

Then, over
6 egg whites
sprinkle
¼ teaspoon salt   *dash monosodium glutamate*
dash celery salt   *2 teaspoons Instant Potato*
dash onion salt

Beat lightly with a fork. Add
1 drop yellow food coloring
Mix and add to the vegetable mixture. Heat in a skillet
2 teaspoons oil
Add the vegetable-egg mixture and brown well on both sides. **Four servings.**

ONE SERVING
Oil — ½ teaspoon   **Protein** — 13 grams
Cholesterol — 0 milligrams   **Carbohydrate** — 6 grams
Saturated fat — negligible   **Calories** — 105
Linoleic acid — 2 grams

Serve with the following soy sauce:
Thicken
1 can bouillon or 1 bouillon cube dissolved in 1½ cups water
with
1 tablespoon cornstarch
Heat slowly, stirring constantly, until smooth. Add
2 teaspoons soy sauce
¼ teaspoon monosodium glutamate

MEATLESS SPAGHETTI

Prepare sauce, then cook
¾ pound spaghetti (about 2½ cups)
Drain, rinse quickly with hot water, and serve.

SAUCE:

In a deep skillet or Dutch oven combine

1½ cups vegetable-burger
2 cups tomatoes
1 large onion, chopped
1 clove garlic, chopped
1 4-ounce can mushrooms
1 8-ounce can tomato sauce
1 sprig parsley, chopped
½ teaspoon monosodium
   glutamate

⅛ teaspoon pepper
1 can bouillon (undiluted)
   or 1 bouillon cube
   dissolved in 1½ cups hot
   water
2 teaspoons Kitchen Bouquet
½ teaspoon chili powder

Mix well and cook over low heat 45 minutes. **Four large servings.**

ONE SERVING

Oil — 0 teaspoons
Cholesterol — 0 milligrams
Saturated fat — negligible
Linoleic acid — 1 gram

Protein — 31 grams
Carbohydrate — 78 grams
Calories — 465

MEATLESS SPANISH RICE

In a saucepan with a tight-fitting lid combine

2 cups vegetable-burger
1 cup chopped onion
1 cup chopped celery
1 green pepper, chopped

3½ cups tomatoes
2 teaspoons salt
½ teaspoon pepper
½ teaspoon chili powder

Mix well. Add

½ cup uncooked enriched white rice

Cover and cook over high heat until the mixture starts to steam. Then turn heat very low and steam 35 minutes without raising the lid. **Four servings.**

ONE SERVING

Oil — 0 teaspoons
Cholesterol — 0 milligrams
Saturated fat — negligible
Linoleic acid — 2 grams

Protein — 25 grams
Carbohydrate — 40 grams
Calories — 290

MEATLESS STUFFED PEPPERS

Parboil for 5 to 10 minutes in a tightly covered saucepan in very little salted, boiling water

    6 medium-size green peppers

Slice off tops, hollow out the seeds and membranes, and fill with the following mixture

½ cup vegetable-burger	*1 cup tomatoes, chopped*
1 tablespoon chopped onion	*¾ to 1 teaspoon salt*
1½ cups cooked rice	*dash of pepper*
1 cup sieved skim milk cottage cheese	

Fit into a baking dish. Sprinkle the top of each stuffed pepper with bread crumbs and bake in a moderate oven (350° F.) 30 minutes. **Six servings.**

ONE SERVING

Oil — ⅔ teaspoon	**Protein** — 12 grams
Cholesterol — 3 milligrams	**Carbohydrate** — 17 grams
Saturated fat — negligible	**Calories** — 145
Linoleic acid — 2 grams	

MEATLESS STUFFED TOMATOES

Cut off the stem ends and with a teaspoon scoop out the insides from

    6 firm tomatoes

Fill with the following mixture

1½ cups whole-kernel corn	*3 tablespoons chopped onion*
1½ cups bread crumbs	*½ cup vegetable-burger*
3 tablespoons chopped green pepper	*½ teaspoon salt*
	2 teaspoons paprika

Place in a baking dish, add 2 tablespoons water, and bake in a moderate oven (350° F.) 30 minutes. **Six servings.**

ONE SERVING

Oil — 0 teaspoons	**Protein** — 8 grams
Cholesterol — 0 milligrams	**Carbohydrate** — 26 grams
Saturated fat — negligible	**Calories** — 135
Linoleic acid — 1 gram	

VEGETABLE-BURGER LOAF

Simmer until tender
   1 *small onion, chopped*
   1 *bouillon cube*
in
   ¼ cup water or meat stock
and add to
   2 *cups vegetable-burger*   2 *tablespoons whole-wheat*
   ½ cup bread crumbs   *flour*
   2 *egg whites*   *salt and pepper to taste*
   ¼ cup wheat germ

Mix, form into a loaf, and place in a baking dish lined with heavy wax paper. Place loaf pan in a pan containing a small amount of water (as in baking a custard) and bake at 350° F. 1 hour. Serve with any desired sauce (not included in calculations). **Six servings.**

ONE SERVING
   Oil — 0 teaspoons   **Protein** — 17 grams
   Cholesterol — 0 milligrams   **Carbohydrate** — 9 grams
   Saturated fat — 3 grams   **Calories** — 120
   Linoleic acid — 1 gram

VEGETABLE-BURGER PATTIES

Mix together
   2 *cups vegetable-burger*
   1 *bouillon cube*
dissolved in
   2 *tablespoons warm water*
Add
   ¼ cup wheat germ   *salt and pepper to taste*
   ½ cup bread crumbs   *¼ teaspoon monosodium*
   2 *egg whites*   *glutamate*
   1 *tablespoon oil*

Mix and form into patties. Place in covered casserole or individual baking dishes. Place in a pan containing a small amount of water. Bake 30 minutes at 350° F. **Six servings.**

ONE SERVING
   Oil — ½ teaspoon   **Protein** — 17 grams
   Cholesterol — 0 milligrams   **Carbohydrate** — 7 grams
   Saturated fat — 1 gram   **Calories** — 140
   Linoleic acid — 2 grams

Try these variations for vegetable-burger patties:

1. Pour Spanish Sauce★ over patties. Bake uncovered 30 minutes at 350° F.

2. **Ginger Vegetable-Burger Patties with Pineapple.** Add ½ teaspoon powdered ginger to the recipe for Vegetable-Burger Patties. Mix. Form into patties and cover with pineapple chunks. Bake uncovered for 30 minutes at 350° F.

3. **Vegetable-Burgers and Sauerkraut.** Cover patties with sauerkraut and bake uncovered 30 minutes at 350° F.

4. **Curried Vegetable-Burger Patties.** Add to the recipe for Vegetable-Burger Patties:

1 cup peas	1 teaspoon curry powder
1 4-ounce can mushrooms	
2 carrots, chopped	
1 medium-size onion, chopped and cooked in a small amount of water	

Mix well and shape into patties. Cover with the following sauce:
1 can bouillon
thickened with
2 tablespoons flour
Add
½ teaspoon curry powder
¼ teaspoon pepper
½ teaspoon Kitchen Bouquet
Bake uncovered in moderate oven (350° F.) 30 minutes.

VEGETABLE-BURGER STEAKS WITH MUSHROOM SAUCE

Simmer until well heated
6 vegetable-burger steaks (18 ounces)
in the following sauce
juice from 1 4-ounce can mushrooms
made up to 2 cups with
meat stock (or bouillon cube dissolved in hot water)
Thicken with
3 tablespoons flour
Add
mushrooms

Season with
>½ teaspoon salt
>pepper
>¼ teaspoon monosodium glutamate

Six servings.

ONE SERVING
>**Oil** — 0 teaspoons
>**Cholesterol** — 0 milligrams
>**Saturated fat** — negligible
>**Linoleic acid** — 1 gram

>**Protein** — 18 grams
>**Carbohydrate** — 6 grams
>**Calories** — 115

MEATLESS SWISS STEAK

Make a gravy by adding
>3 tablespoons flour
shaken with
>juice from vegetable-burger steaks
to
>1 can bouillon, undiluted
>or 1½ cups meat stock

Heat, stirring constantly, until thickened. Add
>1 teaspoon Kitchen Bouquet for darker color
>salt and pepper to taste
Pour over
>6 vegetable-burger steaks (18 ounces)
in a skillet or casserole. Cover and bake 1 hour in slow oven (300° F.).

Six servings.

ONE SERVING
>**Oil** — 0 teaspoons
>**Cholesterol** — 0 milligrams
>**Saturated fat** — negligible
>**Linoleic acid** — 2 grams

>**Protein** — 19 grams
>**Carbohydrate** — 7 grams
>**Calories** — 125

MEATLESS SUKIYAKI

Brown in deep skillet or Dutch oven with tightly fitting lid
>4 vegetable-burger steaks (12 ounces), *thinly sliced in
>small pieces*
in
>1 teaspoon oil

Add

½ cup soy sauce

2 tablespoons sugar

1 bunch celery, coarsely chopped

2 bunches green onions, including tops, chopped

1 bunch chard, coarsely chopped

1 4-ounce can mushrooms, drained

2½ cups cooked bean sprouts, drained

Cover tightly and steam over high heat until vegetables are well heated but still crunchy. **Six servings.**

ONE SERVING

Oil — ⅙ teaspoon

Cholesterol — 0 milligrams

Saturated fat — negligible

Linoleic acid — 1 gram

Protein — 15 grams

Carbohydrate — 16 grams

Calories — 150

QUICK SUPPER DISH

Mix in a casserole

2 cups canned kidney beans

1 large red onion, sliced in rings

1 clove garlic, minced

½ cup red wine

1 cup vegetable-burger

Heat in 300° F. oven 30 minutes or until onions are cooked. **Four servings.**

ONE SERVING

Oil — 0 teaspoons

Cholesterol — 0 milligrams

Saturated fat — negligible

Linoleic acid — 1 gram

Protein — 19 grams

Carbohydrate — 27 grams

Calories — 200

MEATLESS CHILI

Mix

2 cups vegetable-burger

with

1 bouillon cube

dissolved in

½ cup hot water

Let stand 15 minutes. Meanwhile, in a large saucepan or Dutch oven, combine

6 cups cooked kidney beans
3½ cups tomatoes
2 onions, sliced
2 teaspoons Kitchen
   Bouquet

2 tablespoons sugar
2 teaspoons chili powder
¼ teaspoon pepper
¼ teaspoon monosodium
   glutamate

Add

vegetable-burger and bouillon
salt to taste

Cook 1 to 2 hours over low heat. **Eight servings.**

ONE SERVING

   Oil — 0 teaspoons
   Cholesterol — 0 milligrams
   Saturated fat — negligible
   Linoleic acid — 1 gram

   Protein — 23 grams
   Carbohydrate — 44 grams
   Calories — 285

Serve on brown rice or Curds and Rice★. This dish may be served a second day, as the flavor improves with reheating.

BAKED LENTILS

Wash and soak 5 to 6 hours and cook slowly 1 hour
   1 cup lentils
Before the cooking period is up, add
   1 teaspoon salt
Mix together and add to the lentils

1 cup vegetable-burger
1 cup tomato sauce
½ cup water
½ cup finely chopped onion

¼ cup finely chopped celery
2 tablespoons chopped
   parsley

Bake in a slow oven (325° F.) 1 hour. **Six servings.**

ONE SERVING

   Oil — 0 teaspoons
   Cholesterol — 0 milligrams
   Saturated fat — negligible
   Linoleic acid — negligible

   Protein — 16 grams
   Carbohydrate — 26 grams
   Calories — 177

BAKED BEANS

Soak 5 to 6 hours
   2 cups navy, kidney, or red beans

Cook 1 hour and drain. Combine

½ cup vegetable-burger	*3 cups canned tomatoes*
4 sweet pickles, chopped	*1 teaspoon salt*
½ cup chopped onion	*½ teaspoon pepper*
1 clove garlic, chopped	*½ teaspoon paprika*
½ cup chopped celery	

Bring these ingredients to the boiling point. Pour over the beans and bake in oven at 350° F. 2 hours. **Six servings.**

ONE SERVING

Oil — 0 teaspoons	**Protein** — 19 grams
Cholesterol — 0 milligrams	**Carbohydrate** — 53 grams
Saturated fat — negligible	**Calories** — 300
Linoleic acid — negligible	

BOSTON BAKED BEANS

Cover
    4 cups pea beans
with
    cold water

Soak 5 or 6 hours. Pour beans and water in which they soaked into bean pot. Combine and add to the beans

1 teaspoon salt	*3 tablespoons brown sugar*
½ teaspoon mustard	*1 cup boiling water*
2 to 4 tablespoons blackstrap molasses (according to taste)*	

Cover bean pot and bake in a 250° F. oven 6 to 8 hours. Add water as needed during cooking. **Twelve servings.**

ONE SERVING

Oil — 0 teaspoons	**Protein** — 15 grams
Cholesterol — 0 milligrams	**Carbohydrate** — 48 grams
Saturated fat — negligible	**Calories** — 260
Linoleic acid — negligible	

COTTAGE CHEESE AND EGGPLANT CASSEROLE

Peel and cube
    1 eggplant

* 4 tablespoons used in recipe analysis.

Put in saucepan with
>   *½ cup water*

and cook, covered, 15 minutes. Add with stirring

>   *1 egg white, unbeaten*   *1 pimiento, chopped*
>   *2 slices bread, flaked*   *1 teaspoon salt*
>   *½ onion, sliced*   *3 to 4 drops Tabasco*
>   *1 cup skim milk cottage*   *dash marjoram*
>   *cheese*   *pepper to taste*
>   *1 green pepper, chopped*

Pour into casserole, sprinkle with paprika. Bake at 350° F. 45 minutes.
Six servings.

ONE SERVING

>   **Oil** — 0 teaspoons   **Protein** — 9 grams
>   **Cholesterol** — 3 milligrams   **Carbohydrate** — 12 grams
>   **Saturated fat** — 0 grams   **Calories** — 85
>   **Linoleic acid** — 0 grams

DUCHESS COTTAGE POTATO

Shake in a covered jar
>   *⅓ cup skim milk*
>   *¼ cup skim milk powder*

Beat into
>   *3 cups leftover or freshly cooked mashed potatoes*

Add
>   *1½ cups sieved skim milk cottage cheese*
>   *salt and pepper to taste*

Beat well, turn into casserole, dust with
>   *paprika*

and bake in hot oven until brown on top. Add
>   *chopped parsley*

before serving. **Six servings.**

ONE SERVING

>   **Oil** — 0 teaspoons   **Protein** — 15 grams
>   **Cholesterol** — 7 milligrams   **Carbohydrate** — 22 grams
>   **Saturated fat** — negligible   **Calories** — 170
>   **Linoleic acid** — 2 grams

HOT POTATO COTTAGE CHEESE SALAD

Heat over boiling water in the lightly oiled top of a double boiler
> 3 cups cooked, diced potatoes, hot or cold
> ½ cup sliced celery
> 2 tablespoons minced onion
> 2 tablespoons chopped pickle
> 1 tablespoon chopped green pepper or pimiento or both
> ¼ teaspoon sweet basil
> ½ teaspoon salt

Warm in a pan over hot water but not over direct heat
> 1½ cups skim milk cottage cheese
> ¼ cup Fat Free Salad Dressing★

Blend together
> ¼ cup Fat Free Salad Dressing★
> 1 tablespoon tarragon vinegar
> ½ teaspoon salt

Toss potato mixture, cottage cheese, and dressing together and serve at once. **Six servings.**

ONE SERVING
> **Oil** — 0 teaspoons
> **Cholesterol** — 5 milligrams
> **Saturated fat** — 0 grams
> **Linoleic acid** — 0 grams

> **Protein** — 12 grams
> **Carbohydrate** — 17 grams
> **Calories** — 120

CHEESE AND RICE CASSEROLE

Blend together well
> 1½ cups sieved skim milk cottage cheese
> 3 cups cooked rice
> 3 egg whites
> ½ cup skim milk
> 1 teaspoon onion juice
> ½ green pepper, grated
> salt and pepper to taste

Bake in baking dish 45 minutes at 350° F. **Six servings.**

ONE SERVING
> **Oil** — 0 teaspoons
> **Cholesterol** — 5 milligrams
> **Saturated fat** — 0 grams
> **Linoleic acid** — 0 grams

> **Protein** — 13 grams
> **Carbohydrate** — 23 grams
> **Calories** — 145

Serve with Spanish Sauce★ if desired.

CURDS AND RICE

Mix together just before serving
   3 cups cooked enriched white rice
   1½ cups skim milk cottage cheese
Four servings.

ONE SERVING

Oil — 0 teaspoons
Cholesterol — 6 milligrams
Saturated fat — negligible
Linoleic acid — negligible

Protein — 17 grams
Carbohydrate — 33 grams
Calories — 205

VARIATION:

3 cups mashed potatoes may be substituted for the rice.

Use Curds and Rice★ to add protein to any dish served with rice, such as Sukiyaki★, India Curry★, Chicken and Pineapple★, or Creamed Tuna★.

CHAPTER XIV

Soups

THE sight and aroma of steaming bowls of soup being ladled from a tureen are an appetizing beginning for any dinner. Hearty soups can be a substantial part of lunch or supper. Soups play an important part in a diet restricted in saturated fat and cholesterol, since their nutritive content can be high while at the same time the saturated fat and cholesterol content can be kept very low.

Invest in an attractive soup tureen and ladle if you do not already have one. Have a variety of attractive bowls, cups, casseroles, and mugs to glamorize the presentation of soup at the table. Ladle hot soups into warmed dishes and serve cold soups in chilled bowls. Accompany them with appropriate crackers or breads and garnishes (see pages 185–86).

Commercially prepared soups containing fats and meat should not be used, as it is difficult to remove the fat from them. When making soups from commercially canned or packaged products or when including commercial products such as noodles and pastes, read the labels to be sure only acceptable foods are included. Creamed soups in cans or packages cannot be used, since they usually contain saturated fats and cholesterol. Acceptable commercially prepared bouillon, consommé, beef broth, bouillon cubes, chicken broth, and clam juice are available to use as bases for soups and sauces. It is advisable to test them for their fat content by chilling them (the prepared liquids in the case of dry products) and examining them for any congealed visible fat. If any fat is apparent, such products should always be chilled and the visible congealed fat removed with a paper towel (see page 170).

Homemade Stocks

If defatted according to the directions on page 170, these are easy and economical to prepare. Simmering a mixture of meat bones or fish and vegetables or vegetable juices results in *stock*. Stocks are the basis of wonderful flavors for sauces, gravies, aspics, soups, and stews, and they add flavor when used instead of water for cooking vegetables. You can prepare them from many nutritious by-products of cooking that otherwise would be thrown away. Keep a covered jar in your refrigerator for liquids from cooked or canned vegetables, such as green beans, peas, asparagus, and mushrooms. Add to it defatted meat drippings (see pages 84–85). Save celery and onion tops, tender parings or pods from carrots, beans, peas, and asparagus to add to your stock pot. Save meat trimmings, scraps and bones from beef and veal. Skin, giblets* (which you are not allowed to eat), and carcasses of chicken and turkey can become the basis for delicious soups. Keep fishbones and heads and leftovers of fresh or cooked shellfish† for future fish stock. All these can be stored in labeled plastic bags in the freezer until you are ready to prepare the stock. The following vegetables are in general use for soup stock: carrots, celery, onions, parsley, lettuce, tomatoes, parsnips, and leeks. The following seasonings are often used in soups or soup stock: salt, pepper or peppercorns, paprika, thyme, savory, marjoram, bay leaves, whole cloves, allspice, celery seed or celery salt, cayenne, garlic, mace, and rosemary. These may be added when making the stock or added later when making the final soup.

Get in the gourmet habit of having a supply of various stocks in your freezer. Stocks can be frozen in ice cube trays and the frozen cubes can be stored in your freezer in labeled heavy plastic bags.

In your "Frozen Stock Pantry" keep:

1. **Beef or poultry stock** for broths, soups, sauces, stews, and aspics.
2. **Lamb stock** for Scotch Broth★, curry sauce, and curries.
3. **Ham or bacon stock** can do much to provide the taste of ham and bacon for dishes that usually depend on these flavors for their distinctive taste. Beans cooked in ham or bacon stock will taste like old-fashioned beans baked with salt pork. Use the stock as a base for split-pea, lentil, or bean soup. Cook in this ham stock cereals that you plan to fry as a breakfast meat replacement.
4. **Fish stock** for chowders, fish soups, fish sauces, and fish dishes.

* Be sure to clarify stock if giblets are used.
† See page 76, "What You Should Know About Meat."

BASIC MEAT STOCK

For 3 to 4 quarts stock, place in an 8- to 10-quart kettle about
  2 quarts of 2- to 3-inch pieces of raw or cooked veal, beef,
    or poultry
and
  3 quarts cracked beef, veal, or poultry bones
Add, until ingredients are covered, about
  5 quarts cold water
Bring to boil and simmer 5 minutes, removing scum with spoon or
skimmer as it accumulates. Add

1 tablespoon salt	*2 medium-size celery stalks*
6 to 8 peppercorns	*and leaves*
2 whole cloves	*3 sprigs parsley*
2 medium-size carrots,	*¼ teaspoon thyme (or 2*
scraped	*sprigs fresh thyme)*
3 medium-size onions, sliced	*1 small bay leaf*

And if desired
  2 split and washed leeks
  2 unpeeled garlic cloves
Add more boiling water if necessary to cover, bring to simmer, and
simmer covered (do not boil) 3 to 4 hours or until broth has a rich
flavor. Occasionally skim off accumulated fat and scum. Strain stock
through cheesecloth put over a strainer. Cool quickly and keep well
chilled until fat is removed. Do not, however, remove fat until stock
is to be used or frozen as the layer of fat protects the stock from
spoilage. Never try to keep stock in the refrigerator longer than 3 days.
It can be kept frozen for weeks.

To remove fat from soup and soup stock: Chill the soup or stock,
allowing sufficient time for the fat to cake on top.

1. **For jellied stock:** Run a knife around the edge of the bowl.
Carefully remove the fat cake from the top. Wipe off any remaining
fat from the jelly and the bowl with a damp, warm cloth.

2. **Unjellied stock or soup:** Spoon off as much fat as possible. Pass
pieces of absorbent paper, such as facial tissue, or paper towels or
napkins, over the surface.

To clarify soup stock: Remove the fat from the jellied stock. Avoid
using any of the sediment* that may be at the bottom of the jellied
stock.

* The sediment is likely to be high in cholesterol content.

For clear, sparkling soups, melt
 jellied stock
Measure the stock. Add any extra
 seasoning
For each quart of stock, combine and add
 2 egg whites, slightly beaten
 ¼ cup cool stock
Stir thoroughly through the cool stock, then add
 2 eggshells broken into small pieces
Heat and stir until the stock begins to simmer. Simmer 5 minutes
without stirring. Allow it to settle undisturbed in a warm place
25 minutes. Remove the liquid with a ladle without disturbing the
sediment. Strain through a strainer lined with a double thickness of
cheesecloth.

WHITE STOCK

For white stock, use veal or poultry bones and an equal weight of
raw veal or poultry. Veal knuckles contain much gelatin and are
especially good to give the stock body. Raw veal in simmering releases
a large amount of granular scum that must be removed if the stock
is to be clear.

Cut up meat into small pieces and place meat and equal weight
of bones in large soup kettle. For 3 quarts of stock, use about
 3 pounds veal and/or poultry
 3 pounds cracked veal and/or poultry bones
Cover with about
 4 quarts cold water
Add vegetables and seasonings and proceed as in recipe for Basic Meat
Stock★.

BROWN STOCK

This stock is usually made with beef and veal bones and meat
that are first browned either in a roasting pan in the oven or in a
skillet on top of the stove. Transfer the browned meat bones and
scrapings to the soup kettle and proceed as in recipe for Basic Meat
Stock★. Brown stock is used for consommé, brown sauces, and stews.

HAM OR BACON STOCK

Place in a 4-quart pan
  1 *ham hock* or 4 *cups cubed slab bacon, including the rind*
  2 *quarts water*
Bring to boil and simmer 1½ to 2 hours. Cool overnight in the refrigerator. Remove fat as in Basic Meat Stock★ preparation.

LAMB STOCK

Place in a 6- to 8-quart pan
  3 *to 4 pounds lamb scraps and bones*
  1 *teaspoon salt*
Cover with 2 quarts cold water. Bring to boil and simmer for 1½ to 2 hours. Proceed as in Basic Meat Stock★ preparation.

FISH STOCK

In a 6- to 8-quart soup kettle, place
  2 *to 3 pounds fresh or frozen fish, fish heads and bones, or cooked shellfish* *leftovers*
Cover with
  4 *quarts cold water*
Add

1 *teaspoon salt*	8 *parsley stems*
1 *onion, sliced*	(*omit leaves for light stock*)
1 *teaspoon lemon juice*	⅓ *cup mushroom stems or*
1 *slice lemon*	*pieces*

Bring to simmer, skim, and simmer 45 minutes uncovered. Proceed as in recipe for Basic Meat Stock★.

By using these principles for preparing fat free stocks, you can modify your own favorite soups or invent other delicious kinds. A variety of recipes is presented to start you on your way.

★ See pages 79–80.

Some Hearty Soups

LENTIL SOUP

Wash in a fine-meshed sieve
    2 cups dried brown lentils
Place the lentils in an 8-quart soup kettle and add

    3 quarts Ham or Bacon   *¼ cup chopped parsley*
      Stock★ or White Stock★   *1 clove garlic, squeezed*
    2 onions, finely chopped   *through a garlic press*
    2 carrots, finely chopped   *1 teaspoon dried savory*
    3 celery stalks and leaves,   *salt to taste*
      finely chopped   *pepper to taste*

Simmer slowly with occasional stirring 3 hours. Soup can be served at once or, if desired, it can be puréed and then reheated to serve. **Twelve servings.**

ONE SERVING

    Oil — 0 teaspoons   **Protein** — 15 grams
    Cholesterol — 0 milligrams   **Carbohydrate** — 24 grams
    Saturated fat — 0 grams   **Calories** — 155
    Linoleic acid — 0 grams

FISH CHOWDER

Heat to boiling

    1 quart Fish Stock★ or water   *1 teaspoon salt*
    ¼ cup chopped parsley   *⅛ teaspoon pepper*
    ½ bay leaf   *½ teaspoon dried orange peel*
    ½ teaspoon dried thyme   *2 fennel seeds*

Add and simmer 15 minutes

    1 pound boned haddock, halibut, rock fish, snapper, or other
      fish

Remove fish from broth and chop into small pieces. Prepare

    1 cup chopped onion
    1 cup chopped celery
    3 medium-size potatoes, sliced thin

Add to fish broth and cook until potatoes are done. Add

    2 cups skim milk

Heat to simmer and add chopped fish. Simmer but don't allow to boil. **Six servings.**

ONE SERVING

Oil — 0 teaspoons	**Protein** — 22 grams
Cholesterol — 44 milligrams	**Carbohydrate** — 18 grams
Saturated fat — 1 gram	**Calories** — 190
Linoleic acid — negligible	

SCOTCH BROTH

Soak overnight in the refrigerator
   ½ cup barley
   ½ cup dried yellow peas
in
   2½ quarts Lamb Stock★
Add

1 teaspoon salt	1 turnip, chopped
2 onions, chopped	1 small cabbage, shredded
2 carrots, chopped	

Bring to boil and simmer 1 hour. Add

salt to taste	¾ cup chopped parsley
pepper to taste	1 carrot, grated

Simmer 15 minutes and serve. **Eight servings.**

ONE SERVING

Oil — 0 teaspoons	**Protein** — 10 grams
Cholesterol — 0 milligrams	**Carbohydrate** — 30 grams
Saturated fat — negligible	**Calories** — 165
Linoleic acid — negligible	

SALMON BISQUE

Blend in a blender

4 cups Fish Stock★ or chicken broth	3 tablespoons oil
	½ cup cooked mushrooms
1 cup skim milk powder	1 cup cooked asparagus
3 tablespoons flour	(optional but good)

Heat, stirring constantly, until thickened and smooth. Add
   1 can (7½ ounces) pink salmon
   salt to taste
   pepper to taste
Six servings.

ONE SERVING

    Oil — 1½ teaspoons
    Cholesterol — 30 milligrams
    Saturated fat — 1 gram
    Linoleic acid — 4 grams

Protein — 14 grams
Carbohydrate — 11 grams
Calories — 155

LEEK AND POTATO SOUP

Simmer, partially covered, until tender
    4 cups diced potatoes
    4 cups sliced leeks (white portion only)
    1 teaspoon salt
in
    1 quart White Stock★ or chicken broth
Purée in a blender or put through a sieve. Blend or beat together
    1 cup skim milk
    5 tablespoons skim milk
      powder
    2 tablespoons oil
    ½ teaspoon lecithin
      granules
    ¼ teaspoon butter flavor
Add to puréed vegetables and heat. Add
    salt to taste
    white pepper to taste
Garnish with
    minced chives or parsley
Eight servings.

ONE SERVING

    Oil — ¾ teaspoon
    Cholesterol — 2 milligrams
    Saturated fat — 1 gram
    Linoleic acid — 2 grams

Protein — 6 grams
Carbohydrate — 21 grams
Calories — 140

QUICK ONION SOUP

Simmer until tender
    2 cups very thinly sliced onions
in
    1 cup water
    2 teaspoons Kitchen Bouquet
Add
    1 can clear, fat free chicken broth
    1 can condensed bouillon (beef broth)

Heat thoroughly and add
    salt and pepper to taste
Makes about 4 cups. **Four servings.**

ONE SERVING

Oil — 0 teaspoons	**Protein** — 8 grams
Cholesterol — 0 milligrams	**Carbohydrate** — 5 grams
Saturated fat — 0 grams	**Calories** — 50
Linoleic acid — 0 grams	

BEAN SOUP MADE WITH MILK

Soaking and cooking beans in skim milk requires longer cooking time but pays off by the greatly increased protein content of the bean dish thus prepared. In this recipe more than 1 quart skim milk (33 grams protein) has been added.

Soak 4 to 6 hours in the refrigerator
    1 cup soup beans
in
    2 cups skim milk
Place beans and milk in the top of a double boiler and add
    1 medium-size onion,   *½ teaspoon Hickory Salt*
      chopped   *(Spice Islands)*
    1 clove garlic, chopped   *1 teaspoon salt*
Heat over water until beans are tender (6 to 8 hours), adding more milk as necessary. Usually requires adding
    about 3½ cups warmed skim milk
Purée through a sieve or in an electric blender a small amount at a time. Put back into double boiler, reheat, and add
    2 teaspoons lemon juice
    salt and pepper to taste
Makes about 5 cups. **Six servings.**

ONE SERVING

Oil — 0 teaspoons	**Protein** — 15 grams
Cholesterol — 7 milligrams	**Carbohydrate** — 33 grams
Saturated fat — 0 grams	**Calories** — 200
Linoleic acid — 0 grams	

BEAN SOUP

Soak 4 to 6 hours
  1 cup navy beans
in
  6 cups Ham or Bacon Stock★ or water
Simmer in soaking water until beans are tender. Add

1 clove garlic, chopped	*1 cup chopped celery*
1 small onion, chopped	*1 cup canned tomatoes*
2 tablespoons chopped	*1 cup chopped cabbage or*
parsley	*carrots (if desired)*

Simmer ½ hour longer, adding more water if necessary. Makes about 5 cups. **Six servings.**

Oil — 0 teaspoons	**Protein** — 8 grams
Cholesterol — 0 milligrams	**Carbohydrate** — 25 grams
Saturated fat — negligible	**Calories** — 135
Linoleic acid — negligible	

SPLIT-PEA SOUP

Soak 4 to 6 hours in the refrigerator
  1 pound split peas
in
  2 cups skim milk
Mix in a large soup kettle

1 cup Ham or Bacon Stock★	*pinch pepper*
1 can chicken broth	*½ teaspoon Hickory Salt*
1 medium onion stuck with	*(Spice Islands)*
1 clove	*¼ teaspoon monosodium*
2 carrots, chopped	*glutamate*
1 small clove garlic, chopped	*½ teaspoon salt*

Simmer slowly over very low heat 2½ hours or until peas are mushy. Stir occasionally and add more skim milk as necessary. Usually requires
  2 more cups warmed skim milk
Purée through a sieve or in an electric blender a small quantity at a time. Put back in kettle, reheat, salt to taste. Add more warmed skim milk if the soup is too thick. Makes about 6 cups. **Six servings.**

ONE SERVING

Oil — 0 teaspoons	**Protein** — 25 grams
Cholesterol — 5 milligrams	**Carbohydrate** — 58 grams
Saturated fat — 0 grams	**Calories** — 340
Linoleic acid — 0 grams	

MINESTRONE SOUP

Typical of every Italian eating place, this famous soup has as many variations as there are Italian kitchens. It lends itself to imagination and ingenuity and to what is on hand to add to it as no other dish does. Here is one suggestion. Combine in a soup pot and let simmer until vegetables are tender

3 cups water
3 bouillon cubes
few slices of carrot
3 or 4 thin slices of onion
2 or 3 tablespoons chopped
   celery

½ clove garlic, minced
¼ cup spaghetti or macaroni
½ cup sliced cabbage

Before serving add

1 cup tomatoes or tomato
   juice
¼ teaspoon sweet basil

Italian seasoning to taste
salt and pepper to taste

Heat until piping hot and serve. Makes about 4 cups. **Six servings.**

ONE SERVING

Oil ___ 0 teaspoons
Cholesterol ___ 0 milligrams
Saturated fat ___ 0 grams
Linoleic acid ___ 0 grams

Protein ___ 4 grams
Carbohydrate ___ 9 grams
Calories ___ 70

If the soup is used as a main luncheon dish, cottage cheese curd may be served in the soup. Other ingredients typical of minestrone are:

Red beans (cooked before
   using)
Parsley
Peas

Green onions with tops
String beans
Green pepper
Pinch of sage

Leftover vegetables may be substituted for some of the others. "Musts," however, are

onion, garlic, basil, tomatoes

If simmering reduces the volume, add more water before serving. This soup may be served a second day with even finer blending of flavors. Make it with a base of good soup stock if you wish. The use of bouillon cubes is given as a short cut.

Cream Soups

Skim milk with skim milk powder added makes excellent cream soup (see method below) and provides another means of attaining a daily intake of 1 quart of skim milk. *For a richer soup 2 tablespoons of oil may be added in making the white sauce.*

BASIC CREAM SOUP

Make a white sauce by shaking together in a jar
1 cup skim milk
2 tablespoons flour
2 tablespoons skim milk powder
Place in a saucepan and cook slowly, stirring until thickened and smooth. Add

1 tablespoon finely chopped onions (optional)
2 cups skim milk
1 to 2 cups vegetable purée or cooked minced vegetables*

1 teaspoon salt
¼ teaspoon monosodium glutamate
pepper

Each portion may be topped with
1 teaspoon or more of beaten egg white
dash of paprika
Makes about four cups. **Four servings.**

ONE SERVING WITHOUT OIL
Oil — 0 teaspoons
Cholesterol — 6 milligrams
Saturated fat — 0 grams
Linoleic acid — 0 grams

Protein — 8 grams
Carbohydrate — 16 grams
Calories — 95

ONE SERVING WITH OIL†
Oil — 1½ teaspoons
Cholesterol — 6 milligrams
Saturated fat — 1 gram
Linoleic acid — 4 grams

Protein — 8 grams
Carbohydrate — 16 grams
Calories — 160

VEGETABLE CHOWDER

Shake together in a jar
1 cup skim milk
2 tablespoons flour
2 tablespoons skim milk powder

---

* Suggested vegetables: carrots, celery, peas, green beans, lima beans, asparagus, cabbage, potatoes, corn, spinach, onions.
† See page 179.

Place in a saucepan and cook slowly, stirring until thickened and smooth. Add

1 cup skim milk   1 cup chopped carrots
1 cup shredded lettuce or   ¾ cup finely chopped onion
  cabbage

Simmer, covered, until vegetables are tender. Add

1 cup skim milk   ¼ teaspoon monosodium
1 teaspoon salt   glutamate
                                    pepper

Heat thoroughly but do not boil. Season to taste. Makes about 3½ cups. **Four servings.**

ONE SERVING WITHOUT OIL
    Oil — 0 teaspoons   **Protein** — 9 grams
    Cholesterol — 6 milligrams   **Carbohydrate** — 19 grams
    Saturated fat — 0 grams   **Calories** — 110
    Linoleic acid — 0 grams

ONE SERVING WITH OIL*
    Oil — 1½ teaspoons   **Protein** — 9 grams
    Cholesterol — 6 milligrams   **Carbohydrate** — 19 grams
    Saturated fat — 1 gram   **Calories** — 180
    Linoleic acid — 4 grams

CREAM OF ASPARAGUS SOUP

Prepare
    3 cups thin White Sauce★ in top of double boiler
Heat in saucepan
    2 cups puréed asparagus and juice
At serving time combine white sauce and asparagus; season with salt and pepper. Sprinkle each serving with
    paprika
    chopped parsley
Makes about 5 cups. **Six servings.**

ONE SERVING WITHOUT OIL
    Oil — 0 teaspoons   **Protein** — 6 grams
    Cholesterol — 3 milligrams   **Carbohydrate** — 11 grams
    Saturated fat — 0 grams   **Calories** — 70
    Linoleic acid — 0 grams

* See page 179.

ONE SERVING WITH OIL*
   Oil — 1 teaspoon
   Cholesterol — 3 milligrams
   Saturated fat — negligible
   Linoleic acid — 3 grams

   Protein — 6 grams
   Carbohydrate — 11 grams
   Calories — 115

CREAM OF MUSHROOM SOUP

Make a white sauce as in Basic Cream Soup★. Add
   2 cups skim milk
   1 teaspoon salt
   ⅛ teaspoon monosodium
      glutamate
   pepper

   ¼ pound mushrooms, washed
      and chopped (about
      1¼ cups chopped
      mushrooms)

Heat until mushrooms are tender. Do not boil. Makes about 4
cups. **Four servings.**

ONE SERVING WITHOUT OIL
   Oil — 0 teaspoons
   Cholesterol — 6 milligrams
   Saturated fat — 0 grams
   Linoleic acid — 0 grams

   Protein — 8 grams
   Carbohydrate — 14 grams
   Calories — 130

ONE SERVING WITH OIL*
   Oil — 1½ teaspoons
   Cholesterol — 6 milligrams
   Saturated fat — 1 gram
   Linoleic acid — 4 grams

   Protein — 8 grams
   Carbohydrate — 14 grams
   Calories — 150

CREAM OF TOMATO SOUP

Make a white sauce by shaking together in a jar
   2 cups skim milk
   2 tablespoons flour
   2 tablespoons skim milk
      powder

   1 to 2 drops Tabasco
   ¼ teaspoon monosodium
      glutamate

* See page 179.

Place in a saucepan and cook slowly, stirring until thickened and smooth. Heat

> 2½ cups canned or stewed tomatoes
> 1 small bay leaf
>
> ½ teaspoon salt
> ¼ cup sliced onions

Sieve and reheat. Just before serving add the heated tomato juice *very slowly* to the white sauce.

NOTE: Cream of tomato soup will separate or curdle on standing or on reheating. It may be made smooth again by beating with a rotary beater. Makes 4½ cups. **Four servings.**

ONE SERVING WITHOUT OIL
> **Oil** — 0 teaspoons
> **Cholesterol** — 4 milligrams
> **Saturated fat** — 0 grams
> **Linoleic acid** — 0 grams
>
> **Protein** — 7 grams
> **Carbohydrate** — 18 grams
> **Calories** — 100

ONE SERVING WITH OIL*
> **Oil** — 1½ teaspoons
> **Cholesterol** — 4 milligrams
> **Saturated fat** — 1 gram
> **Linoleic acid** — 4 grams
>
> **Protein** — 7 grams
> **Carbohydrate** — 18 grams
> **Calories** — 170

Light Soups

TOMATO BOUILLON

Simmer 10 minutes and strain

> 3 cups soup stock or
> 3 bouillon cubes and 3
> cups water
>
> 2 cloves
> 1 teaspoon sweet basil
> ⅓ teaspoon celery salt

Add water to recover loss by evaporation, if any, or add still more water if desired. Just before serving add

> 2 cups tomato juice
> salt to taste
> pinch of monosodium glutamate

Makes about 5 cups. **Six servings.**

* See page 179.

ONE SERVING

    Oil — 0 teaspoons

    Cholesterol — 0 milligrams

    Saturated fat — 0 grams

    Linoleic acid — 0 grams

    Protein — 3 grams

    Carbohydrate — 4 grams

    Calories — 30

SPRING SOUP

To

    2 cups chopped celery

    2 medium onions, chopped

    4 carrots, chopped

    2 tablespoons chopped bell pepper

    2 tablespoons chopped parsley

add

    3 cups soup stock (1 can bouillon, diluted)

    1 cup canned tomatoes

    1 cup water

    1½ cups shredded lettuce

Bring to a boil and add

    4 tablespoons rice

Simmer 30 minutes. Season with

    salt

    paprika

Makes about 5 cups. **Six servings.**

ONE SERVING

    Oil — 0 teaspoons

    Cholesterol — 0 milligrams

    Saturated fat — 0 grams

    Linoleic acid — 0 grams

    Protein — 3 grams

    Carbohydrate — 15 grams

    Calories — 70

Cold Soups

JELLIED BOUILLON

Soak

    1½ tablespoons gelatin

in

    ½ cup cold water

Combine in saucepan

    2 cups beef stock or canned beef bouillon

    1 cup chicken stock or canned chicken bouillon

    1 small onion, sliced

    ½ teaspoon salt

    sprig of parsley

    pepper to taste

Heat to boiling and then simmer 10 minutes. Add the
softened gelatin
Stir and let stand 10 minutes. Strain through cheesecloth. Pour into
bouillon cups and chill until firm. Just before serving, lightly break
up the jelly and garnish with a few very thin slices of stuffed olives.
Makes about 3 cups. **Six servings.**

ONE SERVING

Oil — 0 teaspoons

Cholesterol — 0 milligrams

Saturated fat — 0 grams

Linoleic acid — 0 grams

Protein — 5 grams

Carbohydrate — 3 grams

Calories — 30

JELLIED TOMATO BOUILLON

To
3½ cups tomato bouillon
add
2 tablespoons gelatin
soaked in
½ cup cold tomato bouillon or water
Heat over boiling water until gelatin is dissolved. Allow to congeal in
the refrigerator; cut into cubes. Serve with a paper-thin slice of lemon
for garnish. Makes about 4 cups. **Six servings.**

ONE SERVING

Oil — 0 teaspoons

Cholesterol — 0 milligrams

Saturated fat — 0 grams

Linoleic acid — 0 grams

Protein — 6 grams

Carbohydrate — 4 grams

Calories — 40

VICHYSSOISE

Fold
1 tablespoon oil
into
½ cup Whipped Topping II★ (without sugar)
Stir into chilled Leek and Potato Soup★
salt to taste
Serve at once in chilled bowls. Sprinkle with
chopped chives
Eight servings.

ONE SERVING

Oil — 1 teaspoon

Cholesterol — 2 milligrams

Saturated fat — 1 gram

Linoleic acid — 5 grams

Protein — 9 grams

Carbohydrate — 22 grams

Calories — 170

GAZPACHO

Put in electric blender

4 ripe peeled tomatoes cut in quarters

½ green pepper, seeded and sliced

½ small onion, peeled and sliced

1 clove garlic, peeled

1 cucumber, peeled and coarsely cut

1 teaspoon salt

¼ teaspoon pepper

2 tablespoons oil

3 tablespoons wine vinegar

½ cup ice water

1 tablespoon paprika

Blend at high speed for 10 seconds. Chill thoroughly. Pour in chilled bowls or individual casseroles. Garnish with thin slices of cucumber and finely chopped parsley. **Four servings.**

ONE SERVING

Oil — 1½ teaspoons

Cholesterol — 0 milligrams

Saturated fat — 1 gram

Linoleic acid — 4 grams

Protein — 3 grams

Carbohydrate — 8 grams

Calories — 110

Soup Accompaniments and Garnishes

Care must be used in selecting soup accompaniments, since many that are commonly used contain animal fat or are high in vegetable fat. Many noodles contain egg yolk and are therefore not acceptable. Many commercial crackers are made from lard, not vegetable shortening. Check the label before using. Following are some suggested accompaniments and garnishes:

Dash of paprika on creamed soups

Finely chopped parsley, chives, watercress

Hard-cooked egg white pressed through a ricer and added in place of rice will help increase protein intake.

Stiffly beaten egg white or blended cottage cheese curd floated on soup will also increase protein intake.

Salted skim milk yogurt floated on soup as a substitute for sour cream

Very thin lemon slices

Cooked macaroni, spaghetti, vermicelli, or Chinese noodles may re-place conventional egg noodles.

Substitutions for crackers:

Cubes or strips of bread toasted in the oven may be floated on soup or substituted for crackers

Melba toast

Cold-water crackers

Rye and wheat wafers (such as Ry-Krisp, Shredded Ralston)

Bread sticks

Matzos (without egg)

Try also:

French bread or

Hard-crusted French rolls with Onion Soup★

Toasted Tortillas★ with Gazpacho★

Rice crackers with Tomato Bouillon★

CHAPTER XV

Yeast Breads and Quick Breads

IF YOU enjoy the warm fragrance of bread or rolls fresh from the oven, if you delight in serving and eating golden brown rolls at dinner, piping hot muffins with lunch, or spicy coffeecake for breakfast, all this and more can still be part of your baking and eating pleasure. None of your favorite yeast breads or quick breads need to be excluded if you follow the principles set forth in this chapter and make allowances for these delicacies in terms of daily oil and caloric allowances as described in Chapter IV. This does not mean that you must now make all your breads at home. Some commercially baked products are acceptable. Since many, however, are not, this chapter will provide recipe guides for making these at home.

What Yeast Breads to Buy

Bakery yeast bread is usually made with some lard or saturated fats,* but the amount per slice is so small that you may use the commercial loaf of yeast bread. Choose 100 per cent whole-wheat bread or enriched bread. Practically all other commercially baked breads, such as rolls, coffeecake, Danish pastry, sweet rolls and buns, are high in saturated fat and contain egg yolk. Principles and recipes for making acceptable products of these kinds are given in this chapter.

Make Your Quick Breads at Home

Most of the bakery quick loaf breads (such as fruit breads and brown breads), muffins, and biscuits are made with whole milk and/or egg yolk and are high in saturated fat. Some English muffins are made without fat and are acceptable—again, read labels carefully for ingredients or ask your baker specifically regarding content of whole eggs

* Sour French and Italian bread usually contain no fat.

and butter and type of shortening used. Make your own quick breads, biscuits, and muffins following our principles for substituting for whole milk, egg yolks, and butter or solid shortening.

What About Mixes, Packaged Rolls, and Partially Baked Breads and Rolls?

Unless the kind and amount of fat contained in mixes and packaged and partially baked rolls are specified on the label and prove to be acceptable under the principles of our diet, you should not use them. If the words "milk solids" are used with no specification as to whether or not these are skim milk, or if the terms "vegetable oil" or "vegetable fats" are used without specifying which vegetable oils, do not accept the products without further clarification from the manufacturer.

The Advantages of Homemade Breads

Homemade breads made from ingredients acceptable in this diet and using an acceptable vegetable oil are a help in restricting saturated fat and cholesterol. If you make your breads at home, you can serve a greater variety of them. Other advantages enjoyed by you as a home baker are the varied flavors and the increased food value that you can give your bread by the use of such ingredients as skim milk powder, whole-wheat flour, wheat germ, molasses, and dried fruits.

USE A VARIETY OF GRAINS

Wheat Germ. Wheat germ should be toasted lightly before using or the bread will not rise properly. No more than ⅓ cup wheat germ should be substituted for an equal amount of white flour per cup of all-purpose enriched white flour specified in the recipe.

Whole-wheat or graham flour. Do not attempt to sift these flours; instead, stir lightly before measuring. The finely milled whole-wheat flours can be substituted for the entire amount of white flour in recipes. The coarsely grained flours should be substituted for no more than ½ the amount of the total flour called for. The rising time for breads made with dark flour will increase by at least ½ hour.

Soy (or soya) flour and grits. These are highly desirable for this diet because of their high protein content. It has been difficult for us to find a soy flour whose fat content is stated, but the kind of fat presents no problem as to saturation. The full fat soy flour can be used, since it is high in polyunsaturated fats and very low in saturated fat. Full fat soy flours should be creamed with the oil or blended with the liquids in making bread. Two tablespoons of soy flour may be substituted for an equal amount of white flour per cup of white flour specified in the recipe.

Corn Meal. We prefer water-ground yellow corn meal because of its higher Vitamin A content and because the germ is retained in milling.

Oatmeal. More nutrient value is retained in the steel-cut oats than in rolled oats and therefore, if possible, steel-cut oats should be used in baking. Oats may replace up to ⅓ of each cupful of enriched white regular flour specified in recipe.

Summary of grain replacements *per cup flour* specified in bread recipes:

Type of Flour or Grain	Maximum Amount to Replace Equal Amount of White Flour
Wheat germ	2 tablespoons to ⅓ cup
Whole-wheat or graham	1 cup
(finely milled)	complete replacement
Whole-wheat	½ cup
(coarsely milled)	2 tablespoons
Soy flour	⅓ cup
Oatmeal	⅓ cup
Rye flour*	

SUBSTITUTE ACCEPTABLE VEGETABLE OIL FOR SOLID SHORTENINGS AND BUTTER IN YOUR BREAD RECIPES

In most quick and yeast bread recipes, you can substitute unsaturated vegetable oil for solid shortening or butter and still have a satisfactory product. You will have to do a little experimenting, but, in general, you can make equal substitutions of oil for solid shortening up to 2 tablespoons of fat. Above this amount, use a little less oil than the solid shortening called for—we suggest about ⅛ less. For example, if the recipe calls for 1 cup of butter, use ⅞ cup of vegetable oil.

These substitutions may result in a bread that is a little heavier in texture than you are accustomed to, especially if you have been eating the usual commercially baked breads. Some of today's commercial breads are so light and fluffy as to resemble angel cake. We have grown very fond of the more chewy texture of the home-baked breads, and we trust that you will too. Since many of our recipes call for less fat and none of the artificial preservatives to prevent drying and mold-

---

* Exception is a rye bread recipe.

ing, it will be important to be careful about the storage of your precious home-baked breads and rolls. When they are thoroughly cooled after baking, wrap in plastic sacks and close tightly. Keep in a cool, dry place. The refrigerator makes an excellent breadbox.

We suggest that you bake extra loaves or extra rolls, wrap them well in plastic wrap or bags, and store them in your freezer for future use.

If any of your bread should become too dry to eat, save it for bread crumbs for many uses (e.g., Bread Crumb Griddlecakes★).

USE OUR SUBSTITUTE EGG YOLKS WHEN YOUR RECIPES CALL FOR WHOLE EGGS*

For each EGG YOLK: Beat lightly together
  ¼ teaspoon lecithin granules
  1 egg white
Add
  1½ teaspoons oil
and beat lightly.

For each WHOLE EGG: Beat lightly
  ¼ teaspoon lecithin granules
  2 egg whites
Add
  1½ teaspoons oil
and beat lightly.

See Chapter VI for the use of egg white powder.

USE SKIM MILK OR RECONSTITUTED SKIM MILK IN PLACE OF WHOLE MILK CALLED FOR IN BREAD RECIPES

We find this substitution can be made without significantly changing the final product.

Yeast Breads

Making your own yeast breads and rolls offers you an opportunity to put variety in your bread basket and fill your home with delicious aromas; at the same time, the kneading process provides you with marvelous exercise for your arm, shoulder, back, and abdominal muscles.

* Not the same nutritionally as whole eggs. The use of this substitute is to provide for a similar final product in terms of taste and appearance.

If you have never baked your own bread or rolls, consult a basic cookbook on the general techniques of the mixing, kneading, and rising processes of breadmaking. For the recipes that follow, we recommend dry granular yeast and all-purpose enriched white flour unless otherwise specified.

The Low-Sodium White Yeast Bread★ is suitable for regular diets with the addition of 1½ teaspoons of salt to the recipe. This makes extra good white bread or rolls, which can be modified with the addition of dried fruits or with the substitution of other grains.

WHITE BREAD

Dissolve
> 2 *tablespoons sugar*
> 1 *package active dry yeast or 1 yeast cake*

in
> ¼ *cup warm water*

Shake together in a jar and add to the yeast mixture

2 *cups warm water*	1 *cup skim milk powder*
2 *teaspoons salt*	2 *tablespoons oil (optional)*

Sift and measure
> 6 *to 6½ cups all-purpose enriched white flour*

Add about half the flour. Beat the batter until it is smooth. Add more flour gradually, using sufficient to make a dough stiff enough to handle. Knead on a lightly floured board until smooth and elastic and the dough does not stick to the hands or to the unfloured board (about 10 minutes). Shape in a ball and place in an oiled deep crockery bowl.* Turn dough over so oiled surface is up. Cover the bowl with a damp cloth and set in a warm place to rise until double in bulk. Without removing from bowl, punch down, cover with a damp cloth, and let rise again until double in bulk. (This second rising isn't necessary, but it improves the texture and flavor of the bread.) Turn the dough out of the bowl and shape into 2 loaves; place in lightly oiled pans, having pans nearly half full. Cover with a damp cloth and let rise until double in bulk. Bake in a hot oven (425° F.) 15 minutes. Reduce the heat to moderate (375° F.) and bake until done (30 to 35 minutes longer).

Rolls can be made from this dough. Bake rolls in hot oven (425° F.)

* The heavy bowl maintains warmth for the rising process.

15 to 20 minutes. Refer to variations for rolls, pages 194–97. **Makes 2 loaves (28 slices) or 3 to 4 dozen rolls.**

ONE SLICE

Oil — 0 teaspoons	**Protein** — 3 grams
Cholesterol — 1 milligram	**Carbohydrate** — 20 grams
Saturated fat — negligible	**Calories** — 90
Linoleic acid — negligible	

If oil is used, add ⅓ teaspoon oil, 9 calories

When baked, remove yeast bread from the pan at once and cool on a wire rack in place free from drafts.

RAISIN BREAD

Refer to the recipe above. Before kneading, add
  2 cups seedless raisins floured with 2 tablespoons flour
  2 to 4 tablespoons additional sugar
Makes 2 loaves (28 slices).

ONE SLICE

Oil — 0 teaspoons	**Protein** — 4 grams
Cholesterol — 1 milligram	**Carbohydrate** — 30 grams
Saturated fat — negligible	**Calories** — 135
Linoleic acid — negligible	

If oil is used, add ⅓ teaspoon oil, 9 calories

100% WHOLE-WHEAT BREAD

Dissolve
  1 yeast cake or package active dry yeast
  1 tablespoon sugar
  2 tablespoons molasses
in
  ¼ cup warm water
Shake together in a jar and add to the yeast mixture

2 cups warm water	*½ cup skim milk powder*
2 teaspoons salt	*1 tablespoon oil (optional)*

Sift and measure
  5½ cups fine 100 per cent whole-wheat flour
Add the flour gradually, beating until well mixed, using sufficient flour to make a dough stiff enough to handle. Knead thoroughly on a

lightly floured board, keeping the dough rather soft. Shape the dough into a ball and place it in an oiled deep crockery bowl. Turn dough over so oiled side is up. Cover with a damp cloth and set in a warm place to rise until double in bulk. Punch down and shape into 2 loaves. Place in lightly oiled pans, having the pans nearly half full. Cover with a damp cloth and let rise until double in bulk. Bake in moderate oven (375° F.) until done (50 to 60 minutes). **Makes 2 loaves** (28 slices.

ONE SLICE

Oil — negligible	**Protein** — 4 grams
Cholesterol — negligible	**Carbohydrate** — 18 grams
Saturated fat — negligible	**Calories** — 90
Linoleic acid — negligible	

If oil is used, add neg. teaspoons oil, 5 calories

BUTTERMILK ROLLS

Dissolve in a large bowl
  1 package active dry yeast
in
  ¼ cup warm skim milk or skim milk buttermilk
Add

1¾ cups skim milk or skim milk buttermilk	*2 tablespoons sugar*
2 tablespoons oil	*1 teaspoon salt*
	¼ teaspoon soda

Sift together
  3 cups sifted all-purpose flour
  ¼ teaspoon baking powder
Beat this flour into liquids. Add
  1 cup flour
and knead. Form into rolls (see pages 194–97) and refrigerate at least 2 hours. Let rise in a warm place 1½ hours. Bake 20 minutes at 400–25° F. **Makes 2 dozen rolls.**

EACH ROLL

Oil — ¼ teaspoon	**Protein** — 3 grams
Cholesterol — negligible	**Carbohydrate** — 15 grams
Saturated fat — negligible	**Calories** — 85
Linoleic acid — negligible	

POTATO REFRIGERATOR ROLLS

In a large bowl dissolve
    2 packages active dry yeast
in
    1⅓ cups warm potato water* or water
In a smaller bowl beat lightly
    3 egg whites
    ¼ teaspoon lecithin granules
Add, with continued beating

1 tablespoon oil	*⅝ cup oil*
⅔ cup sugar	*1 cup lukewarm mashed*
2 teaspoons salt	*potatoes*

Add potato mixture to yeast mixture. Mix in with your hand until dough is easy to handle
    7 to 7½ cups sifted all-purpose flour
Turn onto lightly floured board and knead until smooth and elastic (about 10 minutes). Form into a large ball and place in deep oiled bowl. Turn over so oiled side of dough is up. Cover with wax paper and then a damp cloth and refrigerate.

This dough can be kept in the refrigerator for 5 days; occasionally you may need to punch it down.

Two hours before baking, shape dough into desired rolls or rings (see variations, pages 194–97). Cover and let rise until double in volume. Bake until golden brown:

Plain rolls, about 12 to 15 minutes at 400° F.

Cinnamon or fruit rolls, about 15 to 20 minutes at 375° F.

Tea ring, about 35 to 40 minutes at 350° F.

Makes 48 medium-size rolls.

EACH ROLL

Oil — ¾ teaspoon	**Protein** — 2 grams
Cholesterol — 0 milligrams	**Carbohydrate** — 15 grams
Saturated fat — 1 gram	**Calories** — 100
Linoleic acid — 2 grams	

This dough may also be frozen, either in a large ball or in rolls or coffee rings. The ball of dough should be wrapped in plastic wrap and placed in sealed, labeled plastic sack. The rolls may be frozen on baking sheets and the frozen rolls assembled into labeled plastic bags for storing in the freezer.

Remove them from the freezer 2 hours before you plan to bake. Arrange on greased pans or sheets about 1 inch apart. Cover and put

* Water in which potatoes have been boiled.

in warm place until they have thawed and double in volume. Bake according to suggestions above.

PLAIN ROLLS

Refer to recipe for Potato Refrigerator Rolls★, Buttermilk Rolls★, or White Bread★. When the dough is ready to be shaped:

1. With floured hands, pinch off dough about the size of an egg.
2. Shape into a ball.
3. Set close together on a lightly oiled pan.
4. Cover with a damp cloth.
5. Let rise until double in bulk.
6. If desired, brush with roll glaze.
7. Bake in a hot oven (400–25° F.) until done (15 to 20 minutes).

PARKER HOUSE ROLLS

Refer to recipe for Potato Refrigerator Rolls★, Buttermilk Rolls★, or White Bread★. When the dough is ready to be shaped:

1. Roll the dough gently to about ⅓ inch thick.
2. Cut with a biscuit cutter.
3. Place on a lighty oiled pan.
4. Let rise about 15 minutes.
5. Brush lightly with oil.
6. Crease deeply with the handle of a knife. Fold over and press edges together.
7. Place about 1 inch apart on an oiled pan.
8. Cover with a damp cloth.
9. Let rise until double in bulk.
10. Brush with roll glaze if desired.
11. Bake in a hot oven (400–25° F.) until done (15 to 20 minutes).

CLOVERLEAF ROLLS

Refer to recipe for Potato Refrigerator Rolls★, Buttermilk Rolls★, or White Bread★. When the dough is ready to be shaped:

1. With floured hands pinch off small pieces of dough about the size of a small walnut.
2. Shape into balls.

3. Place 3 balls in each lightly oiled muffin cup.
4. Cover with a damp cloth.
5. Let rise until double in bulk.
6. Brush with roll glaze if desired.
7. Bake in a hot oven (400–25° F.) until done (15 to 20 minutes).

VARIATIONS:

Place 2 to 7 balls in each muffin cup. The greater the number of balls in each cup, the smaller the ball of dough should be. For 7 balls, the dough should be about the size of a small marble.

BREADSTICKS

With the hands, form long, very thin sticks. Put in an oiled pan. Cover with a damp cloth and let rise. Bake in 425° F. until done. These are good with salad or soup.

CHUTNEY ROLLS

Follow Variation 1 under Sweet Rolls★, substituting
    chutney (or other desired relish)
Omit the icing. These make good cocktail rolls.

SWEET ROLLS
(higher in calories)

Potato Refrigerator Rolls★ and Buttermilk Rolls★ can be made into sweet rolls. Make them in any desired shape, using a variety of ingredients. Bake sweet rolls in a 375° F. oven 15 to 20 minutes. Some suggestions for sweet rolls are:

1. Roll out part of the dough to about ¼ to ½ inch thick. Sprinkle generously with
    brown sugar
    cinnamon
    raisins (or currants)
Roll up, moisten edges, and seal. Cut in 1-inch slices. Place close together on a lightly oiled baking pan. Cover with a damp cloth and

let rise until double in bulk. Bake. While hot, frost with icing made by mixing

powdered sugar	*vanilla*
skim milk	*¼ teaspoon oil (optional)*

2. Roll out the dough as above and sprinkle with

cinnamon
powdered sugar

Roll up, moisten edges, and seal. Cut in 1-inch slices. Cook until slightly thickened

½ package dates, chopped
½ cup brown sugar
¼ cup water

Pour into 8-inch pan and place rolls close together on this mixture. When baked, turn out immediately (bottom side up) on a plate to cool.

3. Follow Variation 1. After the dough is rolled, place the slices close together in a pan with a layer of one of the following in the bottom:

molasses, corn syrup, or honey
walnut pieces (optional)

When baked, turn out immediately (bottom side up) on a plate to cool.

4. Follow Variation 1, substituting

brown sugar
a little ginger
candied orange or lemon peel, chopped

5. Follow Variation 1, substituting

brown sugar
cinnamon
chopped, cored, and peeled apple

6. Follow Variation 1. Do not slice, but form the rolled-up dough into a ring. Every 1½ to 2 inches clip part way through with scissors to form a tea ring. Bake 35 to 40 min. at 350° F.

7. Press part of the dough to ¾-inch thickness into a lightly oiled 8-inch pan. Pare, core, and slice

sour apples

Press the sharp edges of the apples into the dough. Sprinkle with

brown sugar
cinnamon
seedless raisins

Cover with a damp cloth and let rise until double in bulk. Bake in a 350° F. oven until done, about 30 minutes.

YEAST ROLL EGG GLAZE

Beat lightly (not enough to foam)
   1 egg white
Add
   1 tablespoon water
Brush tops of yeast rolls with glaze before baking. This makes a glossy crust. Its use is optional.

QUICK BREADS

Remove quick breads from the pans immediately when they are done and cool on a wire rack in a place free from drafts. A double-acting baking powder is used in the recipes.

PRUNE BREAD

Cream together
   1 tablespoon vegetable oil
   1 cup sugar
Add
   1 egg white
   ¼ teaspoon lecithin granules
Beat well. Combine
   ½ cup prune juice
   1 cup cultured skim milk (such as skim milk yogurt or skim milk buttermilk)
Add the liquid to the sugar mixture alternately with
   2 cups fine whole-wheat flour
Sift together 3 times and add to the above mixture
   1 cup sifted enriched white flour
   2 tablespoons baking powder
   ½ teaspoon salt
Add

   1½ cups cooked, pitted, chopped prunes   *¼ cup wheat germ (optional)*
   ½ cup cooked, chopped apricots   *¼ cup cooked low fat soya granules (optional)*

Turn into lightly oiled baking pan. Bake at 350° F. 1 hour. **Makes 2 5 by 9 loaves** (20 slices).

ONE SLICE

Oil —— negligible
Cholesterol —— negligible
Saturated fat —— negligible
Linoleic acid —— negligible

Protein —— 5 grams
Carbohydrate —— 46 grams
Calories —— 215

BANANA BREAD

Sift together 3 times
    1¾ cups sifted enriched
      white flour
    2 teaspoons baking powder
    ¼ teaspoon soda
    ½ teaspoon salt
    ⅔ cup sugar
Combine
    1¼ cups mashed ripe bananas
    2 tablespoons skim milk
    ¾ teaspoon grated lemon rind
Add flour mixture to the banana and milk mixture. Add small amounts at a time, beating after each addition. Fold in
    1 egg white, stiffly beaten
Put the batter into a lightly oiled bread pan and bake in a moderate oven (350° F.) about 1 hour, or until done. **Makes 1 loaf** (12 slices).

ONE SLICE

Oil —— 0 teaspoons
Cholesterol —— 0 milligrams
Saturated fat —— 0 grams
Linoleic acid —— 0 grams

Protein —— 2 grams
Carbohydrate —— 28 grams
Calories —— 120

VARIATIONS (these variations add carbohydrate):

1. Add 1 cup seedless raisins to the flour mixture.
2. Add 1 cup chopped dates to the flour mixture.
3. Add ½ cup chopped walnuts to flour mixture. This variation adds 8 teaspoons oil.

SOY DATE BREAD

Preheat oven to 350° F. Add
    ½ cup cut-up dates
to
    ¾ cup boiling water

and allow to cool. Mix

¾ cup enriched white flour	½ cup soya granules
½ teaspoon salt	2 teaspoons baking powder

Beat lightly

2 egg whites	3 tablespoons oil
¼ teaspoon lecithin granules	1 tablespoon molasses

and add to dry ingredients. Gradually beat in water and dates. Bake in oiled 2 by 3 by 6 inch pan 1 hour at 325° F. **Makes 20 slices.**

ONE SLICE

Oil — negligible	**Protein** — 2 grams
Cholesterol — 0 milligrams	**Carbohydrate** — 8 grams
Saturated fat — negligible	**Calories** — 70
Linoleic acid — 1 gram	

DARK FRUIT BREAD

Preheat oven to 350° F. Mix

1 cup graham flour	1 teaspoon salt
1 cup enriched white flour	1½ teaspoons baking powder

Mix and beat lightly

¼ teaspoon soda
1 cup skim milk
1 tablespoon oil

Gradually add liquid ingredients to dry ingredients. Add

½ cup currants or raisins
½ cup chopped nuts

Pour into oiled loaf pan. Bake at 350° F. 1 hour. **Makes 20 slices.**

ONE SLICE

Oil — negligible	**Protein** — 3 grams
Cholesterol — negligible	**Carbohydrate** — 13 grams
Saturated fat — negligible	**Calories** — 90
Linoleic acid — 1 gram	

CORN BREAD

Sift together 3 times

1 cup sifted enriched white flour	¼ cup sugar (or less, if desired)
1 cup enriched yellow corn meal	3 teaspoons baking powder
	1 teaspoon salt

Mix together
> 1 cup skim milk
> 1½ tablespoons vegetable oil

Combine ingredients, beat well, and fold in
> 2 egg whites, stiffly beaten

Pour into a shallow, lightly oiled pan. Bake 20 minutes in a hot oven (450° F.). **Eight servings.**

ONE SERVING

Oil — ½ teaspoon	**Protein** — 5 grams
Cholesterol — 1 milligram	**Carbohydrate** — 32 grams
Saturated fat — negligible	**Calories** — 175
Linoleic acid — 2 grams	

BOSTON BROWN BREAD

Combine
> 2 cups corn meal or 1 cup   ½ cup wheat germ
> corn meal and 1 cup rye   1 teaspoon salt
> flour   ¼ teaspoon soda
> ½ cup graham flour   4 teaspoons baking powder

Combine in a separate bowl
> ¾ cup molasses
> 2½ cups skim milk
> 2 cups seedless raisins

Add the liquid ingredients to the dry ingredients. Beat the mixture thoroughly. Pour it into a lightly oiled mold until it is about two-thirds full. Cover closely and place the mold on a rack in a kettle of boiling water. Cover closely. Keep the water boiling and add more as needed. The water should be kept halfway or more up the mold during the cooking. Steam the bread 3½ hours. If smaller molds are used, the batter can be steamed 2 hours. Baking powder cans with covers or tin cans covered with heavy wax paper held in place with rubber bands make excellent molds. Either dark or light molasses may be used. Light molasses gives a more delicately flavored, lighter-colored bread. **Makes 4 No. 2 cans** (32 slices).

ONE SLICE

Oil — 0 teaspoons	**Protein** — 2 grams
Cholesterol — 0 milligrams	**Carbohydrate** — 22 grams
Saturated fat — 0 grams	**Calories** — 100
Linoleic acid — 0 grams	

VARIATION:

For a finer-textured bread use 1 cup white flour, 1 cup corn meal, 1 cup graham flour.

QUICK ORANGE-RAISIN BREAD

Sift together twice
    3 cups sifted enriched white flour
    4 teaspoons baking powder
    1 teaspoon salt
Add
    1 cup raisins
Combine and beat
    2 egg whites
    1 cup skim milk
    2 tablespoons vegetable oil
Mix the dry and wet ingredients together well. Stir in
    ½ cup marmalade
Put into greased loaf pan and let stand 20 minutes. Bake in a moderate oven (350° F.) 45 to 60 minutes. **Makes 1 loaf** (14 slices).

ONE SLICE
    Oil — ½ teaspoon   **Protein** — 4 grams
    Cholesterol — negligible   **Carbohydrate** — 33 grams
    Saturated fat — negligible   **Calories** — 165
    Linoleic acid — 1 gram

RAISIN WHOLE-WHEAT BREAD

Combine
    1¾ cups sifted whole-wheat flour
    ½ cup sifted enriched white flour
Sift together twice with
    1 teaspoon salt
    2 teaspoons baking powder
    1 teaspoon soda
Stir in
    ¾ cup brown sugar, firmly packed
    1 cup raisins
Quickly add
    1½ cups skim milk buttermilk

Stir slightly. Bake in a lightly oiled loaf pan at 350° F. 1½ to 2 hours. Wax paper in the bottom of the pan is a time-saver when trying to remove the loaf. Also, we found that when baked in round cans (empty fruit cans) this recipe seems almost like cake. **Makes 1 loaf** (14 slices).

ONE SLICE

Oil — 0 teaspoons
Cholesterol — 0 milligrams
Saturated fat — 0 grams
Linoleic acid — 0 grams

Protein — 4 grams
Carbohydrate — 35 grams
Calories — 155

IRISH SODA BREAD

Mix in a large bowl
   4 cups unsifted enriched
    white flour
   3 teaspoons baking powder
Cut in with pastry blender
   ¼ cup oil
Stir in
   2 cups currants
Beat slightly and add to dry ingredients
   2 egg whites
   1 drop yellow food coloring

1 teaspoon baking soda
¼ cup sugar
⅛ teaspoon cardamom

¼ teaspoon lecithin granules
1¾ cups buttermilk

Turn out on floured board and knead 3 minutes. Divide dough in half and shape into round loaves and press into oiled 8-inch cake or pie pans. Cut a large cross on top of loaf about ½ inch deep and ½ inch wide. Bake in 375° F. oven 35 to 40 minutes. **Makes 2 loaves** (24 slices).

ONE SLICE

Oil — ½ teaspoon
Cholesterol — negligible
Saturated fat — negligible
Linoleic acid — 3 grams

Protein — 3 grams
Carbohydrate — 33 grams
Calories — 170

REFRIGERATOR COFFEECAKE

Beat
> *⅔ cup granulated sugar*
> *3 tablespoons oil*

Beat together
> *2 egg whites*
> *¼ teaspoon lecithin granules*
> *1½ teaspoons oil*

and stir into sugar mixture. Stir in
> *5 tablespoons skim milk*

Sift together
> *1¼ cups enriched white flour*
> *1½ teaspoons baking powder*

and add gradually to above liquids. Cut together with pastry blender
for topping
> *2 tablespoons enriched white flour*
> *1 tablespoon oil*
> *½ cup sugar*

Pour batter into oiled 8 by 8 inch cake pan and spread topping over.
This coffeecake can be baked immediately or after being refrigerated
2 or 3 days. Bake at 350° F. 30 minutes. **Six servings.**

ONE SERVING

Oil —— 2¼ teaspoons   **Protein** —— 5 grams
Cholesterol —— negligible   **Carbohydrate** —— 4 grams
Saturated fat —— 1 gram   **Calories** —— 345
Linoleic acid —— 6 grams

BAKING POWDER BISCUITS

Sift before measuring
> *2 cups enriched white flour*

Resift twice with
> *3 teaspoons baking powder*
> *⅔ teaspoon salt*

Add
> *¼ cup vegetable oil*

Cut the shortening into the flour mixture with a pastry blender or 2
knives until the mixture resembles coarse meal. Make a well in the
flour mixture; add all at once
> *⅔ to ¾ cup skim milk*

Mix only until the flour is dampened. Turn the dough onto a floured board; knead lightly for a few seconds to smooth the dough. Pat or roll the dough to desired thickness (about ½ to ¾ inch); cut with a floured biscuit cutter. Using a spatula, place the biscuits close together on an oiled baking sheet. If crusty sides are desired, however, place them at least ½ inch apart. Bake in a hot oven (425° F.) until done and the crust is golden-brown (12 to 15 minutes). **Makes 12 medium-size biscuits.**

ONE BISCUIT

Oil — 1 teaspoon	**Protein** — 3 grams
Cholesterol — 0 milligrams	**Carbohydrate** — 15 grams
Saturated fat — 1 gram	**Calories** — 115
Linoleic acid — 3 grams	

WHOLE-WHEAT BISCUITS

Follow the directions for Baking Powder Biscuits★. Use
fine whole-wheat flour for all or part of the white flour
Makes 16 to 18 small biscuits.

ORANGE BISCUITS

Follow the directions for Baking Powder Biscuits★. Add to the dry ingredients
grated rind of 1 orange
1 tablespoon sugar
Bake on a greased baking sheet. **Makes 16–18 small biscuits.**

DROP BISCUITS

Follow the directions for Baking Powder Biscuits★. Add
skim milk (about 2 tablespoons more)
to make the dough soft enough to drop from a spoon. Do not knead or roll the dough. Drop by the spoonful on a lightly oiled baking sheet. Bake in a hot oven (425° F.) until done and the crust is golden brown. **Makes 18 small biscuits.**

BISCUITS DELUXE

Sift together
  2 cups enriched white flour   ½ teaspoon cream of tartar
  4 teaspoons baking powder   2 tablespoons sugar
Cut into this with pastry blender
  ½ cup oil
Proceed as in Baking Powder Biscuits★. Bake at 450° F. 15 minutes.
Makes 12 medium-size biscuits.

ONE BISCUIT
  Oil — 2 teaspoons   **Protein** — 2 grams
  Cholesterol — 0 milligrams   **Carbohydrate** — 16 grams
  Saturated fat — 1 gram   **Calories** — 160
  Linoleic acid — 5 grams

PLAIN MUFFINS

Sift together twice
  2 cups sifted flour   3 tablespoons sugar
  5 teaspoons baking powder   ½ teaspoon salt
Beat slightly
  2 egg whites
  ¼ teaspoon lecithin granules
Combine with
  1 cup skim milk
  3 tablespoons oil
Pour the liquid ingredients into the dry ingredients, mixing quickly
and only until the dry ingredients are moistened. The batter will look
lumpy. Turn at once into lightly oiled muffin pans. Bake in a hot
oven (425° F.) 15 minutes. Reduce the temperature to 350° F. and bake
until muffins are brown. Remove from the pans immediately. **Makes
12 medium-size muffins.**

ONE MUFFIN
  Oil — ¾ teaspoon   **Protein** — 3 grams
  Cholesterol — 0 milligrams   **Carbohydrate** — 18 grams
  Saturated fat — 1 gram   **Calories** — 120
  Linoleic acid — 2 grams

VARIATIONS:

1. Add 1 cup seedless raisins, chopped dates, or finely chopped apple to the dry ingredients.
2. Put a small amount of jam into the center of each muffin before baking.

WHOLE-WHEAT MUFFINS

Measure and mix together in a bowl

1 cup fine 100 per cent whole-wheat flour	2 teaspoons baking powder
	2 tablespoons sugar
½ cup wheat germ	½ teaspoon salt

Beat slightly

1 egg white
¼ teaspoon lecithin granules

Blend together with

2 tablespoons vegetable oil
1 cup skim milk

Pour the liquids into the dry ingredients, mixing quickly and only enough to dampen the flour. Do not stir until smooth. Turn into lightly oiled tins and bake at 425° F. until done (15 to 20 minutes). **Makes 8 medium-size muffins.**

ONE MUFFIN

Oil — ¾ teaspoon	**Protein** — 5 grams
Cholesterol — 1 milligram	**Carbohydrate** — 17 grams
Saturated fat — 1 gram	**Calories** — 120
Linoleic acid — 2 grams	

OATMEAL FRUIT MUFFINS

Blend in a blender until the texture of coarse flour

3½ cups rolled oats

Mix in large bowl with

½ cup sugar	1 cup currants or ½ cup
1¼ teaspoons salt	raisins and ½ cup
3¼ teaspoons baking powder	pitted and chopped dates

In separate bowl beat lightly together in order

4 egg whites	7 tablespoons oil
¼ teaspoon lecithin granules	1 cup skim milk

Make well in dry ingredients. Pour in liquid and mix with as few strokes as possible (12 to 15 maximum). Fill oiled muffin pans two-thirds full. Bake about 25 minutes in hot oven (425° F.). **Makes 12 3-inch muffins.**

ONE MUFFIN

Oil — 1¾ teaspoons
Cholesterol — 1 milligram
Saturated fat — 1 gram
Linoleic acid — 5 grams

Protein — 5 grams
Carbohydrate — 33 grams
Calories — 240

WHEAT GERM GRIDDLECAKES

(There are acceptable commercial griddlecake mixes.)

Combine

¾ *cup graham flour*
½ *cup sifted enriched white*
  flour
½ *cup wheat germ*

¼ *cup corn meal*
5 *teaspoons baking powder*
1½ *teaspoons salt*
2 *teaspoons sugar*

Add

2½ *cups skim milk*

Mix well. Bake on a hot, lightly oiled griddle until bubbles appear on the surface and begin to burst. Turn and brown on the other side. Wipe griddle with an oiled cloth before baking each griddlecake, using for the whole recipe not more than

2 *teaspoons oil*

Makes 20 small cakes.

ONE CAKE

Oil — negligible
Cholesterol — 1 milligram
Saturated fat — negligible
Linoleic acid — negligible

Protein — 3 grams
Carbohydrate — 8 grams
Calories — 55

VARIATIONS:

Add sliced bananas or drained pineapple to the batter and serve the griddlecakes with powdered sugar and strawberries. These variations add carbohydrate.

BREAD CRUMB GRIDDLECAKES

Dry your unused bread and spin it in the blender to make bread crumbs for these delicious griddlecakes. In a jar, shake together
  1¼ *cups water*
  ½ *cup skim milk powder*
Beat lightly
  2 *egg whites*
  ¼ *teaspoon lecithin granules*
  3 *tablespoons oil*
Add milk and egg mixture to
  1 *cup dry bread crumbs*
Beat until stiff
  2 *egg whites*
Fold into batter. Sift together

  ½ *teaspoon salt*   2 *tablespoons brown sugar*
  2 *teaspoons baking powder*   ½ *teaspoon cinnamon*
  ½ *cup all-purpose enriched*
    white flour

Add to batter and stir lightly. Bake on oiled or Teflon-coated griddle or skillet. **Makes about 16 4-inch cakes.**

ONE GRIDDLECAKE
  Oil — ½ teaspoon   **Protein** — 3 grams
  Cholesterol — 1 milligram   **Carbohydrate** — 10 grams
  Saturated fat — negligible   **Calories** — 75
  Linoleic acid — 2 grams

FRENCH PANCAKES

Sift together
  ¾ *cup enriched white flour*   ½ *teaspoon salt*
  2 *tablespoons powdered*   1½ *teaspoons baking powder*
    sugar
Beat lightly in order
  3 *egg whites*   1 *cup skim milk*
  ¼ *teaspoon lecithin granules*   ½ *teaspoon vanilla*
  1 *tablespoon oil*
Combine liquid ingredients with dry ingredients. Beat lightly until well mixed.

Place Teflon-lined frying pan over moderate heat. When pan is hot, pour in small circle of batter and tip pan so batter is spread in thin layer over the bottom, to make pancake 6 inches in diameter. Brown on both sides. **Makes 12 to 14 6-inch pancakes.**

These can be spread with jam or filled with mashed or diced fruit, rolled up and dusted with powdered sugar.

They may also be frozen and used as needed. Put small sheets of plastic film between cakes, roll into cylinder shape, and freeze. Store in labeled plastic bag.

ONE PANCAKE

Oil — ¼ teaspoon
Cholesterol — negligible
Saturated fat — negligible
Linoleic acid — 1 gram

Protein — 2 grams
Carbohydrate — 9 grams
Calories — 55

FRENCH TOAST

Beat with rotary beater
  1 egg white
  1 tablespoon skim milk
  1 teaspoon sugar
Soak in this mixture
  2 slices bread

2 or 3 drops yellow food coloring
1 drop butter flavor if desired

Cook on a lightly oiled griddle, using low heat, and turn frequently to brown evenly (or they may be broiled). Serve with powdered sugar, a sprinkling of cinnamon and sugar, maple syrup, molasses, honey, or jam.

ONE SLICE

Oil — negligible
Cholesterol — negligible
Saturated fat — negligible
Linoleic acid — negligible

Protein — 4 grams
Carbohydrate — 18 grams
Calories — 90

CREPES

Beat well
  5 egg whites
  ½ teaspoon lecithin granules
  4½ tablespoons oil
Add and beat
  1½ cups skim milk
Sift together into the batter
  1½ cups sifted flour
  ¼ teaspoon salt

Beat until the consistency of heavy cream. Let stand for at least 30 minutes. Bake as described in French Pancakes★, above. **Makes 12 to 14 7-inch crepes.**

These are good served with hot fillings (see page 372).

They can be stored for weeks in your freezer (see method under French Pancakes★).

ONE CREPE

 Oil — 1 teaspoon   **Protein** — 4 grams
 Cholesterol — 1 milligram   **Carbohydrate** — 12 grams
 Saturated fat — 1 gram   **Calories** — 110
 Linoleic acid — 3 grams

POPOVERS

Beat lightly until foamy
 3 egg whites
 1 teaspoon lecithin granules
Add and beat
 1 cup skim milk
Sift together into the batter
 1 cup sifted flour
 ¼ teaspoon salt
Beat until smooth, like heavy cream. Fill oiled Teflon-coated muffin tins half full. Place in cold oven on center rack. Turn on heat at 450° F. and bake 25 minutes. Reduce heat to 350° F. and bake 15 minutes or until golden brown. *Do not open oven door for the first 40 minutes* of baking time, since this may cause them to fall. Remove from pan and serve at once. If desired, small slit may be cut in each to let steam escape. **Makes 12 popovers.**

ONE POPOVER

 Oil — 0 teaspoons   **Protein** — 3 grams
 Cholesterol — 1 milligram   **Carbohydrate** — 8 grams
 Saturated fat — negligible   **Calories** — 45
 Linoleic acid — negligible

Popovers are also good served with fillings:

 Creamed Tuna★
 Low Calorie Creamed Chicken★
 Creamed Chicken★
 Curried Chicken★
 "Special" Cottage Cheese★ and jam or marmalade
 "Special" Cream Cheese★ and jam or marmalade

WAFFLES

Preheat waffle iron. Sift together
   1½ cups sifted flour
   2 teaspoons baking powder
   ½ teaspoon salt
Beat well
   2 egg whites
   2 tablespoons oil
   ½ teaspoon lecithin granules
Add and mix
   1½ cups skim milk
Add liquids to dry ingredients and combine with a few strokes. Beat
until stiff
   2 egg whites
Fold beaten egg whites into batter. Fill the waffle iron two thirds full.
Bake until done—usually 4 to 5 minutes. **Makes 6 waffles.**

ONE WAFFLE
   Oil — 1 teaspoon   **Protein** — 6 grams
   Cholesterol — 2 milligrams   **Carbohydrate** — 10 grams
   Saturated fat — negligible   **Calories** — 125
   Linoleic acid — 3 grams

DUMPLINGS

Sift together
   2 cups all-purpose flour
   ¼ teaspoon salt
   2½ teaspoons baking powder (double-acting)
Add and stir until blended
   ¾ cup skim milk
Drop into hot liquid of dish in which it is to be used, cover, and cook
15 minutes without lifting cover. **Makes 8 dumplings.**

TOTAL RECIPE
   Oil — 0 teaspoons   **Protein** — 4 grams
   Cholesterol — 1 milligram   **Carbohydrate** — 22 grams
   Saturated fat — negligible   **Calories** — 105
   Linoleic acid — negligible

CHAPTER XVI

How to Prepare and Cook Vegetables to Save Nutrients

THE most important rules in preparing vegetables are to use them as quickly as possible after they have been harvested and to guard against overcooking.

It has been said that the proof of a good cook lies in her ability to prepare vegetables well. In the low saturated fat, low cholesterol diet, vegetables play an important part because they supply vitamins and minerals. Because the vitamins are partially destroyed by cooking, uncooked vegetables should be used whenever possible. However, some vegetables are not palatable or are too fibrous to be eaten raw, and these vegetables should be carefully cooked to preserve as much of the food value as possible. Vegetables are well cooked when they have firmness, good color and taste, and when all possible nutrients have been preserved.

In order to accomplish these purposes, apply the following principles:

1. Purchase vegetables that are in season, firm, fresh, and of good color and quality.
2. Fresh vegetables should be washed, dried, and kept chilled in a dark place until ready to cook.
3. Winter vegetables should be kept in a cool, dark, dry place.
4. Frozen vegetables should be kept well frozen until they are used. Do not thaw before cooking, as the vitamins are rapidly lost in defrosting.
5. Do not soak vegetables, as some of the vitamins and minerals dissolve in water. The exceptions to this rule are the dried vegetables, such as dried peas, beans, and lentils, which may require soaking before cooking to replace some of the moisture removed in drying.

They should be slowly cooked until tender in the water in which they were soaked.

6. Always save and use in other dishes the water in which vegetables have been cooked. Often as much as 50 per cent of the vitamins and minerals are contained in it.

7. Scrape, pare, or peel vegetables only when necessary, as these procedures result in the loss of food values. Some vegetables have thick skins and require paring. Paring *after* cooking results in less loss of nutrients.

8. Do not add soda when cooking vegetables, as it destroys vitamins.

9. Add salt when the vegetables have been cooked until tender. Cooking with salt toughens the vegetables and draws out the nutrients and flavor into the cooking water. Use iodized salt, as it provides essential iodine in the diet.

10. Cook vegetables until they are barely tender. Time for cooking varies with the age of the vegetables and the hardness of the water in which they are cooked. Test the vegetables for tenderness by pricking with a fork.

11. When using diced, chopped, or shredded vegetables, do not cut or chop until time to cook, as the vitamins and flavor rapidly disappear after such preparation.

12. Serve vegetables immediately after cooking unless they are to be chilled for salad.

13. Season vegetables well. A dash of paprika for color, a little chopped parsley, pepper, or skim milk white sauce gives variety to vegetables.

14. Lemon juice adds a piquant flavor to many vegetables and improves the color; for example, yellow squash, yams, sweet potatoes, and most green vegetables.

15. If canned vegetables are to be served hot, they should be heated in their own liquid. Do not allow canned vegetables to boil, as they are already cooked and further boiling destroys the flavor, color, and nutrients.

16. Try to avoid reheating vegetables, as this further destroys the food value.

Boiling

Boil in as little water as possible and cook only until tender. Put the water into a pan with a tight-fitting lid and bring it to a boil. Add the vegetables and cover. Keep the water boiling until the steam is visible, then turn the heat to simmer and cook until barely tender. Add more boiling water during cooking if necessary.

Broiling

Broiling is an excellent method of preparing some vegetables, as the initial heat is rapid, the cooking time is short, and no added moisture is needed. After the vegetable is heated, broil more slowly to retain its attractive appearance. Vegetables may be tossed with oil or brushed with oil.

Waterless Cooking

Cooking vegetables in a heavy pan on top of the stove with little or no water added is a good method. The lid must fit tightly enough so that no steam can escape.

Steaming

Cooking vegetables in a steamer is an excellent method, but care must be taken not to overcook. Vegetables should be left uncut and unpeeled whenever possible.

Pressure Cooking

Follow the directions given with the pressure cooker. Cook only until the vegetables are tender. Time carefully. Overcooking at high temperatures is especially harmful to vegetables.

Baking

Baking vegetables in an open pan or in a covered dish in the oven is preferable to boiling. Whenever possible, bake vegetables un-peeled. If the vegetables are pared and sliced, bake in a tightly covered casserole.

Cooking in Skim Milk

Many vegetables are delicious cooked in skim milk instead of water. The nutrients dissolve less readily in milk. The vegetables should be simmered until tender. Do not boil. The milk should be served with them or retained for soups, sauces, gravies, or other dishes. Vegetables that are particularly good simmered in skim milk are:

Asparagus	Broccoli
Bean sprouts	Brussels sprouts
Beets	Cabbage
Brown rice	Carrots

Cauliflower	New potatoes
Celery	Onion
Celery root	Oyster plant
Corn	Peas
Dried beans (soak in milk)	Potatoes
Green lima beans	Rutabagas
Kohlrabi	String beans

Cooking in Vegetable Oil

This is the Chinese stir-fry method.

The addition of polyunsaturated vegetable oil is often desirable in the preparation and serving of vegetables. Sautéing in a frying pan is a good method for many vegetables. After washing the vegetables, dry them thoroughly. Use 2 tablespoons vegetable oil in the pan or toss the vegetables with the oil to coat thoroughly. Stir while cooking over medium heat. If the vegetables require longer than 5 minutes to cook, add 1 to 2 tablespoons hot water, cover tightly, and reduce the heat. Cook until barely tender. Add salt and pepper to taste.

Cooking in Broth

Many vegetables are delicious cooked in broth. The broth may be canned, made with a bouillon cube, or homemade. If homemade, chill the broth and remove the fat. (See Chapter XIV, pages 170–71.) The vegetable liquid should be served with the vegetable, saved for soups and sauces, or used in other dishes.

Cooking in Heavy-duty Foil

Fresh or frozen vegetables may be cooked in heavy-duty foil. The nutrients are not lost in liquid with this method, and the natural flavor is retained. Add 1 to 2 tablespoons vegetable oil, 1 to 2 tablespoons water and salt, as needed. Seal the foil around the vegetables so that no steam can escape. Place in a shallow pan and bake in a 375° F. oven 45 minutes to 1 hour, depending on the type of vegetable.

Cooking in Teflon-coated Containers

Teflon-coated cooking containers are excellent for the preparation of vegetables, as little or no added moisture is needed. The vessel must have a lid that fits tightly. Read the manufacturer's instructions.

Green and Green Leafy Vegetables

Try various cooking methods in preparing greens, and for greater variety and enjoyment experiment in combinations of green and green leafy vegetables. The following is a list of edible greens rich in nutrients.

Asparagus (green)	Leaf lettuce
Beet greens	Mustard greens
Broccoli	Parsley
Chicory	Peas
Dandelion greens	Spinach
Endive	Swiss chard
Escarole	Turnip greens
Green beans	Watercress
Kale	

Yellow Vegetables

Various parts of the world produce different edible vegetables, and all are desirable. Take advantage of the vegetables that are best in your area, and learn to use as wide a variety of vegetables as your community affords. Here is a partial list of common yellow vegetables.

Carrots	Squash, yellow and orange
Corn, yellow	Sweet potatoes
Pumpkin	Yams
Rutabagas	

How to Serve Vegetables

1. Young, tender vegetables, such as carrots, celery, cauliflower, all kinds of greens, onions, green peppers, tomatoes, cucumber, and cabbage are delicious served raw and should be used in that form whenever possible.

2. Vegetables retain their color and flavor best when cooked quickly without the addition of other foods.

3. The addition of White Sauce★ to such vegetables as peas, carrots, string beans, cabbage, broccoli, cauliflower, celery, onions, or potatoes lends variety and adds protein to the diet.

4. Other foods that may be added to vegetables for flavor and variety include:

Mushrooms (fresh or canned)	Lemon
Chopped celery	Lime
Chopped parsley	Vinegar

Tomato   Herbs
Pimiento   Orange Oil★
Chopped onion   Herb Oil★
Mint

VEGETABLE RECIPES

STEAMED VEGETABLES

Wash, cut off woody ends, and pare the stems of
  *2 pounds asparagus (or 1 pound green beans or 2 pounds
    shelled peas)*
Cut diagonally into 1-inch pieces. In a heavy kettle, preferably Teflon-coated, heat slowly (do not overheat)
  2 tablespoons vegetable oil
Add asparagus and toss in the oil until coated. Sprinkle with
  ½ teaspoon salt
Wet 4 or 5 outer leaves of lettuce and cover asparagus. Cover kettle tightly and cook on low heat until asparagus is just tender. Shake pan occasionally during cooking. **Four servings.**

ONE SERVING (MADE WITH ASPARAGUS)

Oil — 1½ teaspoons	**Protein** — 4 grams
Cholesterol — 0 milligrams	**Carbohydrate** — 5 grams
Saturated fat — 1 gram	**Calories** — 100
Linoleic acid — 4 grams	

STUFFED ARTICHOKE

Wash, trim, and remove center choke from
  4 artichokes, medium size
Mix together

1 cup dry bread crumbs	*2 tablespoons chopped*
1 tablespoon wheat germ	* parsley*
1 clove garlic, minced or	*enough bouillon to moisten*
* put through a garlic press*	*½ teaspoon salt*

Stuff the artichokes, working the mixture down into the leaves. Drizzle over the artichokes
  4 teaspoons vegetable oil
Steam until tender (45 minutes to 1 hour) in bouillon or water.
Four servings.

ONE SERVING

    Oil — 1 teaspoon
    Cholesterol — 0 milligrams
    Saturated fat — 1 gram
    Linoleic acid — 3 grams

    Protein — 3 grams
    Carbohydrate — 15 grams
    Calories — 115

HARVARD BEETS

Wash, cook, remove the skins, and cut into thin slices or cubes
    6 large beets
Mix together
    ½ cup sugar
    1 tablespoon cornstarch
    ½ teaspoon salt
Add
    ½ cup vinegar
Cook 5 minutes, stirring constantly. Pour the boiling liquid over the beets and let stand a few minutes before serving. **Six servings.**

ONE SERVING

    Oil — 0 teaspoons
    Cholesterol — 0 milligrams
    Saturated fat — 0 grams
    Linoleic acid — 0 grams

    Protein — 1 gram
    Carbohydrate — 7 grams
    Calories — 30

SHERRIED BEETS

Place in a heavy frying pan
    2 cups canned small, whole beets
Drain and save the juice. Combine
    3 tablespoons beet juice
    ¼ teaspoon salt
Pour over the beets and heat, turning frequently. When hot, add
    3 tablespoons sherry
Cover and heat 1 to 2 minutes. **Four servings.**

ONE SERVING

    Oil — 0 teaspoons
    Cholesterol — 0 milligrams
    Saturated fat — 0 grams
    Linoleic acid — 0 grams

    Protein — 1 gram
    Carbohydrate — 7 grams
    Calories — 30

BROCCOLI

Choose a skillet with a tight-fitting cover. Slice and spread over the bottom of the skillet
  1 small onion
  1 clove garlic
Wash and cut so that the sections of stem are of about the same thickness
  1 large bunch of broccoli
Place on top of onions. Sprinkle with
  ¼ teaspoon celery salt
  dash of monosodium glutamate
Add
  ½ cup cold water
Cover tightly and steam 5 to 8 minutes, or until the stems are tender. **Six servings.**

ONE SERVING

Oil — 0 teaspoons		**Protein** — 3 grams	
Cholesterol — 0 milligrams		**Carbohydrate** — 7 grams	
Saturated fat — 0 grams		**Calories** — 40	
Linoleic acid — 0 grams			

STIRRED BROCCOLI

Wash and cut from stems
  1½ pounds broccoli
Separate into small flowerets. In a large frying pan, preferably Teflon-coated, sauté
  1 large clove garlic, minced
  1 tablespoon minced candied ginger (or 1½ teaspoons minced fresh ginger)
in
  1 tablespoon vegetable oil
Add broccoli. Stir, toss, and add
  4 tablespoons water
  ¼ teaspoon monosodium glutamate
  1 tablespoon soy sauce
Cover and steam 5 to 7 minutes or until broccoli is tender. Serve at once. **Four servings.**

ONE SERVING

Oil —— ¾ teaspoon

Cholesterol —— 0 milligrams

Saturated fat —— 1 gram

Linoleic acid —— 2 grams

Protein —— 4 grams

Carbohydrate —— 10 grams

Calories —— 85

SCALLOPED EGGPLANT AND TOMATOES

Peel and dice
   1 medium eggplant
Sprinkle with salt and pepper. In a frying pan, sauté
   ⅓ cup finely chopped onion
in
   2 tablespoons vegetable oil
Blend in
   3 tablespoons flour
Add
   1 large can tomatoes (3½ cups)
Cook until thickened. Arrange alternate layers of the eggplant and the tomato mixture in an oiled casserole. Crush and sprinkle over the top
   ½ cup corn flakes
Bake in a 350° F. oven 45 minutes. **Six servings.**

ONE SERVING

Oil —— 1 teaspoon

Cholesterol —— 0 milligrams

Saturated fat —— 1 gram

Linoleic acid —— 3 grams

Protein —— 3 grams

Carbohydrate —— 14 grams

Calories —— 115

SCALLOPED ZUCCHINI AND TOMATOES

Substitute 2 pounds zucchini for the eggplant in the recipe above.

CABBAGE AND APPLES

Combine in a pan
> 2 cups shredded cabbage
> 1 apple, chopped
> ¼ cup cider vinegar
> ¼ cup hot water
> ½ teaspoon salt
> 2 tablespoons sugar

Cook, tightly covered, until tender. **Four servings.**

ONE SERVING

Oil — 0 teaspoons
Cholesterol — 0 milligrams
Saturated fat — 0 grams
Linoleic acid — 0 grams

Protein — 1 gram
Carbohydrate — 14 grams
Calories — 60

MASHED CARROTS

Wash, scrape, cut into small pieces, and cook until tender
> 10 medium-size carrots

When cooked, put through a ricer or mash. Add
> warm skim milk to moisten (about ¼ cup)
> ½ teaspoon salt
> dash of pepper

Serve at once. **Six servings.**

ONE SERVING

Oil — 0 teaspoons
Cholesterol — negligible
Saturated fat — 0 grams
Linoleic acid — 0 grams

Protein — 2 grams
Carbohydrate — 9 grams
Calories — 45

VARIATION:

Form nests of mashed carrots and fill with cooked peas.

PARSLEY CARROTS

Wash, scrape, cut into slices or dice, and cook until tender
> 10 medium-size carrots

Mix together
> 2 tablespoons lemon juice
> 1 tablespoon finely chopped parsley

Mix with the carrots, salt to taste, and serve at once. **Six servings.**

ONE SERVING
    Oil — 0 teaspoons   **Protein** — 2 grams
    Cholesterol — 0 milligrams   **Carbohydrate** — 8 grams
    Saturated fat — 0 grams   **Calories** — 40
    Linoleic acid — 0 grams

HOMINY GRITS

Boil
    4 cups water
    1 teaspoon salt
Add slowly, stirring constantly
    1 cup hominy grits
Reduce heat and simmer 1 hour. **Six servings.**

ONE SERVING
    Oil — 0 teaspoons   **Protein** — 4 grams
    Cholesterol — 0 milligrams   **Carbohydrate** — 25 grams
    Saturated fat — 0 grams   **Calories** — 115
    Linoleic acid — 0 grams

Serve with a fat free gravy. Grits are similar to rice and may be served as a cereal.

BLACK-EYED PEAS

Cover with water and soak 5 to 6 hours
    2 cups dried black-eyed peas
Cook slowly 1 hour. Add
    1 cup canned tomatoes   *1 teaspoon salt*
    1 onion, chopped   *¼ to ½ teaspoon*
    ⅛ teaspoon black pepper   *monosodium glutamate*
Continue cooking slowly until peas are tender. **Six servings.**

ONE SERVING
    Oil — 0 teaspoons   **Protein** — 17 grams
    Cholesterol — 0 milligrams   **Carbohydrate** — 43 grams
    Saturated Fat — 0 grams   **Calories** — 255
    Linoleic acid — 0 grams

MASHED POTATOES

Cook in their jackets until tender
   4 large potatoes
Remove skins and mash the potatoes. Blend or shake together in a covered jar until smooth

   1 tablespoon vegetable oil   *1 teaspoon salt*
   ½ cup potato cooking water   *pepper to taste*
   ⅓ cup skim milk powder

Heat and beat into the mashed potatoes. Add hot potato cooking water if more moisture is needed to make the potatoes light and fluffy. Serve at once. **Six servings.**

ONE SERVING

Oil — ½ teaspoon   **Protein** — 4 grams
Cholesterol — 2 milligrams   **Carbohydrate** — 18 grams
Saturated fat — negligible   **Calories** — 100
Linoleic acid — 1 gram

STUFFED POTATOES

Scrub and prick
   6 medium-size potatoes
Bake in 400° F. oven about 45 minutes or until cooked through. Cut the potatoes lengthwise, scoop out insides without breaking the shells, and mash the potato pulp. Blend or shake together in a covered jar until smooth

   1 tablespoon vegetable oil   *⅓ cup skim milk powder*
   ½ cup skim milk   *salt and pepper to taste*

Heat and add to mashed potatoes. Thin with skim milk if necessary. Beat until light and fluffy. Refill the potato shells. Sprinkle with

   bread crumbs   *chopped parsley*
   wheat germ   *dash of paprika if desired*

Return to oven and brown slightly. **Twelve servings.**

ONE SERVING

Oil — ¼ teaspoon   **Protein** — 3 grams
Cholesterol — 1 milligram   **Carbohydrate** — 12 grams
Saturated fat — negligible   **Calories** — 65
Linoleic acid — 1 gram

VARIATIONS:

Add 2 tablespoons onion, chopped, steamed, or sautéed
Add 2 tablespoons chopped parsley
Add 2 egg whites, stiffly beaten

These should be added to the mixture used in refilling the potato shells.

SCALLOPED POTATOES

Peel and slice very thin enough potatoes to make
   4 cups potatoes
Mix together
   3 tablespoons flour
   ⅛ teaspoon pepper
   1½ teaspoons salt
Put a layer of potatoes in a lightly oiled casserole. Sprinkle with
the seasoned flour. Repeat until potatoes are all used. Mix
   2 tablespoons vegetable oil
   1½ cups hot skim milk
Pour over the potatoes. Bake in a moderate oven (350° F.) 1½ hours.
Cover tightly for the first hour, then remove cover and allow to
brown. Grated onion and chopped parsley may be added for extra
flavor. **Six servings.**

ONE SERVING

Oil — 1 teaspoon
Cholesterol — 2 milligrams
Saturated fat — 1 gram
Linoleic acid — 3 grams

Protein — 4 grams
Carbohydrate — 23 grams
Calories — 155

BAKED POTATO PUFFS

Cook in their jackets by steaming over boiling water in a tightly
covered pan
   4 large potatoes
When tender, remove skins and mash or rice the potatoes. Blend or
shake together in a covered jar until smooth
   ½ cup skim milk
   ⅓ cup skim milk powder
   1 teaspoon salt

Heat and stir into the mashed potatoes. Beat until frothy
   1 egg white
Add to potato mixture and whip until fluffy. Shape into 6 balls.
Roll the balls in wheat germ and heat in a moderate oven (350° F.)
until lightly browned. **Six servings.**

ONE SERVING

Oil — negligible	**Protein** — 5 grams
Cholesterol — 2 milligrams	**Carbohydrate** — 23 grams
Saturated fat — 0 grams	**Calories** — 110
Linoleic acid — 0 grams	

OVEN FRENCH FRIES

Peel and cut into French-fry size
   4 medium-size potatoes
Remove all excess moisture and place the potatoes in a medium-size
bowl.* Sprinkle with
   2 tablespoons vegetable oil
Toss the potatoes as if making a tossed green salad. When the oil
and potatoes are thoroughly mixed, spread the potatoes out on a cookie
sheet and place in a hot oven (475°–500° F.) 35 minutes. Turn
the potatoes so they will brown evenly on both sides. For added
browning, place under the broiler 1 to 2 minutes. Sprinkle with salt
before serving. **Six servings.**

ONE SERVING

Oil — 1 teaspoon	**Protein** — 2 grams
Cholesterol — 0 milligrams	**Carbohydrate** — 14 grams
Saturated fat — 1 gram	**Calories** — 110
Linoleic acid — 3 grams	

OVEN-BROWNED POTATOES

Steam whole until barely done
   4 medium-size potatoes
Remove skins and place potatoes in a small flat pan. Dissolve
   2 vegetable bouillon cubes (or fat free meat drippings)
in
   ½ cup boiling water
   1 tablespoon oil

* *Alternate method:* Place the potatoes in a saucepan. Sprinkle with vegetable oil.
Put lid on the pan and shake vigorously.

Pour over potatoes. Sprinkle with
  paprika if desired
Brown in a hot oven (400° F.) about 30 minutes.* Add water if
needed. For added browning, place under the broiler 1 to 2 minutes.
Four servings.

ONE SERVING

Oil — ¾ teaspoon   **Protein —** 4 grams
Cholesterol — 0 milligrams   **Carbohydrate —** 21 grams
Saturated fat — 1 gram   **Calories —** 135
Linoleic acid — 2 grams

GREEN PEAS AND MUSHROOMS

Shell enough peas to make
  2 cups peas (or use 2 packages frozen peas)
Wipe, trim, and slice
  ½ pound fresh mushrooms
Simmer peas and mushrooms in
  1 cup skim milk
  ½ teaspoon salt
When peas are tender, thicken liquid with
  2 to 3 teaspoons cornstarch
mixed with
  a little water
Stir gently until cornstarch is cooked. Serve in sauce dishes with sauce.
Sauce may be omitted. Drain peas and mushrooms and save the liquid
for soup. **Six servings.**

ONE SERVING

Oil — 0 teaspoons   **Protein —** 5 grams
Cholesterol — 1 milligram   **Carbohydrate —** 11 grams
Saturated fat — 0 grams   **Calories —** 75
Linoleic acid — 0 grams

Substitute: Any vegetable listed under "Cooking in Skim Milk" (pages
215–16).

GREEN PEAS AND CELERY

Shell enough peas to make
  2 cups peas (or use 2 packages frozen peas)

* *Alternate method:* Broil (with care) when in a hurry.

Combine with

½ cup thinly sliced celery
½ to 1 teaspoon salt (depends how salty broth is)
1 cup fat free chicken broth

Cover and cook gently until peas and celery are tender. Thicken liquid with

2 to 3 teaspoons cornstarch

mixed with a little water. Serve in sauce dishes. Sauce may be omitted. Drain peas and celery and save the broth for soup. **Six servings.**

ONE SERVING

Oil — 0 teaspoons	**Protein** — 3 grams
Cholesterol — 0 milligrams	**Carbohydrate** — 5 grams
Saturated fat — 0 grams	**Calories** — 30
Linoleic acid — 0 grams	

SEASONED SPINACH OR GREENS

Wash and boil until just tender

2 pounds spinach, Swiss chard, or other greens

Chop fine and place in serving dish. Combine and heat

2 tablespoons vinegar   *¼ teaspoon monosodium*
2 tablespoons water   *glutamate*
¼ teaspoon salt

Add and simmer until tender

3 tablespoons chopped green pepper

Add

2 tablespoons chopped pimiento

Pour the sauce over the chopped greens and serve at once. **Four servings.**

ONE SERVING

Oil — 0 teaspoons	**Protein** — 5 grams
Cholesterol — 0 milligrams	**Carbohydrate** — 10 grams
Saturated fat — 0 grams	**Calories** — 65
Linoleic acid — 0 grams	

MIXED GREENS

Cook together in little water until tender

½ pound spinach   *½ pound mustard greens*
½ pound Swiss chard   *½ pound tender turnip tops*

Salt when almost cooked. Chop and season with
freshly ground pepper
vinegar or lemon juice if desired
Six servings.

ONE SERVING

Oil — 0 teaspoons   **Protein** — 4 grams
Cholesterol — 0 milligrams   **Carbohydrate** — 7 grams
Saturated fat — 0 grams   **Calories** — 50
Linoleic acid — 0 grams

RICE IN BROTH

Bring to a boil
2½ cups consommé, bouillon, beef or chicken broth
Add
½ teaspoon salt (or as needed)
1 cup enriched white rice or enriched brown rice
Cover tightly and cook over low heat about 25 minutes. If a drier rice
is desired, remove cover and cook 5 minutes longer over low heat.
Six servings.

ONE SERVING

Oil — 0 teaspoons   **Protein** — 3 grams
Cholesterol — 0 milligrams   **Carbohydrate** — 27 grams
Saturated fat — 0 grams   **Calories** — 120
Linoleic acid — 0 grams

VARIATIONS:

Substitute 1¼ cups water and 1¼ cups tomato juice or vegetable
juice for the broth.

VEGETABLES IN FOIL

Frozen or fresh carrots, peas, corn, or green lima beans may be
substituted for the string beans in this recipe. (Calculations are for
string beans.)

Remove from the freezer and allow to thaw until the frozen block can
be broken apart
*1 package (10 ounces) frozen string beans (or prepare 1 pound
fresh string beans)*

Place beans in center of a square of aluminum foil. Sprinkle with

½ teaspoon salt	2 tablespoons water
¼ teaspoon pepper	1 tablespoon vegetable oil
1 teaspoon monosodium glutamate	½ teaspoon orégano

Fold foil over the beans and seal edges to make an airtight package. Place in a shallow pan and bake at 375° F. 55 minutes. **Three servings.**

ONE SERVING

Oil — ½ teaspoon	**Protein** — 1 gram
Cholesterol — 0 milligrams	**Carbohydrate** — 3 grams
Saturated fat — negligible	**Calories** — 45
Linoleic acid — 2 grams	

STRING BEANS AND TOMATOES

Combine and simmer 10 minutes

1 small onion, chopped	1 teaspoon sugar
2 cups canned tomatoes	1 teaspoon salt
1 bay leaf	dash of pepper

Add

2 cups cut uncooked string beans

Cover tightly and cook until almost tender. Mix together

2 tablespoons flour
2 tablespoons water

Add slowly, stirring constantly, and cook until the mixture thickens and beans are tender. **Six servings.**

ONE SERVING

Oil — 0 teaspoons	**Protein** — 2 grams
Cholesterol — 0 milligrams	**Carbohydrate** — 11 grams
Saturated fat — 0 grams	**Calories** — 50
Linoleic acid — 0 grams	

SCALLOPED SWEET POTATOES AND PINEAPPLE

Cook, and when tender scrape and slice
   3 medium-size sweet potatoes
Arrange in a baking dish. Combine
   1 cup crushed pineapple
   ¼ teaspoon salt
Pour over the sweet potatoes. Bake uncovered in a moderate oven
(350° F.) 30 minutes, or until light brown. Serve from the baking dish.
Four servings.

ONE SERVING

Oil — 0 teaspoons	**Protein —** 2 grams
Cholesterol — 0 milligrams	**Carbohydrate —** 42 grams
Saturated fat — 0 grams	**Calories —** 185
Linoleic acid — 0 grams	

BAKED ACORN SQUASH

Cut in half and remove seeds and membranes from
   2 acorn squash
Place cut side down in a pan with about ½ inch water and bake in
350° F. oven 45 minutes to 1 hour. Turn over and sprinkle with
   1 teaspoon brown sugar
   ¼ teaspoon salt
Add
   ½ teaspoon oil
to each half squash. Bake until sugar melts. **Four servings.**

ONE SERVING

Oil — ½ teaspoon	**Protein —** 2 grams
Cholesterol — 0 milligrams	**Carbohydrate —** 21 grams
Saturated fat — negligible	**Calories —** 115
Linoleic acid — 1 gram	

This recipe may be used with any yellow squash.

BROILED TOMATOES

Cut in half and place in a shallow baking dish
> 6 *tomatoes*

Mix together
> ¼ *cup bread crumbs*   2 *tablespoons minced onion*
> 2 *tablespoons chopped green*   *salt and pepper*
>   *pepper*

Sprinkle over the tomatoes. Bake in a moderate oven (350° F.) 30 minutes, then broil until golden brown on top. **Six servings.**

ONE SERVING
> **Oil** — 0 teaspoons   **Protein** — 2 grams
> **Cholesterol** — 0 milligrams   **Carbohydrate** — 10 grams
> **Saturated fat** — 0 grams   **Calories** — 50
> **Linoleic acid** — 0 grams

BAKED TOMATOES WITH BEANS

Soak 5 or 6 hours and cook until not quite tender
> 2 *cups kidney beans*

Add
> 1 *large onion, sliced thin*
> *salt*
> *pepper*

Continue cooking until beans are tender. Remove top and scoop out centers from
> 6 *large, well-shaped tomatoes*

Fill tomatoes with beans, fit into a baking dish, and add
> 2 *tablespoons water*
> *salt*
> *pepper*

Bake in moderate oven (350° F.) until tomatoes are tender. **Six servings.**

ONE SERVING
> **Oil** — 0 teaspoons   **Protein** — 17 grams
> **Cholesterol** — 0 milligrams   **Carbohydrate** — 49 grams
> **Saturated fat** — 0 grams   **Calories** — 275
> **Linoleic acid** — 0 grams

VEGETABLE BOWL

Scald, peel, and slice into a saucepan
  2 ripe medium-size tomatoes
Cut from the cob with a sharp knife and add to the tomatoes
  3 medium-size ears of corn
Add

*½ green pepper, coarsely
  chopped*
1 cup sliced celery
*1 medium-size onion,
  chopped*

1 teaspoon honey
1 tablespoon water

Cook gently, *tightly covered*, about 15 minutes, or until the celery and onion are barely tender. Season with
  salt and pepper to taste
Serve at once. **Six servings.**

ONE SERVING

Oil — 0 teaspoons
Cholesterol — 0 milligrams
Saturated fat — 0 grams
Linoleic acid — 0 grams

Protein — 3 grams
Carbohydrate — 15 grams
Calories — 75

CANDIED YAMS

Boil in water until tender, peel, and slice lengthwise into a baking dish
  6 medium-size yams
Mix together and boil until thickened

¾ cup brown sugar
*⅛ teaspoon cinnamon or
  nutmeg*

¼ teaspoon salt
½ cup water

Pour over yams. Bake in a moderate oven (350° F.) 20 minutes.
Six servings.

ONE SERVING

Oil — 0 teaspoons
Cholesterol — 0 milligrams
Saturated fat — 0 grams
Linoleic acid — 0 grams

Protein — 2 grams
Carbohydrate — 65 grams
Calories — 270

CANDIED VEGETABLES

This method can be used to glaze or candy other vegetables, such as carrots, squash, or sweet potatoes.

LEMONY YAMS

Steam, without peeling, until tender
  6 *medium-size yams*
Peel and mash with juice of
  1 *lemon*
Blend or shake together in a covered jar until smooth
  ½ cup skim milk
  ⅓ cup skim milk powder
  ½ to ¾ teaspoon salt
Add to the mashed yams. Add water for additional moisture if needed. Beat hard until smooth and fluffy. **Six servings.**

ONE SERVING

Oil — 0 teaspoons		**Protein** — 4 grams	
Cholesterol — 2 milligrams		**Carbohydrate** — 42 grams	
Saturated fat — 0 grams		**Calories** — 195	
Linoleic acid — 0 grams			

BAKED ZUCCHINI BOATS

Scrub and remove stems ends from
  6 *young, well-shaped zucchini*
Cook in boiling water 3 minutes, then salt. Slice the zucchini lengthwise and hollow out the centers. Chop the centers and mix with
  ¼ cup bread crumbs   *salt*
  2 tablespoons chopped onion   *pepper*
  1 tablespoon chopped parsley   *paprika*
Moisten with zucchini cooking water. Fill the zucchini boats with the mixture. Mix
  ¾ cup bread crumbs
with
  2 tablespoons oil

Spread over zucchini boats. Bake in moderate oven (350° F.) 30 minutes. **Six servings.**

ONE SERVING

Oil — ½ teaspoon
Cholesterol — 0 milligrams
Saturated fat — negligible
Linoleic acid — 1 gram

Protein — 2 grams
Carbohydrate — 10 grams
Calories — 70

CHAPTER XVII

Salad Dressings and Salads

Good salad dressings are important to the making of a successful salad. Salads are a fine addition to any meal, or they can be a meal in themselves. They provide raw greens, vegetables, and fruits and should be included daily. The addition of small amounts of the acceptable meats or skim milk cheeses can make a complete meal of the salad. Your choice of a salad and the type and amount of salad dressing will depend upon your Daily Food Guide. The number of calories and the amount of polyunsaturated oil needed in the diet will influence this choice. The only oils to be used are safflower, soybean, corn, walnut, sesame seed, sunflower, or cottonseed. Other commonly used oils are too highly saturated for use in this diet.

We have included many salad dressings in this chapter. Some are made without oil, using instead Skim Milk Yogurt★, skim milk buttermilk, and fruit juices. These are helpful when the fats and calories must be limited. There are mayonnaise substitutes, such as "Special" Fat Free Dressing★ and Cooked Salad Dressing★, a mayonnaise made without egg yolk, fat free French dressing, and basic French dressing made with oil, in addition to many others. The basic dressings can be varied in flavor by adding flavored vinegars, herbs, spices, and seeds as well as chopped vegetables, fruits, catsup, chili sauce, or pickles. The salad dressing contributes additional food and caloric values to be added to the values shown for the salad itself.

What Salad Dressing Goes with What Salad?

SALAD DRESSING
(Recipes in this chapter)

FRUIT SALAD
Citrus Fruit Salad   Celery Seed Dressing
Melon Salad

Mixed Fruit Salad (see page 236)

Claret Honey Dressing
Citrus Dressing
Cranberrry Dressing
Fruit Salad Dressing
Low Fat French Dressing:
 variation
Pineapple-Yogurt Dressing
Sherry Dressing
Tart French Dressing

Waldorf Salad

Mayonnaise
Pineapple Salad Dressing
"Special" Fat Free Dressing

GREEN LEAFY SALAD

Coleslaw
Lettuce Wedges

Cooked Salad Dressing
Thousand Island Dressing
Chili Dressing

Mixed Greens Salad (see page 253)

Basic French Dressing
Buttermilk Dressing
Cooked Salad Dressing
Curry Dressing
Fat Free French Dressing
Fluffy Dressing
Herb Dressing
Italian Dressing
Low Fat French Dressing
Tomato French Dressing
Yogurt Dressing I
Yogurt Dressing II

Spinach Salad

Basic French Dressing

Tossed Salad with Wine Dressing

Dressing included in recipe

Tossing a Green Salad (see page 255)

Dressing included in
 instructions

MOLDED GELATIN SALAD

Carrot-Pineapple Salad

"Special" Fat Free Dressing
Mayonnaise

Molded Cucumber Salad

"Special" Fat Free Dressing
Mayonnaise

Molded Grapefruit-Persimmon Salad	"Special" Fat Free Dressing Mayonnaise
Molded Pineapple-Grapefruit Salad	"Special" Fat Free Dressing Mayonnaise
Pear Cellophane Salad	"Special" Fat Free Dressing Mayonnaise
Tomato Aspic Salad	"Special" Fat Free Dressing Mayonnaise

SALADS WITH ADDED PROTEIN

Chicken Salad	Dressing included in recipe
Cottage Cheese Salad	Dressing included in recipe
Fish Salad	Dressing included in recipe
Fish Aspic	Cucumber Sauce Yogurt Sauce
Frozen Cheese and Pineapple Salad	Mayonnaise
Fruit and Crab Salad	Tart French Dressing
Jellied Cottage Cheese Mold	Mayonnaise "Special" Fat Free Dressing
Mexican Tomatoes	Dressing included in recipe
Stuffed Pear Salad	Dressing included in recipe
Stuffed Tomato Salad	Dressing included in recipe
Salmon in Aspic	Cucumber Sauce Yogurt Sauce
Tuna Salad Bowl	Dressing included in recipe
Turkey Salad	Dressing included in recipe

VEGETABLE SALAD

Cabbage and Carrot Salad	"Special" Fat Free Dressing Mayonnaise
Italian Lima Bean Salad	Dressing included in recipe
Mixed vegetables (raw or cooked)	Basic French Dressing Fluffy Dressing Spanish Dressing

Sliced Tomato Salad

Basic French Dressing
Herb Dressing
Mayonnaise
Spicy Cottage Cheese
Dressing

A salad should be pleasing to the eye, which in turn stimulates the appetite. Many attractive garnishes can be added to the salad to make it appetizing and to add food values:

Radishes
Pickles
Green bell pepper
Red bell pepper
Green onion
Parsley
Croutons (made at home using
    polyunsaturated oil)
Chives
Mint

Pimiento
Watercress
Carrots
Beets
Celery
Lemon
Lime
Hard-cooked egg white
Skim milk cottage cheese
Baker's cheese

SALAD DRESSING RECIPES

"SPECIAL" FAT FREE DRESSING

Shake in a jar until smooth
   1 *cup skim milk*
   2 *tablespoons cornstarch*
Pour in a pan and cook over low heat until thick, stirring constantly.
Remove from heat and add
   ½ *teaspoon salt*
   ½ *teaspoon mustard*
Cool thoroughly and add
   2 *tablespoons vinegar*
   1 *to 2 drops yellow food coloring if desired*
Beat until smooth.
Beat until stiff and fold into thickened milk mixture
   1 *egg white*
Makes 1¼ cups.

ONE TABLESPOON

Oil — 0 teaspoons

Cholesterol — negligible

Saturated fat — 0 grams

Linoleic acid — 0 grams

Protein — 1 gram

Carbohydrate — 1 gram

Calories — 10

COOKED SALAD DRESSING

Combine in a bowl

2 *tablespoons sugar*

½ *teaspoon dry mustard*

½ *teaspoon salt*

¼ *cup oil*

¼ *cup vinegar*

Stir in a pan until thoroughly mixed

2 *tablespoons cornstarch*

1 *cup cold water*

Cook over low heat, stirring constantly, until mixture boils and becomes clear. Remove from heat and continue stirring about 1 minute. Pour this hot mixture into the ingredients in the bowl. Beat vigorously with a rotary beater until smooth. Add, if desired, dash of paprika or 1 drop yellow food coloring. Chill. **Makes 1½ cups.**

ONE TABLESPOON

Oil — ½ teaspoon

Cholesterol — 0 milligrams

Saturated fat — negligible

Linoleic acid — 1 gram

Protein — negligible

Carbohydrate — 2 grams

Calories — 30

VARIATIONS:

To "Special" Fat Free Dressing★ or Cooked Salad Dressing★, add chopped chives, chopped parsley, or finely chopped celery.

THOUSAND ISLAND DRESSING

To

½ *cup "Special" Fat Free Dressing★ or Cooked Salad Dressing★*

Add

½ *cup chili sauce or catsup*

If desired, add a little chopped celery or green pepper or pickle if catsup is used. **Makes 1 cup.**

ONE TABLESPOON
    Oil — 0 teaspoons
    Cholesterol — negligible
    Saturated fat — 0 grams
    Linoleic acid — 0 grams

Protein — negligible
Carbohydrate — 2 grams
Calories — 10

BLENDER MAYONNAISE

Place in the electric blender
    1 egg white (or 2 tablespoons
       reconstituted egg white
       powder, see page 66)
    ½ teaspoon lecithin granules
       (optional)

2 tablespoons vinegar or
   lemon juice
½ teaspoon dry mustard
¼ cup oil

Cover the blender and blend at high speed. Remove cover and add gradually, blending after each addition
    ¾ cup oil
When smooth and thickened, store in the refrigerator. **Makes approximately 1½ cups.**

ONE TABLESPOON
    Oil — 2 teaspoons
    Cholesterol — 0 milligrams
    Saturated fat — 1 gram
    Linoleic acid — 5 grams

Protein — negligible
Carbohydrate — negligible
Calories — 90

MAYONNAISE

Mix together in a bowl and beat with a rotary egg beater
    ½ teaspoon sugar
    ½ teaspoon salt

½ teaspoon dry mustard
1 egg white

Add, beating constantly, a few drops at a time
    ½ cup oil
Continue beating and add alternately until all is used
    ½ cup oil
    1 tablespoon cider vinegar
    1 tablespoon lemon juice
Store in refrigerator in a covered container. Depending on the use, increase the vinegar or lemon juice if desired. **Makes approximately 1 cup.**

ONE TABLESPOON

Oil — 3 teaspoons
Cholesterol — 0 milligrams
Saturated fat — 2 grams
Linoleic acid — 8 grams

Protein — negligible
Carbohydrate — negligible
Calories — 130

FLUFFY DRESSING

Combine in a bowl and chill together several hours

½ cup Mayonnaise★
2 tablespoons chopped chives (or grated onion)
1 clove garlic, minced
1 tablespoon tarragon vinegar
1 tablespoon lemon juice
3 tablespoons finely chopped parsley

3 tablespoons chopped anchovy (optional) (Wash in a sieve before chopping to remove olive oil.)
salt to taste
coarsely ground pepper to taste

Prepare chilled bowl and beaters. Beat together in chilled bowl until it forms soft peaks

¼ cup ice water
¼ cup skim milk powder

Fold mayonnaise mixture into the whipped milk. **Makes 1½ cups.**

ONE TABLESPOON

Oil — 1 teaspoon
Cholesterol — 0 milligrams
Saturated fat — 1 gram
Linoleic acid — 3 grams

Protein — negligible
Carbohydrate — 1 gram
Calories — 50

CHEESE DRESSING

Mix together in a blender

¾ cup skim milk cottage cheese (or ¾ cup baker's cheese)

3 tablespoons Mayonnaise★
2 tablespoons scraped onion
¼ teaspoon garlic salt

Blend until smooth. Thin, if desired, with skim milk.
May be served on sliced tomatoes, salad greens, vegetables, or hot baked potatoes. **Makes 1 cup.**

ONE TABLESPOON

Oil — ⅓ teaspoon
Cholesterol — 1 milligram
Saturated fat — negligible
Linoleic acid — 2 grams

Protein — 2 grams
Carbohydrate — negligible
Calories — 30

VARIATION:

Omit scraped onion and add one of the following: chopped green onion; chopped chives; 1-inch piece of cucumber, grated; 1 tablespoon chopped green pepper; or 1 tablespoon chopped celery.

FRUIT SALAD DRESSING

Combine in a saucepan
½ cup sugar (or light corn syrup)
4 teaspoons flour
Gradually stir in
½ cup vinegar
Cook slowly, stirring constantly, until thickened. Add and mix well

1 teaspoon salt
1 teaspoon paprika
1 teaspoon dry mustard

1 teaspoon celery seed
1 tablespoon finely minced onion

Pour into the mixture very slowly, beating constantly with a rotary beater
¾ cup oil
Store the dressing in a covered container in the refrigerator for several hours to blend the flavors before serving. **Makes 2 cups.**

ONE TABLESPOON

Oil — 1 teaspoon
Cholesterol — 0 milligrams
Saturated fat — 1 gram
Linoleic acid — 4 grams

Protein — negligible
Carbohydrate — 5 grams
Calories — 60

LOW FAT FRENCH DRESSING

Crush in a bowl
1 clove garlic (optional)
Add, blend together well, and let stand 30 minutes

3 tablespoons cider or wine vinegar
2 tablespoons cold water
½ teaspoon salt

⅛ teaspoon pepper
⅛ teaspoon dry mustard
½ teaspoon sugar (optional)

Remove garlic and add
   2 *tablespoons oil*
Shake in a jar or beat until well blended. **Six servings.**

ONE TABLESPOON
   Oil — 1 teaspoon   **Protein** — 0 grams
   Cholesterol — 0 milligrams   **Carbohydrate** — 1 gram
   Saturated fat — 1 gram   **Calories** — 50
   Linoleic acid — 4 grams

VARIATION:

   Omit garlic. Substitute lemon or lime juice for vinegar.

FAT FREE FRENCH DRESSING

   Crush in a bowl
      1 clove garlic (optional)
   Add, blend together well, and let stand 30 minutes
      3 tablespoons cider or wine   *⅛ teaspoon pepper*
         vinegar   *⅛ teaspoon dry mustard*
      3 tablespoons cold water   *½ teaspoon sugar (optional)*
      ½ teaspoon salt
   Remove garlic. **Four servings.**

ONE TABLESPOON
   Oil — 0 teaspoons   **Protein** — 0 grams
   Cholesterol — 0 milligrams   **Carbohydrate** — 1 gram
   Saturated fat — 0 grams   **Calories** — 5
   Linoleic acid — 0 grams

BASIC FRENCH DRESSING

   Put into a covered jar
      ⅓ cup cider vinegar   *¼ teaspoon pepper*
      2 tablespoons water   *⅔ cup oil*
      ½ teaspoon salt
   Shake together until blended. **Makes 1 cup.**

ONE TABLESPOON
   Oil — 2 teaspoons   **Protein** — 0 grams
   Cholesterol — 0 milligrams   **Carbohydrate** — negligible
   Saturated fat — 1 gram   **Calories** — 90
   Linoleic acid — 5 grams

ITALIAN DRESSING

Prepare, using wine vinegar instead of cider vinegar
  1 cup Basic French Dressing★
Add
  ½ teaspoon dry mustard
  ½ teaspoon paprika
  1 clove garlic, crushed
Refrigerate for several hours to blend flavors. Remove garlic and shake well before using. **Makes 1 cup.**

ONE TABLESPOON

Oil — 2 teaspoons	**Protein** — negligible
Cholesterol — 0 milligrams	**Carbohydrate** — negligible
Saturated fat — 1 gram	**Calories** — 90
Linoleic acid — 5 grams	

CURRY DRESSING

Combine
  1 cup Basic French Dressing★
  ½ teaspoon curry powder
Makes 1 cup.

ONE TABLESPOON

Oil — 2 teaspoons	**Protein** — negligible
Cholesterol — 0 milligrams	**Carbohydrate** — negligible
Saturated fat — 1 gram	**Calories** — 90
Linoleic acid — 5 grams	

HERB DRESSING

Put in a blender
  1 cup Basic French Dressing★
  ¼ cup parsley, stems removed
  ½ teaspoon dried herb (such as marjoram, dill, orégano, basil, or tarragon)

If fresh herbs are used, a few sprigs or leaves are sufficient. Blend until herbs are fine. **Makes approximately 1¼ cups.**

ONE TABLESPOON

Oil — 2 teaspoons   **Protein** — 0 grams
Cholesterol — 0 milligrams   **Carbohydrate** — negligible
Saturated fat — 1 gram   **Calories** — 90
Linoleic acid — 5 grams

VARIATION:

Prepare the Basic French Dressing★ with wine vinegar instead of cider vinegar.

CHILI DRESSING

Put in a blender
    1 cup Basic French Dressing★   1 whole pimiento (canned)
    3 tablespoons chili sauce   several sprigs watercress
    2 green onions and tops,
        coarsely cut

Blend until finely chopped. Lacking a blender, chop vegetables and herbs finely and add to the French dressing. Shake together in a covered jar until mixed, and refrigerate several hours to blend flavors. **Makes approximately 1½ cups.**

ONE TABLESPOON

Oil — 1½ teaspoons   **Protein** — negligible
Cholesterol — 0 milligrams   **Carbohydrate** — 1 gram
Saturated fat — 1 gram   **Calories** — 75
Linoleic acid — 4 grams

BUTTERMILK DRESSING

    ½ cup skim milk buttermilk   1 tablespoon prepared
    1 teaspoon sugar   horseradish
    ⅛ teaspoon dry mustard   pepper
    ¼ teaspoon salt

Combine all ingredients and mix. Chill before using. **Makes ½ cup.**

ONE TABLESPOON
Oil — 0 teaspoons
Cholesterol — 1 milligram
Saturated fat — negligible
Linoleic acid — 0 grams

Protein — negligible
Carbohydrate — 1 gram
Calories — 5

TOMATO FRENCH DRESSING

Measure into a jar
1 cup tomato juice
½ cup oil
¼ cup vinegar
2 tablespoons sugar
1 teaspoon dry mustard

1 teaspoon paprika
1 teaspoon salt
1 teaspoon Worcestershire
sauce
1 clove garlic, peeled

Cover tightly and shake well. Chill several hours, then remove garlic.
Makes 2 cups.

ONE TABLESPOON
Oil — ¾ teaspoon
Cholesterol — 0 milligrams
Saturated fat — 1 gram
Linoleic acid — 3 grams

Protein — negligible
Carbohydrate — 1 gram
Calories — 40

CITRUS DRESSING

Chill bowl and beaters and beat together until it forms soft peaks
¼ cup ice water
¼ cup skim milk powder
Mix together
3 tablespoons honey
3 teaspoons orange, lemon, or lime juice
Fold the honey mixture into the whipped milk. Serve at once. **Makes
1 cup.**

ONE TABLESPOON
Oil — negligible
Cholesterol — negligible
Saturated fat — negligible
Linoleic acid — negligible

Protein — negligible
Carbohydrate — 4 grams
Calories — 15

SPICY COTTAGE CHEESE DRESSING

Into the blender put

½ cup skim milk cottage
    cheese
½ cup water
¼ cup skim milk powder
1 teaspoon salt
1 teaspoon paprika

2 tablespoons lemon juice
½ garlic clove, sliced
½ green pepper, cut in strips
4 radishes
2 green onions, including
    tops, coarsely cut

Cover and blend on high speed 10 seconds or until vegetables are finely chopped. Lacking a blender, chop the vegetables finely and beat dressing with a rotary beater. **Makes 1½ cups.**

ONE TABLESPOON

Oil — 0 teaspoons
Cholesterol — negligible
Saturated fat — negligible
Linoleic acid — negligible

Protein — 1 gram
Carbohydrate — 1 gram
Calories — 10

COTTAGE CHEESE DRESSING

Sieve or blend in electric blender

1 cup skim milk cottage cheese

Add and blend in

⅓ cup Fat Free French Dressing★
little onion juice (optional)
½ teaspoon sugar

Six servings.

ONE TABLESPOON

Oil — 0 teaspoons
Cholesterol — 3 milligrams
Saturated fat — negligible
Linoleic acid — 0 grams

Protein — negligible
Carbohydrate — negligible
Calories — 10

PINEAPPLE YOGURT DRESSING

Combine in a bowl and beat with a fork

1 cup Skim Milk Yogurt★
½ cup pineapple juice

2 tablespoons honey
⅛ teaspoon salt

Twelve servings.

ONE TABLESPOON

Oil — 0 teaspoons
Cholesterol — 1 milligram
Saturated fat — negligible
Linoleic acid — 0 grams

Protein — 1 gram
Carbohydrate — 5 grams
Calories — 25

YOGURT DRESSING I

Mix together
   ½ cup Skim Milk Yogurt★
   2 tablespoons lemon juice
     (or tarragon or wine
     vinegar)
   ¼ teaspoon dry mustard

   ½ teaspoon salt
   ½ to 1 teaspoon paprika
   1 clove garlic, minced
   1 small onion, grated

If the yogurt is tart, omit the lemon juice or vinegar. **Six servings.**

ONE TABLESPOON

Oil — 0 teaspoons
Cholesterol — negligible
Saturated fat — negligible
Linoleic acid — 0 grams

Protein — 1 gram
Carbohydrate — 3 grams
Calories — 15

YOGURT DRESSING II

Crush together in a bowl
   1 clove garlic
   1 teaspoon salt
Add and beat with a fork until thoroughly blended
   1 teaspoon paprika
   dash of Tabasco sauce
   1 cup Skim Milk Yogurt★
   3 tablespoons oil

   1½ tablespoons claret
     (or 1 tablespoon wine
     vinegar)

Remove garlic just before serving. **Twelve servings.**

ONE TABLESPOON

Oil — ¾ teaspoon
Cholesterol — 1 milligram
Saturated fat — 1 gram
Linoleic acid — 2 grams

Protein — 1 gram
Carbohydrate — 1 gram
Calories — 40

CRANBERRY DRESSING

Blend well
    3 tablespoons lemon juice   2 tablespoons cranberry jelly
    3 tablespoons cold water   salt
Four servings.

ONE TABLESPOON
    Oil — 0 teaspoons   **Protein** — negligible
    Cholesterol — 0 milligrams   **Carbohydrate** — 8 grams
    Saturated fat — 0 grams   **Calories** — 30
    Linoleic acid — 0 grams

SHERRY DRESSING

Blend well
    ¼ cup sherry   salt
    ¼ cup sugar   ¼ teaspoon celery seed
    ¼ cup lemon juice   (optional)
Let stand 30 minutes. **Six servings.**

ONE TABLESPOON
    Oil — 0 teaspoons   **Protein** — negligible
    Cholesterol — 0 milligrams   **Carbohydrate** — 10 grams
    Saturated fat — 0 grams   **Calories** — 50
    Linoleic acid — 0 grams

CLARET HONEY DRESSING

Combine in a jar
    ⅓ teaspoon salt   3 tablespoons claret
    2 tablespoons lemon juice   2 tablespoons honey
    ¼ cup oil
Beat well with a fork or shake until blended. **Makes ¾ cup.**

ONE TABLESPOON
    Oil — 1 teaspoon   **Protein** — 0 grams
    Cholesterol — 0 milligrams   **Carbohydrate** — 3 grams
    Saturated fat — 1 gram   **Calories** — 60
    Linoleic acid — 3 grams

TART FRENCH DRESSING

Place in a bowl and beat slightly

1 egg white   ½ teaspoon paprika
½ teaspoon mustard   ¼ teaspoon salt

Pour into a jar and add

2 teaspoons cider vinegar   1 clove garlic, crushed
2 tablespoons lemon juice   ¾ cup oil

Shake together well. Chill in the refrigerator for several hours to blend flavors. Remove garlic and shake before serving. **Makes about 1⅓ cups.**

ONE TABLESPOON

Oil — 1¾ teaspoons   **Protein** — negligible
Cholesterol — negligible   **Carbohydrate** — negligible
Saturated fat — 1 gram   **Calories** — 75
Linoleic acid — 5 grams

CELERY SEED DRESSING

Mix together in a saucepan

1 tablespoon sugar   ½ teaspoon onion salt
1 tablespoon cornstarch   ½ teaspoon dry mustard
1 teaspoon paprika   ¼ teaspoon salt
1 teaspoon celery seed

Gradually add and stir until smooth

¼ cup wine vinegar
1 cup water

Bring to a boil, stirring constantly, until mixture thickens and becomes clear. Chill in the refrigerator. Stir well with a fork before using. **Makes 1 cup.**

ONE TABLESPOON

Oil — 0 teaspoons   **Protein** — 0 grams
Cholesterol — 0 milligrams   **Carbohydrate** — 1 gram
Saturated fat — 0 grams   **Calories** — 5
Linoleic acid — 0 grams

SPANISH DRESSING

Combine
  1 green pepper, chopped
  1 large white onion, chopped
  1 whole pimiento (canned), chopped
Combine and add
  ¾ teaspoon salt   ½ teaspoon dry mustard
  ¾ teaspoon paprika   2 tablespoons sugar
  ½ teaspoon black pepper   2 tablespoons catsup
Mix well. Combine and add
  ¼ cup white vinegar
  juice of 1 lemon
  1 cup oil
Mix well. **Makes approximately 2 cups.**

ONE TABLESPOON
  Oil ___ 1 teaspoon   **Protein** ___ 3 grams
  Cholesterol ___ 0 milligrams   **Carbohydrate** ___ 1 gram
  Saturated fat ___ 0 grams   **Calories** ___ 55
  Linoleic acid ___ 1 gram

PINEAPPLE DRESSING

Combine
  ½ cup pineapple juice
  juice of 1 lemon
Add slowly to
  1 tablespoon cornstarch
Cook over low heat until thick and clear, stirring constantly. Remove
from fire. Fold in
  2 egg whites, stiffly beaten
Six servings.

ONE TABLESPOON
  Oil ___ 0 teaspoons   **Protein** ___ 2 grams
  Cholesterol ___ 0 milligrams   **Carbohydrate** ___ 5 grams
  Saturated fat ___ 0 grams   **Calories** ___ 30
  Linoleic acid ___ 0 grams

SALADS

It is important to know some general principles about salads: the basic kinds of materials to use, how to select and handle them, and how to combine them with dressings. To select an appropriate dressing, see page 236. You may experiment with other salad and salad dressing combinations. Some salad pointers are contained in this section.

Green Leafy Salads

These may vary from a simple tossed lettuce salad to a delightful combination of greens, or greens with vegetable or fruits. Learn to use a wide variety of greens, such as

Leaf lettuce	Spinach
Romaine	New Zealand spinach
Watercress	Swiss chard
Endive	Peppergrass
Butter lettuce	Parsley
Escarole	Cabbage

Salad greens require careful handling and storing to preserve all the vitamins and minerals. Here are some precautions to observe:

1. Purchase only fresh greens and refrigerate promptly.
2. Store in a covered refrigerator pan.
3. Wash greens rapidly in cold water, rinse, drain, and dry thoroughly by whirling in a cheesecloth bag, or in a wire basket made for this purpose.
4. Do not soak greens, even to freshen them, as the nutrients dissolve into the water.
5. Mix salads in a chilled bowl.
6. As soon as salads are prepared, return them to the refrigerator until time to serve.
7. Add the salad dressing just before serving (see page 255 for a good method).
8. Serve on chilled plates.

Other Vegetables and Fruits

1. Select only fresh vegetables and fruits in season.
2. Wash carefully and quickly in cold water.
3. Dry gently with a towel.

4. Store vegetables in a covered refrigerator pan. Store ripe fruit in the refrigerator, except oranges, lemons, grapefruit, apples, and bananas, which have thick protective skins and do not require refrigeration. These and unripe fruits of other varieties should be stored in a cool, dark place. All fruits should be chilled before preparing and serving.
5. All vegetables and fruits may be used freely except avocado and olives, which are high in fat.

Vegetable Salads

Vegetables should be used raw whenever possible. They may be sliced, grated, or shredded. Unless the skins are tough, it is well not to peel vegetables such as tomatoes or carrots, as the skins are high in nutritive values. Raw, tender buds such as broccoli and asparagus tips give variety to salads. If you have leftover cooked vegetables, it is preferable to use them in salads rather than incur further losses of nutrients by reheating.

If vegetables are to be cooked specifically for salad, they should be cooked until barely tender in as little water as possible. If canned vegetables are used in salad, they should be thoroughly chilled. Save the liquid drained from canned vegetables to use in soups, aspics, sauces, and other dishes, as it is rich in food value. Frozen vegetables may be cooked for salads and chilled before serving.

Fruit Salads

Fresh raw fruits are both refreshing and nutritious in salads. They may be used alone or in combination with vegetables, "Special" Cottage Cheese★, or gelatin. Dried, frozen, and canned fruits may be used, particularly when fresh fruits are not in season.

Molded Gelatin Salads

Fruits, fish, meat, and vegetables may also be served in gelatin salads. It is wise to prepare the gelatin with fruit juices, full strength or diluted, rather than water. Aspic salads should utilize leftover vegetable stock or be made with vegetable juices. Use "Special" Cottage Cheese★ in gelatin and aspic salads for added protein.

Salads with Added Protein

Salads that include dried beans, lentils, meats or fish, "Special" Cottage Cheese★, baker's cheese, or hard-cooked egg white are doubly important because of their protein content. A sprinkling of wheat germ adds vitamins as well as a nutty flavor to salads.

Dressing a Tossed Salad

An excellent method of dressing a leafy green salad is to add the vegetable oil to the salad first, tossing quickly and thoroughly, so that the oil coats the leaves. Little oil is needed to do this. To avoid bruising the leaves, toss in a large shallow bowl. Combine the vinegar and spices and add the mixture to the salad. Toss well again to distribute the seasonings throughout the salad. Serve at once. This method will require a little practice to attain the desired flavor in the salad. Once skill is achieved, this will undoubtedly be your preferred method, as the salad retains all the crispness and flavor in the fresh greens. This is a good method for those restricting calories, since it requires very little oil.

SALAD RECIPES

CABBAGE AND CARROT SALAD

Mix together
   ½ cup "Special" Fat Free Dressing★
   1 teaspoon grated onion (or finely cut chives)
   2 teaspoons finely cut parsley
Chill. At serving time, prepare
   2 cups shredded, chilled cabbage
   ⅔ cup shredded, chilled carrot
Combine all ingredients and add to taste
   salt
   lemon juice
Six servings.

ONE SERVING
   Oil — 0 teaspoons
   Cholesterol — negligible
   Saturated fat — 0 grams
   Linoleic acid — 0 grams

   Protein — 1 gram
   Carbohydrate — 5 grams
   Calories — 25

COTTAGE CHEESE SALAD

Slice as thin as possible
   8 *medium radishes*
   1 *small cucumber*
Chop very fine
   4 *scallions (both the white and green parts)*
Add the mixture to
   2 *cups skim milk cottage cheese*
Mix together well and add
   salt to taste
Serve chilled on leaf of lettuce. **Four servings.**

ONE SERVING

Oil — 0 teaspoons	**Protein** — 20 grams
Cholesterol — 8 milligrams	**Carbohydrate** — 7 grams
Saturated fat — negligible	**Calories** — 115
Linoleic acid — 0 grams	

ITALIAN LIMA BEAN SALAD

Cook until tender, drain, and rinse in cold water (save cooking water for soups or sauces)
   2 *cups green lima beans*
Mix together

4 *tablespoons oil*	2 *tablespoons chopped parsley*
1½ to 2 *tablespoons wine vinegar*	1 *garlic bud, finely chopped*
	salt
2 *tablespoons chopped onion*	*pepper*

Mix the dressing thoroughly through the beans and chill. Serve on crisp greens surrounded by 12 slices tomato garnished with 12 slices green pepper. **Six servings.**

ONE SERVING

Oil — 2 teaspoons	**Protein** — 4 grams
Cholesterol — 0 milligrams	**Carbohydrate** — 10 grams
Saturated fat — 1 gram	**Calories** — 145
Linoleic acid — 5 grams	

VARIATION:

Any green or dried bean, cooked, may be substituted for lima beans.

SPINACH SALAD

Mix together
  ½ pound spinach, coarsely
    shredded
  1 head romaine, shredded
  1 bunch radishes, chopped
    fine
  6 green onions, chopped fine
Six servings.

ONE SERVING
  Oil — 0 teaspoons
  Cholesterol — 0 milligrams
  Saturated fat — 0 grams
  Linoleic acid — 0 grams

  Protein — 2 grams
  Carbohydrate — 4 grams
  Calories — 25

STUFFED TOMATO

Core the centers from
  4 tomatoes
Turn upside down and allow to drain. Mix together
  1 tablespoon skim milk
  ¾ cup skim milk cottage cheese (or ¾ cup baker's cheese)
Chop and add to the cheese
  1 stalk celery
  ¼ green pepper
  2 to 3 green onions
  salt and pepper to taste
Fill the tomatoes with the cheese, chill, and serve on salad greens.
Garnish the tomato with a sprig of parsley and a little paprika.
Four servings.

ONE SERVING
  Oil — 0 teaspoons
  Cholesterol — 3 milligrams
  Saturated fat — 0 grams
  Linoleic acid — 0 grams

  Protein — 10 grams
  Carbohydrate — 10 grams
  Calories — 90

STUFFED PEARS

Mix together
  ½ cup skim milk cottage cheese (or baker's cheese)
  ¼ cup crushed pineapple
  ½ teaspoon lemon juice

Core and fill with cheese mixture
   4 fresh pears
Fresh fruit or canned fruit may be used. Place on lettuce leaves.
Four servings.

ONE SERVING

Oil — 0 teaspoons   **Protein** — 5 grams
Cholesterol — 2 milligrams   **Carbohydrate** — 16 grams
Saturated fat — negligible   **Calories** — 85
Linoleic acid — negligible

VARIATIONS:

1. Use canned pears instead of fresh. (Adds 40 calories to one serving.)
2. Substitute fresh peaches for fresh pears.

MEXICAN TOMATOES

Drain the liquid from
   2 cups canned kidney beans
Marinate in
   ½ cup Fat Free French   *½ teaspoon salt*
      Dressing★   *⅛ teaspoon pepper*
   ½ teaspoon chili powder
Add
   2 tablespoons chopped celery
   2 tablespoons chopped green onion
   2 tablespoons chopped parsley
Scoop out centers from
   6 firm and well-shaped tomatoes
Chop some of the centers and mix with the beans. Fill the tomato
cases with the bean mixture. Top with chopped parsley and a dash of
paprika. **Six servings.**

ONE SERVING

Oil — 0 teaspoons   **Protein** — 6 grams
Cholesterol — 1 milligram   **Carbohydrate** — 23 grams
Saturated fat — 0 grams   **Calories** — 115
Linoleic acid — 0 grams

TOSSED SALAD WITH WINE DRESSING

In a salad bowl toss
   1 head romaine   3 green onions, sliced
   3 tomatoes, cubed   ½ cucumber, sliced thin
   4 small carrots, sliced   2 tablespoons oil
Mix together
   2 tablespoons lemon juice   ¼ cup dry white or red wine
   1 teaspoon sugar   (turned, leftover dry wine is
   ½ teaspoon salt   very good for this purpose)
   ⅛ teaspoon pepper
Add to salad and toss lightly. **Six servings.**

ONE SERVING
   Oil — 1 teaspoon   **Protein** — 3 grams
   Cholesterol — 0 milligrams   **Carbohydrate** — 11 grams
   Saturated fat — 1 gram   **Calories** — 110
   Linoleic acid — 3 grams

WALDORF SALAD

Prepare
   1 cup cubed apples   ½ cup sliced bananas
   ¼ cup diced celery   ¼ cup pitted and diced dates
Soak the fruit 30 minutes in
   ½ cup orange or pineapple juice
Serve on crisp lettuce. **Four servings.**

ONE SERVING
   Oil — 0 teaspoons   **Protein** — 2 grams
   Cholesterol — 0 milligrams   **Carbohydrate** — 25 grams
   Saturated fat — 0 grams   **Calories** — 110
   Linoleic acid — 0 grams

Molded and Frozen Salads

CARROT-PINEAPPLE MOLDED SALAD

Drain juice from
   ½ cup crushed pineapple
Use juice with sufficient water to prepare
   1 package lime or lemon gelatin
When cool but not firm, add the drained pineapple and
   ½ cup grated carrots
   1 tablespoon vinegar
   ½ teaspoon salt
Pour into a mold and chill until firm. Unmold on crisp greens.
Four servings.

ONE SERVING

   Oil — 0 teaspoons   **Protein** — 9 grams
   Cholesterol — negligible   **Carbohydrate** — 27 grams
   Saturated fat — negligible   **Calories** — 115
   Linoleic acid — 0 grams

JELLIED COTTAGE CHEESE MOLD

Soak 5 minutes
   1 tablespoon gelatin
in
   ½ cup water
Dissolve it by placing over boiling water, and then add the gelatin to
   1 cup orange juice   *1 cup puréed skim milk cottage*
   2 tablespoons lemon juice   *cheese (or 1 cup baker's*
   1 tablespoon sugar   *cheese)*
Turn into a ring mold or a square pan and place in refrigerator to
set. **Six servings.**

ONE SERVING

   Oil — 0 teaspoons   **Protein** — 8 grams
   Cholesterol — 3 milligrams   **Carbohydrate** — 8 grams
   Saturated fat — 0 grams   **Calories** — 65
   Linoleic acid — 0 grams

If ring mold is used, fill the center with mixed fruits to serve. If square
pan is used, cut into cubes and garnish with fruits.

MOLDED CUCUMBER SALAD

Dissolve
> *1 package lemon gelatin*

in
> *1½ cups boiling water*

When cool add
> *¼ cup finely chopped celery*   *1 cup grated cucumber*
> *¼ cup finely chopped green*   *1 onion, grated*
>   *pepper*

Put into a mold and chill until firm. Serve on crisp greens. **Four servings.**

ONE SERVING
> **Oil** —— 0 teaspoons   **Protein** —— 3 grams
> **Cholesterol** —— 0 milligrams   **Carbohydrate** —— 25 grams
> **Saturated fat** —— 0 grams   **Calories** —— 110
> **Linoleic acid** —— 0 grams

Molded cucumber salad can be sliced and served on toast as canapés.

MOLDED GRAPEFRUIT-PERSIMMON SALAD

Drain juice from
> *2½ cups unsweetened canned grapefruit (No. 2 can)*

Mix juice with
> *enough ginger ale to make 1 pint*

Soften
> *1 tablespoon gelatin*

with
> *¼ cup of the liquid*

Dissolve over boiling water. Cool. Arrange the grapefruit segments in rows in a square pan or ring mold together with
> *thin slices of ½ unpeeled red apple*
> *larger sections of 1 ripe persimmon*

Pour the gelatin mixture over the fruit. Sprinkle
> *2 tablespoons chopped Chinese preserved ginger*

over the top. Place in refrigerator to set. To serve, cut into squares and arrange in lettuce cups. **Six servings.**

ONE SERVING
> **Oil** —— 0 teaspoons   **Protein** —— 2 grams
> **Cholesterol** —— 0 milligrams   **Carbohydrate** —— 39 grams
> **Saturated fat** —— 0 grams   **Calories** —— 170
> **Linoleic acid** —— 0 grams

PEAR CELLOPHANE SALAD

Prepare according to package directions
>*1 package lime or lemon gelatin*

Cover the bottom of a flat pan with the gelatin to a depth of about ½ to ¾ inch. Place in the refrigerator and allow to become partially set. Prepare
>*6 fresh cored pear halves*
>*6 maraschino cherries*

Place in the center of each pear 1 large maraschino cherry. Place the pears cherry side down at least 2 inches apart on the gelatin. Return to the refrigerator until gelatin becomes firm. To serve, cut around each pear with 1 inch or more margin and, using a pancake turner, scoop out each pear, turning it cherry side up into a crisp lettuce cup. Garnish the salad with a sprig or two of watercress. **Six servings.**

ONE SERVING

Oil — 0 teaspoons	**Protein** — 2 grams
Cholesterol — 0 milligrams	**Carbohydrate** — 30 grams
Saturated fat — 0 grams	**Calories** — 130
Linoleic acid — 0 grams	

MOLDED PINEAPPLE-GRAPEFRUIT SALAD

Drain and mix juice from
>*½ cup unsweetened grapefruit broken into bite-size pieces*
>*¾ cup unsweetened pineapple tidbits*

Prepare according to package directions
>*1 package lemon gelatin*

using
>*1 cup juice mixture*

Mix together and reserve for topping
>*2 tablespoons juice mixture*
>*¾ cup skim milk cottage cheese*

Cool gelatin and stir in
>*1 cup skim milk cottage cheese*

Arrange drained fruit in individual molds or a single large mold. Pour the gelatin mixture over the fruit. Place in the refrigerator to set. To serve, unmold on crisp lettuce and put 1 tablespoon of the reserved skim milk cottage cheese on top of each serving. Needs no added dressing. **Six servings.**

ONE SERVING
  Oil — 0 teaspoons
  Cholesterol — 3 milligrams
  Saturated fat — 0 grams
  Linoleic acid — 0 grams

  Protein — 7 grams
  Carbohydrate — 21 grams
  Calories — 110

TOMATO ASPIC SALAD

Heat together
  1¾ cups tomato juice
  ½ teaspoon salt

  ⅛ teaspoon pepper
  1 bay leaf

Remove bay leaf and add
  ½ teaspoon paprika
  1 teaspoon lemon juice
  1 tablespoon onion juice
Soak
  1 tablespoon gelatin
in
  ¼ cup cold water
Combine tomato juice and gelatin and cool. Stir in finely chopped
  ½ cup celery
  ¼ cup green onion
  2 tablespoons parsley
Pour into individual molds and place in refrigerator to set. **Six servings.**

ONE SERVING
  Oil — 0 teaspoons
  Cholesterol — 0 milligrams
  Saturated fat — 0 grams
  Linoleic acid — 0 grams

  Protein — 2 grams
  Carbohydrate — 4 grams
  Calories — 25

Almost like a gelatin salad because it is frozen firm is:

FROZEN CHEESE AND PINEAPPLE SALAD

Press through sieve and reserve
  1½ cups skim milk cottage cheese or baker's cheese
Measure into a bowl and beat or blend with an electric blender to the
consistency of whipped cream
  5 tablespoons water
  4 tablespoons skim milk
    powder

  2 teaspoons lemon juice
  1½ tablespoons sugar

Fold the sieved cottage cheese into the whipped skim milk mixture. Mix together and fold in

¼ cup "Special" Fat Free
    Dressing★
¾ cup drained, crushed
    pineapple

½ cup pitted, finely sliced
    dates
3 tablespoons lemon juice

Pour into a waxpaper-lined refrigerator tray. Freeze at lowered temperature. Cut in slices; arrange on lettuce cups. **Six servings.**

ONE SERVING

Oil — 0 teaspoons
Cholesterol — 6 milligrams
Saturated fat — 0 grams
Linoleic acid — 0 grams

Protein — 12 grams
Carbohydrate — 26 grams
Calories — 150

Suggested Combinations for Salads

1. Lettuce wedges with Yogurt Dressing★.
2. Lettuce wedges with Basic French Dressing★ and chopped hard-cooked egg white.
3. Grated carrot with pineapple chunks or raisins, lemon juice, and grated lemon rind.
4. Banana, citrus fruit, pineapple with Cranberry Dressing★.
5. Orange and grapefruit sections with Yogurt Dressing★.
6. "Special" Cottage Cheese* or baker's cheese with peach, pineapple, or pear.
7. Prunes stuffed with "Special" Cottage Cheese★ on orange slices.
8. Fruit cup on lettuce leaves with Yogurt Dressing I★.
9. Melon balls in half a cantaloupe.
10. Cantaloupe and pineapple with Sherry Dressing★ or Pineapple Yogurt Dressing★.
11. Grapefruit, pineapple, and strawberries with Citrus Dressing★.
12. Carrot and pineapple, shredded, with "Special" Fat-Free Dressing★ or Mayonnaise★.
13. Chicory, endive, and grapefruit with Basic French Dressing★.
14. Potato, onion, green pepper, pimiento, hard-cooked egg white with "Special" Fat Free Dressing★ or Mayonnaise★.

Meat and Fish Salads

Salads that contain meat or fish are not to be included in a meal containing other meat. They are excellent for luncheon or supper as a main course. Appropriate dressings are listed on page 236 and contribute corresponding additional food and calorie values.

TUNA SALAD BOWL

Line a salad bowl with washed, dried, and trimmed
    greens (romaine, endive, or any desired lettuce)
Arrange on the greens
    1 7-ounce can water-packed
        tuna, flaked
    1 tomato, cut into 8 wedges
    1 cucumber, sliced

    1 cup bean sprouts
    1 green pepper, cut in strips
    2 pimientos (canned), cut in
        strips
Season with
    ¼ cup Basic French Dressing★
Sprinkle with
    dill weed
    4 green onions, sliced
Four servings.

ONE SERVING (CONTAINS 1½ OUNCES FISH)
    Oil — 2 teaspoons
    Cholesterol — 31 milligrams
    Saturated fat — 2 grams
    Linoleic acid — 5 grams

    Protein — 12 grams
    Carbohydrate — 8 grams
    Calories — 190

VARIATION:

Substitute for the tuna 1 cup cooked fish, flaked, or 1 7-ounce can salmon, flaked.

CHICKEN SALAD

Cut into bite-size pieces
    2 cups cooked chicken (without skin or removable fat)
    1 cup diced celery
    1 tablespoon diced pimiento (canned)

Combine with
> ¾ cup Mayonnaise★

Season to taste with
> salt
> paprika
> lemon juice

Serve on a plate of greens. **Eight servings.**

ONE SERVING (CONTAINS 1¼ OUNCES CHICKEN)

Oil — 4½ teaspoons	**Protein** — 10 grams
Cholesterol — 23 milligrams	**Carbohydrate** — 1 gram
Saturated fat — 4 grams	**Calories** — 255
Linoleic acid — 13 grams	

Garnish with tomato wedges, green pepper strips or rings, cucumbers, sliced, any desired raw or cooked vegetables, or fruits such as grapes, pineapple, or citrus fruit.

FISH SALAD

In the recipe for Chicken Salad★, substitute flaked fish for the chicken.

ONE SERVING (CONTAINS 2 OUNCES FISH)

Oil — 4½ teaspoons	**Protein** — 11 grams
Cholesterol — 31 milligrams	**Carbohydrate** — 1 gram
Saturated fat — 3 grams	**Calories** — 255
Linoleic acid — 11 grams	

TURKEY SALAD

Peel and slice
> 2 tomatoes
> 1 cucumber
> 1 green pepper

Arrange on a combination of greens, such as lettuce, tender spinach leaves, and watercress, which have been tossed with
> 2 tablespoons Basic French Dressing★

Cut julienne strips from
> 8 ounces roasted turkey breast (without skin)

Arrange the meat over the vegetables and drizzle over all
> 2 tablespoons Basic French Dressing★

Garnish with pickles, paprika, and parsley. **Four servings.**

ONE SERVING (CONTAINS 2 OUNCES TURKEY)

Oil — 2 teaspoons	**Protein** — 18 grams
Cholesterol — 36 milligrams	**Carbohydrate** — 7 grams
Saturated fat — 1 gram	**Calories** — 215
Linoleic acid — 3 grams	

FISH ASPIC

Tie in cheesecloth
  1 pound cod, halibut, or sole, fresh or frozen
Combine and bring to the boiling point
  4 cups water   *1 small onion, sliced*
  2 stalks celery (including   *2 tablespoons lemon juice*
    leaves), sliced   *½ teaspoon salt*
Simmer 2 to 3 minutes. Lower fish into the liquid, cover, and simmer
(do not allow to boil). As soon as the fish is tender (5 to 10 minutes
for fresh fish—longer if the fish is frozen), remove from the liquid
and remove cloth. Cool. Remove the skin and bones from the fish,
flake, and chill. Save the liquid, as the aspic is to be made from this.
The liquid in which the fish was cooked is known as court bouillon.
Soak
  2 tablespoons gelatin
in
  ¼ cup cold water
Add
  2 cups boiling court bouillon
Stir until gelatin is dissolved. Add
  2 tablespoons vinegar
  1 tablespoon capers
  salt to taste
Chill. When the gelatin is about to jell, put a layer of the gelatin in a
wet mold, then the chilled, flaked fish and the remainder of the
gelatin. Chill until firm. To serve, turn the aspic onto a plate and
garnish with parsley, pickled beets, and lemon wedges. **Six servings.**

ONE SERVING (CONTAINS 2 OUNCES FISH)

Oil — 0 teaspoons	**Protein** — 19 grams
Cholesterol — 43 milligrams	**Carbohydrate** — 1 gram
Saturated fat — negligible	**Calories** — 110
Linoleic acid — negligible	

SALMON IN ASPIC

Soak
>   1 package unflavored gelatin

in
>   ¼ cup cold chicken broth

Add
>   1 cup boiling chicken broth

Stir until dissolved. Add
>   1½ tablespoons lemon juice (or vinegar)
>   salt
>   paprika

Chill. When the gelatin is about to jell, stir in
>   7 ounces canned pink salmon, well drained and flaked

Pour the aspic into a wet mold. Chill until firm. Unmold and garnish with parsley and lemon wedges. **Four servings.**

ONE SERVING (CONTAINS 1½ OUNCES SALMON)

Oil — 0 teaspoons	**Protein** — 10 grams
Cholesterol — 31 milligrams	**Carbohydrate** — 1 gram
Saturated fat — negligible	**Calories** — 70
Linoleic acid — negligible	

VARIATION:

Substitute water-packed tuna for salmon.

CHAPTER XVIII

Sauces and Stuffings

THE addition of a sauce to meats, meat-substitute dishes, vegetables, or desserts often will improve the flavor and make the dish more attractive. Sauces may be varied in taste by the use of seasonings, flavorings, and spices.

What Sauce Goes with What Food?

These are suggestions, and you may experiment with other combinations.

	SAUCES AND RELISHES (Recipes in this book)
DESSERTS	
Cake	Angel Food Cake Sauce
	Citrus Sauce
	Cocoa Sauce
	Fruit Sauce
	Fruit Juice Topping
	Hard Sauce
	Lemon Sauce
	Marshmallow Sauce
	Strawberry Sauce
	Whipped Topping
Ice Cream	Butterscotch Sauce
	Cocoa Sauce
	Fruit Juice Topping
	Marshmallow Sauce
	Strawberry Sauce
	Whipped Topping
Pie	Whipped Topping

Puddings	Butterscotch Sauce
	Custard Sauce
	Foamy Custard Sauce
	Fruit Sauce
	Hard Sauce
	Whipped Topping
FISH	Celery Sauce
	Cucumber Sauce
	Curry Sauce
	Egg Sauce
	Fish Sauce
	Mushroom Sauce
	Spicy Relish
	Tartar Sauce I
	Tartar Sauce II
	Tomato Sauce for Fish
	White Sauce (thin or medium)
	Vermouth Sauce
	Yogurt Sauce
MEAT	
Beef, Veal, Lamb, Ham, or Pork	Basting Sauce for Beef
	Basting Sauce for Poultry (lamb)
	Bouillon Sauce
	Celery Sauce
	Curry Sauce
	Horseradish Sauce
	Mint Sauce (lamb)
	Sauce for Broiled Meat
	White Sauce (thin or medium)
	White Sauce (thick, binding for croquettes)
POULTRY	Basting Sauce for Poultry
	Cranberry Relish
	White Sauce (thin or medium)

VEGETABLES

Bouillon Sauce
Celery Sauce
Cheesy Sauce
Curry Sauce
Egg Sauce
Horseradish Sauce
Mushroom Sauce
Mustard Sauce
White Sauce (thin or medium)

MISCELLANEOUS

Biscuit

Fruit Sauce

Creamed Soups

White Sauce (thin or medium)

Gravy

White Sauce (thin or medium)

Potato

Cheese Dressing (see Salad
   Dressings)
White Sauce (thin or
   medium)

Pancakes

Fruit Sauce

Rice or Macaroni

Mushroom Sauce
Spanish Sauce

Stuffings for Meats

Apple Dressing (veal roast)
Bread Dressing (poultry)
Bread Stuffing (fish)
"Sour Cream" Stuffing (fish)
Spinach Dressing (poultry)

Whipped Cream Substitutes

Marshmallow Sauce
Whipped Topping

SAUCE RECIPES

WHITE SAUCE

Pour into a jar
  1 cup skim milk
Add
  2 tablespoons flour
Shake vigorously until smooth. Pour into a pan and cook over low heat or boiling water until thickened, stirring constantly. Add
  ½ teaspoon salt
Add, if desired
  seasonings
  few drops butter flavoring
  few drops yellow food coloring

TOTAL RECIPE

Oil — 0 teaspoons		**Protein** — 9 grams	
Cholesterol — 7 milligrams		**Carbohydrate** — 22 grams	
Saturated fat — negligible		**Calories** — 125	
Linoleic acid — negligible			

VARIATIONS:

1. For greater richness, add 1–2 tablespoons skim milk powder.
2. For thin sauce, reduce flour to 1 tablespoon.
3. For thick sauce, increase flour to 3–4 tablespoons.
4. One tablespoon polyunsaturated oil to each tablespoon of flour may be added to the sauces after cooking. Stir well to blend. This makes a smoother and richer sauce. It increases the calories and adds polyunsaturated fats to the diet.

TOTAL RECIPE (WHITE SAUCE WITH OIL)

	Thin	Medium	Thick
Oil	3 teaspoons	6 teaspoons	9 teaspoons
Cholesterol	7 milligrams	7 milligrams	7 milligrams
Saturated fat	2 grams	4 grams	6 grams
Linoleic acid	8 grams	16 grams	24 grams
Protein	9 grams	9 grams	10 grams
Carbohydrate	17 grams	22 grams	27 grams
Calories	230	356	525

BOUILLON SAUCE

Make
   1 cup medium White Sauce★ omitting salt
Add
   1 beef or chicken bouillon cube
Stir until dissolved. **Makes 1 cup.**

CELERY SAUCE

Make
   1 cup medium White Sauce★ omitting salt
Add
   1 teaspoon celery salt
Stir in until blended. **Makes 1 cup.**

CURRY SAUCE

Make
   1 cup medium White Sauce★
mixing with the flour
   ¼ teaspoon curry powder
Add
   1 teaspoon instant onion
Simmer and stir until onion is tender. **Makes 1 cup.**

HORSERADISH SAUCE

Combine
   1 tablespoon instant horseradish
   3 tablespoons water
Let stand for 10 minutes. Make
   1 cup medium White Sauce★
substituting the horseradish mixture for 3 tablespoons skim milk in the
recipe. **Makes 1 cup.**

MUSTARD SAUCE

Make
>1 cup medium White Sauce★

Add
>1 tablespoon prepared mustard
>⅛ teaspoon pepper

Stir until well blended. **Makes 1 cup.**

TARTAR SAUCE I

Combine
>1 cup "Special" Fat Free Dressing★
>4 tablespoons finely chopped sweet or sour pickles
>1 tablespoon chopped parsley (or more)

Mix and add
>salt to taste
>pepper
>yellow food coloring if desired

Makes 1½ cups.

TOTAL RECIPE

Oil — 0 teaspoons	**Protein** — 6 grams
Cholesterol — negligible	**Carbohydrate** — 14 grams
Saturated fat — 0 grams	**Calories** — 80
Linoleic acid — 0 grams	

VARIATIONS:

1. Add 1 tablespoon minced onion.
2. Add 1 tablespoon minced capers.

TARTAR SAUCE II

Blend together
>½ cup Mayonnaise★   2 teaspoons capers
>1½ tablespoons minced green   pinch of crushed dill weed
>   onion
>1½ tablespoons minced sour
>   pickle (or sweet pickle)

Season to taste with
salt
freshly ground pepper
lemon juice
Makes ⅔ cup.

TOTAL RECIPE

Oil — 24 teaspoons	**Protein** — 2 grams
Cholesterol — 0 milligrams	**Carbohydrate** — 0 grams
Saturated fat — 5 grams	**Calories** — 1035
Linoleic acid — 64 grams	

CHEESY SAUCE

Shake in a jar until smooth
2 tablespoons flour
1 cup skim milk
Stir over heat in the top half of double boiler until mixture thickens.
Place over boiling water and add
½ cup skim milk cottage cheese mashed, blended, or sieved
(or ½ cup baker's cheese)
Season with

⅛ teaspoon minced onion	*dash pepper*
⅛ teaspoon dry mustard	*3 drops of butter flavor*
1 to 2 drops Tabasco	*paprika or yellow food*
½ teaspoon salt	*coloring*

Continue cooking over boiling water a few minutes. **Makes 1½ cups.**

TOTAL RECIPE

Oil — 0 teaspoons	**Protein** — 28 grams
Cholesterol — 16 milligrams	**Carbohydrate** — 25 grams
Saturated fat — 0 grams	**Calories** — 215
Linoleic acid — 0 grams	

MINT SAUCE

Heat
¼ cup water
Dissolve in it
1 tablespoon sugar
Add and bring to boiling
½ cup strong cider vinegar

Pour over

  ⅓ cup minced mint leaves

Cover and keep in a warm place 30 minutes before serving. **Makes ¾ cup.**

TOTAL RECIPE

  Oil — 0 teaspoons

  Cholesterol — 0 milligrams

  Saturated fat — 0 grams

  Linoleic acid — 0 grams

  Protein — 0 grams

  Carbohydrate — 16 grams

  Calories — 65

MUSHROOM SAUCE

Shake together in a jar until smooth

  ⅓ cup skim milk powder

  1½ tablespoons flour

  1 cup water

Cook, stirring constantly, until the mixture thickens. Add

  ¼ teaspoon salt

  ⅛ teaspoon pepper

  2 teaspoons lemon juice

  2 teaspoons brandy

  1 teaspoon vinegar

  ½ cup chopped mushrooms

  drop of yellow food coloring

    (optional)

  salt to taste

Makes 1⅔ cups.

TOTAL RECIPE

  Oil — 0 teaspoons

  Cholesterol — 7 milligrams

  Saturated fat — 0 grams

  Linoleic acid — 0 grams

  Protein — 12 grams

  Carbohydrate — 25 grams

  Calories — 150

VARIATIONS:

  1. Add 2 tablespoons chopped mustard pickles.

  2. Add ¼ cup capers.

YOGURT SAUCE

Combine

  ½ cup Mayonnaise★

  ½ cup Skim Milk Yogurt★

  lemon juice (omit if the

    yogurt is tart)

  salt to taste

Makes 1 cup.

TOTAL RECIPE

Oil — 24 teaspoons
Cholesterol — 4 milligrams
Saturated fat — 16 grams
Linoleic acid — 64 grams

Protein — 6 grams
Carbohydrate — 9 grams
Calories — 1070

CUCUMBER SAUCE

Combine
  ½ cup Mayonnaise★
  ¼ cup grated cucumber
  1 teaspoon chopped parsley
Makes ¾ cup.

  1 teaspoon chopped chives
  ½ teaspoon lemon juice
  salt to taste

TOTAL RECIPE

Oil — 24 teaspoons
Cholesterol — 0 milligrams
Saturated fat — 16 grams
Linoleic acid — 64 grams

Protein — 2 grams
Carbohydrate — 5 grams
Calories — 1035

EGG SAUCE

Blend and cook, while stirring, until thickened
  1 cup skim milk
  2 tablespoons flour
Add
  2 hard-cooked egg whites,
    chopped
  ¼ teaspoon salt
  ⅛ teaspoon pepper
  1 tablespoon chopped
    pimiento
Makes 1¾ cups.

  1 tablespoon finely chopped
    parsley
  drop of yellow food coloring
    (optional)

TOTAL RECIPE

Oil — 0 teaspoons
Cholesterol — 7 milligrams
Saturated fat — 0 grams
Linoleic acid — 0 grams

Protein — 17 grams
Carbohydrate — 22 grams
Calories — 155

SPANISH SAUCE

Drain juice from
   2 cups cooked tomatoes
Add
   2 tablespoons flour
Cook, while stirring, until thickened. Add
   the cooked tomatoes   *1 teaspoon sugar*
   ¼ cup chopped onion   *¼ teaspoon salt*
   2 stalks celery, chopped   *dash pepper*
   ⅓ cup chopped green pepper   *1 bay leaf, crushed*
   1 tablespoon chopped parsley *dash Tabasco*
Simmer a few minutes to blend the flavors. Taste and add extra salt
if desired. **Makes 2 cups.**

TOTAL RECIPE
   Oil — 0 teaspoons   **Protein** — 17 grams
   Cholesterol — 0 milligrams **Carbohydrate** — 43 grams
   Saturated fat — 0 grams   **Calories** — 200
   Linoleic acid — 0 grams

BROILED MEAT SAUCE

In a saucepan combine
   2 medium onions, sliced   *1 teaspoon salt*
   ¾ cup catsup   *½ teaspoon black pepper*
   ¾ cup water   *1 teaspoon paprika*
   2 tablespoons vinegar   *1 teaspoon chili powder*
   2 tablespoons Worcestershire
      sauce
Cook until onions are tender. **Makes 2 cups.**

TOTAL RECIPE
   Oil — 12 teaspoons   **Protein** — 2 grams
   Cholesterol — 0 milligrams **Carbohydrate** — 17 grams
   Saturated fat — 8 grams   **Calories** — 580
   Linoleic acid — 32 grams

BASTING SAUCE FOR BEEF

Combine in a saucepan

½ cup red table wine
2 tablespoons wine vinegar
¼ cup oil
½ cup consommé
1 clove garlic, crushed
2 tablespoons grated onion
2 tablespoons chili sauce (or catsup)

2 teaspoons Worcestershire sauce
½ teaspoon salt
¼ teaspoon pepper
1 teaspoon dry mustard
½ teaspoon rosemary
½ teaspoon marjoram

Heat the sauce to blend flavors. Baste the meat with warm sauce while baking or broiling. Remaining sauce may be poured over meat when it is served. **Makes 1½ cups.**

TOTAL RECIPE

Oil — 12 teaspoons
Cholesterol — 0 milligrams
Saturated fat — 8 grams
Linoleic acid — 32 grams

Protein — 2 grams
Carbohydrate — 17 grams
Calories — 580

FISH SAUCE

Combine in a saucepan

¼ cup dry sherry
2 tablespoons wine vinegar
⅓ cup chicken broth
2 tablespoons soy sauce

½ teaspoon Worcestershire sauce
¼ teaspoon paprika

Heat sauce. Use it warm, basting the fish while it is cooking. Remaining sauce may be poured over fish when it is served. **Makes ¾ cup.**

TOTAL RECIPE

Oil — 0 teaspoons
Cholesterol — 0 milligrams
Saturated fat — 0 grams
Linoleic acid — 0 grams

Protein — 2 grams
Carbohydrate — 15 grams
Calories — 70

VERMOUTH SAUCE FOR FISH

Combine

½ cup dry vermouth	2 tablespoons chopped chives
¼ cup oil	1 teaspoon salt
⅓ cup lemon juice	½ teaspoon pepper

Follow the directions for oven broiling or baking of fish on pages 117–19 using the above sauce for basting fish to be broiled, or for pouring over fish for baking. Use 2 pounds fish fillets or steaks. Marinate fish to be *broiled* in the sauce 4 hours before broiling, turning occasionally. **Makes approximately 1¼ cups.**

TOTAL RECIPE

Oil — 12 teaspoons
Cholesterol — 0 milligrams
Saturated fat — 8 grams
Linoleic acid — 32 grams

Protein — 0 grams
Carbohydrate — 11 grams
Calories — 550

TOMATO SAUCE FOR FISH

Combine

2 tablespoons oil	½ clove garlic, chopped fine
2 tablespoons lemon juice	1 8-ounce can tomato sauce
⅓ cup chopped onion (or 1½ tablespoons instant minced onion)	1 tablespoon Worcestershire sauce
2 tablespoons chopped green pepper	1 tablespoon sugar
	1 teaspoon salt
	¼ teaspoon pepper

Follow the directions for oven broiling or baking of fish on pages 117–19 using the above sauce for basting fish to be broiled, or for pouring over fish for baking. Use 2 pounds fish fillets or steaks. Marinate fish to be *broiled* in the sauce 30 minutes before broiling, turning occasionally. **Makes approximately 2 cups.**

TOTAL RECIPE

Oil — 6 teaspoons
Cholesterol — 0 milligrams
Saturated fat — 4 grams
Linoleic acid — 16 grams

Protein — 4 grams
Carbohydrate — 38 grams
Calories — 420

BASTING SAUCE FOR POULTRY

Combine in a saucepan
½ cup white wine
2 tablespoons wine vinegar
½ cup chicken broth
¼ cup oil
½ teaspoon rosemary
½ teaspoon orégano
1 clove garlic, crushed
1 tablespoon grated onion
½ teaspoon salt
½ teaspoon soy sauce
½ teaspoon Worcestershire sauce

Heat sauce and use it warm to baste meat while baking or broiling. Remaining sauce may be served with the meat. **Makes approximately 1½ cups.**

TOTAL RECIPE
Oil — 12 teaspoons
Cholesterol — 0 milligrams
Saturated fat — 8 grams
Linoleic acid — 32 grams
Protein — 2 grams
Carbohydrate — 7 grams
Calories — 540

SPICY RELISH

Combine
½ cup catsup
2 tablespoons India relish
Makes approximately ¾ cup.

TOTAL RECIPE
Oil — 0 teaspoons
Cholesterol — 0 milligrams
Saturated fat — 0 grams
Linoleic acid — 0 grams
Protein — 0 grams
Carbohydrate — 42 grams
Calories — 170

CRANBERRY RELISH

Put through a food chopper
    4 cups fresh cranberries (2 pounds)
    2 oranges (quartered and seeded with skins)
Add
    2 cups sugar
Mix well and chill in the refrigerator in a covered container. Makes 1 quart. **Sixteen servings.**

TOTAL RECIPE
    Oil — 0 teaspoons
    Cholesterol — 0 milligrams
    Saturated fat — 0 grams
    Linoleic acid — 0 grams

    Protein — negligible
    Carbohydrate — 272 grams
    Calories — 1120

STUFFINGS

APPLE DRESSING

Combine
    1 cup dry bread crumbs
    ½ cup chopped tart apples
    ¼ cup chopped celery
    1 tablespoon chopped onion

    ¼ teaspoon salt
    ⅛ teaspoon pepper
    ½ teaspoon poultry seasoning

Moisten with
    ¼ cup skim milk
    1 tablespoon vegetable oil
This dressing is cooked after it is stuffed into poultry or meat. Excellent for veal, chicken, or Cornish game hens. **Makes 1¾ cups.**

TOTAL RECIPE
    Oil — 3 teaspoons
    Cholesterol — negligible
    Saturated fat — 2 grams
    Linoleic acid — 8 grams

    Protein — 6 grams
    Carbohydrate — 52 grams
    Calories — 375

APPLE STUFFING FOR FISH

Combine and cook until tender
¾ cup chopped onion (or 3 tablespoons instant minced onion
    plus 3 tablespoons water)
1½ tablespoons oil
Combine
2½ cups chopped, peeled   ⅓ cup lemon juice
    apple   ½ teaspoon salt
⅓ cup chopped celery   ⅛ teaspoon thyme
⅓ cup chopped parsley
Combine the 2 mixtures and mix thoroughly. **Makes approximately 2 cups.**

TOTAL RECIPE
Oil — 4½ teaspoons   **Protein** — 3 grams
Cholesterol — 0 milligrams **Carbohydrate** — 56 grams
Saturated fat — 3 grams   **Calories** — 425
Linoleic acid — 12 grams

BREAD STUFFING FOR FISH

Combine
1 teaspoon finely chopped   1 tablespoon finely chopped
    parsley   celery stalk and leaves
1 teaspoon finely chopped   ½ teaspoon finely chopped
    onion (or ¼ teaspoon   capers
    instant minced onion)   2 cups fresh bread crumbs
Toss lightly. Add
salt and pepper to taste
any other seasonings desired
liquid to moisten
Makes approximately 2 cups.

TOTAL RECIPE
Oil — 0 teaspoons   **Protein** — 8 grams
Cholesterol — 0 milligrams **Carbohydrate** — 61 grams
Saturated fat — negligible **Calories** — 275
Linoleic acid — negligible

VARIATIONS:

1. Add 2 tablespoons oil.
2. Add ⅛ teaspoon each of thyme, marjoram, and sweet basil.
3. Add 2 tablespoons chopped broiled mushrooms or 1 teaspoon chopped sweet gherkins.
4. Or omit capers and any of the above ingredients.

"SOUR CREAM" STUFFING FOR FISH

Combine and cook until tender
  ¾ cup chopped celery .
  ½ cup chopped onion (or 2 tablespoons instant minced onion plus 2 tablespoons water)
  ¼ cup oil
Combine

1 quart dry bread crumbs	*3 tablespoons lemon juice*
½ cup Skim Milk Yogurt★	*1 teaspoon paprika*
2 tablespoons grated lemon rind	*1 teaspoon salt*

Combine the 2 mixtures and mix thoroughly. This dressing will need added moisture if cooked separately or baked on top of the fish. **Makes approximately 4 cups.**

TOTAL RECIPE

Oil — 12 teaspoons	**Protein** — 22 grams
Cholesterol — 4 milligrams	**Carbohydrate** — 143 grams
Saturated fat — 8 grams	**Calories** — 1165
Linoleic acid — 32 grams	

BREAD STUFFING FOR POULTRY

Prepare
  4 cups dry bread crumbs (bread that is at least a day old is better than fresh, but fresh bread can be dried out in a very slow oven)
Add

½ to 1 teaspoon poultry seasoning, according to taste	*½ to 1 teaspoon salt, according to taste*
3 tablespoons chopped onion	*pepper to taste*

Moisten with hot water, vegetable stock, or meat broth. Mix gently. Allow 1 cup dressing for each pound of poultry. **Makes approximately 4 cups.**

TOTAL RECIPE

Oil ___ 0 teaspoons

Cholesterol ___ 0 milligrams

Saturated fat ___ negligible

Linoleic acid ___ 0 grams

Protein ___ 16 grams

Carbohydrate ___ 122 grams

Calories ___ 625

VARIATION:

One or both of the following may be added:

1 cup chopped celery

½ cup chopped parsley

SPINACH DRESSING FOR POULTRY

Prepare

7 cups dry bread crumbs

Add

1½ cups cooked chopped spinach (save stock to moisten crumbs)

½ cup finely chopped celery

1 cup finely chopped onion

¼ cup finely chopped parsley

1 clove garlic, chopped

2 tablespoons poultry seasoning

2 teaspoons salt

¼ teaspoon pepper

Moisten with spinach stock if needed. One half of the recipe is sufficient for a large chicken. Whole recipe is sufficient for a 14-pound turkey.

TOTAL RECIPE

Oil ___ 0 teaspoons

Cholesterol ___ 0 milligrams

Saturated fat ___ negligible

Linoleic acid ___ 0 grams

Protein ___ 34 grams

Carbohydrate ___ 231 grams

Calories ___ 1060

DESSERT SAUCES

COCOA SAUCE

Mix together in a saucepan
  ⅔ cup sugar
  ⅓ cup cocoa
Add
  1 tablespoon oil
  ⅔ cup water
Cook about 5 minutes, stirring constantly. Add
  1 teaspoon vanilla
  pinch of salt
May be stored, tightly covered, in refrigerator for months. **Makes approximately 1 cup.**

TOTAL RECIPE
  Oil — 3 teaspoons   **Protein** — 5 grams
  Cholesterol — 0 milligrams   **Carbohydrate** — 149 grams
  Saturated fat — 4 grams   **Calories** — 785
  Linoleic acid — 8 grams

MARSHMALLOW SAUCE

In a saucepan combine
  ¼ cup water
  ¾ cup sugar
  ⅓ cup white corn syrup
Boil until the mixture spins a thread. Remove from heat and gently mix in
  15 marshmallows, cut into small pieces
When well mixed, fold into
  2 egg whites, stiffly beaten
If kept covered in a clean container, this will keep for a long time in the refrigerator. **Makes approximately 2 cups.**

TOTAL RECIPE
  Oil — 0 teaspoons   **Protein** — 11 grams
  Cholesterol — 0 milligrams   **Carbohydrate** — 297 grams
  Saturated fat — 0 grams   **Calories** — 1230
  Linoleic acid — 0 grams

HARD SAUCE

In a bowl mix
  ⅔ cup powdered sugar
  ⅓ cup skim milk powder
Add and mix well, until the sauce is of proper consistency
  1½ ounces rum or brandy
  3 drops butter flavoring (optional)
  3 drops yellow food coloring
This will keep indefinitely in a covered jar in the refrigerator. Allow to warm to room temperature before using. Rum or brandy not included in the analysis. 1½ ounces is approximately 110 calories. **Makes approximately 1 cup.**

TOTAL RECIPE
  Oil — 0 teaspoons
  Cholesterol — 14 milligrams
  Saturated fat — 0 grams
  Linoleic acid — 0 grams

  Protein — 16 grams
  Carbohydrate — 112 grams
  Calories — 510

CITRUS SAUCE

Mix together
  ½ cup sugar
  1½ tablespoons cornstarch
  ⅛ teaspoon salt
Add
  1 cup cold water
Cook over low heat until thickened, stirring constantly. Add
  3 tablespoons orange juice
  1 tablespoon lemon juice
Beat until smooth. **Makes aproximately 1½ cups.**

TOTAL RECIPE
  Oil — 0 teaspoons
  Cholesterol — 0 milligrams
  Saturated fat — 0 grams
  Linoleic acid — 0 grams

  Protein — 0 grams
  Carbohydrate — 117 grams
  Calories — 465

LEMON SAUCE

Follow recipe for Citrus Sauce★ but omit the orange and lemon juice and add

2 *tablespoons lemon juice*   ½ *teaspoon grated lemon rind*

TOTAL RECIPE
  Oil — 0 teaspoons   **Protein** — 0 grams
  Cholesterol — 0 milligrams   **Carbohydrate** — 117 grams
  Saturated fat — 0 grams   **Calories** — 465
  Linoleic acid — 0 grams

ANGEL FOOD CAKE SAUCE

Bring to a boil
  ½ *cup brown sugar*
  ½ *cup water*
Remove from fire and add
  2 *tablespoons brandy*
Makes ½ cup.

TOTAL RECIPE
  Oil — 0 teaspoons   **Protein** — 0 grams
  Cholesterol — 0 milligrams   **Carbohydrate** — 106 grams
  Saturated fat — 0 grams   **Calories** — 480
  Linoleic acid — 0 grams

FOAMY CUSTARD SAUCE

Blend together in a saucepan
  1 *egg white*   *pinch of salt*
  1 *tablespoon sugar*   1 *cup skim milk*
Cook over low heat, stirring constantly. Do not boil. When thick, remove from heat and fold in
  1 *stiffly beaten egg white*
  1 *teaspoon vanilla (or rum or sherry to taste)*
Makes 1½ cups.

TOTAL RECIPE
  Oil — 0 teaspoons   **Protein** — 16 grams
  Cholesterol — 7 milligrams   **Carbohydrate** — 24 grams
  Saturated fat — 0 grams   **Calories** — 160
  Linoleic acid — 0 grams

CUSTARD SAUCE

Shake together in a covered jar

2 cups skim milk or ½ cup
skim milk powder and 2
cups water
2 tablespoons skim milk
powder

1 tablespoon oil
2 tablespoons cornstarch
¼ cup sugar
⅛ teaspoon salt

Pour into a pan and cook over low heat until thickened, stirring constantly. When slightly cooled, add

1 teaspoon vanilla (or sherry or rum)
1 drop of yellow food coloring

Makes 2½ cups.

TOTAL RECIPE

Oil — 3 teaspoons
Cholesterol — 17 milligrams
Saturated fat — 2 grams
Linoleic acid — 8 grams

Protein — 19 grams
Carbohydrate — 91 grams
Calories — 565

BUTTERSCOTCH SAUCE

Boil until the mixture becomes a heavy syrup

⅓ cup light corn syrup
¾ cup light brown sugar
pinch of salt

Remove from heat and allow to cool. Beat together

2 tablespoons skim milk powder
4 tablespoons water
few drops butter flavoring

Beat into first mixture. Serve hot or cold. **Makes 1 cup.**

TOTAL RECIPE

Oil — 0 teaspoons
Cholesterol — 3 milligrams
Saturated fat — 0 grams
Linoleic acid — 0 grams

Protein — 3 grams
Carbohydrate — 243 grams
Calories — 984

RUM SAUCE

Combine in a saucepan
    2 tablespoons cornstarch
    ¼ cup sugar
    ⅛ teaspoon salt
Add and blend in
    1 cup water
Cook over low heat, stirring constantly, until sauce is thick and clear.
Remove from heat and add
    1 tablespoon rum
Serve warm. **Makes 1 cup.**

TOTAL RECIPE
    Oil — 0 teaspoons
    Cholesterol — 0 milligrams
    Saturated fat — 0 grams
    Linoleic acid — 0 grams

    Protein — 0 grams
    Carbohydrate — 63 grams
    Calories — 250

VARIATION:

Use brandy or sherry instead of rum.

FRUIT SAUCE

Blend together
    1 cup fruit jam
    ¾ cup light corn syrup
Makes 1¾ cups.

TOTAL RECIPE
    Oil — 0 teaspoons
    Cholesterol — 0 milligrams
    Saturated fat — 0 grams
    Linoleic acid — 0 grams

    Protein — 0 grams
    Carbohydrate — 404 grams
    Calories — 1615

STRAWBERRY SAUCE

Put in a saucepan and mash slightly
   1 cup fresh strawberries
Remove 2 tablespoons juice from the berries and mix until smooth with
   1 teaspoon cornstarch
Add to the berries the cornstarch mixture and
   2 tablespoons lemon juice
   3 tablespoons sugar
Heat to boiling, stirring constantly, then 1 to 2 minutes longer until
thickened. **Makes approximately ½ cup.**

TOTAL RECIPE
   Oil — 0 teaspoons   **Protein** — 1 gram
   Cholesterol — 0 milligrams   **Carbohydrate** — 53 grams
   Saturated fat — 0 grams   **Calories** — 220
   Linoleic acid — 0 grams

VARIATION:

Substitute 10 ounces frozen berries for fresh and omit sugar.

CHAPTER XIX

Desserts and Icings

THE purpose of dessert is chiefly to please the appetite. An attractive dessert, well served, can make even the simplest meal delightful. A dessert can also be used to balance the menu, supplying needed nutrients. For example, if the daily diet plan is lower in protein than is desirable, a dessert made with skim milk, skim milk powder, skim milk cheese, skim milk yogurt or egg white affords additional protein. Puddings, sherbets, and imitation ice cream containing these products are delicious and nourishing.

Fruits are easy to serve and are among our most wholesome desserts, providing vitamins and minerals as well as being refreshing and satisfying. Use fresh fruits in season and dried, canned, or frozen fruits when fresh fruits are not available.

The food chosen for dessert must be in keeping with your calorie allowance. It must contain little or no saturated fat. We have included a collection of acceptable desserts in this chapter. Others can be made from many of your own favorite recipes by substituting polyunsaturated oils for the saturated fats, as explained throughout this book. Our recipes for pies, cakes, and high-calorie desserts made with polyunsaturated oils are to be used only if the rest of your daily food intake has been low enough in calories and in meeting your fat and oil allowance to permit their inclusion.

The frequent consumption of high-carbohydrate desserts is not recommended, especially for those people who are inclined to be overweight.

Avoid the use of chocolate, breakfast cocoa, coconut, coconut oil, peanut butter, butter, solid margarine, hydrogenated shortenings, lard, egg yolk, whole milk, cream, sour cream, or cheese except skim milk cheeses. Nondairy creams, nondairy whips, low fat and imitation ice creams, and imitation sour creams usually contain saturated fat. Some products labeled "low fat" are not suitable for the diet, as the fat they contain may be saturated fat. Read the labels carefully, and if you are in doubt about a product, do not use it. Substitute for these foods which are high in saturated fat the following, which are low in saturated fat: cocoa (not the "breakfast" type; "low fat," if you can get it), the recommended vegetable oils, skim milk powder, liquid skim milk, skim milk cheeses, skim milk yogurt, skim milk buttermilk, and egg whites or egg white powder.

Some acceptable desserts can be purchased ready-made from bakeries or food markets, such as plain angel food cake or meringue shells. The cake may be iced at home, using an icing made without saturated fat, or it may be served with fruit or a suitable sauce. Fill the meringue shells with fruit or homemade imitation ice cream, ices, or sherbets, made as directed in this chapter. Some partially prepared desserts with none of the forbidden ingredients can be purchased to be finished at home, such as gelatin, certain package puddings, packaged angel food cake, and certain packaged sherbets. Finish these products using skim milk and egg whites whenever possible. The acceptable packaged puddings and custards make good sauces for other desserts.

The baking powder used in our baking is the double-acting type (combination type).

Our dessert calculations do not include icings, toppings, or sauces. See the recipes for these and add their values to the calculation of calories, fat, and cholesterol.

FROZEN DESSERTS

FRUIT ICE

Boil together for 2 minutes
  ⅔ cup granulated sugar
  1½ cups water
  dash of salt
When cool add
  2 cups pineapple juice
  ⅓ cup lemon juice
Put in refrigerator tray and freeze until mushy. Beat until smooth
Fold in
  2 egg whites, stiffly beaten
Add
  green food coloring (optional)
Continue freezing until firm, stirring once. **Six servings.**

ONE SERVING

Oil — 0 teaspoons
Cholesterol — 0 milligrams
Saturated fat — 0 grams
Linoleic acid — 0 grams

Protein — 2 grams
Carbohydrate — 34 grams
Calories — 145

Delicious served on melon or fresh peaches.

1. Orange Ice:

Substitute orange juice for pineapple juice. Omit green food coloring.

2. Cranberry Ice:

Substitute cranberry juice for pineapple juice. Omit green food coloring.

BUTTERMILK SHERBET

Blend thoroughly

2 cups skim milk buttermilk
⅔ cup confectioner's sugar
1 teaspoon vanilla

1½ cups drained crushed
pineapple
¼ teaspoon salt

Put into a refrigerator tray. Stir occasionally and serve when mushy. If it becomes too firm, beat to a mushy consistency before serving. **Six servings.**

ONE SERVING

Oil — 0 teaspoons
Cholesterol — 4 milligrams
Saturated fat — 0 grams
Linoleic acid — 0 grams

Protein — 4 grams
Carbohydrate — 46 grams
Calories — 200

VARIATION:

Substitute crushed strawberries for the pineapple.

IMITATION ICE CREAM

In an electric blender put

½ cup oil
⅓ cup skim milk powder
¼ cup granulated sugar

⅛ teaspoon salt
½ cup hot skim milk

Beat at high speed until thickened and smooth. Turn the blender to low speed and gradually add

1 cup hot skim milk

Turn back on high speed for a few seconds. Cool. In a saucepan cook together

2 tablespoons cocoa
2 tablespoons granulated sugar
2 tablespoons water

Cool. Combine the milk and cocoa mixtures and blend. Pour mixture into a refrigerator tray and freeze. When almost frozen, remove and beat until very smooth. Fold in

1 egg white, stiffly beaten

Freeze. Remove from the freezer about 10 minutes before serving. (An electric beater or a rotary beater may be used in place of the electric blender. The beating time will be longer.) **Six servings.**

ONE SERVING

Oil — 4 teaspoons

Cholesterol — 3 milligrams

Saturated fat — 3 grams

Linoleic acid — 11 grams

Protein — 4 grams

Carbohydrate — 18 grams

Calories — 260

Berry Ice Cream:

Omit the cocoa mixture. Use only 2 tablespoons sugar. Substitute 1 10-ounce package frozen berries, partially thawed. **Six servings.**

ONE SERVING

Oil — 4 teaspoons

Cholesterol — 3 milligrams

Saturated fat — 3 grams

Linoleic acid — 11 grams

Protein — 4 grams

Carbohydrate — 25 grams

Calories — 285

BASIC ICE CREAM

Sprinkle

¾ cup skim milk powder

Over

1 cup lukewarm water

Beat until light and fluffy. Continue beating and add slowly

4 tablespoons oil   *¾ teaspoon vanilla*
¼ cup granulated sugar   *dash of salt*

Pour into a freezing tray and freeze until firm. Remove mixture, put into a bowl, and beat with an electric beater until smooth. Return to freezing tray and finish freezing or freeze in serving dishes. **Four servings.**

ONE SERVING

Oil — 3 teaspoons	**Protein** — 5 grams
Cholesterol — 4 milligrams	**Carbohydrate** — 19 grams
Saturated fat — 2 grams	**Calories** — 220
Linoleic acid — 8 grams	

1. Chocolate Ice Cream:

Increase sugar to ⅓ cup and decrease vanilla to ½ teaspoon. Mix in a saucepan and cook until thick

¼ cup cocoa
½ cup water

Cool and add to the Basic Ice Cream★ recipe.

ONE SERVING

Oil — 3 teaspoons	**Protein** — 6 grams
Cholesterol — 4 milligrams	**Carbohydrate** — 26 grams
Saturated fat — 2 grams	**Calories** — 265
Linoleic acid — 8 grams	

2. Pineapple Ice Cream:

Fold into the Basic Ice Cream★ recipe

½ cup canned crushed pineapple, well drained

Lemon juice may be substituted for vanilla if desired.

ONE SERVING

Oil — 3 teaspoons	**Protein** — 5 grams
Cholesterol — 4 milligrams	**Carbohydrate** — 25 grams
Saturated fat — 2 grams	**Calories** — 245
Linoleic acid — 8 grams	

3. Strawberry Ice Cream:

Omit vanilla in Basic Ice Cream★ and increase sugar to ⅓ cup. Fold into the mixture

¾ cup crushed hulled strawberries

ONE SERVING

Oil — 3 teaspoons	**Protein** — 8 grams
Cholesterol — 4 milligrams	**Carbohydrate** — 25 grams
Saturated fat — 2 grams	**Calories** — 240
Linoleic acid — 8 grams	

4. Fresh Peach Ice Cream I:

Omit vanilla in Basic Ice Cream★ and increase sugar to ⅓ cup. Add
1 teaspoon lemon juice and fold into the mixture
   ¾ cup fresh peaches, crushed

ONE SERVING

Oil — 3 teaspoons	**Protein** — 5 grams
Cholesterol — 4 milligrams	**Carbohydrate** — 26 grams
Saturated fat — 2 grams	**Calories** — 250
Linoleic acid — 8 grams	

5. Coffee Ice Cream:

Substitute 1 cup strong coffee for 1 cup water in Basic Ice Cream★,
or add 1½ teaspoons powdered coffee to the recipe.

ONE SERVING

Oil — 3 teaspoons	**Protein** — 5 grams
Cholesterol — 4 milligrams	**Carbohydrate** — 19 grams
Saturated fat — 2 grams	**Calories** — 220
Linoleic acid — 8 grams	

6. Toffee Ice Cream:

Substitute 1 tablespoon rum for 1 tablespoon water in Coffee Ice
Cream★.

ONE SERVING

Oil — 3 teaspoons	**Protein** — 5 grams
Cholesterol — 4 milligrams	**Carbohydrate** — 19 grams
Saturated fat — 2 grams	**Calories** — 255
Linoleic acid — 8 grams	

PEACH ICE CREAM II

   Crush and measure
      2 cups canned peaches
Add
      ⅓ cup granulated sugar
In a separate bowl measure
      1 cup water
      1½ tablespoons lemon juice
Sprinkle over it
      ¾ cup skim milk powder

Beat with an electric beater until well blended and light. Combine with the peach mixture. Add

   2 to 3 drops almond extract

Pour into the freezing tray and freeze until firm. Remove to a mixing bowl and beat with an electric beater until smooth. Return to the freezing tray and finish freezing. **Six servings.**

ONE SERVING

   Oil — 0 teaspoons
   Cholesterol — 3 milligrams
   Saturated fat — 0 grams
   Linoleic acid — 0 grams

   Protein — 3 grams
   Carbohydrate — 33 grams
   Calories — 145

MARSHMALLOW PINEAPPLE MOUSSE

Beat together until thick
   ½ cup skim milk powder
   ¾ cup pineapple juice
   1 cup crushed pineapple

   3 tablespoons chopped
      maraschino cherries
   8–10 marshmallows, quartered

Freeze. **Four servings.**

ONE SERVING

   Oil — 0 teaspoons
   Cholesterol — 3 milligrams
   Saturated fat — 0 grams
   Linoleic acid — 0 grams

   Protein — 4 grams
   Carbohydrate — 38 grams
   Calories — 170

APRICOT SHERBET

Combine and boil together 20 minutes
   2½ cups granulated sugar
   4 cups water

Cool, add the strained juice of
   4 lemons
   4 oranges

Press through a sieve and add to the mixture
   12 fresh or canned apricots

Fold in
   2 egg whites, beaten stiff

Turn into a freezing tray. When the mixture is firm, remove from the refrigerator, put into a bowl, and beat until smooth. Return to the refrigerator to complete freezing. Makes about 2 quarts. **Eight servings.**

ONE SERVING

Oil — 0 teaspoons	**Protein** — 2 grams
Cholesterol — 0 milligrams	**Carbohydrate** — 80 grams
Saturated fat — 0 grams	**Calories** — 330
Linoleic acid — 0 grams	

CREAMY SHERBET

Place in a saucepan
2 *cups diced, unpeeled rhubarb*
½ *cup granulated sugar*
pinch of salt
Cover and simmer until rhubarb is tender. Cool. Combine
1 *cup skim milk*
1 *tablespoon lemon juice*
¼ *teaspoon vanilla*
Add rhubarb and mix thoroughly. Freeze in a refrigerator tray until firm. Beat until stiff
2 *egg whites*
Gradually add, beating constantly
¼ *cup granulated sugar*
In a chilled bowl break frozen rhubarb mixture into chunks. Beat until fluffy, but not melted, with a rotary beater or electric mixer. Fold into the egg white mixture and return at once to the freezing tray. Freeze until firm. This procedure gives a very nice texture to the sherbet. **Six servings.**

ONE SERVING

Oil — 0 teaspoons	**Protein** — 3 grams
Cholesterol — 1 milligram	**Carbohydrate** — 28 grams
Saturated fat — 0 grams	**Calories** — 125
Linoleic acid — 0 grams	

LEMON SHERBET

Combine and cook 5 minutes
¾ *cup granulated sugar*
¾ *cup water*
pinch of salt

Add

½ cup skim milk

Then add

½ cup lemon juice

Pour into a refrigerator tray and freeze until firm. Turn into a chilled bowl and beat well. Beat

2 egg whites

Gradually add

2 tablespoons granulated sugar

Fold into frozen mixture. Return to the freezing tray and freeze until firm.

Six servings.

ONE SERVING

Oil — 0 teaspoons	**Protein** — 2 grams
Cholesterol — 0 milligrams	**Carbohydrate** — 31 grams
Saturated fat — 0 grams	**Calories** — 130
Linoleic acid — 0 grams	

One-half cup drained crushed pineapple may be added with the lemon juice if desired.

ORANGE SHERBET

Combine in the top of a double boiler and heat until melted

20 marshmallows

1⅓ cups strained orange juice

Cool. Add

2 tablespoons lemon juice

Pour into a freezing tray and freeze until mushy. Beat until stiff

2 egg whites

Add

2 teaspoons granulated sugar

⅛ teaspoon salt

Fold the sherbet into this mixture and return to the freezing tray. Stir again when mushy, then continue freezing until it reaches the desired consistency. **Six servings.**

ONE SERVING

Oil — 0 teaspoons	**Protein** — 2 grams
Cholesterol — 0 milligrams	**Carbohydrate** — 27 grams
Saturated fat — 0 grams	**Calories** — 115
Linoleic acid — 0 grams	

Lemon Sherbet:

Substitute ⅓ cup lemon juice and 1 cup water in place of orange juice.

Pineapple Sherbet:

Substitute 1 cup unsweetened pineapple juice and ⅓ cup water in place of orange juice.

FRESH PEACH SHERBET

Scald
3 cups skim milk
Add
1 cup granulated sugar
Stir to dissolve the sugar. Cool and add

½ cup light corn syrup   *1 tablespoon lemon juice*
2 cups mashed fresh peaches   *1 teaspoon vanilla*
½ cup orange juice

Place in a freezing tray and freeze until firm. Beat until stiff
2 egg whites
Gradually add, beating constantly
¼ cup granulated sugar
In a chilled bowl break up the frozen peach mixture into chunks. Beat until fluffy but not melted. Fold into egg white mixture and return at once to the freezing tray. Freeze until firm. **Eight servings.**

ONE SERVING

Oil — 0 teaspoons   **Protein** — 4 grams
Cholesterol — 3 milligrams   **Carbohydrate** — 64 grams
Saturated fat — 0 grams   **Calories** — 270
Linoleic acid — 0 grams

FRUIT DESSERTS

FRUIT CHILLED WITH COINTREAU

Combine in a large bowl
    1 cup fresh pineapple, diced   1 box strawberries, washed
        (or 1 small can, 9 ounces,   and hulled
        diced pineapple)   1 cup seedless grapes,
    2 oranges, peeled and sliced   stemmed
Pour over the fruit
    1 ounce Cointreau*
Chill in the refrigerator 1 hour. One banana, sliced, may be added just
before serving. **Six servings.**

ONE SERVING
    Oil — 0 teaspoons   **Protein** — 1 gram
    Cholesterol — 0 milligrams   **Carbohydrate** — 23 grams
    Saturated fat — 0 grams   **Calories** — 115
    Linoleic acid — 0 grams

CLARET GLAZED PEARS

Mix together and cook slowly until sugar is dissolved
    1 cup claret
    ¼ cup granulated sugar
Peel
    4 large pears (firm-textured)
Prick pears with a fork in several places so wine will permeate. Add
pears and
    1 piece stick cinnamon
    20 whole cloves
Cook covered 20 minutes, turning at least once. When done, remove
stick cinnamon and cloves. Serve juice with the pears. **Four servings.**

ONE SERVING
    Oil — 0 teaspoons   **Protein** — 1 gram
    Cholesterol — 0 milligrams   **Carbohydrate** — 40 grams
    Saturated fat — 0 grams   **Calories** — 165
    Linoleic acid — 0 grams

* Approximately 20 calories per serving. Not included in the analysis.

HONEY ORANGE GLAZED BANANAS

Combine
  ¼ cup orange juice
  ¼ cup honey
Peel and slice in half lengthwise
  4 bananas
Place in an oiled baking dish and pour honey orange mixture over all, coating well. Sprinkle with ¼ cup chopped walnuts. Bake at 350° F. 10 minutes or until bananas are easily pierced with a fork. **Four servings.**

ONE SERVING
  Oil — 1 teaspoon
  Cholesterol — 0 milligrams
  Saturated fat — 0 grams
  Linoleic acid — 3 grams

  Protein — 1 gram
  Carbohydrate — 42 grams
  Calories — 215

PEACHES IN CARAMEL SAUCE

Combine
  ½ cup light corn syrup
  ½ cup brown sugar
  ¼ cup white, port, muscatel, or sherry wine
Bring to a boil, stirring until sugar is dissolved. Simmer, stirring occasionally, 5 minutes. Add
  8 fresh or canned peach halves
Simmer 5 minutes. **Four servings.**

ONE SERVING
  Oil — 0 teaspoons
  Cholesterol — 0 milligrams
  Saturated fat — 0 grams
  Linoleic acid — 0 grams

  Protein — 1 gram
  Carbohydrate — 68 grams
  Calories — 275

Serve warm with Whipped Topping★.

APPLE WHIP

Combine in a bowl
  ½ cup water
  1 tablespoon lemon juice

Sprinkle over and whip until very stiff
   ⅓ cup skim milk powder
Add and beat in
   2 tablespoons granulated sugar
   ¼ teaspoon vanilla
Fold in
   2 cups cold thick applesauce
Pile into serving dishes and serve immediately. **Six servings.**

ONE SERVING
   Oil — 0 teaspoons   **Protein —** 2 grams
   Cholesterol — 0 milligrams   **Carbohydrate —** 26 grams
   Saturated fat — 0 grams   **Calories —** 110
   Linoleic acid — 0 grams

APRICOT MARSHMALLOW DELIGHT

Mash or sieve
   ½ cup unsweetened, cooked dried apricots
Combine in the upper part of a double boiler with
   16 marshmallows, quartered
   ½ cup cooking liquid from apricots
   1 tablespoon lemon juice
Heat over hot water until marshmallows are melted. Pour into serving
glasses and chill. **Three servings.**

ONE SERVING
   Oil — 0 teaspoons   **Protein —** 2 grams
   Cholesterol — 0 milligrams   **Carbohydrate —** 35 grams
   Saturated fat — 0 grams   **Calories —** 150
   Linoleic acid — 0 grams

ORANGE MALLOW

Heat
   2 cups orange juice
Add and stir until dissolved
   ½ pound marshmallows
Add and mix in
   juice 1 lemon
Put into sherbet glasses. **Six servings.**

ONE SERVING
> **Oil** — 0 teaspoons
> **Cholesterol** — 0 milligrams
> **Saturated fat** — 0 grams
> **Linoleic acid** — 0 grams

> **Protein** — 2 grams
> **Carbohydrate** — 40
> **Calories** — 165

Chill and serve with Whipped Topping★.

QUICK APRICOT WHIP

Combine in the top of a double boiler
> 6 egg whites
> 2 teaspoons grated lemon peel
> 2 tablespoons lemon juice
> ¼ cup apricot juice (drained
>   from the canned appricots,
>   below)

> dash of salt
> ⅔ cup granulated sugar

Beat with a rotary beater while cooking over boiling water until mixture fluffs up and holds its shape. Add
> 1 cup chopped canned apricots, drained

Turn into serving dishes and cool. **Six servings.**

ONE SERVING
> **Oil** — 0 teaspoons
> **Cholesterol** — 0 milligrams
> **Saturated fat** — 0 grams
> **Linoleic acid** — 0 grams

> **Protein** — 4 grams
> **Carbohydrate** — 34 grams
> **Calories** — 150

Serve with Custard Sauce★.

SPICED APRICOT WHIP

Soak
> 1 tablespoon gelatin

in
> 2 tablespoons cold water

Then dissolve in
> 3 tablespoons hot water

Purée
> 1 cup cooked dried apricots (no added sugar)

Combine with
> ⅓ cup granulated sugar
> ⅛ teaspoon ginger
> ⅛ teaspoon cloves

Cool the mixture. Add
    8 marshmallows, cut into small pieces
    ½ tablespoon lemon juice
    1 teaspoon vanilla
Combine apricot and gelatin mixtures. Beat until stiff
    5 egg whites
Fold apricot-gelatin mixture into beaten egg whites. Beat slightly until
well mixed. Pile into serving dishes and chill. **Eight servings.**

ONE SERVING

Oil — 0 teaspoons	**Protein** — 5 grams
Cholesterol — 0 milligrams	**Carbohydrate** — 20 grams
Saturated fat — 0 grams	**Calories** — 100
Linoleic acid — 0 grams	

More sugar may be added if desired.

BROILED GRAPEFRUIT

  Cut in half, separate pulp from the skin with a sharp knife, remove
seeds and fibrous centers from
    3 grapefruits
Sprinkle with
    6 tablespoons granulated or brown sugar*
Broil until grapefruit is hot. Set far enough away from flame so that
the grapefruit broils rather slowly. **Six servings.**

ONE SERVING

Oil — 0 teaspoons	**Protein** — 1 gram
Cholesterol — 0 milligrams	**Carbohydrate** — 26 grams
Saturated fat — 0 grams	**Calories** — 110
Linoleic acid — 0 grams	

A tablespoon of brandy or sherry may be added if desired. This is also
an excellent appetizer.

UNCOOKED PRUNE WHIP

  Drain, pit, and put through a ricer
    1½ pounds prunes, stewed (makes 1½ cups pulp)
Combine in a bowl
    ½ cup water
    1½ tablespoons lemon juice

* Amount of sugar may be varied to taste. Adjust calorie count accordingly.

Sprinkle over it and beat until very stiff
  ⅓ cup skim milk powder
Stir into the mixture and blend well
  1½ cups prune pulp
  3 tablespoons granulated sugar
  ⅛ teaspoon salt

Pile into sherbet glasses and serve chilled. **Six servings.**

ONE SERVING
  Oil ___ 0 teaspoons   **Protein** ___ 3 grams
  Cholesterol ___ 0 milligrams   **Carbohydrate** ___ 73 grams
  Saturated fat ___ 0 grams   **Calories** ___ 315
  Linoleic acid ___ 0 grams

PRUNE WHIP
(baked)

Cook until tender
  1 pound dried prunes
in water to cover. Remove stones and chop prunes (or "scramble"
them with an electric mixer until they are well broken up. Beat until
stiff but not dry
  5 egg whites
Beat in
  ½ cup granulated sugar   *¼ teaspoon lemon juice*
  ⅛ teaspoon salt   *½ teaspoon cinnamon*
Fold in
  prune pulp
Place in a 9-inch baking dish set in a pan of hot water. Bake in a
slow oven (275° F.) until firm (50 minutes to 1 hour). Do not overcook. **Six servings.**

ONE SERVING
  Oil ___ 0 teaspoons   **Protein** ___ 5 grams
  Cholesterol ___ 0 milligrams   **Carbohydrate** ___ 61 grams
  Saturated fat ___ 0 grams   **Calories** ___ 265
  Linoleic acid ___ 0 grams

PUDDINGS, DUMPLINGS, AND COBBLERS

CORNSTARCH PUDDING

Mix together
   3 tablespoons cornstarch   *2 tablespoons skim milk*
   ⅓ cup granulated sugar   *powder*
   ⅛ teaspoon salt
Add
   ⅓ cup skim milk
Scald in double boiler
   1⅔ cups skim milk
Add the cornstarch mixture to the scalded milk and cook, stirring occasionally, until thickened and smooth. Cover and let cook 15 minutes.
Add
   1 teaspoon vanilla
   3 drops butter flavoring
   3 drops yellow food coloring
Pour into individual molds or into dessert dishes, cover, and let cool. Then chill in the refrigerator. **Four servings.**

ONE SERVING
   Oil — 0 teaspoons   **Protein** — 5 grams
   Cholesterol — 4 milligrams   **Carbohydrate** — 28 grams
   Saturated fat — 0 grams   **Calories** — 130
   Linoleic acid — 0 grams

Serve with crushed fresh or frozen berries, sweetened.

MAPLE RICE PUDDING

Stir into 2 cups boiling water
   ⅓ cup rice
   ¼ teaspoon salt
Steam 1 hour in the top of a double boiler, stirring occasionally. To
   1 cup skim milk
Add
   ¾ cup skim milk powder

Beat until smooth. Combine with the rice and cook slowly 10 minutes. Soak

> 1 tablespoon gelatin

in

> ½ cup water

Remove the rice from the heat and stir in

> soaked gelatin
> ¼ cup granulated sugar
> ¼ cup brown sugar, firmly
>   packed

> ¾ teaspoon maple flavoring
> drop of yellow food coloring

Cool until slightly thickened and turn into mold. Chill until well set. **Six servings.**

ONE SERVING

> **Oil** — 0 teaspoons
> **Cholesterol** — 4 milligrams
> **Saturated fat** — 0 grams
> **Linoleic acid** — 0 grams

> **Protein** — 7 grams
> **Carbohydrate** — 31 grams
> **Calories** — 150

Serve plain or with Whipped Topping★.

TAPIOCA PUDDING

Mix together

> 1 egg white, slightly beaten
> ⅓ cup granulated sugar
> 3 tablespoons tapioca

> ⅛ teaspoon salt
> 2¾ cups skim milk

Let stand 5 minutes. Cook over medium heat, stirring constantly until mixture comes to a full boil and is slightly thickened. Stir in

> ¾ teaspoon vanilla

Serve warm or chilled. **Four servings.**

ONE SERVING

> **Oil** — 0 teaspoons
> **Cholesterol** — 5 milligrams
> **Saturated fat** — 0 grams
> **Linoleic acid** — 0 grams

> **Protein** — 7 grams
> **Carbohydrate** — 34 grams
> **Calories** — 165

VARIATION:

Fluffy Tapioca Pudding: Beat 1 egg white until foamy. Add 2 tablespoons sugar and beat until it forms soft peaks. Very slowly add hot tapioca mixture to the egg white, stirring until blended well.

YOGURT WHIP

Make up a package of fruit gelatin using
   1 cup boiling water
   1 cup fruit juice
Chill until almost set. Beat until fluffy. Add and fold in
   1 cup Skim Milk Yogurt★
Put into serving dishes and chill. Serve with ¼ cup fresh or canned fruit over the top of each serving. **Six servings.**

ONE SERVING

Oil ___ 0 teaspoons   **Protein** ___ 3 grams
Cholesterol ___ 1 milligram   **Carbohydrate** ___ 25 grams
Saturated fat ___ 0 grams   **Calories** ___ 110
Linoleic acid ___ 0 grams

HOLIDAY PERSIMMON PUDDING

Cream together
   1 tablespoon oil
   ⅔ cup granulated sugar
Stir in
   ½ teaspoon salt
   1 teaspoon cinnamon
Mix and stir until dissolved
   1 teaspoon soda
   2 cups ripe persimmon pulp
Combine both mixtures with
   ½ cup skim milk buttermilk   *⅓ cup bread crumbs (not*
   * or sour skim milk*   *   too dry)*
   1 teaspoon vanilla   *½ cup flour*
Turn into a baking pan and bake in a medium oven (350° F.) until barely firm. **Four servings.**

ONE SERVING

Oil ___ ¾ teaspoon   **Protein** ___ 4 grams
Cholesterol ___ 1 milligram   **Carbohydrate** ___ 66 grams
Saturated fat ___ 1 gram   **Calories** ___ 315
Linoleic acid ___ 2 grams

Serve with Hard Sauce★, Foamy Custard Sauce★, or Rum Sauce★.

CORN FLAKE STRUDEL

Oil a 9-inch pan. Crush slightly
   2 cups corn flakes
Combine
   ½ cup brown sugar   *½ teaspoon nutmeg*
   ½ cup granulated sugar   *1 teaspoon cinnamon*
   ¼ teaspoon salt
Mix with the corn flakes and place half the mixture in the bottom of
the pan. Peel and core 3 pounds tart apples and slice thinly over the
corn flakes. Sprinkle remaining corn flake mixture over the apples. Drizzle over the top
   ¼ cup oil
Bake in 350° F. oven 40 minutes. Serve warm or cold. **Six servings.**

ONE SERVING
   Oil — 2 teaspoons   **Protein** — 1 gram
   Cholesterol — 0 milligrams   **Carbohydrate** — 72 grams
   Saturated fat — 1 gram   **Calories** — 380
   Linoleic acid — 5 grams

MERINGUE SHELLS

Beat until stiff
   4 egg whites
Add gradually, beating constantly
   1¼ cups granulated sugar
Beat until mixture is fine-grained and holds its shape. Add and beat in
   ⅛ teaspoon cream of tartar
   ½ teaspoon vanilla
Shape the meringues with a pastry tube or spoon on a cookie sheet
lined with aluminum foil. Bake in a slow oven (275° F.) 1 hour.
Makes 8 large meringues. **Eight servings.**

ONE SERVING
   Oil — 0 teaspoons   **Protein** — 2 grams
   Cholesterol — 0 milligrams   **Carbohydrate** — 31 grams
   Saturated fat — 0 grams   **Calories** — 130
   Linoleic acid — 0 grams

Fill meringues with Imitation Ice Cream★, fruit, Sherbet★, or Ices★.

CRUNCH TORTE

Beat until frothy
   3 egg whites
Add
   ¼ teaspoon cream of tartar
Beat until stiff but not dry. Add and stir in
   ½ teaspoon vanilla
Crush coarsely and then measure
   1 cup corn flakes
Mix with
   1 cup granulated sugar
Fold into the egg white mixture together with
   ½ cup chopped walnuts
Pour into an oiled 9-inch pie pan and bake 30 minutes at 325° F.
Cut into 6 wedges and serve with
   *1 cup raspberries or strawberries sugared or a package of
      partially thawed frozen berries*
Six servings.

ONE SERVING

Oil — 1½ teaspoons		**Protein** — 4 grams	
Cholesterol — 0 milligrams		**Carbohydrate** — 45 grams	
Saturated fat — negligible		**Calories** — 260	
Linoleic acid — 4 grams			

Top with Whipped Topping★.

MARMALADE SOUFFLE

Whip until stiff
   6 egg whites
Gradually add, beating constantly
   6 tablespoons granulated sugar
Then add
   5 tablespoons orange marmalade
Pour into an oiled double-boiler top and cook over simmering water
1½ hours or until done in the middle. (This soufflé can be held
over hot water for sometime without falling.) **Six servings.**

ONE SERVING
> **Oil** — 0 teaspoons
> **Cholesterol** — 0 milligrams
> **Saturated fat** — 0 grams
> **Linoleic acid** — 0 grams

> **Protein** — 4 grams
> **Carbohydrate** — 24 grams
> **Calories** — 110

Serve with Rum Sauce★.

FUDGE PUDDING

Sift together
> 1 cup cake flour
> 2 teaspoons double-acting
>   baking powder

> ¼ teaspoon salt
> 3 tablespoons cocoa

Add and mix well
> ½ cup skim milk
> 2 tablespoons oil
> 1 cup chopped walnuts

Spread into an oiled 8-inch square pan. Mix together
> 2½ tablespoons cocoa
> 1 cup brown sugar

Sprinkle evenly over the top of the pudding. Pour carefully onto the back of a tablespoon over the pudding
> 1¾ cups hot water

Bake in 350° F. oven 45 minutes. **Six servings.**

ONE SERVING
> **Oil** — 3 teaspoons
> **Cholesterol** — 1 milligram
> **Saturated fat** — 2 grams
> **Linoleic acid** — 9 grams

> **Protein** — 5 grams
> **Carbohydrate** — 55 grams
> **Calories** — 385

Cut in squares and serve with Whipped Topping★.

FRUIT DUMPLINGS

Sift before measuring
> 1 cup flour

Resift with
> 1½ teaspoons double-acting baking powder
> ½ teaspoon salt
> 2 tablespoons granulated sugar

Make a well in the flour mixture and add all at once
   ½ cup skim milk
Mix only until the flour is dampened. Combine and heat to boiling
   *1 No. 2½ can sliced peaches (3½ cups) (add a little lemon
      juice)*
   ⅓ cup brown sugar, firmly packed
Pour into a 2-quart casserole with a tightly fitting lid. Drop dumpling
batter by tablespoonfuls on hot fruit mixture. Cover tightly. Bake in a
hot oven (450° F.) 20 minutes, or until dumplings are lightly browned.
Serve at once. **Six servings.**

ONE SERVING

Oil — 0 teaspoons	**Protein** — 3 grams
Cholesterol — 1 milligram	**Carbohydrate** — 49 grams
Saturated fat — 0 grams	**Calories** — 210
Linoleic acid — 0 grams	

VARIATION:

For peaches substitute any suitable fruit or berries.

APPLE COBBLER

Peel and slice into a baking dish
   5 medium-size apples
Combine and sprinkle over the apples
   ¾ cup granulated sugar   *2 teaspoons lemon juice*
   ¼ teaspoon cinnamon   *⅛ teaspoon salt*
Bake 30 minutes in a 350° F. oven. While the apples are cooking, sift
   1 cup cake flour
   ⅛ teaspoon salt
   1 teaspoon baking powder
Cut into it
   ¼ cup oil
   ¼ cup skim milk
Turn onto a floured board and pat until the dough will cover baking
dish. Place the dough on top of the apples and cut slits for the
steam to escape. Bake 20 minutes in a 450° F. oven. Boil together
   ¼ cup granulated sugar
   ¼ cup water
Pour over the cobbler and bake 10 minutes more. Serve warm. **Six
servings.**

ONE SERVING

Oil — 2 teaspoons	**Protein** — 2 grams
Cholesterol — negligible	**Carbohydrate** — 62 grams
Saturated fat — 1 gram	**Calories** — 335
Linoleic acid — 5 grams	

VARIATION:

Use 2 cups fresh or canned fruit instead of apples and bake only until tender or sugar is melted.

APPLE BETTY

Combine and put in a baking dish
  4 cups sliced tart apples   *1⅓ teaspoons cinnamon*
  1½ cups soft bread crumbs
  *½ cup brown sugar, firmly
    packed*
Pour over the apples
  1 cup water
Mix together and sprinkle over top of apples
  ½ cup soft bread crumbs
  1 tablespoon oil
Cover and bake in a moderate oven (350° F.) until apples are tender (35 to 40 minutes). **Six servings.**

ONE SERVING

Oil — ½ teaspoon	**Protein** — 1 gram
Cholesterol — negligible	**Carbohydrate** — 39 grams
Saturated fat — 1 gram	**Calories** — 180
Linoleic acid — 1 gram	

Serve with Custard Sauce★.

LOW FAT SOY GRITS APPLE BETTY

Combine and put in a casserole
  4 cups sliced tart apples   *½ cup brown sugar, firmly
  1¾ cups soft whole-wheat   packed
    bread crumbs*   *1½ teaspoons cinnamon*
  ¼ cup cooked low fat soy   *1 tablespoon wheat germ*
    grits
Pour over all
  1 cup boiling water

Cover and bake in a moderate oven (350° F.) until apples are tender (35 to 40 minutes). **Six servings.**

ONE SERVING

Oil — 0 teaspoons
Cholesterol — negligible
Saturated fat — negligible
Linoleic acid — negligible

Protein — 3 grams
Carbohydrate — 40 grams
Calories — 170

Serve with Custard Sauce★.

CHEESECAKE

Cheesecake has been a favorite among users of this book. Because of the generous amount of protein supplied by one serving, this dessert is particularly useful when a low protein main dish is served.

Let soak until softened, then place over slow heat, stirring until dissolved
2 tablespoons gelatin
¼ cup skim milk
Press through a sieve or blend in an electric blender until smooth
4 cups skim milk cottage cheese (or 4 cups baker's cheese)
Add and stir until well mixed
¼ cup skim milk powder
1¼ cups granulated sugar
1 ounce chopped almonds
Add
1 teaspoon vanilla   *½ cup skim milk*
½ teaspoon almond flavoring   *pinch of salt*
½ cup chopped raisins   *the dissolved gelatin*
Turn into a pan 8 by 8 by 2 inches or into a 9-inch cake pan; place in refrigerator until firm. Crush with a rolling pin or with the side of a tumbler
¼ cup corn soya dry cereal or corn flakes
Sprinkle over the top for a crust. Cut into squares and serve. **Eight servings.**

ONE SERVING

Oil — ½ teaspoon
Cholesterol — 8 milligrams
Saturated fat — negligible
Linoleic acid — negligible

Protein — 24 grams
Carbohydrate — 48 grams
Calories — 305

The use of an electric blender makes a smoother cheesecake.

PIECRUST

Sift into a bowl
 1⅓ cups sifted all-purpose flour
 1 teaspoon salt
Mix together
 ⅓ cup oil
 3 tablespoons cold skim milk
Add all at once to the flour and stir until mixed. Using the hands, form the mixture into a smooth ball. Roll the dough between 2 sheets of wax paper on a dampened board until it is a circle about 11 inches in diameter. Remove one sheet of the wax paper. Turn the crust into a 9-inch pan. Remove wax paper. Flute the edge of the crust. Bake in a 400° F. oven 12 minutes or until lightly browned.

If the crust is to be baked with a filling, follow the cooking directions for the filling. **Six servings.**

ONE SERVING

Oil —— 2⅔ teaspoons	**Protein** —— 3 grams
Cholesterol —— negligible	**Carbohydrate** —— 20 grams
Saturated fat —— 2 grams	**Calories** —— 210
Linoleic acid —— 7 grams	

Double the recipe for a double-crust pie.

APPLE PIE

Line a 9-inch pie tin with Piecrust★. Peel and slice and arrange in the tin
 7 tart medium-size apples
Mix and sprinkle evenly over the apples
 ½ cup granulated sugar *1½ tablespoons cornstarch (or*
 ½ teaspoon cinnamon *flour)*
 ¼ teaspoon nutmeg *1 tablespoon wheat germ*
 ⅛ teaspoon salt
Sprinkle over all
 1 tablespoon oil
 1 tablespoon lemon juice
Cover with an inverted pie tin (punched with a hole to let out the steam) that will fit inside the crust to allow the edge of the crust

to brown. Bake in a 450° F. oven 15 minutes, reduce heat to 325° F., and cook 45 minutes more. **Six servings.**

ONE SERVING

Oil — 3 teaspoons	**Protein** — 3 grams
Cholesterol — 0 milligrams	**Carbohydrate** — 57 grams
Saturated fat — 2 grams	**Calories** — 375
Linoleic acid — 8 grams	

APRICOT MERINGUE PIE

Blend together
  ½ cup granulated sugar
  3 tablespoons cornstarch
  ¼ teaspoon salt
Add
  1 cup cooked dried apricots, drained
  1 cup crushed pineapple, drained
  1 cup juice from apricots and pineapple
Cook over low heat, stirring constantly until thick. Cool. Pour into a baked Piecrust★ shell and cover with Meringue for Pies★. Bake as directed. **Six servings.**

ONE SERVING

Oil — 2⅔ teaspoons	**Protein** — 5 grams
Cholesterol — 0 grams	**Carbohydrate** — 65 grams
Saturated fat — 2 grams	**Calories** — 395
Linoleic acid — 7 grams	

GLAZED BERRY PIE

Mix in a saucepan
  2 tablespoons cornstarch   *⅓ cup water*
  1 cup granulated sugar   *1 tablespoon lemon juice*
  pinch of salt   *2 cups crushed strawberries*
  ½ teaspoon nutmeg
Cook over direct heat, stirring constantly until thickened. Remove from heat and promptly add
  2 cups whole strawberries
Cool. Turn into a baked Piecrust★ and chill. **Six servings.**

ONE SERVING

Oil — 2⅔ teaspoons
Cholesterol — 0 milligrams
Saturated fat — 2 grams
Linoleic acid — 7 grams

Protein — 4 grams
Carbohydrate — 64 grams
Calories — 390

VARIATION:

For strawberries substitute boysenberries, youngberries, or other berries. If desired, top with Whipped Topping★ flavored with lemon juice, vanilla, and nutmeg.

PUMPKIN PIE

Combine
⅔ cup granulated sugar
½ cup skim milk powder
½ teaspoon salt
½ teaspoon cinnamon

½ teaspoon ginger
½ teaspoon nutmeg
pinch cloves

Add and stir in well
1½ cups canned pumpkin
Add
1 teaspoon vanilla
1½ cups skim milk (or 1½
cups water and add 6
tablespoons skim milk
powder to dry ingredients)

½ teaspoon grated orange
rind (optional)
3 egg whites, slightly beaten

Beat with a rotary beater until smooth. Pour into an unbaked Piecrust★ shell that has been lightly sprinkled with flour. Bake in a hot oven (450° F.) 10 minutes to cook the crust. Reduce the temperature to 325° F. and bake until a knife inserted comes out clean. **Six servings.**

ONE SERVING

Oil — 2⅔ teaspoons
Cholesterol — 3 milligrams
Saturated fat — 2 grams
Linoleic acid — 7 grams

Protein — 9 grams
Carbohydrate — 52 grams
Calories — 360

MERINGUE FOR PIES

Beat until stiff but not dry
   2 egg whites (or 2 tablespoons powdered egg white
      reconstituted with 4 tablespoons water)
   ⅛ teaspoon salt
Gradually beat in
   4 tablespoons granulated sugar
   ½ teaspoon vanilla
Swirl on the pie and bake 15 minutes in a slow oven (300° F.).
Six servings.

ONE SERVING

Oil — 0 teaspoons	**Protein** — 1 gram
Cholesterol — 0 milligrams	**Carbohydrate** — 8 grams
Saturated fat — 0 grams	**Calories** — 35
Linoleic acid — 0 grams	

CAKES

ANGEL FOOD CAKE

Beat until frothy
   1¼ cups egg whites
Add and beat until stiff but not dry
   1⅓ teaspoons cream of tartar
   ¼ teaspoon salt
Add gradually, beating constantly
   1 cup sugar
   1¼ teaspoons vanilla
Sift together
   1 cup sifted cake flour
   ½ cup granulated sugar
Sift a small amount at a time over the batter and fold it in until all
the flour mixture is used. Pour into an ungreased 9- or 10-inch tube
pan. Cut through the batter with a knife to remove air bubbles. Bake
in a 325° F. oven 60 minutes. Remove from the oven, invert at once,
and let stand inverted until cold. **Twelve servings.**

ONE SERVING

    Oil —— 0 teaspoons   **Protein** —— 4 grams
    Cholesterol —— 0 milligrams   **Carbohydrate** —— 31 grams
    Saturated fat —— 0 grams   **Calories** —— 140
    Linoleic acid —— 0 grams

DARK ANGEL FOOD CAKE

Beat until frothy
    1¼ cups egg whites
Add and continue whipping until egg whites are stiff but not dry
    1 teaspoon cream of tartar
    ¼ teaspoon salt
Fold in, a tablespoon at a time, beating constantly
    1¼ cups sifted granulated sugar
Add
    1 teaspoon vanilla
Sift together
    ¾ cup sifted cake flour
    ¼ cup cocoa
Sift a small amount at a time over the batter and fold it in until all the flour mixture is used. Bake in a 9-inch ungreased tube pan at 325° F. 50 minutes. Remove from the oven and invert the pan. Let the cake hang until cold before removing from the pan. **Twelve servings.**

ONE SERVING

    Oil —— 0 teaspoons   **Protein** —— 4 grams
    Cholesterol —— 0 milligrams   **Carbohydrate** —— 27 grams
    Saturated fat —— negligible   **Calories** —— 125
    Linoleic acid —— 0 grams
Sprinkle with powdered sugar, ice with any desired icing, or serve with Whipped Topping★.

WHITE CAKE

Sift
    1 cup granulated sugar
Gradually add to
    ½ cup oil

Cream together until light and fluffy. Sift before measuring
  2 cups cake flour
Resift twice with
  ¼ teaspoon salt
  3 teaspoons double-acting baking powder
Add the dry ingredients to the sugar mixture alternately with
  ⅔ cup skim milk (or use ⅔ cup water and add 3 tablespoons
    skim milk powder to dry ingredients)
Beat the batter until smooth after each addition. Beat in
  1 teaspoon vanilla
Beat until stiff but not dry
  3 egg whites
Fold them lightly into the mixture. Pour the batter into 2 lightly
greased and floured 9-inch cake pans. Bake in a moderate oven (350° F.)
about 25 to 30 minutes. **Twelve servings.**

ONE SERVING

Oil — 2 teaspoons	**Protein** — 3 grams
Cholesterol — negligible	**Carbohydrate** — 30 grams
Saturated fat — 1 gram	**Calories** — 220
Linoleic acid — 5 grams	

FEATHERY SPICECAKE

Cream together thoroughly
  ½ cup oil
  ¾ cup granulated sugar
  ¾ cup brown sugar, firmly packed
Sift together

2 cups sifted cake flour	½ teaspoon salt
2 teaspoons double-acting	½ teaspoon cloves
baking powder	1 teaspoon cinnamon

Combine
  ¾ cup skim milk
  1 teaspoon vanilla
To the creamed sugar and oil mixture, add the flour and liquid
alternately, a little at a time, beating slightly after each addition.
Beat stiff but not dry
  4 egg whites
Fold them quickly into the batter. Pour the batter into lightly oiled
cake pans and bake 20 to 25 minutes at 350° F. **Twelve servings.**

ONE SERVING

  Oil —— 2 teaspoons
  Cholesterol —— 1 milligram
  Saturated fat —— 1 gram
  Linoleic acid —— 5 grams

  Protein —— 3 grams
  Carbohydrate —— 39 grams
  Calories —— 250

CHOCOLATE CAKE

Cream together
  ¼ cup oil
  2½ cups brown sugar, firmly packed
Stir in
  4 egg whites
  ½ cup skim milk buttermilk
  2 teaspoons vanilla
Sift together and add to the batter, stirring after each addition
  2¼ cups sifted cake flour
  ½ teaspoon salt
  ⅓ cup cocoa
Dissolve and stir into the batter
  1 teaspoon baking soda
  1 cup boiling water
Beat well. Pour the batter into 2 lightly oiled 9-inch cake pans and bake at 375° F. 25 minutes. **Twelve servings.**

ONE SERVING

  Oil —— 1 teaspoon
  Cholesterol —— negligible
  Saturated fat —— 1 gram
  Linoleic acid —— 3 grams

  Protein —— 3 grams
  Carbohydrate —— 59 grams
  Calories —— 295

APPLESAUCE CAKE

Beat until foamy
  2 egg whites
Add
  ½ cup oil
Sift together and add
  1 cup granulated sugar
  1½ cups sifted cake flour
  ¼ teaspoon salt

  1 teaspoon baking soda
  1 teaspoon cinnamon
  ½ teaspoon cloves

Sift
> ¼ *cup flour*

Over
> ½ *cup chopped walnuts*
> 1 *cup raisins*
> 1 *cup currants*

Stir into the batter with
> 1 *cup sweetened applesauce, heated*

Bake in a lightly oiled loaf pan, 8 by 10 inches, in a 350° F. oven about 40 minutes. **Twelve servings.**

ONE SERVING

Oil —— 2½ teaspoons	**Protein** —— 3 grams
Cholesterol —— negligible	**Carbohydrate** —— 55 grams
Saturated fat —— 2 grams	**Calories** —— 350
Linoleic acid —— 8 grams	

Sprinkle with powdered sugar, or frost if desired.

GINGERBREAD

Sift together 3 times
> 2 *cups sifted cake flour*
> 2 *teaspoons double-acting baking powder*
> ¼ *teaspoon baking soda*
> 2 *teaspoons ginger*
> 1 *teaspoon cinnamon*
> ½ *teaspoon salt*

Cream together
> ⅓ *cup oil*
> ½ *cup granulated sugar*

Stir into the creamed sugar
> 2 *egg whites*
> ⅔ *cup molasses*

Then add, alternately with the flour mixture, beating after each addition
> ¾ *cup Skim Milk Yogurt★*

Bake in lightly oiled 8-inch pan in moderate oven (350° F.) about 40 minutes. **Sixteen servings.**

ONE SERVING

Oil —— 1 teaspoon	**Protein** —— 2 grams
Cholesterol —— negligible	**Carbohydrate** —— 25 grams
Saturated fat —— 1 gram	**Calories** —— 155
Linoleic acid —— 3 grams	

EASY WHITE CUPCAKES

Cream until light and fluffy
>   ½ cup oil
>   1½ cups granulated sugar

Sift together
>   2 cups sifted cake flour
>   2 teaspoons double-acting baking powder
>   ½ teaspoon salt

Combine
>   1 teaspoon vanilla
>   ¾ cup skim milk

To the creamed sugar and oil mixture, add the flour and liquid alternately, a little at a time, and beat after each addition. Beat stiff but not dry
>   4 egg whites

Fold them quickly into the batter. Pour the batter into small cupcake papers. Bake 25 minutes at 350° F. **Makes 24 cupcakes.**

ONE SERVING

Oil — 1 teaspoon	**Protein** — 1 gram
Cholesterol — negligible	**Carbohydrate** — 19 grams
Saturated fat — 1 gram	**Calories** — 125
Linoleic acid — 3 grams	

COTTAGE CHEESE CUPCAKES

Cream together
>   ¼ cup oil
>   ½ cup brown sugar, firmly packed

Add and beat well
>   grated rind of 1 lemon   ½ cup brown sugar, firmly
>   1 egg white   packed
>   1 cup skim milk cottage
>   cheese

Sift together
>   1 cup sifted cake flour
>   ½ teaspoon salt
>   ¼ teaspoon baking soda

Blend with the cottage cheese mixture. Fold in
   ½ cup chopped raisins or dates
Bake in lightly oiled muffin pans at 350° F. 30 to 40 minutes.
Serve warm. **Makes 1 dozen cupcakes** (Twelve servings).

ONE SERVING

Oil — 1 teaspoon
Cholesterol — 1 milligram
Saturated fat — 1 gram
Linoleic acid — 3 grams

Protein — 4 grams
Carbohydrate — 29 grams
Calories — 175

COOKIES

OATMEAL COOKIES

Beat until stiff
   2 egg whites
   ½ teaspoon salt
Gradually fold in
   2 cups granulated sugar
Then fold in
   2 cups rolled oats
   ½ cup chopped walnuts
   1 teaspoon vanilla
Moisten with
   2 tablespoons skim milk
Drop from a teaspoon onto a cookie sheet lined with aluminum foil
or Teflon-coated cookie sheet and bake in a moderate oven (350° F.)
12 minutes. **Makes 4 dozen cookies.**

ONE COOKIE

Oil — negligible
Cholesterol — 0 milligrams
Saturated fat — negligible
Linoleic acid — negligible

Protein — 1 gram
Carbohydrate — 11 grams
Calories — 55

WALNUT KISSES

Beat until stiff but not dry
   3 egg whites
Add gradually, beating constantly
   1 cup granulated sugar
Fold in
   1 teaspoon vanilla
   1 cup chopped walnuts
   pinch of salt
Drop by heaping teaspoonfuls onto a Teflon-coated cookie sheet or a baking sheet lined with aluminum foil. Bake in a slow oven (300° F.) approximately 30 minutes. To test when done, lift one from the sheet with a spatula and let it stand for a minute. If it holds its shape, the cookies can be removed from the oven. **Makes 2 dozen cookies.**

ONE COOKIE
   Oil —— ½ teaspoon   **Protein** —— 1 gram
   Cholesterol —— 0 milligrams   **Carbohydrate** —— 9 grams
   Saturated fat —— 0 grams   **Calories** —— 65
   Linoleic acid —— 2 grams

APPLESAUCE DROP COOKIES

Blend together
   ½ cup oil
   1 cup brown sugar
Add and beat until light and fluffy
   2 egg whites
Sift together
   2 cups flour   *½ teaspoon nutmeg*
   ½ teaspoon baking soda   *½ teaspoon cinnamon*
   ½ teaspoon salt   *½ teaspoon cloves*
Mix together
   ¼ cup strong, cold coffee
   1 cup thick applesauce
Add dry ingredients and liquid mixture alternately, with stirring, to creamed sugar and egg whites. Mix in
   ½ cup chopped raisins
   ¼ cup coarsely chopped walnuts

Drop from a teaspoon onto an oiled cookie sheet. Bake in a 400° F. oven 9 to 12 minutes. **Makes 4 dozen cookies.**

ONE COOKIE

Oil — ½ teaspoon

Cholesterol — 0 milligrams

Saturated fat — negligible

Linoleic acid — 2 grams

Protein — 1 gram

Carbohydrate — 11 grams

Calories — 75

SPICED DROP COOKIES

Sift together

1 cup flour

1 teaspoon double-acting
    baking powder

½ teaspoon cinnamon

¼ teaspoon cloves

¼ teaspoon nutmeg

¼ teaspoon salt

Blend together

¼ cup granulated sugar

⅓ cup corn syrup

⅓ cup oil

½ cup hot mashed potato

Combine mixtures and add

¼ cup seedless raisins

¼ cup chopped walnuts

Drop from a teaspoon on a lightly oiled cookie sheet. Bake in 375° F. oven 20 minutes. **Makes 30 cookies.**

ONE COOKIE

Oil — ½ teaspoon

Cholesterol — 0 milligrams

Saturated fat — negligible

Linoleic acid — 2 grams

Protein — 1 gram

Carbohydrate — 9 grams

Calories — 65

WALNUT DROP COOKIES

Sift together

1¼ cups flour

¼ teaspoon baking soda

¼ teaspoon salt

Blend together

½ cup oil

1¼ cups brown sugar, firmly packed

Add to creamed sugar and beat in thoroughly

1 egg white

Add flour mixture and mix until smooth. Add
1 cup coarsely chopped walnuts
Drop from a teaspoon onto a lightly oiled cookie sheet. Bake in
375° F. oven 10 minutes. **Makes 3½ dozen cookies.**

ONE COOKIE

Oil — 1 teaspoon	**Protein** — 1 gram
Cholesterol — 0 milligrams	**Carbohydrate** — 9 grams
Saturated fat — 1 gram	**Calories** — 75
Linoleic acid — 3 grams	

MOLASSES SQUARES

Blend together
⅓ cup oil
⅓ cup confectioner's sugar
Beat in
⅓ cup molasses
½ teaspoon vanilla
1 egg white
Sift together and add to sugar mixture
1 cup flour
⅛ teaspoon baking soda
Add
½ cup chopped walnuts
Bake in an oiled pan 9 inches square in a 350° F. oven 25 minutes.
Cut into 1½-inch squares and remove from pan when slightly cooled.
Makes 3 dozen cookies.

ONE COOKIE

Oil — ¾ teaspoon	**Protein** — 1 gram
Cholesterol — 0 milligrams	**Carbohydrate** — 6 grams
Saturated fat — negligible	**Calories** — 55
Linoleic acid — 2 grams	

REFRIGERATOR COOKIES
(basic recipe)

Blend together
　1 cup granulated sugar
　½ cup oil
Beat together
　2 egg whites　　　　　　*1 tablespoon oil*
　½ teaspoon lecithin granules　*1 teaspoon vanilla*
Add to creamed sugar, beating well. Sift together
　1¾ cups sifted all-purpose flour
　¼ teaspoon salt
　1½ teaspoons double-acting baking powder
Stir the sifted ingredients into the sugar mixture. Mix well. Shape into
rolls about 2 inches in diameter. Wrap in wax paper. Chill in the
refrigerator 24 hours. Slice in thin slices. Bake on an oiled cookie sheet
in a 400° F. oven about 10 minutes. **Makes 3½ dozen cookies.**

ONE COOKIE

Oil — ¾ teaspoon	**Protein** — 1 gram
Cholesterol — 0 milligrams	**Carbohydrate** — 8 grams
Saturated fat — negligible	**Calories** — 65
Linoleic acid — 2 grams	

VARIATIONS:

Sugar Cookies: Sprinkle with granulated sugar before baking.

Cocoa Cookies: Substitute ¼ cup cocoa for ¼ cup flour and sift with
the dry ingredients.

Nut Cookies: Add ½ cup chopped walnuts after the dry ingredients.

Orange or Lemon Cookies: Omit vanilla. Substitute orange or lemon
juice for skim milk and add 1 teaspoon grated orange or lemon rind to
the recipe.

Spice Cookies: Sift ½ teaspoon each of cinnamon, ginger, and
nutmeg with the dry ingredients.

Ginger Cookies: Substitute 2 tablespoons molasses for 2 tablespoons
sugar and add ¼ cup finely chopped candied ginger or 1 teaspoon
powdered ginger.

Fruit Cookies: Add ½ cup currants, raisins, or finely chopped dried
fruit.

DATE BARS

Sift together
   1½ cups sifted all-purpose flour
   1 teaspoon baking soda
   ¼ teaspoon salt
Add
   1¼ cups rolled oats
   1 cup brown sugar
   ⅓ cup oil
Add slowly and mix well
   2 tablespoons skim milk
Pack one half of the mixture firmly into a lightly oiled 8-inch cake pan.
Cook until thick
   1 package pitted dates,   *1 teaspoon flour*
      chopped   *1 cup hot water*
   ½ cup granulated sugar
Add
   1 teaspoon vanilla
When the date mixture is cool, spread it over the mixture already
in the pan. Sprinkle and pat the remaining half of the cake mixture
evenly over the top. Bake in a moderate oven (350° F.) until golden
brown (about 30 minutes). Cut into bars. **Makes 2 dozen cookies.**

ONE COOKIE
   Oil — ⅔ teaspoon   **Protein** — 2 grams
   Cholesterol — negligible   **Carbohydrate** — 29 grams
   Saturated fat — negligible   **Calories** — 150
   Linoleic acid — 2 grams

FRUIT-STUFFED COOKIES

Cook in double boiler until thick (about 15 minutes)
   1 cup chopped dried fruit (prunes, raisins, apricots, dates, figs, or
      a combination)
   2 tablespoons granulated sugar
   1 cup skim milk
Remove from heat and add
   ½ cup chopped walnuts
   1 teaspoon vanilla

Dough:

Mix

    1 cup granulated sugar
    ⅔ cup oil

Add

    ½ cup skim milk

Sift together and add gradually

    3½ cups sifted all-purpose flour
    ¼ teaspoon baking soda
    ½ teaspoon salt

Roll dough out on a piece of lightly floured wax paper. Cut into 3-inch rounds. Put a teaspoon of filling at the side of each round and fold the other side over. Press edges together with a fork and prick the top. Bake at 350° F. about 30 minutes. **Makes 5 dozen cookies.**

ONE COOKIE

    Oil — ¾ teaspoon   **Protein** — 1 gram
    Cholesterol — negligible   **Carbohydrate** — 11 grams
    Saturated fat — negligible   **Calories** — 75
    Linoleic acid — 2 grams

CORN FLAKE MACAROONS

Beat until stiff but not dry

    2 egg whites

Add gradually, beating constantly

    1 cup granulated sugar

Add

    ½ teaspoon vanilla
    1 cup chopped walnuts
    2 cups corn flakes (or other dry cereal)

Mix well. Drop by spoonfuls onto a baking sheet lined with aluminum foil or Teflon-coated cookie sheet. Bake in a moderately hot oven (400° F.) until the macaroons are a delicate brown. **Makes 3 dozen cookies.**

ONE COOKIE

    Oil — ½ teaspoon   **Protein** — 1 gram
    Cholesterol — negligible   **Carbohydrate** — 8 grams
    Saturated fat — negligible   **Calories** — 55
    Linoleic acid — 1 gram

TOPPINGS AND FILLINGS

FRUIT JUICE TOPPING

Stir in a small saucepan
> ½ teaspoon gelatin
> 2 tablespoons water

Place over low heat, stirring, until completely dissolved. In a chilled bowl put
> ½ cup chilled fruit juice
> 1 teaspoon lemon juice (optional)

Sprinkle over it
> ⅔ cup powdered skim milk

Add the gelatin mixture. Beat at high speed in an electric mixer until stiff. Add and beat in
> 2 tablespoons granulated sugar

Makes 12 servings.

ONE SERVING

Oil — 0 teaspoons	**Protein** — 2 grams
Cholesterol — 1 milligram	**Carbohydrate** — 5 grams
Saturated fat — 0 grams	**Calories** — 30
Linoleic acid — 0 grams	

Serve on cake or pudding.

MERINGUE TOPPING
(for pie or pudding)

Whip until stiff but not dry
> 3 egg whites

Add gradually
> 6 tablespoons granulated or powdered sugar

Continue beating until stiff and glossy, and add
> ⅛ teaspoon vanilla
> pinch of salt

Drop mixture by spoonfuls into a shallow pan filled 1 inch deep with boiling water and bake at 350° F. until light brown. After browned in this way, lift each portion from the water with a spoon and place on top of pudding or dessert. **Yields 12 medium-size meringues.**

ONE SERVING

Oil — 0 teaspoons	**Protein** — 1 gram
Cholesterol — 0 milligrams	**Carbohydrate** — 6 grams
Saturated fat — 0 grams	**Calories** — 30
Linoleic acid — 0 grams	

HARVEST MOON ICING

Blend in the top of a double boiler
   2 egg whites, unbeaten   ⅛ teaspoon salt
   2 cups brown sugar   ¼ cup water
Place over rapidly boiling water and beat with a rotary egg beater
until the mixture thickens and will hold a peak. Remove from the
heat and add
   1 teaspoon vanilla
Beat until the right consistency to spread on cake. Sufficient for the top
and sides of 2 8-inch layers. **Twelve servings.**

ONE SERVING

Oil — 0 teaspoons	**Protein** — 1 gram
Cholesterol — 0 milligrams	**Carbohydrate** — 35 grams
Saturated fat — 0 grams	**Calories** — 145
Linoleic acid — 0 grams	

MOCHA ICING

Combine
   1 cup brown sugar, firmly packed
   ⅓ cup strong coffee
Boil until mixture spins a thread. Do not stir, and keep the pan
covered for the first 3 minutes. Beat until frothy
   2 egg whites
Add
   ¼ teaspoon cream of tartar
Continue beating until the egg whites are stiff. Pour the hot syrup
into the beaten egg whites, beating constantly with a rotary beater. Add
   1 teaspoon vanilla
Beat until the frosting will stay in peaks. Will frost 2 9-inch layers of
cake. **Twelve servings.**

ONE SERVING
    Oil — 0 teaspoons
    Cholesterol — 0 milligrams
    Saturated fat — 0 grams
    Linoleic acid — 0 grams

Protein — 1 gram
Carbohydrate — 18 grams
Calories — 75

ORANGE ICING

Blend in top of double boiler
    2 cups powdered sugar
    1 tablespoon skim milk
    1 tablespoon oil
    3 tablespoons orange juice

1 tablespoon lemon juice
¼ teaspoon grated orange rind
pinch of salt

Do not cook but let stand over hot water for several minutes. Thin with additional skim milk if needed. Beat well and spread on cake. **Twelve servings.**

ONE SERVING
    Oil — ¼ teaspoon
    Cholesterol — 0 milligrams
    Saturated fat — negligible
    Linoleic acid — 1 gram

Protein — 0 grams
Carbohydrate — 22 grams
Calories — 90

BOILED ICING

Mix together in a saucepan
    2 cups granulated sugar
    ⅔ cup water
    2 teaspoons white corn syrup

Boil gently and keep covered for the first few minutes to prevent the formation of large crystals on the side of the pan. Do not stir. Boil to 238° F. or until the syrup spins a thin thread. Beat until stiff
    2 egg whites
    ⅛ teaspoon salt

Pour the syrup slowly over the beaten egg whites while beating constantly. Add
    1 teaspoon vanilla or other flavoring

Continue beating until stiff enough to spread on cake. **Twelve servings.**

ONE SERVING
    Oil — 0 teaspoons
    Cholesterol — 0 milligrams
    Saturated fat — 0 grams
    Linoleic acid — 0 grams

Protein — 1 gram
Carbohydrate — 34 grams
Calories — 140

SEVEN-MINUTE ICING

Blend in top of double boiler

    2 *egg whites, unbeaten*   5 *tablespoons cold water*

    1½ *cups granulated sugar*   ¼ *teaspoon cream of tartar*

Place over rapidly boiling water and beat with a rotary beater 7 minutes, or until the mixture holds a peak. Remove from the heat and add

    1 *teaspoon vanilla*

Beat well and spread on cake. **Twelve servings.**

ONE SERVING

Oil — 0 teaspoons	**Protein** — 1 gram
Cholesterol — 0 milligrams	**Carbohydrate** — 25 grams
Saturated fat — 0 grams	**Calories** — 105
Linoleic acid — 0 grams	

VARIATIONS:

Peppermint Seven-Minute Icing: Omit vanilla. Add 1 stick peppermint candy, crushed, and a few drops peppermint.

Lemon Seven-Minute Icing: In place of the vanilla, add 2 tablespoons lemon juice and a little grated lemon rind.

UNCOOKED CHOCOLATE FROSTING

Sift into bowl

    2 *cups powdered sugar*

    ⅓ *cup cocoa*

    pinch of salt

Add

    1 *tablespoon oil*

    hot, very black coffee

and beat until frosting has desired consistency to spread. Serve on cake. **Twelve servings.**

ONE SERVING

Oil — ¼ teaspoon	**Protein** — 1 gram
Cholesterol — 0 milligrams	**Carbohydrate** — 13 grams
Saturated fat — negligible	**Calories** — 70
Linoleic acid — 1 gram	

ORANGE FILLING

Measure into the top of a double boiler

2 tablespoons cornstarch   ⅓ cup water
½ cup orange juice   pinch of salt
½ cup granulated sugar

Cook over boiling water, stirring constantly, until mixture thickens. Then cook 10 minutes longer, stirring occasionally. Add and beat in

2 egg whites, unbeaten

Cook the mixture a few minutes more. Add

1 teaspoon grated orange rind

Six servings.

ONE SERVING

    Oil — 0 teaspoons   **Protein** — 1 gram
    Cholesterol — 0 milligrams   **Carbohydrate** — 10 grams
    Saturated fat — 0 grams   **Calories** — 45
    Linoleic acid — 0 grams

LUSCIOUS LEMON WHIP

Measure into the top of a double boiler

2 tablespoons cornstarch   ⅔ cup water
2 tablespoons lemon juice   pinch of salt
¾ cup granulated sugar

Cook over boiling water, stirring frequently until mixture thickens. Cook 10 minutes longer, stirring occasionally. Add

1 teaspoon grated lemon rind

Remove from heat, cool, and chill. Measure in a bowl

3 tablespoons water
1 teaspoon lemon juice

Add

3 tablespoons skim milk powder

Whip with a rotary beater or an electric mixer until stiff. Fold into the chilled cornstarch-lemon mixture, combining well. Serve on cake.
Eight servings.

ONE SERVING

    Oil — 0 teaspoons   **Protein** — 1 gram
    Cholesterol — 1 milligram   **Carbohydrate** — 21 grams
    Saturated fat — 0 grams   **Calories** — 90
    Linoleic acid — 0 grams

Serve over slices of angel food cake.

VARIATION:

Use ½ cup orange juice and ¼ cup water in place of the 2 tablespoons lemon juice and ⅔ cup water. Use orange rind in place of the lemon rind.

STRAWBERRY TOPPING

Measure after hulling and mashing
 1 cup fresh strawberries
Place in a bowl and add
 ⅔ cup granulated sugar
 1 egg white
 ⅛ teaspoon salt
Beat with an electric beater at high speed 7 to 10 minutes until the mixture forms peaks. (If a hand beater is used, it will take a longer beating period.) **Eight servings.**

ONE SERVING

Oil — 0 teaspoons	**Protein** — 1 gram
Cholesterol — 0 milligrams	**Carbohydrate** — 17 grams
Saturated fat — 0 grams	**Calories** — 70
Linoleic acid — 0 grams	

Use over sliced white cake. If strawberries are tart, increase sugar.

CHAPTER XX

Beverages

MANY beverages may be enjoyed on the low saturated fat, low cholesterol diet, but those most important are the skim milk drinks that get more of the important skim milk, powdered skim milk, fruits, and vegetables into the diet. For those who do not enjoy drinking skim milk or who desire variety, many palatable drinks can be made by disguising skim milk and skim milk powder with other foods. These beverages can be made by shaking the foods together in a covered container, beating with a rotary beater, or blending in an electric blender. A number of such recipes are included in this chapter.

An electric blender is helpful in making a smoother drink. Fruits and vegetables can be liquefied in a blender to produce a tasty drink rich in nutrients. All fruits and vegetables and their juices are acceptable on this diet. Chilled fresh or canned fruit juices are attractive when decorated with mint or fruit. Vegetable juices may be served chilled or over ice. These drinks go well with meals, as between-meal snacks, or at bedtime.

Drinks may be sweetened. Added sugar adds calories, however, and often is not needed to make the drink enjoyable. If the calories or the carbohydrates in the diet are restricted, confine the choice of a drink to those made without added sugar.

Skim Milk Buttermilk★ (see discussion on page 63) may be substituted for skim milk. If you want to use commercial buttermilk, check with your dairy to be sure butterfat flecks or whole milk has not been added to it. Churned buttermilk without added butterfat is nutritionally the same as skim milk and is a refreshing drink.

Skim Milk Yogurt★ may be used as a drink. It has an entirely different taste from that of skim milk. To drink, beat the yogurt until it reaches the consistency of buttermilk. Yogurt with fruit juices, fruits, or molasses is enjoyed by many.

Fresh egg white, skim milk cottage cheese, or baker's cheese may be added to drinks for more protein.

The addition of polyunsaturated vegetable oil to some drinks makes a smoother drink and provides some of the important unsaturated fat in the diet.

Tea, coffee, alcoholic drinks, and carbonated drinks may be used in accordance with the instructions of your physician. Do not use the artificial sweeteners containing cyclamates.* Saccharin is acceptable.

Coffee substitutes such as Postum may be used, and the decaffeinated coffees replace coffee for many people. Do not add cream or commercial cream substitutes. Canned evaporated skim milk may be used as a substitute for cream. Tea, coffee, and coffee substitutes have no nutritional value but are enjoyed for their flavor, satisfy the appetite, and add to morale. When recipes call for cocoa, use "low fat" cocoa if available; in any event, avoid the "breakfast" type, which is high in saturated fat.

Consommé, bouillon, and broths from which the fat has been removed are good drinks. They are not nutritious but are tasty as a beginning to a meal and satisfying as a warm drink between meals.

BEVERAGE RECIPES

MAPLE MILK

Beat or shake until smooth
  1½ *cups skim milk powder*   6 *cups water*
  2 *tablespoons sugar*   ½ *teaspoon maple flavoring*
Serve cold. **Six servings.**

ONE SERVING
  Oil — 0 teaspoons   **Protein** — 6 grams
  Cholesterol — 5 milligrams **Carbohydrate** — 13 grams
  Saturated fat — 0 grams   **Calories** — 75
  Linoleic acid — 0 grams

MOLASSES MILK

Mix together
  ⅓ *cup molasses*
  6 *cups water*

* See Chapter XXVI, page 401.

Add
   1½ cups skim milk powder
   ¼ teaspoon salt
Beat or shake until smooth. **Six servings.**

ONE SERVING
   Oil — 0 teaspoons
   Cholesterol — 5 milligrams
   Saturated fat — 0 grams
   Linoleic acid — 0 grams

   Protein — 6 grams
   Carbohydrate — 0 grams
   Calories — 110

SPICED MILK

Beat or shake until smooth
   1½ cups skim milk powder
   ½ teaspoon cinnamon
   ½ teaspoon nutmeg
   1 tablespoon sugar

   ¼ teaspoon salt
   6 cups water
   2 drops butter flavor if
      desired
This may be made with spice extract. Omit cinnamon and nutmeg and substitute ½ teaspoon spice extract. **Six servings.**

ONE SERVING
   Oil — 0 teaspoons
   Cholesterol — 5 milligrams
   Saturated fat — 0 grams
   Linoleic acid — 0 grams

   Protein — 6 grams
   Carbohydrate — 11 grams
   Calories — 68

MILK SHAKE I

Beat together
   ⅓ cup skim milk powder
   ½ cup skim milk
   2 tablespoons sugar
Freeze in refrigerator tray. Just before serving, add 1 cup chilled fruit juice or chilled crushed fruit. Whip with a rotary beater. Serve at once. **Two servings.**

ONE SERVING
   Oil — 0 teaspoons
   Cholesterol — 11 milligrams
   Saturated fat — 0 grams
   Linoleic acid — 0 grams

   Protein — 12 grams
   Carbohydrate — 52 grams
   Calories — 255

MILK SHAKE II

Combine
>   2 *tablespoons cooked packaged pudding (any flavor), chilled*
>   1 *cup chilled skim milk*

Blend or beat with a rotary beater. Serve immediately. **One serving.**

ONE SERVING

Oil — 0 teaspoons   **Protein** — 10 grams
Cholesterol — 7 milligrams   **Carbohydrate** — 19 grams
Saturated fat — 0 grams   **Calories** — 115
Linoleic acid — 0 grams

BANANA MILK SHAKE

Peel a fully ripe banana and slice into a bowl. Beat with a rotary beater until smooth. Add and beat in until smooth
>   1 *teaspoon oil*
>   1 *cup cold skim milk*
>   2 *tablespoons skim milk powder*

Two servings.

ONE SERVING

Oil — 1 teaspoon   **Protein** — 12 grams
Cholesterol — 10 milligrams   **Carbohydrate** — 39 grams
Saturated fat — 1 gram   **Calories** — 240
Linoleic acid — 3 grams

STRAWBERRY MILK SHAKE

Combine and beat, shake, or blend together
>   ¼ *cup crushed strawberries*   1 *teaspoon sugar*
>   1 *cup skim milk*   1 *egg white*
>   1 *teaspoon oil*

One serving.

Oil — 1 teaspoon   **Protein** — 12 grams
Cholesterol — 7 milligrams   **Carbohydrate** — 27 grams
Saturated fat — 1 gram   **Calories** — 190
Linoleic acid — 3 grams

Fruit Milk Shakes:

Follow Strawberry Milk Shake★ recipe and substitute any berries, or fruits such as apricot, peach, or pineapple, for strawberries. Sweeten to taste with honey or sugar, and blend until smooth. Additional sugar may be used. If thawed frozen berries are used, omit sugar.

PEACH SHAKE

Cut into an electric blender
  1 fresh peach, peeled (if not available, canned may be used)
Add
  ½ cup skim milk   *½ teaspoon lemon juice*
  ½ cup baker's cheese or skim   *1 teaspoon sugar or honey*
    milk cottage cheese
Blend 10 seconds or until smooth. **One serving.**

ONE SERVING
  Oil — 0 teaspoons   **Protein** — 24 grams
  Cholesterol — 12 milligrams **Carbohydrate** — 31 grams
  Saturated fat — 0 grams   **Calories** — 230
  Linoleic acid — 0 grams

May be thinned with additional skim milk. Other fruits may be substituted for the peach.

EGGNOG

Combine
  6 egg whites   *¼ teaspoon salt*
  1½ cups skim milk powder   *1½ teaspoons vanilla (or*
  1½ quarts skim milk   *grated orange or lemon*
  ⅓ cup sugar   *rind)*
Beat, stir, or shake until smooth. Chill before serving. Sprinkle each serving with nutmeg if desired. **Six servings.**

ONE SERVING
  Oil — 0 teaspoons   **Protein** — 18 grams
  Cholesterol — 12 milligrams **Carbohydrate** — 31 grams
  Saturated fat — 0 grams   **Calories** — 195
  Linoleic acid — 0 grams

QUICK EGGNOG

Combine
 1 egg white   *1 teaspoon sugar*
 1 cup chilled skim milk   *¼ teaspoon vanilla*
 pinch of salt
Beat thoroughly, sprinkle with nutmeg if desired. Serve at once. **One serving.**

ONE SERVING
 Oil — 0 teaspoons   **Protein** — 12 grams
 Cholesterol — 7 milligrams   **Carbohydrate** — 16 grams
 Saturated fat — 0 grams   **Calories** — 110
 Linoleic acid — 0 grams

CAFE AU LAIT

Dissolve
 2 tablespoons skim milk powder
in
 ½ cup skim milk
Heat slowly. Do not boil. Remove from heat and combine with
 ½ cup strong coffee or coffee substitute
 1 teaspoon sugar
Serve hot or iced. **One serving.**

ONE SERVING
 Oil — 0 teaspoons   **Protein** — 7 grams
 Cholesterol — 7 milligrams   **Carbohydrate** — 14 grams
 Saturated fat — 0 grams   **Calories** — 85
 Linoleic acid — 0 grams

HOT OR ICED COCOA

Mix together
 ¼ cup sugar
 ¼ cup cocoa
 ⅛ teaspoon salt
Stir in slowly
 ½ cup water

Boil over low flame 1 or 2 minutes, stirring constantly. Remove from heat and add

4 cups skim milk

Heat thoroughly but do not boil. Cocoa can be made and kept hot in the top of a double boiler. **Six servings.**

ONE SERVING

Oil — 0 teaspoons	**Protein** — 6 grams
Cholesterol — 5 milligrams	**Carbohydrate** — 19 grams
Saturated fat — 2 grams	**Calories** — 100
Linoleic acid — 0 grams	

VARIATIONS:

1. Beat before serving.
2. Add ¾ teaspoon vanilla just before serving. Beat 1 minute.
3. Serve 1 or 2 marshmallows in each cup.
4. Chill and serve with cracked ice.

SPICED COCOA

Combine and beat until smooth

1 egg white
½ teaspoon cinnamon
¼ cup cocoa
⅓ cup water

2 tablespoons skim milk powder
2 tablespoons oil
1 tablespoon sugar

Scald

1 quart skim milk

Slowly add the scalded milk to the cocoa mixture, beating constantly with a rotary beater over low heat. Serve when hot but do not allow to boil. **Six servings.**

ONE SERVING

Oil — 1 teaspoon	**Protein** — 7 grams
Cholesterol — 5 milligrams	**Carbohydrate** — 13 grams
Saturated fat — 1 gram	**Calories** — 125
Linoleic acid — 3 grams	

MOCHA FLOAT

Put into a saucepan

4 tablespoons cocoa
¼ cup water

Bring to a boil and cook 2 minutes. Cool and put into an electric blender. Add

2 teaspoons instant coffee   1½ cups cold skim milk
2 tablespoons sugar   2 tablespoons skim milk
dash of salt   powder

Cover and blend on high speed 15 seconds or until smooth. Pour into 2 tall glasses. **Two servings.**

ONE SERVING

Oil — 0 teaspoons   **Protein** — 9 grams
Cholesterol — 7 milligrams   **Carbohydrate** — 29 grams
Saturated fat — 2 grams   **Calories** — 170
Linoleic acid — negligible

SKIM MILK POWDER COCOA

Mix together in the top of a double boiler

¼ cup sugar   1 cup skim milk powder
¼ cup cocoa   ⅛ teaspoon salt

Add slowly, stirring until smooth

2 cups skim milk

Cook over low heat, stirring constantly, until hot. Do not boil. Add

2 cups skim milk

and heat in double boiler. **Six servings.**

ONE SERVING

Oil — 0 teaspoons   **Protein** — 10 grams
Cholesterol — 5 milligrams   **Carbohydrate** — 25 grams
Saturated fat — 0 grams   **Calories** — 140
Linoleic acid — 0 grams

FRUIT PUNCH

Pour

2 cups boiling water

over

8 teaspoons tea

Cool. Combine

2 cups sugar
2½ quarts hot water

Stir until dissolved and add
   1 cup grated pineapple
   1 cup orange juice
   1 cup grape juice
Add the strong tea and chill. One gallon, or **32 servings.**

ONE SERVING
   Oil — 0 teaspoons   **Protein** — negligible
   Cholesterol — 0 milligrams   **Carbohydrate** — 16 grams
   Saturated fat — 0 grams   **Calories** — 65
   Linoleic acid — 0 grams

CRANBERRY PUNCH

   Combine in a large pitcher
   2 cups cranberry juice cocktail
   2 cups grapefruit juice
   1½ cups pineapple juice
Chill and serve over ice in tall glasses. **Six servings.**

ONE SERVING
   Oil — 0 teaspoons   **Protein** — negligible
   Cholesterol — 0 milligrams   **Carbohydrate** — 33 grams
   Saturated fat — 0 grams   **Calories** — 130
   Linoleic acid — 0 grams

COWELL PUNCH

   Bring to a boil
   1 cup juice from canned fruit (peach, pear, or apricot)
   1 cup water
   ¼ cup sugar
Add these spices and remove at once from heat
   4 whole cloves
   ½ teaspoon nutmeg
   ¼ teaspoon cinnamon
Cool, strain, and add to
   1 cup orange juice
   1 cup pineapple juice
   juice and grated rind of 1 or 2 limes (or 1 lemon)

When ready to serve, add ice cubes made of diluted fruit juice. Add
12 ounces ginger ale
and serve. **Six servings.**

ONE SERVING

Oil — 0 teaspoons   Protein — negligible
Cholesterol — 0 milligrams   Carbohydrate — 31 grams
Saturated fat — 0 grams   Calories — 125
Linoleic acid — 0 grams

SPARKLING FRUIT JUICES

Fill a large glass with cracked ice and pour over it
4 ounces fruit juice
Fill with
sparkling water
One serving.

ONE SERVING

Oil — 0 teaspoons   Protein — negligible
Cholesterol — 0 milligrams   Carbohydrate — 13 grams
Saturated fat — 0 grams   Calories — 50
Linoleic acid — 0 grams

FRUIT JUICE AND MILK SHAKES

Pineapple—Combine equal parts pineapple juice and skim milk in a
covered container and shake. Ice may be added and the mixture may
be stirred in an electric blender.

Many variations of the above recipe can be made by combining
skim milk with juices such as prune juice, grape juice, canned fruit
syrups, grapefruit juice, cranberry juice, or orange juice. An egg white
may be added for extra protein, and it makes a fluffy drink. Both
the juice and the milk should be well chilled. If a blender is used,
whole fruit may be added and blended until liquefied. The drinks may
be sweetened with sugar or honey if desired.

ORANGE-APRICOT NECTAR

Into an electric blender put
2 cups orange juice   *½ cup cooked apricots*
3 tablespoons lemon juice   *1 cup cracked ice*

Blend covered on high speed 10 seconds or until smooth and frothy.
Four servings.

ONE SERVING

Oil — 0 teaspoons
Cholesterol — 0 milligrams
Saturated fat — 0 grams
Linoleic acid — 0 grams

Protein — 2 grams
Carbohydrate — 21 grams
Calories — 85

GINGER ALE PUNCH

Blend and chill
    ¾ cup grapefruit juice
    ¾ cup orange juice
When ready to serve, add
    1 pint ginger ale
    sprig of mint
Makes about 1 quart. **Six servings.**

    ¼ cup lemon juice
    ⅓ cup granulated sugar

ONE SERVING

Oil — 0 teaspoons
Cholesterol — 0 milligrams
Saturated fat — 0 grams
Linoleic acid — 0 grams

Protein — negligible
Carbohydrate — 27 grams
Calories — 110

HOT TOMATO JUICE APPETIZER

Combine in a saucepan
    1½ cups tomato juice
    3 cups water
    ½ teaspoon onion juice
Add and beat until smooth
    ¾ cup skim milk powder
Heat quickly to drinking temperature, stirring constantly. Serve at once.
Six servings.

    ½ teaspoon lemon juice
    1 teaspoon salt
    2 or 3 drops Tabasco

ONE SERVING

Oil — 0 teaspoons
Cholesterol — 3 milligrams
Saturated fat — 0 grams
Linoleic acid — 0 grams

' **Protein** — 4 grams
Carbohydrate — 7 grams
Calories — 45

VEGETABLE FRUIT COCKTAIL

Slice into an electric blender
   1 carrot, scrubbed and unpeeled
Add and blend at high speed
   2 cups pineapple juice
Add

¼ apple, cored and unpeeled
½ banana, peeled
1 small stalk celery, sliced
3 or 4 slices cucumber, unpeeled

½ orange, peeled
2 teaspoons lemon juice
¼ small green pepper, seeds removed

Blend until ingredients are liquefied. **Four servings.**

ONE SERVING
   Oil — 0 teaspoons
   Cholesterol — 0 milligrams
   Saturated fat — 0 grams
   Linoleic acid — 0 grams

   Protein — 1 gram
   Carbohydrate — 25 grams
   Calories — 105

VEGETABLE COCKTAIL

Put into an electric blender and blend at low speed
   2¼ cups tomato juice
   1 sprig parsley
   1 slice lemon, unpeeled
Add

¼ small green pepper, seeds removed
1 stalk celery, sliced
¼ teaspoon salt

⅛ teaspoon Worcestershire sauce
¼ cup chipped ice

Turn on high speed and blend until ingredients are liquefied. **Four servings.**

ONE SERVING
   Oil — 0 teaspoons
   Cholesterol — 0 milligrams
   Saturated fat — 0 grams
   Linoleic acid — 0 grams

   Protein — 1 gram
   Carbohydrate — 5 grams
   Calories — 30

VEGETABLE JUICE COCKTAIL

Blend or stir
  2 *cups vegetable juice, such*
    as tomato juice
  2 *tablespoons lemon juice*
  2 *drops Tabasco*

  ½ *teaspoon* Worcestershire
    sauce
  ½ *teaspoon onion juice*
  ½ *teaspoon salt or to taste*

Chill and serve. **Three servings.**

ONE SERVING
  Oil — 0 teaspoons
  Cholesterol — 0 milligrams
  Saturated fat — 0 grams
  Linoleic acid — 0 grams

  Protein — 1 gram
  Carbohydrate — 6 grams
  Calories — 30

MIXED FRUIT FLIP

Place in 12-ounce glass
  1 *rounded tablespoon Orange Sherbet*★ (*or other fruit sherbet*)
Fill the glass with unsweetened pineapple juice, chilled. **One serving.**

ONE SERVING
  Oil — 0 teaspoons
  Choleseterol — 0 milligrams
  Saturated fat — 0 grams
  Linoleic acid — 0 grams

  Protein — 0 grams
  Carbohydrate — 39 grams
  Calories — 160

Ginger ale may be substituted for the pineapple juice.

FRUIT YOGURT

Beat together until smooth
>   1 cup pineapple juice (or other fruit or berry juices)
>   ¼ cup skim milk powder

Add and beat in
>   1 cup Skim Milk Yogurt★

Serve chilled. **Two servings.**

ONE SERVING

>   **Oil** — 0 teaspoons   **Protein** — 8 grams
>   **Cholesterol** — 0 milligrams **Carbohydrate** — 28 grams
>   **Saturated fat** — 6 grams   **Calories** — 145
>   **Linoleic acid** — 0 grams

Sweeten to taste with honey if desired.

MULLED CIDER

Measure into a saucepan
>   2 cups apple cider

Add
>   6 whole cloves   1 tablespoon lemon juice
>   1-inch cinnamon stick   1 tablespoon sugar

Simmer until hot. Serve at once. **Two servings.**

ONE SERVING

>   **Oil** — 0 teaspoons   **Protein** — negligible
>   **Cholesterol** — 0 milligrams **Carbohydrate** — 37 grams
>   **Saturated fat** — 0 grams   **Calories** — 150
>   **Linoleic acid** — 0 grams

MINT COOLER

Boil together for several minutes
>   1 cup sugar
>   1 cup water

Pour over a large handful of crushed mint leaves. Cool and strain. Squeeze juice (about 15 ounces) from
>   6 lemons
>   2 oranges

Add to mint syrup. Place ⅛ of mixture in each glass, add cracked ice, and fill the glasses with charged water. Garnish with sugared mint leaves. **Eight servings.**

ONE SERVING

Oil — 0 teaspoons
Cholesterol — 0 milligrams
Saturated fat — 0 grams
Linoleic acid — 0 grams

Protein — 1 gram
Carbohydrate — 35 grams
Calories — 140

VARIATION:

Ginger ale may be used instead of charged water.

CHAPTER XXI

Appetizers, Snacks, and
Sandwich Spreads

A common custom is to serve guests a few snacks, hors
d'oeuvres, or canapés with an alcoholic or nonalcoholic drink before dinner. This custom, if enjoyed, need not be discarded. An
attractive and appetizing tray can be assembled in keeping with the
diet, and this luxury may be enjoyed in moderation. Recipes are given
in this chapter, and others can be advised following the principles set
down in this book. To be acceptable in this diet, all canapés, hors
d'oeuvres, and snacks must contain little or no saturated fat. A dieter
must always keep in mind the caloric allowance of his particular diet
and choose accordingly.

Canapés are small, open-faced sandwiches or closed sandwiches cut
into interesting shapes. They are filled with a tasty spread and garnished
to be attractive. The base of the canapé may be any kind of bread
or cracker that meets the low saturated fat, low cholesterol diet requirements. It may be toast, cold-water crackers, rye crackers, melba toast,
Norwegian flat bread, wheat wafers, rice crackers, matzos, or bread.
If bread is used, it should be thinly sliced and the crusts removed.
If toast is desired, preheat the broiler and put the bread on the broiler
rack about three inches from the heat element. It may be toasted
on one side and spread on the other side with a seasoned spread, or
it may be toasted on both sides. If desired, it may be sautéed in
an acceptable vegetable oil in a heavy skillet. When golden brown, drain
on an absorbent paper. Bread may also be used untoasted. Mexican
tortillas do not contain fat. They may be cut into pie-shaped wedges
and fried in a little vegetable oil to use with the cheese dips, or they
may be salted and eaten as a cracker or chip.

The spread may consist of well-seasoned "Special" Cottage Cheese★
combined with chopped celery, cucumber, onion, watercress, or tomato,

moistened with salad dressings given in this book or with lemon, lime, or onion juice, and seasoned with suitable spices. Other canapés may be made of slices of tomato aspic or cucumber aspic or spread with jelly, jam, or chopped dried fruits. "Special" Cottage Cheese★ and the skim milk cheeses afford many possibilities.

Hors d'oeuvres are often arranged on toothpicks so that they may be easily eaten. Stud a grapefruit or a small red cabbage with the filled toothpicks, or use a metal or crockery frame designed to hold the toothpicks. Use pickles, pickled pearl onions, radishes, pickled carrots, celery, beets, brandied fruits, pickled fruits, fresh fruits, well-seasoned mushrooms, cucumber, cauliflower, zucchini, tomato, and dried fruits. Serve dips of blended or sieved "Special" Cottage Cheese★ or baker's cheese thinned with skim milk or Skim Milk Yogurt★ or salad dressing. These should be well seasoned and accompanied with thin toast, tortilla wedges, or raw vegetables such as sliced cucumber, sliced green pepper, celery sticks, carrot sticks, green onions, zucchini sticks, cauliflowerets, or cooked artichoke hearts.

For those who do not care for an alcoholic drink, or for those whose Daily Food Guide does not permit the inclusion of alcohol, a pleasant substitute is vegetable juice, fruit juice, or a cup of hot bouillon, consommé or fat free broth. A thoughtful hostess enjoys providing for these guests.

Any fruit, vegetable, or harmonious combination of juices may be served, garnished with lemon, mint, or lime. If a fruit cocktail is served, it is usually a first course of a meal. It may consist of any fruit (except avocado) or combination of fruits. If desired, a little sherry, brandy, lemon juice, or lime juice may be added to the fruit. A vegetable cocktail may consist of any combination of interesting vegetables. Garnish with chili sauce, catsup, lemon, lime, parsley, onion juice, and spices if desired.

Snacks are for between-meal eating, and their purpose is to supplement the diet or satisfy the appetite. Their nutritional value is enhanced when they are served with a skim milk drink or fruit juice. The snack may consist of a sandwich, canapé, hors d'oeuvre, Brown Bread★ spread with Walnut Butter★, jelly or jam, Banana Bread★, angel food cake, toast, or fresh, dried, or glazed fruits.

Suggestions for Fruit Cocktails

1. Pineapple cubes and cantaloupe balls.
2. Banana, orange, and pineapple garnished with a maraschino cherry and sugar if desired.
3. Orange and grapefruit sections garnished with a sprig of mint.

4. Coarsely chopped unpeeled apple, celery, and green pepper sprinkled with lemon juice.

5. Pineapple, banana, orange, and strawberries with lemon juice and sugar if desired.

6. Watermelon, cantaloupe, and honeydew melon balls with lime juice, garnished with fresh mint leaves.

7. Pears, peaches, raspberries, and pineapple with 1 tablespoon brandy and powdered sugar.

8. Grapefruit and strawberries with 1 tablespoon sherry and powdered sugar. Garnish with a sugared, unhulled strawberry.

9. Hollow out a grapefruit and fill with grapefruit and orange sections, then broil. Garnish with a sprig of watercress.

10. Grapefruit sections combined with any diced fruits, with 1 tablespoon mint jelly cut in pieces.

APPETIZER AND SNACK RECIPES

CHEESE DIP FOR RAW VEGETABLES

Place in an electric blender and beat until smooth (about 1 minute)
¼ cup skim milk (or ⅓ cup skim milk yogurt)
½ cup skim milk cottage cheese
½ teaspoon salt
Turn the cheese mixture into a small bowl. Place in the center of a large round serving plate. Surround with carrot sticks, celery curls, cucumber sticks, radishes, green onions, green pepper sticks, and cauliflowerets.

TOTAL RECIPE (VEGETABLES NOT IN CALCULATIONS)

Oil — 0 teaspoons	**Protein** — 21 grams
Cholesterol — 10 milligrams	**Carbohydrate** — 6 grams
Saturated fat — 0 grams	**Calories** — 110
Linoleic acid — 0 grams	

Add one of the following flavorings:

1. *½ teaspoon celery salt*
⅛ teaspoon monosodium glutamate
dash of onion salt

2. *1 ounce anchovies*
Put the fish in a sieve and run warm water through to remove the oil. Cool, and blend into the cheese; chop.

3. *¼ teaspoon garlic salt*
   1½ teaspoons lemon juice
   dash of Tabasco

COTTAGE CHEESE CANAPE SPREAD

Force through a sieve
   2 cups skim milk cottage cheese
and blend with
   ¼ bouillon cube dissolved in   *2 or 3 drops onion juice*
   3 tablespoons water   *salt*
Beat vigorously and chill. Serve as a spread on cold-water crackers or
toast. Any of these seasonings may also be added:
   ¼ teaspoon celery seeds (or   *⅛ teaspoon sweet basil*
   more)   *1 drop liquid smoke*
   2 or 3 drops tarragon vinegar
Makes approximately 2 cups.

TOTAL RECIPE (CRACKERS OR TOAST NOT IN CALCULATIONS)
   Oil — 0 teaspoons   **Protein** — 76 grams
   Cholesterol — 32 milligrams   **Carbohydrate** — 12 grams
   Saturated fat — 0 grams   **Calories** — 370
   Linoleic acid — 0 grams

CUCUMBER CANAPE

Marinate
   thinly sliced cucumber (medium-size)
in
   Fat Free French Dressing★ (or Low Fat French Dressing★)
Cut and toast
   bread rounds
and arrange the cucumber slices on the toast.
   salt and pepper to taste
Sprinkle with
   paprika
Twelve servings.

TOTAL RECIPE (BREAD NOT IN CALCULATIONS)
   Oil — 0 teaspoons   **Protein** — negligible
   Cholesterol — 0 milligrams   **Carbohydrate** — 4 grams
   Saturated fat — 0 grams   **Calories** — 15
   Linoleic acid — 0 grams

COTTAGE CHEESE SPREAD

Mix together and blend with a fork
<table>
<tr><td>¾ cup skim milk cottage
cheese
¼ teaspoon salt</td><td>1 teaspoon chopped chives
1½ teaspoons grated onion
1 tablespoon Mayonnaise★</td></tr>
</table>

Thin with equal parts skim milk and oil. Refrigerate to blend flavors. Serve on toast or crackers. **Makes approximately 1 cup.**

TOTAL RECIPE (TOAST OR CRACKERS NOT IN CALCULATIONS)

Oil — 3 teaspoons	**Protein** — 29 grams
Cholesterol — 12 milligrams	**Carbohydrate** — 6 grams
Saturated fat — 2 grams	**Calories** — 275
Linoleic acid — 8 grams	

PINEAPPLE CHEESE SPREAD

Mix together
   ½ cup skim milk cottage cheese or baker's cheese
   ¼ cup crushed pineapple
   ½ teaspoon lemon juice
Spread on crackers or toast. **Makes approximately 1 cup.**

TOTAL RECIPE (CRACKERS OR TOAST NOT IN CALCULATIONS)

Oil — 0 teaspoons	**Protein** — 19 grams
Cholesterol — 8 milligrams	**Carbohydrate** — 16 grams
Saturated fat — 0 grams	**Calories** — 145
Linoleic acid — 0 grams	

SEASONED CHEESE DIP

Combine
<table>
<tr><td>1 cup whipped skim milk
cottage cheese or baker's
cheese
1 to 2 tablespoons steak sauce</td><td>1 tablespoon chili sauce
seasoning salts or chopped
parsley, onion, or garlic if
desired</td></tr>
</table>

Makes approximately 1 cup.

TOTAL RECIPE

Oil — 0 teaspoons	**Protein** — 38 grams
Cholesterol — 16 milligrams	**Carbohydrate** — 13 grams
Saturated fat — 0 grams	**Calories** — 215
Linoleic acid — 0 grams	

CHILI DIP

Combine and chill
1 cup Mayonnaise★
¼ cup chili sauce
¼ cup catsup
2 tablespoons horseradish

2 tablespoons lemon juice or
  vinegar
dash of Tabasco or a few
  grains of cayenne

Serve as a dip for crisp raw vegetables. **Makes approximately 1¾ cups.**

TOTAL RECIPE (VEGETABLES NOT IN CALCULATIONS)
Oil — 48 teaspoons
Cholesterol — 0 milligrams
Saturated fat — 32 grams
Linoleic acid — 128 grams

Protein — 4 grams
Carbohydrate — 38 grams
Calories — 2285

BASIC CHEESE DIP

Blend in an electric blender
1 cup baker's cheese or skim
  milk cottage cheese
1 tablespoon lemon juice
2 tablespoons oil

½ teaspoon sugar
3 to 6 tablespoons skim milk
  buttermilk or skim milk
  (as needed to thin)

Blend on high speed 10 seconds. **Makes approximately 1½ cups.**

TOTAL RECIPE
Oil — 6 teaspoons
Cholesterol — 17 milligrams
Saturated fat — 4 grams
Linoleic acid — 16 grams

Protein — 40 grams
Carbohydrate — 10 grams
Calories — 460

Basic recipe is delicious on fruit or berries; for example, with strawberries and brown sugar. It is also a base for dips and spreads.

VARIATIONS:

Add any or all of these seasonings:
2 teaspoons scraped onion
1 teaspoon celery salt
⅛ teaspoon monosodium glutamate
¼ teaspoon dry thyme and marjoram
1 teaspoon minced parsley

Blend well and refrigerate to blend flavors.

NOTE: Many other seasoning salts, spices, herbs, vegetables, and sauces can be used to vary the taste.

SEASONED MUSHROOMS I

Marinate
  ½ cup button mushrooms
in
  Fat Free French Dressing★
Roll in
  finely chopped parsley
Sprinkle with
  paprika
Serve on toothpicks.

TOTAL RECIPE

Oil — 0 teaspoons   **Protein** — 4 grams
Cholesterol — 0 milligrams   **Carbohydrate** — 4 grams
Saturated fat — 0 grams   **Calories** — 30
Linoleic acid — 0 grams

ASPIC CANAPES

Prepare
  Tomato or Cucumber Aspic★
Mold in a small glass or pour a ½-inch layer in a pan. Unmold and slice rounds or cut fancy shapes from the sheet of aspic. Fit onto toast and garnish with
  "Special" Fat Free Dressing★ or Mayonnaise★
    parsley, watercress leaves, or a slice of stuffed green olive
Four servings.

TOTAL RECIPE

Oil — 0 teaspoons   **Protein** — 4 grams
Cholesterol — negligible   **Carbohydrate** — 8 grams
Saturated fat — 0 grams   **Calories** — 48
Linoleic acid — 0 grams

CELERY STICKS

Prepare
  4 celery sticks
Dip in
  "Special" Fat Free Dressing★ or Mayonnaise★

Then dip in
   paprika
Chill.

TOTAL RECIPE

   Oil — 0 teaspoons
   Cholesterol — negligible
   Saturated fat — 0 grams
   Linoleic acid — 0 grams

   Protein — 1 gram
   Carbohydrate — 2 grams
   Calories — 15

STUFFED CELERY

Mix
   *1 cup sieved skim milk
   cottage cheese*
   *2 tablespoons grated
   horseradish*

   *⅛ to ¼ teaspoon Tabasco
   salt*

Fill celery stalks. Sprinkle with
   paprika
Chill.

ONE SERVING

   Oil — 0 teaspoons
   Cholesterol — 2 milligrams
   Saturated fat — negligible
   Linoleic acid — negligible

   Protein — 3 grams
   Carbohydrate — 2 grams
   Calories — 30

WATERCRESS CANAPE

Spread
   2 toast rounds
Generously with
   2 tablespoons "Special" Fat Free Dressing★ or Mayonnaise★
Dip into
   finely minced watercress
Sprinkle with
   salt
Garnish with
   grated hard-cooked egg white

TOTAL RECIPE

   Oil — 0 teaspoons
   Cholesterol — 0 milligrams
   Saturated fat — 0 grams
   Linoleic acid — 0 grams

   Protein — 2 grams
   Carbohydrate — 10 grams
   Calories — 50

FRUIT KEBOBS

Prepare fruit in small bite-size pieces, using
  pineapple   *Orange*
  small melon balls or squares   *Grapefruit*
  peach
Wash and remove stems and hulls from
  berries
  grapes
  cherries
Combine and marinate in
  sherry
Chill in the refrigerator. To serve, alternate the fruits on small sticks
or toothpicks. When fresh fruit is not available, use canned fruit cocktail,
drained.

TASTY CHEESE DIP

Press through a fine sieve or blend in an electric blender for a smoother
dip
  2 cups skim milk cottage cheese or baker's cheese
Add
  ½ cup Skim Milk Yogurt★   *1 tablespoon Worcestershire*
  2 teaspoons seasoning salt   *sauce*
  2 teaspoons chopped parsley
Refrigerate for an hour or more to blend the flavors. Serve in a bowl
surrounded by chilled crisped raw vegetables or suitable toast or crackers. **Makes approximately 2½ cups.**

TOTAL RECIPE (VEGETABLES NOT IN CALCULATIONS)
  Oil — 0 teaspoons   **Protein** — 80 grams
  Cholesterol — 36 milligrams   **Carbohydrate** — 22 grams
  Saturated fat — 0 grams   **Calories** — 425
  Linoleic acid — 0 grams

WALNUT BUTTER

Spin in an electric blender until finely chopped
  1 quart walnut meats (or other acceptable nuts; see page 17)
  ⅓ cup oil
  ½ teaspoon salt
Makes 2 cups.

ONE TABLESPOON

Oil — 2 teaspoons	**Protein** — 2 grams
Cholesterol — 0 milligrams	**Carbohydrate** — 2 grams
Saturated fat — 1 gram	**Calories** — 110
Linoleic acid — 6 grams	

CRUNCHY KRISPS

Put into a heavy skillet
   4 tablespoons oil
   1 teaspoon mustard seed
Heat until seeds begin to pop, then add
   ½ teaspoon curry powder   *Dash of pepper*
   ¼ teaspoon salt   *3 cups puffed rice*
   ¼ teaspoon cinnamon
Stir until heated and well coated with seasonings and oil. Cool and
store in a covered container.

TOTAL RECIPE

Oil — 12 teaspoons	**Protein** — 3 grams
Cholesterol — negligible	**Carbohydrate** — 39 grams
Saturated fat — 8 grams	**Calories** — 670
Linoleic acid — 32 grams	

CEREAL SNACKS

Mix together the following ready-to-eat dry, toasted cereals
   1 cup wheat cereal
   1 cup rice cereal
   1 cup oat cereal
Mix with
   ¼ cup oil
   1½ teaspoons garlic salt
   ¼ teaspoon salt
Stir until the cereals are well coated. Pour into a large flat pan. Toast
in 300° F. oven, stirring frequently, until crisp. Cool and store in a
covered container.

TOTAL RECIPE

Oil — 12 teaspoons	**Protein** — 12 grams
Cholesterol — 0 milligrams	**Carbohydrate** — 78 grams
Saturated fat — 8 grams	**Calories** — 890
Linoleic acid — 32 grams	

POPCORN

In a 3-quart covered kettle or a popcorn popper place
   4 tablespoons oil
Put over high heat until hot and add
   ½ cup popcorn
   ½ teaspoon salt
Cover and shake the kettle until all the corn is popped. Season with more salt, if desired, or seasoning salts such as onion, garlic, celery, or combinations of these salts. Serve hot or cold.

TOTAL RECIPE

Oil — 12 teaspoons	**Protein** — 10 grams
Cholesterol — 0 milligrams	**Carbohydrate** — 62 grams
Saturated fat — 8 grams	**Calories** — 830
Linoleic acid — 32 grams	

SEASONED MUSHROOMS II

Remove stems and clean
   1 pound fresh button mushrooms
Simmer in a covered pan for 10 minutes in
   ⅔ cup chicken broth
   ¼ cup oil
Cool and add
   ½ cup vinegar   *¼ cup oil*
   ½ teaspoon salt   *1 clove garlic, peeled*
   ¼ teaspoon pepper   *1 teaspoon fine herbs*
   1 tablespoon minced parsley
Store in a covered container in the refrigerator to blend flavors before serving. May be stored for a week.

TOTAL RECIPE

Oil — 24 teaspoons	**Protein** — 16 grams
Cholesterol — 0 milligrams	**Carbohydrate** — 29 grams
Saturated fat — 16 grams	**Calories** — 1195
Linoleic acid — 64 grams	

STUFFED EGGS

Hard-cook, cut into halves, and discard the yolks from
   5 *eggs*
In an electric blender put

2 of the hard-cooked egg
   whites
¼ teaspoon dry mustard
1 tablespoon oil
¼ teaspoon lecithin granules
   (optional)

⅛ teaspoon monosodium
   glutamate
¼ teaspoon salt
drop of yellow food coloring

Blend until smooth. Fill the remaining egg halves with the mixture.
Sprinkle with chopped parsley or paprika if desired.

These may be served as hors d'oeuvres or on a salad plate. **Six servings.**

ONE SERVING

Oil — ½ teaspoon
Cholesterol — 0 milligrams
Saturated fat — negligible
Linoleic acid — 1 gram

Protein — 3 grams
Carbohydrate — 0 grams
Calories — 30

BAKED CHEESE

Beat together

1 tablespoon skim milk
   cottage cheese
4 tablespoons reconstituted
   egg whites*
¼ teaspoon lecithin granules
1½ teaspoons oil

drop of yellow food coloring
   if desired
⅛ teaspoon seasoning salt
⅛ teaspoon monosodium
   glutamate
1 teaspoon chopped chives

Bake in a small oiled baking dish in a 350° F. oven until a knife
comes out clean when inserted into the center (about 20 minutes). To
serve, cut into small squares about ¾ inch in size.

TOTAL RECIPE

Oil — 1½ teaspoons
Cholesterol — 1 milligram
Saturated fat — 1 gram
Linoleic acid — 4 grams

Protein — 19 grams
Carbohydrate — 1 gram
Calories — 140

* See Chapter VI, page 66.

MEAT SANDWICH SPREADS

CHICKEN OR TURKEY SPREAD

Combine
> 1 cup chopped cooked   ¼ cup Mayonnaise★
>   chicken or turkey meat   salt to taste
> ½ cup finely chopped celery   pepper to taste

Spread on bread to make 6 sandwiches. Garnish with thin slices of cranberry jelly or Cranberry Relish★ if desired. **Six servings.**

ONE SERVING
> **Oil** — ⅔ teaspoon   **Protein** — 1 gram
> **Cholesterol** — 15 milligrams   **Carbohydrate** — negligible
> **Saturated fat** — 2 grams   **Calories** — 105
> **Linoleic acid** — 6 grams

TUNA SPREAD

Shred
> 1 can water-packed tuna

Add
> ½ cup celery, finely chopped   4 tablespoons French
> 1 tablespoon capers   Dressing★
> 2 tablespoons green onion,
>   finely chopped

Spread on bread to make 4 sandwiches. Garnish with shredded lettuce, sliced cucumber, or sliced tomato if desired. **Four servings.**

ONE SERVING
> **Oil** — 2⅔ teaspoons   **Protein** — 10 grams
> **Cholesterol** — 32 milligrams   **Carbohydrate** — 1 gram
> **Saturated fat** — 2 grams   **Calories** — 150
> **Linoleic acid** — 5 grams

MEAT SANDWICHES

Thinly slice and remove all visible fat or chop
  *2 ounces veal roast, lean beef roast, lean lamb roast or lean
  center cut of ham*

TOTAL RECIPE

Oil — 0 teaspoons	**Protein** — 18 grams
Cholesterol — 46 milligrams	**Carbohydrate** — 0 grams
Saturated fat — 2 grams	**Calories** — 110
Linoleic acid — 0 grams	

Place between bread and add any of the following:
  *Sliced or chopped tomato, sliced or chopped cucumber, sliced
  or chopped onion, shredded lettuce, India relish, chili sauce,
  catsup, pickles, mustard, margarine, or Mayonnaise★*
One serving.

SARDINE SPREAD

Drain the oil from and mash with a fork
  1 can sardines packed in an acceptable vegetable oil
Add
  ½ teaspoon lemon juice   ¼ teaspoon salt
  ⅛ teaspoon pepper   2 tablespoons Mayonnaise★
Mix well and serve on toast. May be put under the broiler for a
short time to warm if desired. Place between bread to make a
sandwich. Garnish with lettuce. **Four servings.**

ONE SERVING

Oil — 2 teaspoons	**Protein** — 5 grams
Cholesterol — 16 milligrams	**Carbohydrate** — negligible
Saturated fat — 1 gram	**Calories** — 90
Linoleic acid — 4 grams	

CHAPTER XXII

What to Eat for Breakfast on a Diet Restricted in Saturated Fats and Cholesterol

BREAKFAST and brunch on this diet can become delicious events with which to start your day. At the same time breakfast offers you the opportunity to include a substantial portion of essential daily nutrients in many interesting dishes that you can prepare for this meal. Fresh citrus fruits, melons, or berries served at breakfast can provide most of the daily requirements of Vitamin C. Steaming bowls of whole-grain cereals, piping hot enriched muffins, breakfast breads, and rolls, griddlecakes, and waffles will increase your intake of B-complex vitamins and iron. Raisins, currants, dates, and nuts may be mixed into these cereal foods to add interesting flavors and at the same time increase considerably your supply of these essential nutrients. The skim milk incorporated into many breakfast dishes contributes substantially to the daily protein intake. Essential protein is also in rich supply in many delicious "egg" dishes made with egg whites modified to taste like whole eggs.

Fruits

All fruits are acceptable in this diet. You should especially favor fresh fruits high in Vitamin C. In addition to the citrus fruits, such as oranges, grapefruit, and tangerines, Vitamin C is high in melons, nectarines, fresh pineapple, raspberries, loganberries, and strawberries. Fruits high in iron, such as dried apricots, currants, dates, figs, prunes, and raisins, can be served stewed or added to cereal, breakfast breads, rolls, and muffins. (See Chapter XV, "Yeast Breads and Quick Breads.")

Many interesting suggestions for serving fruits are described on pages 398–400. Try these to give your breakfasts a lift.

Beverages

Coffee, coffee substitutes, tea, and skim milk beverages are all acceptable. Hot Cocoa★ and Café au Lait★ offer pleasant variations for the 8 ounces of skim milk that should be included in breakfast. The present commercial powdered and liquid cream substitutes are not satisfactory because of their high saturated fat content. For acceptable substitutes for coffee cream, see page 61.

Whole-grain Cereals

Whole-grain cereals play an important part in this diet, and you can make your breakfast cereal dish interesting in many ways.

Dried Cereals: There are several prepared dry cereals fortified with vitamins and minerals which, when served with enriched* skim milk or canned evaporated skim milk, will provide an adequate breakfast on those days when time is limited for preparation of more interesting fare. The bowl of dry cereal can be improved in taste and nutrition by the addition of fresh fruit or raisins, currants, figs, stewed prunes, or apricots.

Cooked Cereals: Keep on hand in covered containers a variety of cereals to cook for breakfast and to use in baking breakfast breads. Include wheat germ, cracked wheat, groats (cracked buckwheat), oatmeal, enriched corn meal, and low fat soybean grits. Be careful about the use of some products on the market which require only the addition of boiling water and no on-the-stove cooking. Be sure to read their labels for ingredients and avoid those that contain unspecified vegetable oils, since they may be highly saturated.

Make your cooked cereals more nutritious by substituting skim milk for the water required in cooking. You can add extra skim milk powder to increase further the protein content. Care must be taken that the milk does not boil over or burn; more frequent stirring and lower heat are required than when cooking cereals with water. The use of a double boiler will help, especially for keeping the cereal warm before serving.

As has been pointed out in Chapter VI, wheat germ is an excellent source of iron and the B-complex vitamins, and at least 1 tablespoon daily is desirable in this diet. Cereal offers a good place for its use. Add 1 or 2 tablespoons of wheat germ to cooked cereal before or after it has been cooked, and sprinkle wheat germ on dry cereal.

* Enriched by adding skim milk powder.

FORTIFIED COOKED CEREAL

Heat just to boiling over direct heat
   1½ cups skim milk
Mix in a measuring cup and stir slowly into the milk
   ½ cup whole-wheat cereal   *3 tablespoons wheat germ*
   3 tablespoons skim milk   *¼ teaspoon salt*
   powder
Continue stirring until well mixed. Place over hot water to thicken and keep warm until served. **Two servings.**

ONE SERVING
   Oil — 0 teaspoons   **Protein** — 13 grams
   Cholesterol — 7 milligrams   **Carbohydrate** — 32 grams
   Saturated fat — negligible   **Calories** — 190
   Linoleic acid — 1 gram

This method can be applied to the preparation of any of the cooked cereals. Try adding cooked dried fruits, such as pitted dates, raisins, cut-up pitted prunes, and cut-up figs to cereals. Add these fruits in small amounts at first and increase according to taste.

Brown sugar, honey, maple syrup, or maple sugar offers a pleasant variation from refined sugar on cereals. For those who do not enjoy cereal without cream, there is a substitute "cream" that may be used (see page 61). This special "cream" may also be used in coffee. Evaporated skim milk, now available in groceries, is also a good cream substitute for these purposes.

Make Meat Substitutes from Cereal

Some cooked cereals are delicious when sautéed and, with the addition of special flavorings, can replace the bacon and sausage that are now eliminated from the breakfast menu.

CRACKED WHEAT CAKES

Mix
   5 tablespoons skim milk powder
   1 cup beef or chicken broth (or 1 cup Bacon or Ham Stock★)
   ½ cup cracked wheat
Cook in top of double boiler until the liquid is absorbed by the cracked wheat. Set aside to cool. (This can be cooked ahead of time

and kept in the refrigerator until ready to sauté.) Add to cooked cereal and mix

1 tablespoon oil	⅛ teaspoon Beau Monde
½ teaspoon salt	Seasoning (Spice Islands)
⅛ teaspoon monosodium glutamate	

Form into patties and brown in a skillet in 1 tablespoon oil. **Makes 2 patties.**

ONE PATTY

Oil — 1½ teaspoons	**Protein** — 5 grams
Cholesterol — 2 milligrams	**Carbohydrate** — 11 grams
Saturated fat — 1 gram	**Calories** — 135
Linoleic acid — 4 grams	

Try also sautéed hominy, sautéed slices of cold cooked corn meal, and squares of cooked oatmeal dusted in flour and browned in oil.

What Breakfast Breads Are Allowed?

Although commercial yeast bread is usually made with some lard, the amount per slice is so small that the plain loaves may be used for breakfast toast. Some commercially prepared English muffins are made without added fat or eggs and are well suited to this diet. Almost all other commercial baked products, such as rolls, muffins, and coffeecakes, are unacceptable because they contain substantial amounts of butter, lard, hydrogenated fats, or egg yolks. Most packaged mixes for coffeecakes, rolls, muffins, biscuits, waffles, and griddlecakes are likewise unsuitable. Again, read the labels and eliminate products that contain prohibited ingredients or vaguely described fats and oils.

Delicious breads that are acceptable for this diet can be made in your own kitchen. Suggestions are given in Chapter XV, "Yeast Breads and Quick Breads," on how to substitute acceptable ingredients in place of solid shortening and whole eggs. Baking at home will enable you to enjoy a wide variety of breakfast breads, including muffins, sweet rolls, coffeecakes, griddlecakes, waffles, French toast, and even popovers. Try these for a change in breakfast fare:

CHEESE BLINTZES

For each blintz, sprinkle inner surface of 1 French Pancake★ with
  ½ teaspoon powdered sugar
  cinnamon to taste

Across the center, place in a strip
>   3 tablespoons "Special" Cottage Cheese★
>   2 tablespoons applesauce

Roll up and place in oiled baking dish. Sprinkle each blintz with
>   ½ teaspoon powdered sugar
>   cinnamon to taste

Bake in moderate oven (350° F.) 15 to 20 minutes.

ONE BLINTZ

Oil — ¼ teaspoon		Protein — 8 grams	
Cholesterol — 4 milligrams		Carbohydrate — 19 grams	
Saturated fat — negligible		Calories — 120	
Linoleic acid — 1 gram			

Filled Crepes

For glamorous brunches we suggest you try Crepes★ with any one of the fillings that can be made with our sauce recipes as a base. Prepare one of the following heated mixtures:

>   Cheesy Sauce★ and chopped cooked asparagus, broccoli, artichokes, or flowerets of cauliflower
>   Cheesy Sauce★ and crab or shredded cooked fish
>   Mushroom Sauce★ and cooked rice
>   Mushroom Sauce★ and shredded tuna or chopped cooked chicken or turkey
>   Spanish Sauce★ and kidney beans
>   "Egg" Sauce★ and shredded pink salmon

For each serving, fill 1 crepe with 2 tablespoons of this mixture. Place filled crepes in an oiled baking dish. Cover with more of the same sauce and bake in oven at 350° F. 15 to 20 minutes. Garnish with paprika or parsley.

What About Eggs?

A wide variety of egg dishes is now possible with the substitutes for whole egg which we have devised (see pages 66–67). This substitute tastes so much like whole egg that you need not be deprived of delicious egg dishes for breakfast.

The following dishes can be made using either fresh egg whites* or reconstituted dried egg whites. It is our impression that fresh egg whites are superior for these recipes.

* See "Feed Plants with Egg Yolks," pages 470–71.

BASIC "SCRAMBLED EGGS"

For each serving, beat lightly with a fork

4 egg whites	1 tablespoon fine bread
1½ teaspoons oil	crumbs
¼ teaspoon lecithin granules	salt and pepper to taste
1 drop yellow food coloring	3 drops Worcestershire sauce
1 teaspoon skim milk	

Place over moderate heat in oiled or Teflon-lined frying pan. Pour in egg mixture and cook, with or without stirring, until eggs are set.

ONE SERVING

Oil —— 1½ teaspoons	**Protein** —— 17 grams
Cholesterol —— negligible	**Carbohydrate** —— 4 grams
Saturated fat —— 1 gram	**Calories** —— 150
Linoleic acid —— 4 grams	

BASIC SOUFFLE

Make a white sauce by shaking together in a covered jar

¾ cup water	½ teaspoon monosodium
⅓ cup skim milk powder	glutamate
4 tablespoons oil	¼ teaspoon white pepper
4 tablespoons flour	½ teaspoon salt

Heat in top of double boiler with constant stirring until thick and creamy. Beat with rotary or electric beater until well mixed

3 egg whites	1 drop yellow food coloring
½ teaspoon lecithin granules	3 tablespoons oil
1 drop butter flavoring	

Pour slowly, with stirring, into hot white sauce. Let sauce mixture cool. At this point, you can add any desired flavoring or ingredients to modify the soufflé (see list, pages 374–75).
Beat until they form peaks

6 egg whites
pinch of cream of tartar

Fold ¾ of the beaten egg whites gently but thoroughly into the cooled sauce mixture. Quickly fold in the remainder of the egg whites. Pour into a well-oiled soufflé dish. Set the dish in a pan containing about 1 inch of warm water and bake in a preheated oven at 350° F. 50 to 60 minutes. **Six servings.**

ONE SERVING

Oil — 2 teaspoons

Cholesterol — 1 milligram

Saturated fat — 2 grams

Linoleic acid — 9 grams

Protein — 8 grams

Carbohydrate — 5 grams

Calories — 195

COTTAGE CHEESE OMELET

For each serving, beat slightly together

4 egg whites

1½ teaspoons oil

¼ teaspoon lecithin granules

1 drop yellow food coloring

1 teaspoon chopped chives
(fresh or dried)

2 drops Worcestershire sauce

*⅛ teaspoon monosodium
glutamate*

*2 tablespoons "Special"
Cottage Cheese★*

2 teaspoons skim milk

salt and pepper to taste

Pour into moderately hot oiled or Teflon-lined frying pan and cook slowly until eggs are set. Fold and serve.

ONE SERVING

Oil — 1½ teaspoons

Cholesterol — 2 milligrams

Saturated fat — 1 gram

Linoleic acid — 4 grams

Protein — 20 grams

Carbohydrate — negligible

Calories — 145

VARIATIONS for Basic "Scrambled Eggs"★

Add any of the following to your taste

chopped mushrooms

chopped chives

chopped parsley

diced tomatoes

diced cucumbers

chopped canned pimientos

chutney

chopped cooked asparagus

chopped cooked spinach

browned chopped onions,
    green peppers, green onions

small cooked Brussels sprouts

cooked flowerets of cauliflower

cooked green peas

minced canned artichoke
    hearts

diced cooked eggplant

diced fried potatoes

lima beans

corn

herbs, such as thyme,
    marjoram, orégano, savory,
    dill

curry powder

chili powder

VARIATIONS for Basic Soufflé★

For soufflés, purée the selected vegetable in a blender or press through a sieve. Add about 1 cup purée to the basic sauce mixture after it has cooled and proceed according to recipe, page 373.

VARIATIONS for Cottage Cheese Omelet★

1. Try substituting skim milk or baker's cheese for the "Special" Cottage Cheese★.
2. Jam or jelly may be spread over the surface of the omelet after browning.
3. A sauce, such as Spanish Sauce★, may be served over the omelet.

"POACHED EGGS" ON TOAST

For each serving, poach
 2 *egg whites*
Place on
 1 *slice whole-wheat toast*
Sprinkle with
 salt
 pepper
 paprika

ONE SERVING

Oil — 0 teaspoons	**Protein** — 12 grams
Cholesterol — 0 milligrams	**Carbohydrate** — 15 grams
Saturated fat — 0 grams	**Calories** — 110
Linoleic acid — 0 grams	

EGGS BAKED IN BREAD CASES

Cut crusts from
 1 *unsliced loaf of bread*
For each serving cut a 2-inch slice and hollow out the center, leaving at least 1 inch thickness on sides and bottom. Brush center and sides with a mixture of
 1 *tablespoon oil*
 ¼ *teaspoon Beau Monde Seasoning*

Place on baking sheet and fill with mixture of

2 egg whites
1 teaspoon oil
1 drop yellow food coloring
⅛ teaspoon lecithin granules
⅛ teaspoon Beau Monde
    Seasoning

⅛ teaspoon monosodium
    glutamate
1½ teaspoons "Special"
    Cottage Cheese★
1 teaspoon chopped chives
salt and pepper to taste

Bake in oven at 350° F. until bread is golden brown and eggs are set (about 20 minutes).

ONE SERVING

Oil — 4 teaspoons
Cholesterol — negligible
Saturated fat — 3 grams
Linoleic acid — 11 grams

Protein — 15 grams
Carbohydrate — 38 grams
Calories — 400

This egg mixture may be baked in oiled porcelain earthenware or Pyrex ramekins set in a pan of boiling water in an oven preheated to 350° F. Bake 7 to 10 minutes or until inserted table knife comes out clean.

ONE SERVING

Oil — 1 teaspoon
Cholesterol — negligible
Saturated fat — 1 gram
Linoleic acid — 3 grams

Protein — 9 grams
Carbohydrate — negligible
Calories — 80

CHAPTER XXIII

How to Choose a Low Saturated Fat, Low Cholesterol Lunch in a Restaurant

"THOSE who find it necessary to eat lunch in a restaurant are confronted with a problem because restaurant menus offer very little which is completely acceptable on the low fat, low cholesterol diet."

Twenty years ago, in the first edition of this book, we began this chapter with the statement above. Unfortunately, today, this statement is still true. The medical literature on controlled studies of the low saturated fat, low cholesterol diet has noted the difficulty in lowering blood cholesterol levels of those study subjects who ate regularly in restaurants.

Your best chance of success in selecting a restaurant meal that conforms to your Daily Food Guide is to follow these suggestions:

1. Learn to recognize the foods that contain saturated fats and cholesterol and avoid them.

2. Become acquainted with the acceptable foods on the menus of the restaurants you patronize.

3. Learn to ask for certain modifications in some restaurant dishes so that you may eat them.

4. Best of all, become a regular customer of a limited number of restaurants and get to know the manager, headwaiter, or chef. Explain to him your dietary needs and suggestions for modifications that will enable you to select acceptable dishes. Ask him to stock certain essentials for your luncheon meals, such as skim milk, acceptable vegetable oil and margarine, and cottage cheese curd or washed cottage cheese. This is discussed more fully on pages 380–81.

Foods that Should Be Avoided

It is of utmost importance to learn to recognize the foods that do contain cholesterol and are high in saturated fats. The usual sandwiches made with hamburger, mayonnaise, and grilled cheese, the French-fried potatoes, the milk shakes, the pie à la mode quickly run up the cholesterol and saturated fat intake and are therefore impossible to include. You should make a careful study of your diet so that you will be thoroughly familiar with the foods to be avoided. In addition to the dishes obviously high in eggs, cream, butter, and saturated fat are the following, which are often on restaurant menus and which should be avoided:

Cream soups	Waffles
Creamed foods and casseroles	Cheese dishes
Croquettes	Soufflés and other egg dishes
Fried foods	French-fried potatoes
Timbales	Potato salad
Frankfurters	Potato chips
Hamburgers	Doughnuts
Cheeseburgers	Sweet rolls
Milk shakes	Desserts other than those
Pancakes	listed in this chapter

Learn What Acceptable Foods Are on the Menu

The following are a few possibilities:

Soups. Clear soups are recommended because most broths have had the fat removed and are very low in cholesterol. Many vegetable, rice, barley, and split-pea soups are made with a low fat broth. If such soups are high in fat, the fat can usually be seen floating in large amounts on the surface.

Two canned soups, available at lunch counters, bouillon and consommé, do not contain meat and are very low in saturated fat.

Salads. As vegetables and fruits do not contain cholesterol and are usually low in saturated fat, you may order a fruit or vegetable salad with a dressing made with vinegar, lemon juice, and acceptable vegetable oil. If the restaurant cannot offer skim milk cottage cheese, low fat or creamed cottage cheese may be accepted if the equivalent of the contained fat is eliminated from another part of your daily food allowance. The following fat equivalents can guide you in making this substitution:

For ½ cup creamed cottage cheese, eliminate 1 teaspoon margarine from your day's menu.

For ½ cup low fat cottage cheese, eliminate ½ teaspoon margarine from your day's menu.

A limited quantity of commercial mayonnaise is allowed. Although the amount of egg yolk in one serving is negligible, if salads are drenched in dressings made with mayonnaise, if quantities are spread on sandwiches, or if large amounts are used in tartar sauce on fish, the "negligible" egg yolk begins to add up to excessive amounts of saturated fat and cholesterol. Ask to have the mayonnaise served on the side so that you may estimate its amount and hold to a minimum the amount you eat.

Avocado may be included in salads as a garnish only. It must be remembered that 1 ounce (2 tablespoons) of avocado plus ½ tablespoon French dressing requires you to decrease your "special" margarine allowance by 1 tablespoon. It is obvious, then, that a stuffed half avocado is not an acceptable salad for this diet.

Vegetables. The vegetables offer many possibilities for hot vegetable plates. You should be sure that they are not seasoned with butter, cooked in egg yolk batter, or contained in a cream sauce, which is usually made with butter, margarine, whole milk, or cream.

Cereals and legumes. Rice, whole-grain cereals, beans, and lentils may be included in the lunch, if they are prepared without adding animal fats. Don't be shy—ask about this. Many restaurants have a good bean dish, and if it is low in fat, it is acceptable. H. J. Heinz and Company prepares canned oven-baked beans that contain no added fat and may be available in the restaurant.

Bread. Most commercial loaf bread is acceptable. Restaurants can generally provide enriched white, whole-wheat, French, rye or Russian rye, all of which are satisfactory. Hard rolls, English muffins, rye crisps, matzos and plain tortillas are also acceptable.

Sandwiches. Acceptable sandwiches include those made with lettuce, tomato, dried fruits, jam, jelly, honey, fish, lean meat, chicken, or turkey. These sandwiches should not to be made with butter or regular margarine or cheese spreads. Ask them to leave the mayonnaise off your sandwiches or at least to go *very* light on it. A *small* amount of commercial mayonnaise is allowed. Mustard, catsup, horseradish, pickle relish, onion, and pickles may be included.

Meat, Poultry, and Fish. Slices of roasted lean beef, veal, turkey, or chicken (without gravy) can be eaten according to the allowance in your Daily Food Guide, provided you carefully remove all visible fat. Broiled lean steaks of beef or fish can be eaten for lunch in amounts allowed in your Daily Food Guide if they are broiled without adding butter or margarine. Practice estimating and then verifying the weights of portions of cooked lean meat at home so that you can make fairly accurate judgments of amounts in your restaurant servings.

Desserts. Desserts that you may order in restaurants include gelatin, water ices, fruit-juice ices, angel food cake, and fresh, dried, or cooked fruits.

Beverages. Acceptable beverages include tea, coffee, skim milk, fat free buttermilk, fruit juices, vegetable juices, and any desired beverage not containing whole milk, eggs, or cream or saturated fat substitutes for cream.

Some people may find it more convenient to eat the dinner meat allowance at noon in the restaurant and prepare a low meat meal for dinner at home. If you do this, you must be certain that your restaurant meal does not exceed the prescribed amount of cholesterol and saturated fat recommended for the main meat meal of the day's diet. The amount of meat allowed is usually less than the average restaurant meat serving, so it is up to you to divide the portion served to you and eat only your proper quota.

Miscellaneous

Though only mints are likely to be offered you in the restaurant, other candies may tempt you as an after-lunch trimming. Refuse the restaurant's mints if they are chocolate-coated. You may treat yourself to hard candy, marshmallows, gumdrops, jelly beans, mints (not chocolate), walnuts, or candied fruit to the extent they fit within your calorie allowance.

You Can Modify Some Restaurant Dishes So They Are Acceptable for Your Diet

Some poultry and lean meat dishes prepared in the restaurant can be made acceptable by proper steps taken at the table. For example, broiled, fried, or baked chicken or squab may be eaten if the skin is discreetly removed and only the meat consumed. Some lean beef or veal dishes that are served with a gravy or sauce may be made acceptable by pushing the sauce aside (uneaten). Even fish of the "fish and chips" variety may be acceptable if the browned batter or breaded covering is discarded and only the cooked flesh is eaten.

Ask for your baked potatoes to be brought to you unopened, together with some acceptable oil or margarine, so that you may avoid the butter usually placed in the split potato before it is brought to the table.

If molded salads or gelatin desserts are served with whipped cream dressings or toppings, these can be scraped off before eating the gelatin. If you have the opportunity, however, you should order them without such toppings.

Creamy frostings on acceptable angel food cake, or whipped cream on fruit, may be left on your plate. The fruit filling in certain pies may be eaten, leaving the high saturated fat crust uneaten.

Ask Your Restaurant to Stock Certain Essentials for Your Diet

If you are a regular customer, you may persuade your restaurant to keep some of the following items on hand to make your dining more pleasant on this diet:

1. Skim milk for drinking.
2. Canned evaporated skim milk as a cream substitute.
3. Canned soups—bouillon, consommé (or they may make soups from fat free broth).
4. Low fat cottage cheese or cottage cheese curd. (You might even persuade them to wash the cream off regular cottage cheese by running water through a portion placed in a sieve.)
5. "Special" margarine.
6. Polyunsaturated oil and assorted dried herbs to be used with vinegar, salt, and pepper to make a dressing for vegetable and fruit salads. The same oil can be used on cooked vegetables and baked potato.
7. Flavored gelatin desserts.
8. Angel food cake, unfrosted.

You may even persuade your restaurant to prepare some acceptable dishes specifically for your diet, such as skim milk soups, vegetable plates, and fish salads. You may be successful in getting them to broil fish, poultry, and beef without adding butter or margarine.

Ask your restaurant to make a no-fat bean or lentil dish for you. One that can be made from canned products (hence in small amounts) uses:

1 can kidney beans (2 cups)   *salt, pepper, chili powder to*
1 small onion, sliced   *taste*
1 can tomatoes, (2 cups)

Some Suggested Restaurant Lunches*

Menu I

Heinz Oven Baked Beans with Tomato Sauce
Salad*—lettuce, sliced tomatoes, cottage cheese
Pickle
2 slices French bread
1 glass skim milk
Stewed prunes and angel food cake
Coffee or tea if desired

Menu II

Consommé with rye crackers
Fried chicken (remove the skin and visible fat)
Baked potato (add oil from your daily fat and oil allowance)
Sliced tomato salad*
2 slices French bread
1 glass skim milk
Fruit gelatin
Coffee or tea if desired

Menu III

Canned bouillon, heated, undiluted (may be spooned over the
  vegetable plate if preferred)
Vegetable plate of:
  carrots (may be raw)
  peas
  beets
  lima beans
  flaky rice
Cottage cheese and apple butter (or applesauce)
2 slices bread
1 glass skim milk
½ cantaloupe filled with lemon ice
Coffee or tea if desired

* These contain no significant amount of fat, so that you may add oil according to your Daily Food Guide.

Menu IV

Broiled halibut steak
Celery and carrot sticks
2 slices French bread
1 glass skim milk
Stewed apricots
Coffee or tea if desired

Menu V

Sliced turkey sandwich (white meat only)
Celery or pickles
Vegetable salad*
Canned fruit
1 glass skim milk
Coffee or tea if desired

Menu VI

Jellied consommé with rye crackers
Salad—chilled fruit (banana plus fruit cocktail, if fresh
    fruits are not available) and cottage cheese*
Whole-wheat toast
1 glass skim milk
Angel food cake topped with strawberries
Coffee or tea if desired

Menu VII

Tuna fish salad*—dressing served separately (see page 379)
Pickles and raw carrot sticks
1 glass skim milk
Fruit ice
Coffee or tea if desired

* These contain no significant amount of fat, so that you may add oil according
to your Daily Food Guide.

CHAPTER XXIV

Box Lunches and Sandwiches

EATING lunch at a restaurant is not easy for those on this diet, though it can be made quite pleasant by following the advice given in Chapter XXIII. For many who must eat lunch away from home, packing a lunch may be the preferred solution.

Preparing a box lunch for this diet is not difficult, as there is a variety of acceptable foods that are appropriate to pack. Follow the Daily Food Guide in Chapter IV for your prescribed diet. Lunch-box menus should include such foods as soups, skim milk and skim milk drinks, skim milk cottage cheese in some form, vegetables (preferably green or yellow), fresh, cooked, or dried fruits, sandwiches made from 100 per cent whole-wheat or enriched white breads and, if you have suitable containers, the no meat or low meat luncheon dishes described in this book. How much you pack will depend upon your calorie restriction.

Plastic bags are indispensable for the box lunch. We have found a number of containers in our local stores which make it easier to pack a variety of foods successfully, such as containers with screw tops for carrying liquids and semisolids, and covered containers of suitable shapes and sizes to carry sandwiches, a wedge of pie, or a piece of cake. A thermos bottle (or two) is a must for this diet, to carry soups and milk beverages. A small cup-shaped thermos is on the market that is excellent for carrying such foods as salads, gelatin desserts, and hot luncheon dishes. The lunch box should be dustproof, well ventilated, easily (and frequently) washed and preferably with divisions to keep the foods from mashing. Wrap each article separately in wax paper, plastic film, or plastic bags and pack compactly so that the food cannot be shaken about.

Pack skim milk. Since it is desirable to consume at least 1 pint of skim milk in the diet daily, it should be included in some form in the lunch-box menu. Skim milk can be drunk plain, made into hot or cold flavored milk drinks, or used in soups and desserts; or skim milk powder can be added in extra amounts to "cream" soups, milk drinks, desserts, hot dishes, and sandwich fillings.

Pack soups. The lunch box is a good place to include a hot "cream" soup made of plain or enriched skim milk. Soups are particularly welcome in cold weather.

Pack "Special" Cottage Cheese★. It is an important food for this diet and should be used in the menu often. It does not always have to be eaten as is, however. We use it as sandwich filling, for stuffing small peppers, and in desserts such as cheesecake, to mention only a few of the ways.

A *meat free or a low meat luncheon dish* (see Chapters XII and XIII) or sandwich may substitute for meat in the box lunch. If you do not use the luncheon meat allowance of your Daily Food Guide, you can include this extra amount in your meat for dinner.

Pack vegetables. Vegetables, especially the green and yellow ones and tomatoes, are excellent and should be packed in the box lunch. Include one or more raw vegetables for munching. Chopped vegetables make good sandwich fillings, or use them raw, canned, or cooked in salads.

Pack fruits. Fruits are excellent food, yellow fruits being especially good. Use only sparingly the high fat fruits, such as olives, avocados, and nuts. Of these, nuts are to be preferred, since, with care in choosing, you can get polyunsaturated fats instead of saturated. Pack whole fruits, such as oranges, peaches, and apricots, and for variety include canned, cooked, or dried fruits.

How to Make the Sandwiches

Sandwiches can be made more appealing and interesting in a packed lunch by the use of a variety of breads. Since whole-grain or enriched breads are recommended for this diet, get variety by using Boston Brown Bread★, rye, 100 per cent whole-wheat, and enriched white breads. Use fresh or day-old bread, leaving the crust on to help keep the sandwiches moist. Spread on a plentiful amount of filling, all the way to the edge of the bread, but do not have it oozing out. If the sandwiches have to stand for any length of time, use fillings that will not soak into the bread. Wrap such moist ingredients as lettuce and tomato separately, to be inserted in the sandwich when it is eaten. Wrap sandwiches carefully so that no portion is exposed to the air.

Use a Variety of Sandwich Fillings

With "Special" Cottage Cheese★, fish, poultry, vegetables, dried fruits, Walnut Butter★, preserves, relishes, and seasonings all being acceptable, sandwiches for this diet need not be humdrum. We have listed here some suggestions for fillings, but with a little experimenting you can devise new and tasty ones to suit your own likes. Use Mayonnaise★ or other salad dressings acceptable in this diet in making these fillings. Try these sandwich fillings:

"Special" Cottage Cheese★

1. "Special" Cottage Cheese★ with finely chopped prunes, dates, raisins, dried figs, or dried apricots. Add salt to season.
2. "Special" Cottage Cheese★ mixed with chowchow, chili sauce, chopped dill pickle, pickled beets, celery, green pepper, parsley, watercress, onion, or chive. Add salt to season.
3. "Special" Cottage Cheese★ mixed with drained crushed pineapple.
4. "Special" Cottage Cheese★ and jelly or marmalade on Boston Brown Bread★.
5. "Special" Cottage Cheese★ mixed with a few caraway or celery seeds. Add enough suitable dressing to give the right consistency for spreading. Add salt to season.
6. See other cottage cheese spreads among the "Appetizers, Snacks, and Sandwich Spreads," Chapter XXI.
7. "Special" Cream Cheese★ and its variations.

Dried Fruits

8. Grind together dried apricots and pitted dates or other dried fruits and add enough lemon juice to brighten up the flavor.
9. Chop pitted prunes or raisins and add enough suitable dressing to give the right consistency for spreading.
10. Chop pitted dates, add a little sweet fruit juice, heat gently, and rub to a smooth paste. Add a little orange or lemon juice. This is good with Boston Brown Bread★.

Vegetables

11. Use thin slices of cucumbers or tomatoes spread with dressing.
12. Mix finely chopped green pepper and celery with grated carrot and chili sauce. Add dressing to moisten.
13. Mix grated carrots and raisins. Add dressing to moisten.

Beans

14. To ½ cup cold baked beans, add 2 tablespoons chili sauce. Mash, mix to a smooth paste, and spread between slices of Boston Brown Bread★.

Fish and Poultry

15. Mix flaked fish or chopped poultry with salad dressing.
16. Sardine Sandwich Spread★ on Russian rye.
17. Tuna Sandwich Spread★ on hard roll.

Nuts

18. Walnut Butter★ on brown bread or pumpernickel.

Section II

CHAPTER XXV

The Dietary Carbohydrate

THE dietary approach to prevention of heart disease is based upon reduction in the blood concentration of certain fatty substances, such as cholesterol. Cholesterol is only one of the fatty substances in blood, though it has a special importance in the formation of deposits within the arteries. The blood also contains neutral fats or triglycerides. A more technical discussion of the chemical composition of fats is given in Chapter XXXII.

Elevated levels of triglycerides are related to an excessive risk of heart disease, just as are elevated levels of cholesterol in the blood. The low saturated fat, low cholesterol diet is directed primarily at the reduction of elevated levels of blood cholesterol, and for most persons this is the major problem. There do exist some persons, however, in whom the risk of premature heart disease is primarily due to elevated levels of triglycerides, the true fats. In some of these persons, a high dietary carbohydrate intake can be deleterious, since it promotes elevation in the level of the triglycerides.

In the case of such patients, physicians have suggested modification of the low saturated fat, low cholesterol diet to ensure a relatively low carbohydrate intake. The restriction of carbohydrate intake should be undertaken only by those persons specifically advised to do so by their physicians. We have made provision for them in this book. In each recipe the carbohydrate content is given. Chapter XXVI is devoted to sugar free and low sugar dessert recipes. Therefore, if a person is advised to restrict carbohydrate intake, the information is here to enable him to stay within such restriction while following the low saturated fat, low cholesterol diet. In most individuals, fortunately, specific restriction of carbohydrate is not required.

The question arises, "Are all carbohydrates alike?" The evidence is clear that ordinary sugar (sucrose) and the more complex carbohydrates, as in cereals or grains, can both raise the blood triglyceride level in sensitive persons. Some, but not all, evidence indicates sucrose to be worse in this regard than the more complex carbohydrates. There is also another factor to be considered in weighing the relative merits of these two kinds of food.

There are many valuable and important nutrients in those foods that contain the complex carbohydrates, such as cereals, grains, and vegetables. Sugar represents what are referred to as "empty calories," meaning calories without the benefit of valuable nutrients other than carbohydrates. For two reasons, therefore, we recommend the choice of such sources of carbohydrate as starchy vegetables, cereals, and grains rather than ordinary sugar. First, supplemental nutrients are thus provided. Second, if the person does have the unusual triglyceride sensitivity to carbohydrates, sugar probably increases his risk more than the unrefined carbohydrates.

The Carbohydrate-controlled Diet

The carbohydrate-controlled diet embraces many of the same principles as the low saturated fat, low cholesterol diet. The meal patterns differ slightly. When carbohydrate is reduced in the diet to maintain the desired level of calories, the protein and fat must be increased.

If your physician has prescribed an intake of carbohydrate that is 25 to 30 per cent of total calories, one of the diet patterns, page 394, can guide you in following that regimen and at the same time in having a satisfying and adequate diet.

How to Reduce the Dietary Carbohydrate

1. *Omit all sugar foods.* Refined sugar, whether granulated, powdered, or cubed, candies, jellies, jams, honey, syrups, carbonated beverages containing sugar, canned and frozen sweetened fruits, and all desserts containing sugar. When sugar calories are replaced with calories of the natural foods rich in essential nutrients, the quality of the diet is improved.

2. *Control the amount of starchy foods and control the amount of fruit.* Have the number of servings of these foods as outlined in your diet pattern, but do not have more. See the Food Groups, for the Bread, Cereal, Cereal Products, and Starchy Vegetable Group, and for the Fruit Group. Have the size of servings as shown. Read the discussion on how to use the Food Groups given on pages 25–26, 473–81.

How to Meet the High Level of Protein

1. *Have baker's cheese or cottage cheese curd every day* in addition to the meat in your diet. You will devise many different ways to use it. Prepare "Special" Cottage Cheese★. This bland dish, like a glass of

skim milk, can become a routine part of a meal every day. Here are some other suggestions: Cheesecake★, Curds and Rice★, shakes— blend some baker's cheese with skim milk, add flavoring, saccharin, and oil, or blend the cheese with fruit or juice. Spreads—"Special" Cream Cheese★, Walnut Butter★ mixed with baker's cheese. Whip some baker's cheese into Mashed Potatoes★. Have "Special" Cottage Cheese★ often for breakfast.

2. *Have gelatin and fat free broths very often.* While these bolster the protein level, they contain negligible carbohydrate, fat, or cholesterol. One tablespoon gelatin or 1 cup of homemade broth, full strength (jells on chilling), together with ½ tablespoon gelatin, can in this diet substitute for ¼ cup baker's cheese or curd. You can add gelatin to broth or add it in dissolved form to your juice or stewed fruit. Make molded gelatin. Try gelatin made with water, artificial fruit flavoring, and saccharin. This can be used added to any meal.

Ways you can use oil

See the suggestions for using oil on pages 69–70.

How to include the sugar free and low sugar desserts in the following chapter

You will observe that the desserts, as such, do not appear in the Diet Patterns, and you may be asking how, therefore, can they be used. When you have a milk pudding, have it in place of a cup of skim milk. When you have a frozen dessert made of fruit or fruit juice, have it in place of a serving of fruit. If you occasionally have a serving of cookie snack or a serving of low sugar cake, have it in place of a slice of bread. If occasionally you want to have a serving of pie, a serving of the crust can substitute for a serving of bread and a fruit filling of the pie for a serving of fruit.*

How to plan your menus

Use pencil and paper to chart the day's menus within the framework of the Diet Pattern. This will help you to distribute and include all of the food factors throughout the day.

* These substitutions approximate only the carbohydrate. Your range of calories will cover the additional oil and protein in the desserts.

DIET PATTERNS FOR LOW CARBOHYDRATE DIETS

	1600–1700 calories	2000–2100 calories	2500–2600 calories
BEEF, LAMB, PORK, OR HAM	3 ounces	3 ounces	3 ounces
FISH, POULTRY, OR VEAL	3 ounces	4 ounces	5 ounces
BAKER'S CHEESE OR CURD	¾ cup (⅜ pound)	1 cup (½ pound)	1 cup (½ pound)
SKIM MILK	2 cups	2 cups	3 cups
EGG WHITES	1–2	1–2	2
VEGETABLES, LOW CALORIE	2 servings	2 servings	2 servings
VEGETABLES, MEDIUM CALORIE	1 serving (or 2 servings of low calorie vegetables)	1 serving (or 2 servings of low calorie vegetables)	1 serving (or 2 servings of low calorie vegetables)
FRUIT	3 servings	3 servings	3 servings
BREADS, CEREALS, CEREAL PRODUCTS, STARCHY VEGETABLES	3 servings	4 servings	6 servings
OIL	4 tablespoons	5 tablespoons	6 tablespoons
"SPECIAL" MARGARINE	1 tablespoon	1 tablespoon	2 tablespoons

Calories: Carbohydrate 28 per cent, saturated fat 7 per cent, total fat 40 per cent or over, linoleic acid 20 per cent or over (values are approximate).

SAMPLE MENUS FOR
LOW CARBOHYDRATE DIETS

1600–1700 CALORIES

Breakfast	Teaspoons Oil	Teaspoons Margarine
½ grapefruit		
add 1 teaspoon oil	1	
1 serving basic Scrambled Eggs★		
1 slice toast		
1 teaspoon "special" margarine		1
1 cup "Special" Whole Milk★ (this contains 2 teaspoons oil)	2	
Coffee		

Lunch

3 ounces broiled ground lean beef with		
½ cup spaghetti		
½ cup seasoned tomatoes		
1 tablespoon oil	3	
1 serving celery, radish, green pepper with		
½ cup "Special" Cottage Cheese★		
1 serving applesauce (saccharine-sweetened)		
Tea		

Dinner

1 cup beef broth with ½ tablespoon gelatin (substitute for ¼ cup curd)		
4 ounces broiled halibut		
1 tablespoon Tartar Sauce★	3	
1 serving green beans		
1 serving lettuce with		
1 tablespoon oil (and vinegar)	3	
1 slice bread		
2 teaspoons "special" margarine		2
1 serving Pineapple Parfait★		
1 cup skim milk		
Coffee		
	12 teaspoons (4 tablespoons)	3 teaspoons (1 tablespoon)

2000–2100 CALORIES

Breakfast	Teaspoons Oil	Teaspoons Margarine
1 serving orange juice		
1 serving oatmeal		
1 serving Poached Eggs★		
on 1 slice toast		
1 teaspoon "special" margarine		1
¾ cup skim milk		
¼ cup "special" coffee cream★	3	
Coffee		

Lunch		
Sandwiches, open-face:		
3 ounces boiled lean beef		
chopped with sour pickle		
mixed with 1 tablespoon		
Mayonnaise★	3	
2 slices bread		
2 teaspoons "special" margarine		2
Salad:		
1 serving grated carrot		
with lemon juice		
and 1 tablespoon Mayonnaise★	3	
½ cup "Special" Cottage Cheese★		
1 serving water-packed peaches		
Tea		

Dinner		
4 ounces roast turkey		
with Fat Free Gravy★		
1 serving asparagus		
1 serving shredded cabbage		
with 2 teaspoons oil	2	
and 1 tablespoon Mayonnaise★	3	
¼ cup "Special" Cottage Cheese★		
1 serving Cranberry Ice★	1	
blended with ¼ cup baker's cheese		
1 cup skim milk		
Coffee		
	15 teaspoons	3 teaspoons
	(5 tablespoons)	(1 tablespoon)

2500–2600 CALORIES

Breakfast	Teaspoons Oil	Teaspoons Margarine
1 serving cantaloupe, sliced with ½ cup "Special" Cottage Cheese★, add 2 teaspoons oil	2	
1 serving shredded wheat		
1 slice toast		
2 teaspoons "special" margarine		2
1 cup "Special" Whole Milk★	2	
Coffee		

Lunch		
5 ounces sliced roast chicken		
1 serving Fat Free Gravy★, add 1 teaspoon oil	1	
1 serving corn, add 1 teaspoon "special" margarine		1
1 serving carrots		
1 serving tossed greens and tomato with 1 tablespoon oil (and vinegar)	3	
1 serving orange, diced, add 2 teaspoons oil	2	
1 Oatmeal Cookie Snack★	1	
1 cup skim milk		

Dinner		
3 ounces lamb chops, broiled		
1 serving summer squash, add 1 teaspoon "special" margarine		1
1 serving Spinach Salad★ with ½ cup baker's cheese and 2 Baked Egg Whites★, sliced		
1 teaspoon oil	1	
1 tablespoon Mayonnaise★	3	
1 slice bread		
2 teaspoons "special" margarine		2
1 serving Apple Cobbler★	1½	
⅛ cup "Special" Coffee Cream★	1½	
¾ cup skim milk		
	18 teaspoons (6 tablespoons)	6 teaspoons (2 tablespoons)

CHAPTER XXVI

Sugar Free and Low Sugar Desserts

In this chapter are recipes for desserts prepared without sugar or with very little sugar. These are suitable for individuals whose physicians have recommended a low sugar regimen, probably for the reasons discussed in Chapter XXV. In appearance and taste, these special desserts are very much like those we are accustomed to, so that substituting them for sugar-filled desserts makes the transition to a low sugar diet easy.

Some of the recipes incorporate oil to add calories where sugar calories have been eliminated. This substitution can aid in keeping the day's total calories at maintenance level for persons of normal weight. Dieters who have been advised to lose weight will select recipes without added oil, since these recipes are lower in calories.

Refined sugar, whether granulated, powdered, or cubed, in syrups, candies, soft drinks, and sweet desserts, yield *"empty calories"* and nothing more. Carbohydrate foods of this kind are completely devoid of mineral values and vitamins. Americans currently consume excessive amounts of sugar, amounts far above those recommended for good nutrition. Not only for those on a low carbohydrate diet, but for others as well, when refined sugar calories are replaced with calories from natural foods rich in essential nutrients, the quality of the diet is greatly improved.

Fruit Dessert*

For a low carbohydrate or diabetic dessert, no wiser, more pleasant choice can be made than fresh fruit in season. What is so good as

    a crisp, spicy apple
    a garden-ripened melon
    a sliced juicy orange
    a delicious winter pear

* For the amount of one serving of fruit, see food groups, pages 478–79.

and all of nature's other delicious fruits—deep ripe persimmon, clusters of grapes, watermelon, cantaloupe, and the many varieties of autumn melons—Persian, crenshaw, honeydew, casaba, Christmas melon—as well as, out of season, the dried fruits, canned fruits, and frozen fruits? All these, served just as they are, are best-of-all desserts.

Sometimes, however, we like to let fresh fruit take on a little more fanciful look to make the dessert course more special. You might try:

Sherbet Fruit Cup: Top fresh, juicy fruit cup with one of the "special" sherbets or ices for which recipes are given in this chapter.

Island Pineapple: Cut fresh ripe pineapple in two, through leaves and all; scoop out center; refill with sliced peaches and pineapple; garnish with berries.

Grapefruit Ginger: Sprinkle a half grapefruit with a teaspoon of slivered crystallized ginger; for color, garnish with threadlike slivers of red apple peel.

Banana Logs: Spread a peeled banana with Walnut Butter★.

Sparkling Grapes: Dip grapes in egg white diluted with equal amount of water. Place on tray. When partly dry, sprinkle with a few grains of sugar per serving of grapes.

Cranberry Grapefruit: Chop in blender fresh raw cranberries and apple; sweeten with saccharin; serve with grapefruit sections in grapefruit shells.

Holiday Fruit Cup: Grate raw apple into orange juice; add unsweetened crushed pineapple and almond flavoring, sweeten with saccharin. Garnish with cranberries.

You will add many ideas to this list, for imagination determines how a fruit dessert is created.

Other simple and elegant combinations taste good together

Pomegranate juice in fruit cup

Rhubarb juice, sweetened with saccharin, on strawberries

Pear half served with "Special" Cream Cheese★

Apple slices, "Special" Cream Cheese★, and walnut halves

Fruits on ice have appetite appeal

Sink a grapefruit shell in a bowl of cracked ice.

Sink half a small cantaloupe filled with berries into a bowl of cracked ice.

Sink a smaller bowl containing fruit into a larger bowl containing ice.

Garnish any of these with sprigs of watercress or parsley, or place around the fruit cup on top of the ice any green, nonedible leaves.

Broiled fruit for winter days

Place a fruit combination in ramekins under the broiler to heat before serving.

Broil halves of grapefruit, plain or filled with sections of grapefruit and tangerine sections mixed together.

Flavor a fruit cup with lime juice, top with a few tiny marshmallows, and toast under broiler.

Broil orange slices dusted lightly with spice, such as cinnamon or nutmeg, and sprinkle lightly with sugar from shaker.

The Out-of-season Forms of Fruit

While summer and fall afford an abundance of fresh, ripe fruits, other seasons offer just as much, though in dried, frozen, and canned forms.

Because of the concentration of *dried fruits*, the size of a serving may appear small when carbohydrate is held within desired limits. Yet this small, concentrated portion, when used in a recipe, gives full flavor and fulfills its satisfying place.

Water-packed fruits are a particularly good choice for low carbohydrate desserts. They contain neither added sugar nor nonnutritive sweeteners. A large can (No. 10, about 3½ quarts) is sold for bakery and restaurant use and is available in many markets. Since small cans are seldom available in the market, buy the large one and repack in smaller containers or in plastic freezer bags. Store them in the deep freezer. Sweeten them, if you like, with saccharin.

Commercially canned fruits are packed with heavy, medium, or light syrups and are therefore not suitable for diabetics. For others on low carbohydrates, this syrup can be drained off and the fruit can be rinsed to remove much of the sugar. Fruit packed in light syrup, when so treated, may contain little enough sugar to permit its use on a low sugar regimen.

Frozen fruit is also packed with sugar or syrup and is similarly unsuitable for diabetics. Fruits that are frozen in large pieces, such as peaches, whole berries, and pineapple, when drained and rinsed will come out with little or no extra sugar content.

Saccharin (acceptable nonnutritive sweetener)

Saccharin is a nonnutritive sweetener with a long history of safe use. It has been found to produce no toxic effects and to be safe even with lifetime usage. When it is cooked with certain foods, it may occasionally develop a slightly bitter flavor, so it is preferably added after foods have been cooked or used with cold foods.

Saccharin is available in tablet, liquid, and powdered forms and in sizes and concentrations that vary proportionately in sweetening power. In the following recipes, we use the equivalent of saccharin in ½-grain tablets. We recommend dissolving it for convenience. To make your own

SACCHARIN LIQUID

Put into a small bottle with a secure top
    ¼ *cup water*
    48 saccharin tablets, ½-grain size
Use only after completely dissolved. One-quarter teaspoon of this solution equals one ½-grain saccharin tablet. The solution is specified in our recipes as "liquid saccharin."

PUDDINGS, PIE FILLINGS, AND PIES

PIECRUST

Follow piecrust recipe given in Chapter XIX, page 317, or use recipe for Walnut Piecrust★.

BLANC MANGE

Mix in the top of a double boiler
⅔ cup skim milk powder
3 tablespoons cornstarch
½ cup water
Add and mix in
1½ cups water
1½ tablespoons oil
½ teaspoon salt
Cook over boiling water, stirring until mixture thickens. Cover and
cook 10 minutes longer. Then add
¾ teaspoon liquid saccharin
½ teaspoon vanilla
Four servings.

ONE SERVING

Oil — 1 teaspoon
Cholesterol — 4 milligrams
Saturated fat — 1 gram
Linoleic acid — 3 grams

Protein — 4 grams
Carbohydrate — 11 grams
Calories — 105
Total fat — 5 grams

FRUIT BLANC MANGE

Prepare Blanc Mange★ and serve with sliced peaches, berries, or
pineapple. Use ¼ cup fruit for each serving. **Six servings.**

ONE SERVING

Oil — ¾ teaspoon
Cholesterol — 2 milligrams
Saturated fat — 1 gram
Linoleic acid — 2 grams

Protein — 3 grams
Carbohydrate — 13 grams
Calories — 100
Total fat — 4 grams

COCOA BLANC MANGE

Mix in the top of a double boiler
⅔ cup skim milk powder
3 tablespoons cornstarch

2 tablespoons cocoa
½ cup water

Add and mix in
>1½ *cups water*
>2 *tablespoons oil*
>½ *teaspoon salt*

Cook over boiling water, stirring until mixture thickens. Cover and cook 10 minutes more, then add
>1 *teaspoon liquid saccharin or more*
>½ *teaspoon vanilla*
>¼ *teaspoon cinnamon*

Four servings.

ONE SERVING

Oil — 1½ teaspoons	**Protein** — 5 grams
Cholesterol — 4 milligrams	**Carbohydrate** — 13 grams
Saturated fat — 1 gram	**Calories** — 135
Linoleic acid — 4 grams	**Total fat** — 7 grams

CUP CUSTARD

Mix in blender (or stir with spoon to mix)
>⅔ *cup skim milk powder*
>¼ *cup powdered egg white*

Add and spin to mix in (or mix in with spoon)
>1 *tablespoon oil*   ½ *teaspoon lecithin granules*
>2 *cups water*   ¼ *teaspoon nutmeg*
>1 *teaspoon vanilla*   1 *teaspoon liquid saccharin**
>¼ *teaspoon salt*

Pour into 4 custard cups, place in pan with water about 1 inch deep, and bake at 325° F. about 20 minutes or until a knife inserted comes out clean. **Four servings.**

ONE SERVING

Oil — ¾ teaspoon	**Protein** — 8 grams
Cholesterol — 4 milligrams	**Carbohydrate** — 6 grams
Saturated fat — 1 gram	**Calories** — 90
Linoleic acid — 2 grams	**Total fat** — 4 grams

* We have found it satisfactory to add saccharin to custard and custard-base desserts before baking, since custard congeals below boiling temperature.

RICE RAISIN CUSTARD

Use recipe for Cup Custard★. Before baking, stir in
   ⅓ cup cooked rice
   2 tablespoons seedless raisins
   dash salt
Pour into custard cups or into one small bowl and bake as for Cup
Custard★. **Four servings.**

ONE SERVING
   Oil — ¾ teaspoon   **Protein** — 8 grams
   Cholesterol — 4 milligrams   **Carbohydrate** — 14 grams
   Saturated fat — 1 gram   **Calories** — 125
   Linoleic acid — 2 grams   **Total fat** — 4 grams

CREAM PIE

Prepare 1½ times the recipe for Blanc Mange★. While it is cooking,
beat until frothy
   2 egg whites (or 2 tablespoons powdered egg white and
      ¼ cup water)
When Blanc Mange is almost completely cooked, stir a small portion
of it into the beaten egg whites. Return this mixture to the rest of the
blanc mange and continue to cook and stir 1 or 2 minutes.
Remove from heat and add
   1 teaspoon liquid saccharin or to taste
   1 teaspoon vanilla
Pour into a baked Piecrust★. **Six servings.**

ONE SERVING
   Oil — 4 teaspoons   **Protein** — 8 grams
   Cholesterol — 4 milligrams   **Carbohydrate** — 30 grams
   Saturated fat — 3 grams   **Calories** — 315
   Linoleic acid — 10 grams   **Total fat** — 18 grams

LOW SUGAR MERINGUE

Beat until frothy
   2 egg whites (or 2 tablespoons powdered egg white and
      ¼ cup water)
   ¼ teaspoon cream of tartar

Add and beat again until the whites stand in stiff peaks
>   2 *tablespoons sugar*
>   ¼ *teaspoon salt*
>   ½ *teaspoon vanilla*

Divide into 4 portions. Float each portion in a heap on top of hot water in a pan. Bake at 350° F. 15 minutes or until lightly browned on top. Then transfer meringues from water to the top of a pie. **Four servings.**

ONE SERVING

Oil — 0 teaspoons	**Protein** — 2 grams
Cholesterol — 0 milligrams	**Carbohydrate** — 6 grams
Saturated fat — 0 grams	**Calories** — 30
Linoleic acid — 0 grams	**Total fat** — 0 grams

BANANA PIE

Prepare Cream Pie★ but reduce the amount of Blanc Mange★ used to the single recipe. Transfer to a baked Piecrust★. After adding
>   *vanilla*

stir in
>   2 *bananas, sliced*

This pie may be covered with Low Sugar Meringue★ or with Sugar Free Whipped Topping★. Topping is not included in calculations. **Six servings.**

ONE SERVING

Oil — 3½ teaspoons	**Protein** — 7 grams
Cholesterol — 3 milligrams	**Carbohydrate** — 34 grams
Saturated fat — 2 grams	**Calories** — 310
Linoleic acid — 9 grams	**Total fat** — 16 grams

PEACH PIE

Prepare
>   4 *cups sliced peeled peaches*

Mix with

2 *tablespoons flour (or 1½ tablespoons cornstarch or quick-cooking tapicoa)*	½ *teaspoon nutmeg*
	1½ *to 2 teaspoons liquid saccharin*
1 *tablespoon oil*	¼ *teaspoon salt*

Transfer to a Piecrust★ and bake in a hot oven (425° F.) 10 minutes; then reduce heat to 350° F. and bake 20 to 30 minutes longer. **Six servings.**

ONE SERVING

Oil ⎯ 3 teaspoons	**Protein** ⎯ 4 grams
Cholesterol ⎯ negligible	**Carbohydrate** ⎯ 31 grams
Saturated fat ⎯ 2 grams	**Calories** ⎯ 275
Linoleic acid ⎯ 9 grams	**Total fat** ⎯ 15 grams

VARIATION:

Substitute apricots, berries, or plums for the peaches.

LOW SUGAR GLAZED BERRY PIE

Prepare Glazed Berry Pie★ but omit sugar. After the cornstarch-berry mixture has been cooked, add 1½ to 2 teaspoons liquid saccharin. Pour over the raw berries, cool, and transfer to a baked Piecrust★. **Six servings.**

ONE SERVING

Oil ⎯ 2⅔ teaspoons	**Protein** ⎯ 4 grams
Cholesterol ⎯ 0 milligrams	**Carbohydrate** ⎯ 30 grams
Saturated fat ⎯ 2 grams	**Calories** ⎯ 255
Linoleic acid ⎯ 7 grams	**Total fat** ⎯ 13 grams

PUMPKIN PIE

Spin in blender
   3 egg whites (or 3 tablespoons powdered egg white and
      6 tablespoons water)
   4 teaspoons oil
   ½ teaspoon lecithin granules
Add and spin again until well mixed

1½ cups canned pumpkin (or cooked pumpkin, puréed)	*¼ teaspoon grated orange rind (optional)*
1 teaspoon cinnamon	*1 tablespoon brown sugar*
½ to 1 teaspoon ginger	*4 teaspoons liquid saccharin*
½ teaspoon nutmeg	*¼ cup oil*
¼ teaspoon cloves	*1½ cups canned evaporated skim milk*
½ teaspoon salt	

Pour into an uncooked Piecrust★ and bake at 400° F. 10 minutes, lower thermostat to 350° F., and bake until a knife inserted comes out clean. **Eight servings.**

ONE SERVING

Oil ⎯ 4 teaspoons
Cholesterol ⎯ 3 milligrams
Saturated fat ⎯ 3 grams
Linoleic acid ⎯ 10 grams

Protein ⎯ 7 grams
Carbohydrate ⎯ 24 grams
Calories ⎯ 295
Total fat ⎯ 19 grams

APPLE COBBLER

Peel and slice into an oiled baking pan
  2 pounds tart apples
Mix in
  1 teaspoon cinnamon (or more)
  1 tablespoon oil
  4 teaspoons flour
  ¼ teaspoon grated lemon rind (or more)
  ½ teaspoon salt

Cover, place in oven at 375° F., and bake until apples are cooked. Remove from oven and stir in
  2 teaspoons liquid saccharin (or to taste)
Prepare a baked crust by mixing
  ¾ cup sifted flour
  ¼ teaspoon salt
Stir in
  3 tablespoons oil
  1½ tablespoons skim milk
Roll out on floured wax paper. Transfer to pie pan or to a cookie sheet, cut into 6 pieces, and bake in a hot oven, 425° F., 12 to 15 minutes. **Six servings.**

ONE SERVING

Oil ⎯ 2 teaspoons
Cholesterol ⎯ negligible
Saturated fat ⎯ 1 gram
Linoleic acid ⎯ 6 grams

Protein ⎯ 2 grams
Carbohydrate ⎯ 32 grams
Calories ⎯ 225
Total fat ⎯ 10 grams

APRICOT COBBLER

Cut, pit, and cook, covered with water, until tender
    2 pounds fresh apricots (or 1 cup dried apricots)
Mix
    1⅓ tablespoons cornstarch
    ⅓ cup cold water
Add to
    1 cup juice from the cooked apricots
and cook with stirring until thickened. Stir in

    2 teaspoons oil   *dash of salt*
    2 teaspoons lemon juice   *¼ teaspoon nutmeg*
    2 teaspoons liquid saccharin

Add the cooked apricots, transfer to a baking dish, and cover with crust.

Crust:

Sift together
    1 cup sifted flour
    2 teaspoons baking powder
    ½ teaspoon salt
Mix in
    1 tablespoon skim milk powder
Add and stir in
    3 tablespoons oil
Add slowly while stirring
    ⅓ cup water
Turn onto floured wax paper, knead 2 or 3 times, roll out, and place crust on top of apricots. Bake 10 minutes at 400° F., then lower temperature to 350° F. until crust is brown (about 12 to 15 minutes). **Six servings.**

ONE SERVING

Oil — 2 teaspoons	**Protein** — 4 grams
Cholesterol — negligible	**Carbohydrate** — 33 grams
Saturated fat — 1 gram	**Calories** — 240
Linoleic acid — 5 grams	**Total fat** — 10 grams

MINCE PIE

Simmer for an hour or more to obtain a plain broth
¼ pound lean beef
1½ cups water
¼ teaspoon salt

Replace water that boils off to 1 cup. Strain to remove the meat, chill broth, and remove the fat. Then add and mix together

½ cup raisins	*½ teaspoon grated lemon*
½ cup currants	*rind*
4 cups chopped apples	*2 tablespoons oil*
½ teaspoon salt	*2 tablespoons molasses*
1 teaspoon cinnamon	*1½ tablespoons cornstarch*
½ teaspoon cloves	

Cook until mixture is thickened and add
1 to 2 teaspoons liquid saccharin (or to taste)

Make single Piecrust★, roll out thin on a floured wax paper. Place inverted pie pan on top and turn pan, crust, and paper all together. Trim crust from edge of pie pan and form into a ball. Roll this out lengthwise and cut into strips. Pour the filling into the lower crust and place the strips of crust on top. Bake at 425° F. 10 to 15 minutes; lower temperature to 350° F. and bake 40 to 50 minutes longer. **Ten servings.**

ONE SERVING

Oil — 2 teaspoons	**Protein** — 2 grams
Cholesterol — negligible	**Carbohydrate** — 32 grams
Saturated fat — 2 grams	**Calories** — 226
Linoleic acid — 6 grams	**Total fat** — 10 grams

PLUM PUDDING

Spin in blender until mixed and chopped
⅔ cup flour
½ cup raisins or dried fruits

Remove most of this mixture to a bowl. Add to blender and spin again

¼ cup oil	*¼ teaspoon grated lemon*
2 tablespoons molasses	*rind*
2 teaspoons cinnamon	*2 teaspoons vanilla*
1 teaspoon ginger	*1½ cups grated carrots (add*
1 teaspoon salt	*gradually)*
2 tablespoons water	

Transfer most of this to raisin and flour mixture. Chop in blender
    ½ cup walnuts
Add to previous mixture. Beat until stiff, not dry
    2 egg whites
Stir about ⅓ of the beaten egg whites into the combined mixture to soften it. Then fold in the rest of the beaten whites. Turn into a pudding mold or into small containers. Place the mold or containers in a pan with water 1 inch or more deep. Bake at 325° F. 1 hour for small containers, 1½ hours for a large container. **Six servings.**

ONE SERVING

Oil — 3 teaspoons	**Protein** — 5 grams
Cholesterol — 0 milligrams	**Carbohydrate** — 28 grams
Saturated fat — 2 grams	**Calories** — 265
Linoleic acid — 9 grams	**Total fat** — 15 grams

Serve with Pudding Sauce★ or with Whipped Topping★.

VARIATION:

For a sweeter pudding, add 1½ to 2 teaspoons liquid saccharin before baking.

PUDDING SAUCE

Mix in saucepan
    1 tablespoon cornstarch
    2 tablespoons water
    1 cup water
    ¼ teaspoon salt
    2 tablespoons oil

    ⅛ teaspoon grated orange rind (or 1 tablespoon orange peel in confetti-size pieces)

Cook, stirring until thickened, then remove from heat and add
    2 tablespoons lemon juice
    ½ teaspoon liquid saccharin (or to taste)
    ½ teaspoon vanilla
    ¼ teaspoon nutmeg

If sauce is to be served warm, place over hot water. **Six servings.**

ONE SERVING

Oil — 1 teaspoon	**Protein** — negligible
Cholesterol — 0 milligrams	**Carbohydrate** — 2 grams
Saturated fat — 1 gram	**Calories** — 55
Linoleic acid — 3 grams	**Total fat** — 5 grams

VARIATIONS:

1. Add rum flavoring to sauce.
2. Add 2 tablespoons chopped raisins or chopped dried fruits.

SHORTCAKE

Sift together
   1 cup sifted enriched flour
   1½ teaspoons baking powder
   ½ teaspoon salt
Stir together with a fork
   2½ tablespoons oil
   3 tablespoons water
   2 tablespoons frozen orange juice concentrate
Add the cold liquids to the flour mixture and mix with fork. Turn
the dough onto a floured wax paper or bread board and knead 3 or
4 times. Pat or roll out, cut into squares or cut with a biscuit
cutter. Transfer to an oiled pan, turn shortcakes to oil both sides
and bake at 425° F. 12 to 15 minutes. **Six servings.**

ONE SERVING
   Oil — 1¼ teaspoons
   Cholesterol — 0 milligrams
   Saturated fat — 1 gram
   Linoleic acid — 3 grams

   Protein — 2 grams
   Carbohydrate — 16 grams
   Calories — 125
   Total fat — 6 grams

STRAWBERRY SHORTCAKE

Chop
   3 cups fresh strawberries
Add
   1 teaspoon liquid saccharin (or more)
Serve on Shortcake★ with Sugar Free Whipped Topping I★ or II★
(or with Whipped Topping I★ or II★). **Six servings.**

ONE SERVING
   Oil — 1¼ teaspoons
   Cholesterol — 1 milligram
   Saturated fat — 1 gram
   Linoleic acid — 3 grams

   Protein — 4 grams
   Carbohydrate — 25 grams
   Calories — 170
   Total fat — 6 grams

WHIPPED TOPPINGS

When Whipped Toppings I★ and II★ are divided among 6 servings, the sugar content of 1 serving is small enough to be almost negligible and may therefore be used on a sugar free or low sugar regimen. However, since saccharin can satisfactorily replace the sugar in these toppings, you will prefer to use it for the sugar free diet.

SUGAR FREE WHIPPED TOPPING I

Prepare Whipped Topping I★, pages 61–62, but substitute ¼ to ½ teaspoon liquid saccharin for the sugar. **Six servings.**

ONE SERVING

Oil — 0 teaspoons	**Protein** — 1 grams
Cholesterol — 1 milligram	**Carbohydrate** — 2 grams
Saturated fat — 0 grams	**Calories** — 10
Linoleic acid — 0 grams	**Total fat** — 0 grams

SUGAR FREE WHIPPED TOPPING II

Prepare Whipped Topping II★, pages 62–63, but substitute ¼ to ½ teaspoon liquid saccharin for the sugar. **Six servings.**

ONE SERVING

Oil — 0 teaspoons	**Protein** — 3 grams
Cholesterol — 1 milligram	**Carbohydrate** — 2 grams
Saturated fat — 0 grams	**Calories** — 20
Linoleic acid — 0 grams	**Total fat** — 0 grams

GELATIN DESSERTS

Follow package directions for measuring and dissolving plain unflavored gelatin. In recipes that call for sugar, omit the sugar or decrease the amount and substitute saccharin for all or part of the sugar. The gelatin may be softened in water before dissolving or it may be placed directly over heat to dissolve, as in many of our recipes.

PLAIN GELATIN MOLD

While plain fruit-flavored gelatin molds can be made with artificial fruit flavoring and coloring in water, with a little lemon juice and saccharin added, we are partial to those made with natural fruit juices, with canned juices, or juices drained from stewed or water-packed fruit or berries.

ORANGE GELATIN MOLD

Place over low heat in a small saucepan and stir until completely dissolved (about 2 minutes)

2 tablespoons cold water
1 tablespoon gelatin

Pour into

1½ cups orange juice   *1 teaspoon liquid saccharin*
2 tablespoons lemon juice   *or to taste*
¼ cup water

Pour into mold and refrigerate. **Four servings.**

ONE SERVING

Oil — 0 teaspoons   **Protein** — 3 grams
Cholesterol — 0 milligrams   **Carbohydrate** — 10 grams
Saturated fat — 0 grams   **Calories** — 55
Linoleic acid — 0 grams   **Total fat** — 0 grams

Clear gelatins are appealing not only in a mold but also as gelatin squares (molded in a sheet and diced), as sparkling gelatin (forced through a ricer); or as whipped gelatin (when partly congealed, whipped with a beater). While these are quick and easy to prepare and light and refreshing after a meal, nutritionally better gelatin desserts are those filled with fruit and other ingredients.

PRUNE MOLD

Place over low heat and stir until dissolved

1 tablespoon gelatin
2 tablespoons water

Add to

1 cup prune juice   *¼ teaspoon cinnamon*
½ cup orange juice   *dash of salt*

Remove pits from
  1 cup cooked prunes
Chop them and add to gelatin mixture along with
  ¼ cup walnuts, coarsely chopped
Stir in
  1 teaspoon liquid saccharin
Pour into mold and refrigerate. **Eight servings.**

ONE SERVING

Oil — ½ teaspoon	**Protein** — 2 grams
Cholesterol — 0 milligrams	**Carbohydrate** — 18 grams
Saturated fat — negligible	**Calories** — 107
Linoleic acid — 1 gram	**Total fat** — 3 grams

Serve prune mold with "Special" Coffee Cream★.

RHUBARB STRAWBERRY MOLD

Boil until very soft
  2 cups sliced rhubarb
  1½ cups water
Drain off
  2 cups rhubarb juice
To this hot juice add and stir to dissolve
  1 tablespoon gelatin
softened in
  2 tablespoons water
Add
  2 teaspoons oil
  2 teaspoons liquid saccharin (or to taste)
Cut into pieces
  2 cups whole strawberries
Add to the rhubarb juice. Pour into mold and refrigerate. Serve as a dessert or salad. **Four servings.**

ONE SERVING

Oil — ½ teaspoon	**Protein** — 3 grams
Cholesterol — 0 milligrams	**Carbohydrate** — 8 grams
Saturated fat — negligible	**Calories** — 80
Linoleic acid — 1 gram	**Total fat** — 4 grams

SPANISH CREAM

Soak to soften
   1 tablespoon gelatin
   2 tablespoons water
Cook in a double boiler, stirring until mixture just begins to coat a spoon
   ⅔ cup skim milk powder   *dash of salt*
   1½ cups water   *1 tablespoon oil*
   3 egg whites
Remove from heat, add softened gelatin, and stir to dissolve. Fold in
   1 egg white, beaten stiff
   1 teaspoon liquid saccharin
   1 teaspoon vanilla
Pour in mold and place in refrigerator to set. Serve with 2 tablespoons chopped or puréed fruit per serving. **Four servings.**

ONE SERVING
   Oil — ¾ teaspoon   **Protein** — 10 grams
   Cholesterol — 4 milligrams   **Carbohydrate** — 9 grams
   Saturated fat — 1 gram   **Calories** — 116
   Linoleic acid — 2 grams   **Total fat** — 4 grams

CHEESECAKE

Soak to soften
   2 teaspoons gelatin
in
   1 tablespoon water
Combine in a saucepan and cook, stirring until mixture thickens
   1 cup water   *1½ teaspoons grated lemon*
   1½ tablespoons cornstarch   *rind*
   ⅛ teaspoon salt
Add the softened gelatin. Pour into a bowl and add slowly, while stirring
   3 tablespoons frozen orange juice concentrate
Spin in blender or whip with beater
   1 cup baker's cheese   *2 tablespoons lemon juice*
   ¼ cup oil   *3 tablespoons water*
   2 teaspoons liquid saccharin

Beat into the cooled cornstarch mixture and set aside. Whip until stiff with an electric beater

½ cup skim milk powder
½ cup water

Fold into the cheese mixture. Prepare 1 Walnut Crust★. Transfer cheese mixture to Walnut Crust★. **Eight servings.**

ONE SERVING

Oil — 3 teaspoons	**Protein** — 9 grams
Cholesterol — 3 milligrams	**Carbohydrate** — 13 grams
Saturated fat — 2 grams	**Calories** — 225
Linoleic acid — 8 grams	**Total fat** — 15 grams

RASPBERRY BAVARIAN CREAM

Stir over low heat until dissolved

1 tablespoon gelatin
¼ cup water

Remove from heat and cool but do not let it set. Add

½ cup skim milk powder
¼ cup water
½ teaspoon liquid saccharin (or more)

Whip with electric beater until stiff. Measure

2 cups fresh raspberries

Crush berries and mix with

2 tablespoons oil

Fold berry mixture into whipped gelatin and pour into mold. Place in refrigerator to set. **Four servings.**

ONE SERVING

Oil — 1½ teaspoons	**Protein** — 6 grams
Cholesterol — 3 milligrams	**Carbohydrate** — 13 grams
Saturated fat — 1 gram	**Calories** — 150
Linoleic acid — 4 grams	**Total fat** — 8 grams

VARIATIONS:

Use other berries or fruit, such as ripe persimmon pulp, water-packed pineapple, or peaches, etc.

WALNUT CRUST

Spin in blender
 ½ cup flour
 ½ cup walnuts
 ¼ teaspoon salt
Transfer to a bowl. Mix with a fork
 1 tablespoon water
 2 tablespoons oil
Stir into the flour and walnut mixture. Place in pie pan and flatten
with a fork dipped in flour or roll out with a small tumbler dusted
with flour. Bake at 350° F. for a few minutes until the crust becomes
light brown. If the edges brown first, cover them with aluminum foil
or paper. **Eight servings.**

ONE SERVING
Oil — 1¾ teaspoons	**Protein** — 2 grams
Cholesterol — 0 milligrams	**Carbohydrate** — 6 grams
Saturated fat — 1 gram	**Calories** — 105
Linoleic acid — 5 grams	**Total fat** — 8 grams

COOKIES, CAKES, AND TOPPINGS

Fruits and juices serve as the principal sweetening ingredients in
the following recipes. Little or no sugar is used. Saccharin may be
added if desired.

OATMEAL DATE COOKIE SNACKS

Spin in blender, half at a time, until almost like flour
 2 cups oatmeal or rolled oats
 ⅔ cup pitted dates
 2 tablespoons brown sugar
Empty into a bowl, then add to blender
 4 egg whites (or 4   *½ cup oil*
   tablespoons powdered egg   *2 teaspoons vanilla*
   white and ½ cup water)   *½ teaspoon salt*
Spin until powdered egg white is dissolved. Add
 ½ cup walnuts

Turn blender on and then off again at once. Spin only long enough to chop the nuts. Pour contents into the bowl with oatmeal and date mixture. Drop by spoonfuls onto an oiled or Teflon-coated cookie sheet to make 20 cookies. Flatten them with a fork dipped in flour. Bake at 350° F. 10 to 12 minutes.

ONE COOKIE

Oil — 1½ teaspoons	**Protein** — 3 grams
Cholesterol — 0 milligrams	**Carbohydrate** — 12 grams
Saturated fat — 1 gram	**Calories** — 130
Linoleic acid — 4 grams	**Total fat** — 8 grams

VARIATIONS:

1. *Oatmeal Date Cookie Snacks, Hand-Chopped:* In place of using blender, chop dates with knife or chop-mix dates and oatmeal with electric mixer.
2. *Spiced Cookie Snacks:* Add ¼ teaspoon each cinnamon and nutmeg and a pinch of cloves.
3. *Oatmeal Raisin Cookies:* Substitute raisins for dates.
4. *Sweetened Cookies:* Stir 3 teaspoons or more of liquid saccharin into the cookie mixture.

(Values are approximately the same.)

DATE NUT PINWHEELS

Cook, stirring, until thick

4 pitted dates, chopped	dash of cinnamon
¼ cup water	dash of salt
1 teaspoon cornstarch	
2 tablespoons chopped walnuts	

Prepare
   Shortcake★

Roll thin and spread with the cooled date mixture. Roll up, cut into 15 slices, place separated slices on an oiled pan, flatten slightly, and bake at 425° F. 10 to 14 minutes. **15 pinwheels.**

ONE PINWHEEL

Oil — ⅔ teaspoon	**Protein** — 1 gram
Cholesterol — 0 milligrams	**Carbohydrate** — 9 grams
Saturated fat — negligible	**Calories** — 65
Linoleic acid — 1 gram	**Total fat** — 3 grams

WHEAT GERM COOKIE SNACKS

Spin in a blender until well chopped
⅔ *cup wheat germ*
⅓ *cup seedless raisins*
Empty into a bowl and then chop in blender
⅓ *cup walnuts*
Add to raisin mixture, then add
⅔ *cup enriched flour*
¼ *teaspoon baking powder*
½ *teaspoon salt*
Beat together and stir into the above mixture

3 *tablespoons water*	1 *teaspoon vanilla*
2 *tablespoons molasses*	1 *teaspoon cinnamon*
3 *tablespoons oil*	2 *teaspoons liquid saccharin*
1 *egg white*	*(optional)*

Divide into 22 cookies. Flatten them with a fork dipped in flour. Bake at 350° F. 8 to 10 minutes. This cookie recipe is high in iron—2 cookies yield over 1 milligram (see Iron, page 470).

ONE SERVING (2 COOKIES)

Oil — 1⅓ teaspoons	**Protein** — 3 grams
Cholesterol — 0 milligrams	**Carbohydrate** — 14 grams
Saturated fat — negligible	**Calories** — 125
Linoleic acid — 3 grams	**Total fat** — 6 grams

VARIATIONS:

1. In place of raisins use ⅓ cup pitted dates.
2. Instead of molasses use 2 tablespoons sugar or brown sugar.

CRISP COOKIES

Mix and sift
3 *cups flour*
3 *teaspoons baking powder*
1 *teaspoon salt*
Mix in
⅔ *cup oil*
1 *teaspoon grated orange rind (or more)*
Stir in to make a dough
½ *cup frozen orange juice concentrate*
2 *teaspoons vanilla*
Turn cold dough into an oiled cookie sheet and, with a floured tumbler or rolling pin, roll out extremely thin. Cut with cookie cutter, picking up trimmings of dough between cookies and rerolling. **Makes 36 cookies.**

Put into a small salt shaker
    2 teaspoons sugar
Sprinkle the cookies evenly with this sugar. Bake at 350° F. 4 to 5
minutes or until they begin to brown. Remove with a pancake turner
any that brown early.

ONE SERVING (ONE COOKIE)

Oil — 1 teaspoon	**Protein** — 1 gram
Cholesterol — 0 milligrams	**Carbohydrate** — 10 grams
Saturated fat — 1 gram	**Calories** — 85
Linoleic acid — 2 grams	**Total fat** — 5 grams

VARIATIONS:

1. Add cinnamon or nutmeg to the sugar to sprinkle over cookies
   before baking.
2. *Lemon Cookies:* Add to recipe 1 teaspoon lemon extract and
   ½ teaspoon grated lemon rind.

ORANGE SPONGECAKE

Beat together
    ½ cup frozen orange juice concentrate
    2 tablespoons oil
    1½ teaspoons liquid saccharin (or more)
In another bowl whip until stiff
    6 tablespoons powdered egg white
    ¾ cup water
    ¼ teaspoon cream of tartar
Sift together
    1 cup flour
    ½ teaspoon baking powder
    ¼ teaspoon salt
and add to the orange juice-oil mixture together with about ⅓ of the
beaten egg whites. Then fold in the remaining egg whites, pour into
an oiled 8 by 8 inch pan or small bread pan and bake at 325° F. 10 to
14 minutes, or until a toothpick inserted comes out clean. **Twelve
servings.**

ONE SERVING

Oil — ½ teaspoon	**Protein** — 3 grams
Cholesterol — 0 milligrams	**Carbohydrate** — 16 grams
Saturated fat — 0 grams	**Calories** — 100
Linoleic acid — 1 gram	**Total fat** — 3 grams

PRUNE CAKE

Measure into a bowl

2 tablespoons oil

¼ cup frozen orange juice
    concentrate

½ teaspoon salt

½ teaspoon nutmeg

½ teaspoon cinnamon

1 teaspoon finely grated
    lemon rind

2 tablespoons water

2 teaspoons liquid saccharin
    (or more)

Sift together and set aside

1 cup sifted flour

1 teaspoon baking powder

Whip with an electric beater (or hand beater) in a large bowl until
fluffy

¾ cup prune juice (unsweetened, bottled)

⅓ cup powdered egg white

¼ teaspoon cream of tartar

Transfer beater to the oil and orange juice concentrate mixture to mix
ingredients. Fold this mixture into the beaten egg whites. Gradually
sift and fold in the flour, then fold in

¼ cup chopped walnuts

Pour into a small oiled bread pan. Bake at 325° F. 12 to 15 minutes
or until a toothpick inserted comes out clean. Or pour into oiled 8-inch
square or 9-inch round cake pan, bake at 325° F. 10 to 12 minutes.
Twelve servings.

ONE SERVING

Oil — 1 teaspoon

Cholesterol — negligible

Saturated fat — 1 gram

Linoleic acid — 2 grams

Protein — 3 grams

Carbohydrate — 15 grams

Calories — 110

Total fat — 4 grams

Top the cake with choice of topping recipes.

RAISIN NUT TOPPING

Spin in blender until raisins are well chopped

½ cup raisins

½ cup water

1 tablespoon flour

⅛ teaspoon salt

2 tablespoons oil

1 teaspoon gelatin

Stop motor. Add and spin again until chopped

⅓ cup walnuts

Transfer to a saucepan and cook, stirring until thickened. Remove from heat and stir in

⅓ cup cold water	*¼ cup skim milk powder*
1 teaspoon liquid saccharin	*½ teaspoon vanilla*

Place in refrigerator until firm. Stir to soften and spread on cake. **Twelve servings.**

ONE SERVING

Oil — 1 teaspoon	**Protein** — 1 gram
Cholesterol — negligible	**Carbohydrate** — 7 grams
Saturated fat — negligible	**Calories** — 70
Linoleic acid — 2 grams	**Total fat** — 4 grams

VANILLA CAKE TOPPING

Put into the top of a double boiler

2 teaspoons gelatin	*2 tablespoons oil*
2 tablespoons cornstarch	*dash of salt*
⅓ cup skim milk powder	*⅛ teaspoon cinnamon*
⅔ cup water	

Place over boiling water and cook, stirring until thickened. Remove, cool, then add

½ teaspoon vanilla
1 teaspoon liquid saccharin (or more, to taste)

Whip with an electric beater or hand beater until stiff

¼ cup skim milk powder
¼ cup water

Fold into the cooled cornstarch mixture, cover, and place in the refrigerator until set. **Twelve servings.**

ONE SERVING

Oil — ½ teaspoon	**Protein** — 2 grams
Cholesterol — 1 milligram	**Carbohydrate** — 3 grams
Saturated fat — negligible	**Calories** — 40
Linoleic acid — 1 gram	**Total fat** — 2 grams

COCOA CAKE TOPPING

Soak to soften

1 teaspoon gelatin
2 tablespoons cold water

Put into the top of a double boiler

2 tablespoons cocoa	dash of salt
¼ cup skim milk powder	1 tablespoon powdered sugar
¼ cup water	few drops of butter flavoring
2 tablespoons oil	(optional)
⅛ teaspoon cinnamon	

Bring to a boil over direct medium heat, stirring until the cocoa is dissolved and the mixture thickened. Stir together

⅓ cup water
1 tablespoon cornstarch

Pour into hot cocoa mixture, stirring vigorously. Place over boiling water and cook, stirring until thickened. Stir in the softened gelatin. Remove from heat and set the mixture aside to cool. Whip with an electric beater until stiff

¼ cup skim milk powder	1 teaspoon vanilla
3 tablespoons water	
1 to 1½ teaspoons liquid saccharin	

Fold this into the cold cornstarch mixture and spread over cake. Place in the refrigerator to set. **Twelve servings.**

ONE SERVING

Oil — ½ teaspoon	**Protein** — 1 gram
Cholesterol — 1 milligram	**Carbohydrate** — 3 grams
Saturated fat — negligible	**Calories** — 40
Linoleic acid — 1 gram	**Total fat** — 3 grams

ORANGE TOPPING

Dissolve, while stirring, over direct medium heat

1 teaspoon gelatin

in

2 tablespoons water

Remove from heat and add

1 tablespoon lemon juice	dash of salt
4 tablespoons frozen orange juice concentrate	½ teaspoon vanilla (optional)
½ teaspoon liquid saccharin (or more, to taste)	

Stir vigorously until the frozen orange juice concentrate is thawed, then add

½ cup skim milk powder

Whip with an electric beater until stiff. Fold in
    2 *tablespoons oil*
    ¼ *teaspoon nutmeg (optional)*
Heap on cake and place in refrigerator. **Twelve servings.**

ONE SERVING

Oil — ½ teaspoon	**Protein** — 1 gram
Cholesterol — 1 milligram	**Carbohydrate** — 4 grams
Saturated fat — negligible	**Calories** — 40
Linoleic acid — 1 gram	**Total fat** — 2 grams

FROZEN DESSERTS

Freeze these desserts in an ice cream freezer, or if this is not available freeze them as follows.

Method of Freezing

Prepare the mixture to be frozen according to the recipe. Pour it into freezing containers and place in the freezer until well frozen. A short time before serving, break up the hard frozen mixture with a spoon, put it into the blender, add liquid according to the recipe, and spin at low speed for a few seconds. Stop blender, push down the frozen mixture, spin again. Repeat a few times. (You may prefer to blend half at a time.) This will give a mushy consistency. Serve at once or hold in deep freeze for only a short time before serving.

ORANGE PARFAIT

Spin in blender (or mix with beater)
    ¾ *cup frozen orange juice*   ¼ *cup oil*
        concentrate   ½ *teaspoon liquid saccharin*
    1¼ *cups water*   *(or more, to taste)*
Apply standard Method of Freezing★, reblending with
    ¼ *cup cold water*
Serve in tall parfait glasses. Streak each serving with 2 teaspoons frozen orange juice concentrate. **Six servings.**

ONE SERVING

Oil — 2 teaspoons	**Protein** — 1 gram
Cholesterol — 0 milligrams	**Carbohydrate** — 14 grams
Saturated fat — 1 gram	**Calories** — 145
Linoleic acid — 5 grams	**Total fat** — 10 grams

CRANBERRY ICE

Spin in blender
> 2 *cups (½ pound) raw*
> *cranberries*
> *water to cover*
> 1 *tablespoon flour*
> 2 *tablespoons oil*

Pour into a saucepan and boil until cranberries are cooked and the mixture slightly thickened. Cool and add
> 2 *tablespoons sugar*
> 1 *teaspoon liquid saccharin (or to taste)*
> ⅛ *teaspoon salt*

Apply standard Method of Freezing★, reblending with
> ¼ *cup water*

Six servings.

ONE SERVING
> **Oil** — 1 teaspoon
> **Cholesterol** — 0 milligrams
> **Saturated fat** — 1 gram
> **Linoleic acid** — 3 grams

> **Protein** — negligible
> **Carbohydrate** — 9 grams
> **Calories** — 80
> **Total fat** — 5 grams

PINEAPPLE PARFAIT

Spin in blender until smooth
> 2 *cups canned water-packed pineapple*
> ¼ *cup oil*
> 1 *teaspoon liquid saccharin*

Apply standard Method of Freezing★, reblending with
> ¼ *cup water (or more)*

Serve in parfait glasses. Streak each serving with
> 1 *tablespoon chopped peach (or apricot)*

Six servings.

ONE SERVING
> **Oil** — 2 teaspoons
> **Cholesterol** — 0 milligrams
> **Saturated fat** — 1 gram
> **Linoleic acid** — 5 grams

> **Protein** — negligible
> **Carbohydrate** — 8 grams
> **Calories** — 115
> **Total fat** — 9 grams

VARIATIONS:

1. *Pineapple Ice:* Substitute 2 cups unsweetened pineapple juice for the pineapple.

2. *Berry Ice:* Substitute 2 cups berries, fresh or water-packed, for the pineapple.
3. *Grape Ice:* Substitute 1⅓ cups grape juice and ⅔ cup water for the pineapple. For final blending, use either water or grape juice.
4. *Peach Ice:* Substitute 2 cups fresh or water-packed peaches for the pineapple. For final blending, use 2 teaspoons lemon juice in ¼ cup water.

LEMON SHERBET

Spin in blender
  3 tablespoons lemon juice   *1½ teaspoons liquid saccharin*
  1 cup water   *⅓ cup skim milk powder*
  2 tablespoons oil   *1 tablespoon sugar*
Apply standard Method of Freezing★, reblending with
  ¼ cup water
  2 tablespoons frozen orange juice concentrate
Six servings.

ONE SERVING
  Oil — 1 teaspoon   **Protein** — 1 gram
  Cholesterol — 1 milligram **Carbohydrate** — 7 grams
  Saturated fat — 1 gram   **Calories** — 75
  Linoleic acid — 3 grams   **Total fat** — 5 grams

ORANGE SHERBET

To the recipe for Orange Parfait★ add
  ⅓ cup skim milk powder
Six servings.

ONE SERVING
  Oil — 2 teaspoons   **Protein** — 2 grams
  Cholesterol — 1 milligram **Carbohydrate** — 16 grams
  Saturated fat — 1 gram   **Calories** — 155
  Linoleic acid — 5 grams   **Total fat** — 9 grams

CRANBERRY SHERBET

To the recipe for Cranberry Ice★ add
    ½ cup skim milk powder
    1 tablespoon oil
Six servings.

ONE SERVING

    Oil — 1½ teaspoons   **Protein** — 2 grams
    Cholesterol — 2 milligrams   **Carbohydrate** — 12 grams
    Saturated fat — 1 gram   **Calories** — 120
    Linoleic acid — 4 grams   **Total fat** — 7 grams

PINEAPPLE SHERBET

To the recipe for Pineapple Parfait★ add
    ½ cup skim milk powder
Six servings.

ONE SERVING

    Oil — 2 teaspoons   **Protein** — 2 grams
    Cholesterol — 2 milligrams   **Carbohydrate** — 11 grams
    Saturated fat — 1 gram   **Calories** — 135
    Linoleic acid — 5 grams   **Total fat** — 9 grams

BERRY SHERBET

To the recipe for Pineapple Parfait★, substitute berries for pineapple and add
    ½ cup skim milk powder
Six servings.

ONE SERVING

    Oil — 2 teaspoons   **Protein** — 2 grams
    Cholesterol — 2 milligrams   **Carbohydrate** — 11 grams
    Saturated fat — 1 gram   **Calories** — 135
    Linoleic acid — 5 grams   **Total fat** — 9 grams

CHAPTER XXVII

How to Restrict the Sodium
on a Low Saturated Fat,
Low Cholesterol Diet

OFTEN a person on a low saturated fat, low cholesterol diet has also to restrict the amount of the mineral sodium in his diet. Sodium is found in almost all the plant and animal tissues that we use as food. Then, most of us add extra sodium to our diet, chiefly by using table salt. Salt, a chemical compound of sodium and chlorine, is 40 per cent sodium. One teaspoon of salt has approximately 2300 milligrams of sodium. We all need some sodium in the diet, but some of us, because of an upset in our body processes, retain sodium to an extent that causes tissue swelling. These persons need much less sodium than we would normally eat. For them, the physician prescribes a restricted sodium diet. Under no circumstances should you adopt a restricted sodium diet without the recommendation and supervision of your physician, because persons in normal health are apt to suffer from sodium insufficiency on such a diet.

To dovetail a low saturated fat, low cholesterol diet with a restricted sodium diet presents a definite challenge. This challenge can be met successfully, however, with ingenuity and planning. As the title of our book states, our chief objective is to aid in planning and executing a low saturated fat, low cholesterol diet regimen. For those who are also restricted as to sodium, we offer suggestions we have found helpful. For a more complete discussion, we recommend the following three booklets and their accompanying leaflets, all published by the American Heart Association:*

Your Mild Sodium-Restricted Diet

* For information about obtaining these, consult your local Heart Association.

Your 1000 Milligram Sodium Diet—Moderate Sodium Restriction
Your 500 Milligram Sodium Diet—Strict Sodium Restriction

The purpose of this chapter is to suggest ways of keeping the food intake low in sodium while using low saturated fat, low cholesterol foods. This usually means more than merely avoiding the addition of sodium chloride (salt) to foods in cooking or at the table. It means selecting foods and using seasonings that, upon chemical analysis, have proved to be low in the mineral, sodium. Our average American diet contains from 3000 to 7000 milligrams of sodium daily. Individual preferences for highly seasoned or salty foods may double this figure. There are all stages of restriction in sodium diets, from 2000 milligrams of sodium a day to as low as 100 milligrams. The extremely restricted sodium diet is often just a modification of the "rice diet." (This diet consists of rice, fruit, fruit juices, and vitamin and mineral supplements.) As the amount of sodium allowed in the diet is increased, your choice of food widens.

Chemical analyses have shown that the sodium content of foods of animal origin, such as meat, skim milk, skim milk cottage cheese, and egg whites, is relatively high. These foods must be restricted in amount but must be included in the diet because of their complete protein value. Fortunately, most fresh fruits and vegetables as well as cereal products are relatively low not only in sodium but also in cholesterol and saturated fat. These foods can therefore be used in abundance to make the diet appetizing and nutritious.

How to Restrict the Sodium in Your Low Saturated Fat, Low Cholesterol Diet

To plan a restricted sodium diet, modify the low saturated fat, low cholesterol Daily Food Guide recommended by your physician according to these additional principles, and make use of the food lists in this chapter:

1. All foods are to be prepared and seasoned without the addition of salt, monosodium glutamate, baking soda (bicarbonate of soda, sodium bicarbonate), or baking powder. For baked goods, use yeast, sodium free baking powder, or potassium bicarbonate instead of baking soda.

2. Read all food labels to note additions of salt or sodium in any form, and avoid those products.

NOTE: Most canned vegetables have salt added to them, even if the label does not list it.

3. Avoid commercially prepared food labeled "salt free" (except upon the advice of your physician or dietitian). Many such products have been proved by chemical analysis to be high in sodium and often not much lower than the regular products. Acceptable products will state the amount of sodium they contain.

4. Avoid sugar substitutes in general, since most of them contain sodium. If you need one, make sure it does not contain sodium.

5. Avoid medications unless prescribed by your physician. Many patent medicines are high in sodium.

6. Avoid bottled soft drinks, since most contain sodium.

7. Check on the sodium content of your drinking water. The American Heart Association suggests that if 1 quart of your tap water contains more than 20 milligrams of sodium, distilled water should be used for drinking and cooking.

Foods to Use and Foods to Avoid on the Restricted Sodium, Low Saturated Fat, Low Cholesterol Diet*

A. MEAT, FISH, AND POULTRY

(1 ounce contains approximately 50 calories and 20 milligrams sodium.)

Use:

6 ounces cooked lean meat, fish, or poultry daily.

NOTE: ¼ cup unsalted cottage cheese† may be substituted for 1 ounce meat. 1 egg white has approximately the same sodium content as 1 ounce meat but less than half as much protein.

Avoid:

Smoked, salted, cured, or corned meats, fish, or poultry.
Frozen fish. (Be sure to rinse fresh fish thoroughly, since it has often been stored in brine (salt and water).

* The amounts of foods listed in this Daily Food Guide are for a 500-milligram sodium diet, which is a strict restriction. The amount of sodium in the diet may easily be increased to meet your physician's recommendation by the addition of appropriate amounts of foods listed on page 439.
† Low fat, low sodium cottage cheese is available commercially from many dairies.

Ham or bacon (imitation variety, too).
Shellfish.
Canned tuna unless it is labeled low sodium, and preferably with
milligrams of sodium per ounce of tuna stated on the label.

B. UNSALTED FATS AND OILS

(1 teaspoon contains approximately 45 calories and practically no
sodium.)

Use:

Polyunsaturated vegetable oils.
Salad dressings, mayonnaise, and "French" dressing made at home
without salt.
Salt free "special" margarine.
Unsalted nuts of the varieties acceptable in the low saturated fat,
low cholesterol diet; nuts are particularly low in sodium.

Avoid:

Salted "special" margarine (1 teaspoon salted margarine contains
about 50 milligrams sodium).*
Salted nuts.

C. SKIM MILK AND SKIM MILK BUTTERMILK

(1 cup contains about 80 calories and 120 milligrams sodium.)

Use:

2 cups skim milk, skim milk buttermilk, or the equivalent in evaporated skim milk or skim milk powder daily.

NOTE: Some dairies add salt to their buttermilk, so check with your
local dairy.

8 ounces skim milk yogurt may be substituted for 1 cup skim milk.
Low sodium skim milk or the equivalent amount of low sodium skim
milk powder, as desired.† Most liquid low sodium milk has 12
milligrams sodium per cup of milk.

* See page 436 for preparing low sodium "special" margarine.
† Many dairies have low sodium skim milk available as a frozen product. Check
at your local dairy or check with your dietitian regarding how to buy it. There
is also a low sodium skim milk powder available.

Avoid:

Any additional milk, unless it is low sodium skim milk.

D. VEGETABLES

(1 serving has from 5 to 35 calories and about 9 milligrams sodium.)

NOTE: Starchy and high calorie vegetables are listed under F. LOW
SODIUM BREADS, CEREALS, CEREAL PRODUCTS, AND STARCHY VEGETABLES.

Use:

All fresh and frozen vegetables except those listed under the heading

Avoid:

Vegetables canned specially without salt (check with your physician).
Low sodium tomato juice.
Limit carrots to 2 servings per week, since they are higher in sodium
content.

Avoid:

All vegetables and vegetable juices canned with salt (½ cup regular
canned tomato juice contains about 200 milligrams sodium).
Frozen peas and lima beans (salt has been added).
In all forms: artichokes, beet greens, beets, celery, chard, dandelion
greens, kale, mustard greens, sauerkraut, spinach, and white turnips.

E. FRUITS

(1 serving fresh fruit contains about 40 calories and 2 milligrams
sodium. For fruit canned in medium syrup, add 40 calories.)

Use:

All types of fresh, frozen, or canned fruits or juices (see comments
on tomato juice under D. VEGETABLES).
Dried apricots and dried prunes.

NOTE: Read the labels on packages of frozen and dried fruit. Sometimes a sodium preservative has been added.

Avoid:

Glazed fruit.
Maraschino cherries.

F. LOW SODIUM BREADS, CEREALS, CEREAL PRODUCTS, AND STARCHY VEGETABLES

(1 serving contains about 70 calories and 5 milligrams sodium.)

Use:

Yeast bread made without salt, baking powder, or other sodium compounds.

Matzos (plain Jewish Passover crackers).

Unsalted cooked cereals (not the quick-cooking variety).

Dry cereals: puffed rice, puffed wheat, and shredded wheat.

Pastes: spaghetti, macaroni, and vermicelli, manufactured and cooked without salt.

Rice.

Barley.

Unsalted popcorn.

Flour—all kinds except self-rising.

Vegetables—Irish potato, sweet potato, corn, lentils, split peas, parsnips, dried lima beans, and green lima beans (except frozen).

Avoid:

All regular bakery bread, rolls, muffins or biscuits (1 slice of regular bread contains approximately 125 milligrams sodium).

All home-baked bakery products that use baking powder or soda.

All commercial crackers such as graham, soda, pretzels, oyster crackers, etc.

All commercial mixes for cakes, waffles, pancakes, etc.

Dry cereals except the three listed above.

All quick cooking and instant cereals.

Potato chips, corn chips, salted popcorn, etc.

Self-rising flour and corn meal.

Frozen green lima beans and frozen peas, since salt is added in the freezing process.

Whole hominy.

G. DIETER'S CHOICE

(The amount used will depend on the caloric value of your Daily Food Guide.) The required calories can be supplied by fruits, low sodium vegetables, low sodium bread, low sodium grain products, walnuts and other nuts low in saturated fats, "special" low sodium desserts, low sodium soups and sweets.

NOTE: Be sure cakes and cookies are made without salt, soda, cream of tartar, baking powder, or self-rising flour.

Avoid:

Commercial flavored gelatin products.*

H. MISCELLANEOUS (little or no calories)

Use servings as desired.
Soups—low sodium bouillon cube.
Beverages—coffee, tea, coffee substitutes.
Gelatin—unflavored; add your own low sodium flavoring.
Seasonings that do not contain sodium: pepper, herbs, spices, vinegar,† lemon juice, saccharin,‡ low sodium catsup, dry mustard (but not prepared mustard).

The following is a menu for a 1200 Calorie Diet with the sodium restricted to 500 milligrams. This menu is planned by combining the 1200 Calorie Daily Food Guide with the rules on how to restrict the sodium on a Low Saturated Fat, Low Cholesterol Diet discussed earlier in this chapter. Any other Daily Food Guide also can be combined in this way.

1200-Calorie (500-Milligram Sodium) Low Saturated Fat, Low Cholesterol Diet (all food is to be prepared without the addition of salt)

6 teaspoons oil allowance (see page 27)

BREAKFAST
½ cup orange juice
¾ cup puffed wheat dry cereal
1 slice whole-wheat toast (low sodium)
1 teaspoon Low Sodium "Special" Margarine★
1 cup skim milk
Coffee or tea if desired

LUNCH
½ cup chilled apple juice
Open-Face Sandwich:

* Acceptable gelatin desserts and aspics can be made at home.
† Choosing a flavorful vinegar is important, since the wine vinegars that are high in acetic acid and wine taste seem to reduce the need for salt in salads; many persons will find simple oil and vinegar dressing tasty without salt.
‡ Avoid saccharin containing sodium.

3 ounces unsalted chicken
1 slice low sodium bread
1 teaspoon low sodium mayonnaise
lettuce
½ cup peas with ½ teaspoon Orange Oil★
Tossed green salad with 1 tablespoon low sodium French Dressing★
1 peach, sliced (or ½ cup water-packed canned peaches)
Coffee or tea if desired

DINNER
Lean roast beef, 3 ounces cooked weight, garnished with lemon slices
½ cup or ½ small baked potato with 1 teaspoon Herbed Oil★
½ cup string beans with 1 teaspoon Orange Oil★
Sliced tomato salad
½ cup water-packed canned apricots
1 cup skim milk
Coffee or tea if desired

NOTE: This menu was prepared by combining the 1200-Calorie Daily Food Guide with the guide for the low sodium diet. You can increase or decrease your calories by choosing a different Daily Food Guide, increase your sodium by adding foods listed on page 439, or do both. Remember that, unless you use low sodium skim milk, the amount of skim milk allowed in the low sodium Daily Food Guide is more restricted than in the other diets, so you will have extra calories in the Dieter's Choice. Since the 1200-Calorie Daily Food Guide recommends 2½ cups milk, while the above menu includes only 2 cups, an extra 40 calories is available as Dieter's Choice. We have used it for the apple juice.

Potpourri (A Few Ideas to Help You)

Foods don't have to be seasoned with salt in order to be tasty. Natural flavors, spices, and herbs magically enliven unsalted dishes. For example, one or more of the herbs orégano, tarragon, basil, rosemary, sage, and thyme can be used in combination with oil and added to either meat or starchy foods for a gourmet dish. We suggest that you experiment in cooking with herbs and spices and discover for yourself the delight of other seasonings.

When the natural food flavors are carefully preserved, there seems to be a decrease in the need for additional seasoning. This is why it is so important, for example, not to overcook vegetables. Not only does overcooking destroy nutrients, but it destroys the vegetable's natural flavor. One of our favorite ways to cook unsalted vegetables is to place the vegetables in a sealed plastic bag, put the bag of vegetables into gently boiling water, and cook until the vegetables are just done.* Then, just before serving, add a bit of natural fruit flavoring such as lemon, lime or orange juice.

Adding natural fruit flavors to foods is an excellent way to lessen the taste need for salt and enhance the flavor of the food. Some suggestions are:

Use Orange Oil★ or Lemon Oil★ on vegetables.
Use lemon juice on all meats, not just fish.
Serve fresh fruit, such as ripe strawberries or pineapple, as an accompaniment to meat on the entree plate. It seems to lessen the need for salting the meat.

Preparing a Low Sodium "Special" Margarine

When we first published *The Low Fat, Low Cholesterol Diet*, it was extremely difficult to find an unsalted margarine. Now, many large grocery stores carry a low sodium "special" margarine. However, for those of you who may not be able to purchase this product readily, we are including our original recipe to transform your "special" margarine into a low sodium "special" margarine.

LOW SODIUM "SPECIAL" MARGARINE

Bring 2 cups water to boil in a small saucepan. Remove the pan from the heat and add ¼ pound "special" margarine that has been cut into several small pieces. Stir until the margarine is entirely melted. Cool the margarine and water mixture. When the margarine has solidified on top of the water, cut a hole in the margarine and pour out the water. Press margarine into mold and store in the refrigerator. Most of the sodium will have dissolved in the liquid and the remaining "special" margarine will be low in sodium.

Dialyzed Skim Milk

Sometimes a diet must be so restricted in sodium that regular skim milk cannot be included, yet the diet needs the nutrients that milk supplies. Then it is necessary either to buy a commercial low sodium skim milk or to improvise and provide it yourself by dialyzing skim milk. In dialyzing, most of the sodium is removed and some of the other minerals of milk are partially lost. However, it is still an excellent source of complete protein and calcium.

* See Cooking in Heavy-Duty Foil, page 216, for another excellent way of cooking unsalted vegetables.

How to Dialyze Skim Milk

Equipment Needed:

1. Cellophane meat casings—the type used in making bologna, liverwurst, and sausage. Most meat markets and wholesale meat-packing firms sell these casings.
2. Common household string.
3. A large container to hold water, with an arrangement by which a continual stream of water may run in and out. For example, the basin of a sink with an overflow outlet.

Directions:

Fill the cellophane casing with skim milk and tie the ends securely so that the milk does not leak out. The result looks like a white frankfurter in a cellophane jacket. Fill the sink or laundry tub with water and adjust the tap so that the overflow outlet can handle the flow. With the string, fasten the cellophane bag into the tub. The bag should be completely submerged and the water should be able to flow freely about the bag. Leave overnight. By osmosis, this process removes most of the sodium from the milk.

Pour the milk into clean jars, cover, and refrigerate. We advise using extra care to keep the milk sweet, since it sours so easily. The cellophane casings may be washed and used again and again. If the casings are not washed completely clean before each use, souring occurs.

What About Salt Substitutes?

Many salt substitutes are available commercially. These substitutes, usually a crystalline preparation containing potassium chloride, differ in taste and form. They are improving each year. The one you choose depends upon your taste and your doctor's recommendation. Be sure to have your doctor approve your choice, for salt substitutes often contain other sodium products and would thus defeat the entire purpose of your diet.

Where Can I Get Low Sodium Bread?

Certain bakeries specialize in low sodium breads and other bakery products. You may ask your physician or dietitian to recommend a bakery of this kind. The best way, though, to ensure having low sodium bread is to bake your own. Try this:

LOW SODIUM WHITE YEAST BREAD OR ROLLS

Place in a large mixing bowl
>2 *tablespoons polyunsaturated oil*
>2 *tablespoons sugar*

Add
>2 *cups boiling water*

Cool to lukewarm. Dissolve
>1 *yeast cake*

in
>¼ *cup lukewarm water*

Add the yeast solution to the lukewarm oil and sugar mixture. Add
>3 *cups sifted bread flour*
>1 *teaspoon finely grated lemon rind*

Mix ingredients well, gradually add to the batter
>3 *cups sifted all-purpose flour*

Mix well with each addition. Use only enough of the flour to prevent sticking. Turn onto floured board and knead until mixture is smooth and elastic to the touch and bubbles may be seen under the surface. Return to bowl, cover, and let rise in warm place until double in bulk. Cut down. Turn onto slightly floured board and knead and shape into loaves or rolls. Place in oiled loaf pans or on oiled baking sheets. Cover and let rise in warm place until double in bulk. Bake bread in hot oven (425° F.) 15 minutes, then reduce to moderate (375° F.) and bake 30 to 35 minutes longer. Recipe makes 2 loaves (28 slices). For rolls, bake in hot oven (425° F.) 15 to 20 minutes.

ONE SLICE

Oil — negligible	**Protein** — 2 grams
Cholesterol — 0 milligrams	**Carbohydrate** — 19 grams
Saturated fat — negligible	**Calories** — 85
Linoleic acid — negligible	

VARIATIONS:

1. WHEAT GERM BREAD

In the recipe for low sodium yeast bread, substitute ⅔ cup toasted wheat germ for ⅔ cup all-purpose enriched flour

2. RAISIN NUT BREAD

Add to either the low sodium yeast bread dough or wheat germ bread dough after it has risen once:
>1 *cup raisins*
>1 *cup walnuts, chopped*

APPROXIMATE SODIUM CONTENT OF FOODS RELATIVELY
HIGH IN SODIUM WHICH MAY BE ACCEPTABLE
FOR MILDLY RESTRICTED SODIUM DIETS*

	Milligrams of Sodium
Egg white, 1 medium-size	50
Skim milk, 1 cup	120
Skim milk buttermilk, 1 cup	310
Skim milk cottage cheese, unwashed, ½ cup	290
Yogurt, skim milk, 1 cup	125
"Special" margarine, 1 teaspoon	50
"Special" mayonnaise, 1 teaspoon	30
Vegetables	
½ cup of the allowed vegetables, if canned with salt	235
Carrots, raw, 2 medium	45
cooked, ½ cup	35
canned with salt, ½ cup	240
Vegetables usually avoided on strict sodium diet	
Celery, raw, 1 stalk	50
Beets, cooked, ½ cup	50
canned with salt, ½ cup	240
Spinach, cooked, ½ cup	50
canned with salt, ½ cup	240
Tomato juice canned with salt, ½ cup	240
Turnips, cooked, ½ cup	50
Turnip greens, canned with salt, ½ cup	240
Peas, frozen, ½ cup	110
Lima beans, frozen, ½ cup	100
Bread, regular, 1 slice	125
Cereal, dry (for example, corn flakes), ¾ cup	250
Crackers, soda, 2	120
Salt, ¼ teaspoon	580

* These figures are approximate and are to be used as a guide for determining
which foods you want to add to your low sodium diet when your physician
allows more than 500 milligrams of sodium.

Foods low in sodium are listed under the individual food groups in the Daily
Food Guide in this chapter.

CHAPTER XXVIII

How to Build a Low or
High Calorie Diet

ALTHOUGH the word "calorie" is used almost glibly by the average person, few actually know just what a calorie is. A calorie is a unit of energy used in specifying the fuel or energy value of a food and also in expressing how much fuel or energy the body must expend in doing a particular task. The amount of energy expended is dependent not only on the task but also on many other factors, such as the size, sex, and age of the individual. Naturally, more units of energy or more calories are used by the individual engaged in physical labor than by the office worker.

The foods eaten supply the caloric requirements or fuel for the body. Each class of foods has a definite caloric or energy value.

1 gram of carbohydrate produces 4 calories
1 gram of protein produces 4 calories
1 gram of fat produces 9 calories

Very few foods are pure carbohydrate, protein, or fat but are a mixture of the three plus noncaloric minerals, vitamins, water, and fiber. The caloric value of a food is dependent upon the proportions of these components. Low calorie or bulky foods such as celery, lettuce, and spinach have a low concentration of carbohydrates, fats, and proteins but have a high concentration of fiber and water. High calorie foods have a higher concentration of carbohydrate, fat, and protein and small amounts of moisture and fiber. As shown above, the caloric value of fat is more than twice as great as that of either carbohydrate or protein; therefore, foods containing a large percentage of fat will be much higher in caloric value than foods containing a similar percentage of protein and carbohydrate.

Fewer Calories Mean Weight Loss

When the intake of calories exceeds the output, the individual gains weight. If you are gaining weight, there is usually only one reason—you are eating too much food. On the other hand, if you are losing weight, you are not eating enough food to meet your calorie needs.

For the individual who wants either to lose or gain weight, calories then take on major importance. Too often, though, the dieter forgets the other goals in nutrition in his pursuit of a low calorie diet. The recommendations for a nutritionally adequate diet should always be followed, whether the diet be for 800 calories or for 3500 calories.

A strict low calorie diet should never, under any circumstances, be undertaken without consulting a physician. This cannot be overemphasized, for there may be other factors of health to consider which only your physician can determine. A diet restricted in calories requires careful planning, for most low calorie diets are lacking in some important vitamins and minerals and require additional supplements.

Accurate Measurement Is the Secret

With the strict low calorie diet, measurements are extremely important. A rounded serving portion here and there adds unsuspected calories. If your menu plan calls for ½ cup of potatoes and you serve ¾ cup, you have added 35 or more extra calories. In teaching low calorie diet regimens, we have found that, when a person realizes the importance of measuring accurately, he loses weight faster. Too often the specified ½ teaspoon of "special" margarine actually becomes 1 teaspoon, which adds 22 calories. Soon the 800-calorie diet becomes a 1000-calorie diet.

Additional Hints for the Low Calorie Dieter

To help remedy the feeling of hunger that often accompanies the low calorie diet, include a large proportion of bulky and chewy foods, such as lettuce sections, celery, or tomato wedges. Saving some of your calories from one meal for an in-between snack also helps to satisfy. The important thing to remember is to eat only the prescribed number of calories during the entire day. Your menu plans, however, may be arranged to suit your own convenience.

Using water-packed canned fruits helps conserve rationed calories and yet provides the same vitamin and mineral content as fruits canned in syrup. One half cup of water-packed fruit gives approximately 40 calories, while ½ cup of fruit canned in heavy syrup gives 80 to 100 calories.

Meet your nutritional requirements with low calorie foods. They are skim milk cottage cheese and skim milk; egg whites and the lean meats, fish and poultry; and the low calorie fruits and vegetables. The concentrated foods should be avoided; this means the exclusion of most sweets* and the limiting of the breads, cereal products, and starchy vegetables.

800-Calorie Low Saturated Fat, Low Cholesterol Diet

> 20 grams total fat, including:
> 4 grams saturated
> 6 grams linoleic
> 2 teaspoons fat and oil allowance
> 130 milligrams cholesterol
> 68 grams protein

A. MEAT, FISH, AND POULTRY—Daily

Use: 5 ounces cooked lean meat, fish, or poultry. Limit the servings of beef, lamb, and pork to 4 a week. These servings (after cooking) must be only 3 ounces each, so that the amount of saturated fat is limited.

For the other meat meals, use poultry, veal, fish, or meat substitutes. The meat servings can be divided among the day's meals as you desire. For example:

A 3-ounce steak for breakfast
Vegetable plate and skim milk for lunch
2 ounces fish for dinner
    or
2 ounces chicken for lunch
3 ounces veal for dinner

Meat substitutes: ¼ cup skim milk cottage cheese or 2 egg whites may be substituted for 1 ounce meat, fish, or poultry. Be sure to note that, although protein values are similar to meat, caloric values are not.

B. FATS AND OILS—Daily

Use: 2 teaspoons. The oil may be used in cooking, added to food, or in salad dressings (see pages 27, 68–69). It is important to use all of the prescribed polyunsaturated oil.

* See page 401 on nonnutritive sweeteners and page 395 for Low Calorie Desserts.

C. SKIM MILK, SKIM MILK BUTTERMILK—Daily

Use: 3 cups fortified with A and D vitamins, or the equivalent in skim milk powder or evaporated skim milk.

D. VEGETABLES—Daily

Use: 3 or more servings to include: 2 or more servings of low calorie vegetables, 1 serving of which should be raw.
One additional serving of vegetable that can be either a low or medium calorie vegetable. One of the vegetables eaten should be either dark green or deep yellow.

E. FRUITS—Daily

Use: 3 servings of fresh, frozen, or canned without additional sugar to include: ½ cup citrus fruit or citrus fruit juice, or, 1 cup tomato juice

F. BREAD, CEREALS, CEREAL PRODUCTS, AND STARCHY VEGETABLES—Daily

Use: 1 serving. This can be 1 slice bread, ½ cup starchy vegetable, or ½ cup cereal

G. DIETER'S CHOICE

Absolutely no additional calories are allowed on the 800-calorie diet.

H. MISCELLANEOUS (contain little or no calories)

Use: Servings as desired.
Soups—clear broth, bouillon
Beverages—coffee, tea, coffee substitutes (without sugar, milk, or cream)
Seasonings—salt, pepper, herbs, spices, vinegar, and lemon juice

Here is a menu that illustrates the application of the 800-calorie diet guide in meal planning:
2 teaspoons oil allowance*
No Dieter's Choice

* The number in parentheses is the teaspoons of oil used in that particular food.

BREAKFAST
>   ½ cup orange juice
>   ½ cup cooked whole-wheat cereal
>   1 cup skim milk
>   Coffee or tea if desired

LUNCH
>   2-ounce serving sliced chicken
>   ½ cup asparagus
>   Large tossed green salad with 1 tablespoon Low Fat French
>   Dressing★   (1)
>   1 fresh peach, sliced, or ½ cup water-packed peaches
>   1 cup skim milk
>   Coffee or tea if desired

DINNER
>   3-ounce serving roast beef
>   ½ cup string beans seasoned with 1 teaspoon Orange Oil★
>   (1)
>   ½ cup carrots
>   Large sliced tomato salad with 1 serving Fat Free French
>   Dressing★
>   ½ cup water-packed canned apricots
>   1 cup skim milk
>   Coffee or tea if desired

1200-Calorie Low Saturated Fat, Low Cholesterol Diet
>   39 grams total fat, including:
>   8 grams saturated
>   16 grams linoleic
>   2 tablespoons (6 teaspoons) fat and oil allowance
>   145 milligrams cholesterol
>   80 grams protein

A. MEAT, FISH, AND POULTRY—Daily

Use: 6 ounces cooked lean meat, fish, or poultry. Limit the servings of beef, lamb, and pork to 4 a week. These servings (after cooking) must be only 3 ounces each, so that the amount of saturated fat is limited.

For the other meat meals, use poultry, veal, fish, or meat substitutes.

The meat servings can be divided among the day's meals as you desire. For example:

2 ounces cooked chicken for lunch
and
4 ounces veal for dinner
or
A 3-ounce steak for breakfast
Fruit plate and skim milk for lunch
3 ounces fish for dinner

Meat substitutes: ¼ cup skim milk cottage cheese or 2 egg whites may be substituted for 1 ounce meat, fish, or poultry. Be sure to note that, although protein values are similar to meat, caloric values are not.

B. FATS AND OILS—Daily

Use: 2 tablespoons (6 teaspoons). 1 teaspoon of this may be "special" margarine. The oil may be used in cooking, added to food, or in salad dressings (see pages 27–28 and 68–69). It is important to use all of the prescribed polyunsaturated oil.

C. SKIM MILK, SKIM MILK BUTTERMILK—Daily

Use: 2½ cups fortified with A and D vitamins, or the equivalent in skim milk powder or evaporated skim milk.

D. VEGETABLES—Daily

Use: 3 or more servings to include: 2 or more servings of low calorie vegetables, 1 serving of which should be raw.

One additional serving of vegetable that can be either a low or medium calorie vegetable. One of the vegetables eaten should be either dark green or deep yellow.

NOTE: High-calorie or starchy vegetables are listed under Bread, Cereals, Cereal Products, and Starchy Vegetables (below).

E. FRUITS—Daily

Use: 3 servings fresh, frozen, or canned without additional sugar to include: ½ cup citrus fruit or citrus fruit juice, or 1 cup tomato juice

F. BREAD, CEREALS, CEREAL PRODUCTS, AND STARCHY VEGETABLES—Daily

Use: 4 servings. A possible choice would include:
1 serving whole-grain cereal for breakfast

2 slices bread
½ cup potato or rice

G. DIETER'S CHOICE

No additional calories are allowed on the 1200-calorie diet other than those supplied by Groups A to F.

H. MISCELLANEOUS (Contain little or no calories)

Use: Servings as desired:
Soups—clear broth, bouillon
Beverages—coffee, tea, coffee substitutes (without sugar, milk, or cream)
Seasonings—salt, pepper, herbs, spices, vinegar, and lemon juice

Here is a menu that illustrates the application of the 1200-calorie diet guide in meal planning:
6 teaspoons fat and oil allowance*
No Dieter's Choice

BREAKFAST
½ cup orange juice
½ cup cooked whole-wheat cereal
½ cup skim milk for cereal
1 slice whole-wheat toast
1 teaspoon "special" margarine (1)
Coffee or tea if desired

LUNCH
Open-face sandwich
   3-ounce serving sliced chicken
   1 slice bread with 1 teaspoon Mayonnaise★ (1)
½ cup carrots
Large tossed green salad with 1 tablespoon Low Fat French Dressing★ (1)
1 fresh pear or ½ cup water-packed pears
1 cup skim milk

DINNER
3-ounce serving roast beef
½ small baked potato with 1½ teaspoons Herbed Oil★ (1½)

* The number in parentheses is the teaspoons of oil or "special" margarine used in that particular food.

½ cup string beans with ½ teaspoon Orange Oil★ (½)
Large sliced tomato salad with 1 teaspoon Mayonnaise★ (1)
½ cup water-packed canned apricots
1 cup skim milk
Coffee or tea if desired

A 2000-calorie diet can be considered a high, medium, or low calorie diet depending upon the individual needs of the dieter. It may therefore be a reducing diet for some of you larger eaters, just a normal calorie diet for others, and, for still others, a diet for gaining weight.

When planning a menu for diets of 2000 calories or more,* include more concentrated foods, such as cereal products and higher calorie fruits, vegetables, and legumes. Sweets such as jams and jellies may be added more frequently as well as sweet desserts.

2000-Calorie Low Saturated Fat, Low Cholesterol Diet

    67 grams fat, including:
        11 grams saturated
        31 grams linoleic
        4 tablespoons (12 teaspoons) fat and oil allowance
    150 milligrams cholesterol
     88 grams protein

A. MEAT, FISH, AND POULTRY—Daily

Use: 6 ounces cooked lean meat, fish, or poultry. Limit the servings of beef, lamb, and pork to 4 a week. These servings (after cooking) must be only 3 ounces each, so that the amount of saturated fat is limited.

For the other meat meals, use poultry, veal, fish, or meat substitutes. The meat servings can be divided among the day's meals as you desire. For example:

    2 ounces cooked chicken for lunch in a sandwich
        and
    4 ounces veal for dinner
        or
    A 3-ounce steak for breakfast
    Skim milk cottage cheese and fruit plate and skim
    milk for lunch
    3 ounces fish for dinner

Meat substitutes: Protein foods to use in addition to, or in place of, meat are: skim milk cottage cheese, skim milk yogurt, dried peas and beans, egg white, walnuts, Walnut Butter★, and vegetable-protein

* See Chapter IV, page 30, for 2600-calorie diet.

meat substitute (see page 475). Be sure to note that, although protein values are similar to meat, caloric values are not.

NOTE: ¼ cup skim milk cottage cheese or 2 egg whites may be substituted for 1 ounce meat, fish, or poultry.

B. FATS AND OILS—Daily

Use: 4 tablespoons (12 teaspoons). 1 tablespoon of this can be "special" margarine. The oil may be used in cooking, added to food or in salad dressings (see pages 28–29 and 69–70). It is important to use all of the prescribed polyunsaturated oil.

C. SKIM MILK, SKIM MILK BUTTERMILK—Daily

Use: 3 cups fortified with A and D vitamins, or the equivalent in skim milk powder or evaporated skim milk.

D. VEGETABLES—Daily

Use: 3 or more servings of any low or medium calorie fresh, frozen, or canned vegetables or vegetable juices. Avoid those commercially frozen and canned vegetables to which fat or cream sauce has been added.

Be sure to include: 1 or more servings of green leafy or yellow vegetables, one of which should be raw.

NOTE: The high calorie or starchy vegetables are listed in Group F. Bread, Cereals, Cereal Products, and Starchy Vegetables (below).

E. FRUITS—Daily

Use: 3 servings fresh, frozen, or canned fruit without additional sugar to include: ½ cup citrus fruit or citrus fruit juice, or 1 cup tomato juice

F. BREAD, CEREALS, CEREAL PRODUCTS, AND STARCHY VEGETABLES—Daily

Use: 7 servings. A possible choice would include:
   1 serving whole-grain cereal for breakfast
   4 slices bread
   2 servings starchy vegetables such as potatoes, corn, or lima beans

G. DIETER'S CHOICE (see list on pages 480–81)—Daily

Use: 200 calories in foods you desire. The calories can be supplied by fruit, vegetables, grain products, nuts, olives, "special" desserts, soups, and sweets. Even though these foods are needed to supply your caloric requirements, try to choose foods that add extra vitamins, minerals, and protein to your diet. Don't choose too many "empty calories" such as in carbonated drinks, sugar, and candy. For your convenience, see the list of acceptable foods and their approximate caloric values, page 480. If you choose foods that contain part of your oil allowance, see pages 28–29.

H. MISCELLANEOUS (contain little or no calories)

Use: Servings as desired
Soups—clear broth, bouillon, and fat free beef-stock soups
Beverages—coffee, tea, coffee substitutes (without sugar, milk, or cream)
Seasonings—salt, pepper, herbs, spices, vinegar, lemon juice, and mustard

Here is a menu that illustrates the application of the 2000-calorie diet guide in meal planning:

12 teaspoons fat and oil allowance*
175–200 Calories Dieter's Choice†

BREAKFAST
½ cup orange juice
½ cup cooked whole-wheat cereal
[½ serving Basic Scrambled Eggs★] (½)
2 Whole-Wheat Muffins★ (1½)
2 teaspoons "special" margarine (2)
[1 teaspoon honey]
[1 teaspoon sugar]
1 cup skim milk
Coffee or tea if desired

* The number in parentheses is the teaspoons of oil or "special" margarine used in that particular food.
† The food enclosed in brackets [ ] is a Dieter's Choice.

LUNCH
Sandwich
  2 slices bread
  3-ounce serving chicken
  2 teaspoons Mayonnaise★ (2)
½ cup carrots
*Large tossed green salad with 1 tablespoon Low Fat French
  Dressing★ (1)*
1 fresh peach, sliced, or ½ cup canned peaches
1 cup skim milk

DINNER
  3-ounce serving roast beef
  ½ small baked potato with 1½ teaspoons Herbed Oil★ (1½)
  ½ cup string beans with ½ teaspoon Orange Oil★ (½)
  Large sliced tomato salad with 1 teaspoon Mayonnaise★ (1)
  ½ cup canned apricots
  [2 Oatmeal Cookies★] (1)
  1 slice whole-wheat bread
  1 teaspoon "special" margarine (1)
  1 cup skim milk
  Coffee or tea if desired

CHAPTER XXIX

Specially Restricted Diets

How to Build a Diet Extremely Low in Fat and Very Low in Cholesterol

UNDER certain conditions, it is necessary for your physician to recommend a very drastic restriction in total fat and cholesterol. The following guide is for such a diet. The saturated fat is very low and just enough oil is allowed to meet the body's requirement for linoleic acid (see page 461).

EXTREMELY LOW FAT AND VERY LOW CHOLESTEROL DIET
Approximately 2600 Calories*
18–20 grams fat
100 milligrams cholesterol
100 grams protein

A. MEAT, FISH, AND POULTRY—Daily

Use: 3 ounces cooked lean meat, fish, or poultry. Limit the servings of beef, lamb and pork to 3 a week. For the 4 other meat meals, use poultry, veal, or fish.

NONMEAT PROTEIN FOODS†

Use: ½ cup of skim milk cottage cheese or baker's cheese 3 or 4 times a week.
Cooked egg white as desired.
1 serving of vegetable-protein meat substitute daily (see Chapter XXXI, and page 475).

* Recommended Daily Allowance (RDA) for a moderately active man 5'8" weighing 154 pounds in the age group 35–55 years is 2600 calories.
† This Daily Food Guide differs from the others in requiring meat substitutes daily.

B. OILS—Daily

Use: 1 teaspoon safflower, soybean, corn, or cottonseed oil

C. SKIM MILK, SKIM MILK BUTTERMILK—Daily

Use: 5 or more cups fortified with A and D vitamins, or, the equivalent in skim milk powder or evaporated skim milk.

D. VEGETABLES—Daily

Use: 3 or more servings of any low or medium calorie fresh, frozen, or canned vegetables or vegetable juices. Avoid those commercially frozen and canned vegetables to which fat or cream sauce has been added.

Your choice of vegetables should include 1 or more servings of green leafy or yellow vegetables, one of which should be raw.

NOTE: The high calorie or starchy vegetables are listed in Group F. Bread, Cereals, Cereal Products, and Starchy Vegetables (below).

E. FRUITS—Daily

Use: 5 or more servings fresh, frozen, dried, or canned fruit to include:

At least 1 cup citrus fruit or citrus fruit juice
1 large serving dried fruit, cooked or uncooked, 3 or 4 times a week

F. BREAD, CEREALS, CEREAL PRODUCTS, AND STARCHY VEGETABLES—Daily

Use: 9 or more servings. A possible choice would include:

1 cup (2 servings) of whole-grain cereal for breakfast
6 slices bread
2 servings starchy vegetables such as potatoes, corn, or lima beans

G. OTHER CALORIES SUPPLIED BY:

2½ tablespoons jelly or jam or their caloric equivalent (125 calories)
2 servings of extremely low fat desserts such as angel food cake, fruit gelatin, and sherbet (see menu following)
2 teaspoons sugar

One Day's Menu for Extremely Low Fat and Very Low Cholesterol Diet:

BREAKFAST
1 cup orange juice
1 cup whole-grain cereal
1 tablespoon wheat germ sprinkled on cereal
½ cup skim milk for cereal
2 teaspoons sugar
2 slices whole-wheat toast
1 tablespoon jelly
1 cup nonfat milk
Coffee or tea if desired

LUNCH
1 cup chilled apple juice
1 serving Meatless Spanish Rice★
½ cup string beans
½ cup cabbage slaw with Fat Free Dressing★
¾ cup stewed dried apricots
1 slice whole-wheat bread
½ tablespoon jam or jelly
1 cup skim milk or skim milk buttermilk
Coffee or tea if desired

DINNER
3-ounce serving very lean roast beef with Fat Free Gravy★
½ cup Mashed Potatoes★
½ cup carrots
Tossed green salad with 1 teaspoon oil in dressing
1½ servings Marshmallow Pineapple Mousse★
1½ cups skim milk
2 slices whole-wheat bread
1 tablespoon jelly
Coffee or tea if desired

BEDTIME SNACK
Fruit flavored gelatin with bananas and Whipped Topping★
1 glass skim milk

Extremely Low Cholesterol

This Extremely Low Fat, Low Cholesterol Diet can be converted into a Vegetarian Diet with a cholesterol content of less than 50 *milli-*

grams by merely substituting a nonmeat protein food such as skim milk cottage cheese or a vegetable protein meat substitute for the 1 daily serving of meat allowed in the above diet.

Diabetic Low Saturated Fat, Low Cholesterol Diets

The person with diabetes on the low saturated fat, low cholesterol diet does have a definite dietary problem, but it is far from a discouraging one. His problem is much the same as that of the individual on a low calorie diet or a low carbohydrate diet. In all three cases, concentrated carbohydrates are forbidden. The generous use of low calorie fresh fruits and vegetables and water-packed canned fruits is a must for the diabetic. He is also able to include generous amounts of whole-grain cereals, cereal products, and skim milk products in his diet.

We have included a chapter on low sugar and sugarless desserts (made without cyclamates), many of which are suitable for diabetic diets (see page 398).

It is especially important that a person with diabetes should check his general diet plans with his physician or dietitian before starting on any diet. Then be sure to adhere strictly to the prescribed diet plan and measure accurately all food eaten.

Many local Heart Associations now have available low saturated fat diet guides planned especially for diabetics. These diets may be obtained from your local Heart Association if prescribed by your physician.

What if My Physician Allows Me to Eat an Egg?

The Daily Food Guides in this book may be increased or decreased in both fat and cholesterol according to your physician's recommendation.

If your physician allows you to eat 2 or 3 whole eggs per week, we suggest you do the following:

1. Choose the Daily Food Guide to fit your caloric requirements.

2. Limit your meat, fish, and poultry to 6 ounces cooked weight per day.

3. Limit the servings of beef, lamb, and pork to 3 per week. The cholesterol of the diet will then be increased to an average of approximately 300 milligrams per day.

Section III

CHAPTER XXX

Nutritional Science

In CHAPTER IV, Daily Food Guides are outlined to show what foods to include in planning menus for the low saturated fat, low cholesterol diets. Why is it necessary for you to follow such a guide? The answer is: to meet your nutritional needs even though you restrict cholesterol and saturated fat. Your nutritional needs are to satisfy your hunger and to provide your body with the materials (nutrients) it requires for growth, repair, and energy. There are three classes of foods—protein, carbohydrate, and fat. These foods plus minerals and vitamins are referred to as nutrients.* Experimental evidence indicates that the human body requires definite amounts of these nutrients daily.

"Since 1940, the Food and Nutrition Board has developed formulation of daily nutrient intakes that were judged to be adequate for the maintenance of good nutrition in the population of the United States. These formulations were designated as 'Recommended Dietary Allowances' (RDA); they were value judgments based on existing knowledge of the nutritional science which were subject to revision as new knowledge became available."† (See chart, page 472).

Why are these nutrient intakes recommended? In what foods are they most abundant? To answer these two questions, many of the nutrients will be briefly considered with particular emphasis on their place in the low saturated fat, low cholesterol diet.

---

* The U. S. Department of Agriculture defines nutrients as "Chemical substances that the body is known to require from food."
† Recommended Dietary Allowances, Publication 1694, Food and Nutrition Board, National Academy of Sciences—National Research Council, Washington, D.C., 1968.

Why Is Protein Essential?

Protein is a vital constituent of all living cells of animals and plants. Protein functions in the human body in many ways. It not only builds new body tissues but replaces worn ones, helps form enzymes and hormones, aids in protecting the body against infections, and promotes full growth and energy.

Proteins are built from units called amino acids. Since there are more than twenty-two separate amino acids widely distributed in nature, many different combinations and variations of proteins are found in foods. The kind and number of amino acids in milk differ from those in meat, yet both are called protein foods. The adult body can manufacture from food all but eight of the amino acids. These eight amino acids, which must be available in the food eaten, since the body cannot make them itself, are called "the essential amino acids."*

Proteins may be rated as complete (or of high nutritional quality), partially complete, and incomplete (or of low nutritional quality). The protein's rating depends upon the number and amount of essential amino acids it contains. A complete protein has all of the essential amino acids, while an incomplete protein lacks a significant amount of some of the essential amino acids.

An adult generally cannot maintain optimum health if his diet contains only proteins of partially complete and incomplete types, since they may all lack the same one or two essential amino acids. Half of an adult's daily protein intake should be in the form of complete protein.

What Protein Foods Are Available for This Diet?

COMPLETE PROTEIN (of excellent nutritional quality)
skim milk
skim milk powder
evaporated skim milk
skim milk cottage cheese
skim milk yogurt
lean meat, fish, or poultry
soy grits and soybeans
wheat germ
skim milk ricotta (if made entirely with skim milk)
baker's cheese
egg white

* Essential amino acids: isoleucine, leucine, lysine, methionine, phenylalanine, threonine, tryptophan, valine. Children require these eight plus histidine.

PARTIALLY COMPLETE PROTEIN (of fair nutritional quality)
   whole-grain cereals
   whole-grain cereal products
   legumes, such as dried beans of all kinds, split peas, and lentils
   walnuts

INCOMPLETE PROTEIN (of low nutritional quality)
   gelatin
   vegetable protein, as in corn
   fruit

Will My Diet Have Enough Protein for Optimum Health?

The RDA (Recommended Daily Allowance) for protein for a man of average size and moderate activity is 65 grams,* while for a woman it is 55 grams. All the Daily Food Guides in this book, including the reducing diets, more than meet this recommendation. Currently nutritionists advise a more liberal allowance than the RDA to provide for less obvious body needs, such as antibody formation and enzyme and hormone synthesis as well as for growth, repair, and maintenance. For this reason, most of the menu guides provide 80 grams or more of protein.

It is easy to plan menus high in protein, with most of the protein of the complete type, when using the guides in the Low Saturated Fat, Low Cholesterol Diet. We have planned even the restricted calorie Daily Food Guides to include at least the equivalent of the following complete protein†:

5 ounces cooked lean meat, fish, or poultry, supplying 40 grams protein
2½ cups skim milk, supplying   20 grams protein
The total complete protein from skim milk and meat is 60 grams protein

Then you will be adding complete and incomplete proteins to your menus from the other foods that you choose, such as:

	Approximate Amount of Protein
1 cup skim milk	8 grams
4 tablespoons skim milk powder	6
½ cup skim milk cottage cheese	19
1 cup skim milk yogurt	8
1 egg white	4
½ cup legumes	8
1 serving bread or grain products	2

* The protein, carbohydrate, and fat content of foods is usually expressed in terms of grams. Twenty-eight grams (or roughly 30) is equivalent to 1 ounce.
† Diet I and the other higher calorie diets allow more meat and skim milk.

As you can see, by following any of the Daily Food Guides you will have enough protein for optimum health.

It is extremely important that complete protein be included in every meal because research indicates that the body's chemical processes require that all of the essential amino acids be present at the same time for cell building and repair of body tissues. The all too common habit of skipping breakfast, eating a light lunch and a heavy evening meal is a very poor one nutritionally. You are then supplying the body with most of its required nutrients all in one meal; therefore, your body cannot utilize these nutrients as efficiently. This is particularly true for protein.

Since most people prefer to use their meat allowance at lunch and dinner, special attention must be given to planning the breakfast menu to include complete protein. With whole eggs restricted, skim milk products and egg whites become important as your complete protein for breakfast (see Chapter XXII). Try to include skim milk for breakfast whenever possible; one cup of skim milk supplies more protein than one whole egg.

If it is necessary to eat your entire meat allowance at one meal, then skim milk cottage cheese, skim milk yogurt, and vegetable protein entrees are excellent foods to incorporate protein into an otherwise protein-deficient meal.

What Part Do Carbohydrates Play in the Low Saturated Fat, Low Cholesterol Diet?

All fruits, vegetables, and cereal products contain large proportions of carbohydrates (sugar, starch, and cellulose*). The sugars and starches are broken down by the body for the production of heat and energy. Some foods, such as potatoes, bread, macaroni, and sugar, have very high proportions of carbohydrate and provide abundant calories or potential energy; while other foods, such as lettuce and tomatoes, are low in carbohydrate and consequently low in calories and in energy value. (See Chapter XXXI for caloric values.) Remember, though, that these low calorie fruits and vegetables are excellent sources of minerals, roughage, and vitamins and should be included in the diet. Carbohydrate foods such as fruits, vegetables, and whole-grain cereal products† are important for their energy value and their vitamin and mineral content.

* Cellulose is a complex carbohydrate that is indigestible by humans. It furnishes no calories but roughage in your diet. Celery fiber is an example.
† Other foods, such as milk and cheese, contain carbohydrates too, but are more important to the diet for their protein content, so are classified as protein foods.

Choosing your carbohydrate foods carefully is important. Too many of us eat "empty" calories (foods that provide calories but none of the essential nutrients) such as sugar and sweets, and carbonated and alcoholic beverages. Fruits, vegetables, and whole-grain cereals should provide most of the carbohydrates of your diet to ensure optimum nutrition.

Occasionally carbohydrate foods need to be carefully controlled, as in reducing diets, diabetic diets, and diets to control certain blood lipids (see Chapter XXV), but this should be done only on the advice of your physician. Too often, popular reducing regimens restrict the carbohydrates so much that health is impaired.

How Much Fat Is Essential in the Diet?

The exact amount of fat required by the human body is not known. Nutritionists agree, though, that the essential fatty acid, linoleic,* must be present daily in the diet. Even on the strictest of reducing diets, at least 1 teaspoon of liquid polyunsaturated vegetable oil should be included, since these oils are excellent sources of linoleic acid. The Low Saturated Fat, Low Cholesterol Diet more than meets this recommendation. Fat is important in the diet, for it serves as a concentrated source of food energy, carrier of fat soluble vitamins and part of the structure of cells. It is also important as a padding around vital organs if you don't store too much.

What Are Fats and Oils?

Fats and oils are composed of fatty acids chemically combined with glycerol. One classification is according to their fatty acid content—a useful classification for this diet. Each chemical unit (molecule) of fat is composed of a glycerol unit combined with three fatty acid units. There are hundreds of fatty acids.

The identifying portion of a fatty acid is composed of a straight chain of two or more carbon atoms (some have dozens) attached to each other and to hydrogen. In *saturated* fatty acids, each carbon is joined to the next one by a single bond. In *unsaturated* fatty acids, one or more pairs of carbon atoms are partially depleted of hydrogen atoms, thus freeing the bonds that would have held hydrogen and allowing the carbon atoms to be joined by a double bond. If there are two or more such double bonds in a fatty acid, it is *polyunsaturated*. *Monounsaturated* fatty acids are those with one double bond.

* Many fatty acids are found in food and body fat; an essential fatty acid is one that is necessary for normal nutrition and that cannot be synthesized by the body from other substances.

Glycerol
portion

Fatty acid
portion

This is a structural formula showing three fatty acids, a saturated (stearic), a monounsaturated (oleic), and a polyunsaturated (linoleic), combined with glycerol to form a triglyceride, or fat.

Hydrogenated fats are vegetable oils that have been solidified by hydrogenation, a process in which unsaturated double bonds are lost by saturating them with hydrogen. In this process at least some of the polyunsaturates are changed to monounsaturates and saturates. How saturated the oil becomes depends upon how many of the double carbon bonds are caused to take up hydrogen.

Saturation (or unsaturation) of a food fat is a matter of degree. Saturated, monounsaturated, and polyunsaturated fatty acids are all usually present in any single fatty food but in varying amounts. See the chart, page 484, for the fatty acid content of food fats. A food fat is termed *polyunsaturated* if most of its fatty acid content is polyunsaturated. *Saturated* fats are ones in which most of the fatty acid content is saturated. The ratio of the amount of polyunsaturated fatty acids in a fat, food, or food mixture to the amount of saturated fatty acids is sometimes given as the P/S (or PUS/S) ratio (or value).

Food tables often give the content of stearic, oleic, and linoleic acids in foods as an indication of the degree of saturation (or unsaturation) of the fat in the food. These are the fatty acids that occur in the largest amounts in most foods.

As the diagram above shows, stearic acid has an 18-carbon chain and is completely saturated, containing no double bonds. Fats with a high percentage of this acid are listed as "saturated."

Linoleic acid has an 18-carbon chain with two double bonds. Fats containing a high percentage of acids of this type are termed "polyunsaturated." We use the linoleic acid content of foods as a guide in selecting foods with high polyunsaturated fat content for our Daily Food Guides.

Oleic acid has an 18-carbon chain with one double bond and is, therefore, a monounsaturated fatty acid.

The oils containing a high percentage of unsaturated fatty acids such as linoleic are the ones to use on this diet. As can be seen from the table on page 484, these are: corn, cottonseed, safflower, sesame, soybean, sunflower seed, and walnut oil.

Vitamins

Vitamins are complex chemical substances found in food that play an important role as body regulators. They are required by the body for growth and good health. It is unwise, however, and could be dangerous to take large doses of any vitamin preparation without consulting a physician.

Vitamins are usually classified by their solubility as fat soluble vitamins and water soluble vitamins. The fat soluble vitamins—A, D, E, and K—are not destroyed by ordinary cooking methods and may be stored in the human body. The water soluble vitamins—the B complex and Vitamin C—can be destroyed by improper cooking methods, lost down the kitchen drain with the soaking and cooking liquids, or discarded in the manufacturing process of our highly refined foods. Water soluble vitamins are not usually stored by the body, so they must be included daily in the diet.

Fat Soluble Vitamins

VITAMIN A

Vitamin A is essential for normal growth and development and aids in maintaining resistance to infections, developing smooth healthy skin, and preventing night blindness. As can be seen by referring to the chart of Recommended Dietary Allowances (page 472) the RDA is a minimum of 5000 International Units of Vitamin A daily.

How can we provide enough Vitamin A without butter, cream, or whole milk, the excellent natural sources of this vitamin?* If fortified skim milk and "special" margarine are used in the amounts suggested in the Daily Food Guides, over half of your requirement will be met.† Fortunately the body is able to convert the carotene found in green leafy vegetables, yellow vegetables, and dried fruits into Vitamin A. Therefore, use these foods regularly in the low saturated fat, low cholesterol diet.

* Foods not allowed on the low saturated fat, low cholesterol diet are not, for obvious reasons, listed as sources for vitamins or minerals.
† Most skim milk and margarines are fortified with Vitamins A and D. If the dairy you patronize does not do this, we suggest you request it.

Vitamin D

Since the body can make Vitamin D under the influence of the sun's rays, this vitamin is often called the "sunshine" vitamin. Vitamin D helps build and maintain strong bones and teeth and prevents the disease rickets. Although the RDA is 400 International Units of Vitamin D daily, the National Research Council states that the exact adult requirement still is not known. The National Research Council does state, though, that most adults can meet their Vitamin D requirement by skin irradiation. This is encouraging since the foods high in Vitamin D are cream, butter, eggs, and liver. However, persons who have no opportunity for exposure to clear sunshine (the beneficial rays in sunlight are filtered out by ordinary window glass, fog, and smoke) should be sure to include "special" margarine and skim milk in their diet that is Vitamin D fortified.

Vitamin E

With the increased use of polyunsaturated fats in the diet, renewed interest has been shown in Vitamin E. Current research indicates that if the diet is high in polyunsaturated fats, as in our Daily Food Guides, the need for Vitamin E is increased. The exact role of Vitamin E in human nutrition is not known, but it seems to prevent oxidation of unsaturated fatty acids in the body, to maintain healthy cells, and to influence other vitamin utilization. Vitamin E is widely distributed in common foods acceptable in this diet, such as vegetable oils, margarine, wheat germ, dark green leafy vegetables, nuts, and whole-grain cereals.

Vitamin K

Vitamin K, actually a family of vitamins, is essential for human blood coagulation, the process that stops wounds from bleeding. Since the body can synthesize Vitamin K in the intestines and because Vitamin K is found in many foods such as cabbage, cauliflower, soybeans, soybean oil, spinach, and other green leafy vegetables, a Vitamin K deficiency is rare. Because reliable information is lacking concerning the amount of the human requirement for Vitamin K, a definite daily allowance has not been established for it.

Water-soluble Vitamins

Vitamin C or Ascorbic Acid

From ancient times, extreme deficiencies of ascorbic acid or Vitamin C have caused widespread occurrence of scurvy. Today, with the increased use of fresh fruits and vegetables, scurvy itself isn't prevalent, but milder forms of Vitamin C deficiency are all too common.

Ascorbic acid plays a complex and vital role in the body processes. It is needed for the proper growth of bone and teeth as well as for the production of strong intercellular material or connective tissue (which is very important in wound healing). Vitamin C is also involved in helping the cells to use oxygen, in the enzyme system, in the metabolism of the amino acids and in the utilization of other vitamins and iron. Evidence seems to indicate that during times of body stress the need for ascorbic acid is increased, e.g., during fevers and infections.

Fruits and vegetables are the main sources of ascorbic acid. Foods containing this vitamin in large amounts are the citrus fruits—oranges, lemons, and grapefruit. A 4-ounce glass of orange juice will supply your daily recommended allowance of 55 milligrams of ascorbic acid. Strawberries, tomatoes, honeydew melon, casaba, cantaloupe, watercress, green pepper, parsley, broccoli, and raw cabbage also supply liberal amounts of this vitamin. Potatoes, too, are a good source of Vitamin C. Since the body does not seem to store Vitamin C, the homemaker should plan to include one serving of citrus juice plus another serving of fresh fruit or vegetable in her daily menu plan.

Of all the vitamins, ascorbic acid is the most easily destroyed by exposure to air and by heat. That is the reason for storing all fruit juices in covered containers in the refrigerator. In cooking, the fruits and vegetables should be cooked in the shortest time possible and cooked in the smallest amount of water possible, for ascorbic acid is extremely water soluble. Much of this vitamin can be be lost in improper food preparation. (See Chapter XVI.)

THE B-COMPLEX

The need of the human body for adequate amounts of the B-complex vitamins is vital and cannot be overemphasized. Yet, owing to the use of highly refined foods, the average American diet is usually lacking in the B vitamins. What is commonly thought of as Vitamin B is in reality a group of vitamins including:

Thiamin or B_1	Vitamin B_{12}
Riboflavin or B_2	Folic acid (Folacin)
Niacin	Biotin
The B_6 group—pyridoxine,	Inositol
pyridoxal, and pyridoxamine	Choline
Pantothenic acid	Betaine

These collectively are known as the B-complex.

THIAMIN

Perhaps the best known member of the B-complex is thiamin. Many descriptive names are attached to it, such as the appetite vitamin, the pep vitamin, or the nerve vitamin. Each of these names describes one of its diversified functions. A lack of thiamin is often the cause of easy fatigue, loss of appetite, nervousness, a feeling of depression, muscle cramps, and constipation. In addition, the utilization of carbohydrate in the body requires thiamin, as does the enzyme system of the body.

Excellent sources of thiamin are all the whole-grain cereals, legumes, soy grits, unpolished rice or brown rice, nuts, yeast, and especially wheat germ. Special note should be made that green leafy vegetables are a good contributor of thiamin, provided the vitamins are not destroyed by overcooking.

NIACIN

Niacin receives considerable publicity as one of the antipellagra vitamins. Pellagra exemplifies a deficiency of vitamins in an extreme form (actually, pellagra is a multiple deficiency). A slight deficiency, however, can be harmful too, for niacin is necessary for utilization of food and for keeping the body tissues healthy; it is a vital part of the enzyme system. The more calories a person consumes, the more niacin he seems to require. This vitamin is not found abundantly in most fruits and vegetables, except mushrooms, but it is found in meat, legumes, skim milk, and whole grain cereals.

RIBOFLAVIN

A deficiency of riboflavin has many of the same effects as the lack of thiamin does, such as the loss of appetite and a feeling of fatigue. Riboflavin is noted particularly for its effect upon growth, its important role in maintaining healthy eyes, and its essential role in protein, fat, and carbohydrate metabolism. Meeting the riboflavin requirement is easy on the low saturated fat, low cholesterol diet because skim milk provides a rich source of this vitamin. It is important to protect the milk from prolonged exposure to sunlight, since riboflavin is easily destroyed by light. One half or more of the riboflavin in milk may be destroyed if exposed to sunlight for two hours. Other foods containing a high concentration of riboflavin are egg whites, green leafy vegetables, lean meats, and legumes.

Others of the Vitamin B Complex*

The current revision of the Recommended Daily Allowances suggests probable human requirements for folacin, the Vitamin B_6 group and Vitamin B_{12}. Vitamin research continues to determine more fully the exact functions in the body of these vitamins as well as all the others of the B-complex.

Folacin or Folic Acid is essential in humans for formation of body protein and for normal fat metabolism. It is also related to the production of red blood cells. Many foods contain folic acid; for example, beef, veal, fish, nuts, legumes, deep green vegetables, and whole-grain cereals.

Vitamin B_{12}, a truly potent vitamin, is another vitamin involved in blood formation and is given for the treatment of certain anemias. Muscle meat, fish, dairy products, and green leafy vegetables are good sources of this vitamin.

Vitamin B_6 Group, Pantothenic Acid and Biotin are all involved in fat, protein, and carbohydrate metabolism. Good food sources for pantothenic acid are legumes and whole-grain cereals, while the vitamins of the B_6 group are found in meat, particularly lamb and veal, as well as legumes, potatoes, and wheat germ. Biotin is fairly well distributed in food sources, although a biotin deficiency can be caused by using large quantities of uncooked egg white in the diet.

Choline and Betaine are believed by researchers to protect the body's liver against becoming a "fatty liver" and to promote the body's growth. Current research indicates *inositol* to be synthesized by the body, so it is not needed from dietary sources. Choline is distributed widely in plant and animal tissue, so a deficiency of choline is not likely to occur either.

Even a brief discussion of the B-complex shows the vital role these vitamins play in human nutrition. In menu planning, the number of different vitamins in this complex is not a serious problem to the homemaker because food rich in one of these vitamins usually contains several of the other B vitamins. Since liver is eliminated from the low cholesterol diet, more emphasis must be placed on using the whole-grain cereals, which are rich in the B-complex vitamins.

The use of highly refined foods and the modern milling of our cereal products can seriously deplete the B vitamins from our diets. Modern milling removes the outer layers of grains and the embryo or wheat germ. (10/11ths of the thiamin is removed from the wheat in milling.) Even so-called enriched flours do not return all the vital nutrients that were removed during the milling process. Although for

---

* Although liver and organ meats are excellent sources of several of the B-complex vitamins, they are not listed since they are not allowed on this diet because of their high cholesterol content.

digestion's sake the husk and some of the outermost layers of the seed must be removed, not nearly so much needs to be removed as the modern miller seems to think. The outer parts of the seed contain valuable nutrients; most of the protein and mineral salts are located in the outer coat, and most of the vitamins are located in the wheat germ. Fortunately, wheat germ may be purchased commercially, and the wise homemaker will use it liberally in her menu planning.

Whole wheat contains so many valuable nutrients that it is almost a complete food. The drawing shows how the vitamins, minerals, proteins, fat, and starch are distributed in the wheat kernel.

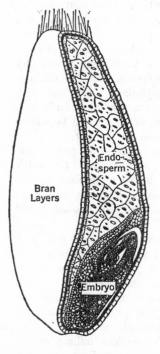

ENDOSPERM: The inner part of the wheat kernel, called the endosperm, consists mostly of starch and a small amount of protein (known as "gluten"). The endosperm contains almost no vitamins or minerals. White flour is made from this part of the kernel, which is low in those nutrients other than carbohydrates and proteins upon which we depend for our health.

BRAN LAYERS (the outside coat), in which are found: large amounts of VITAMINS; large amounts of MINERALS (iron to make good red blood and phosphorus for nerves and bones); PROTEINS of very good quality.

THE EMBRYO, or "wheat germ": This is the life-giving part from which the wheat plant sprouts and is one of the richest known sources of B vitamins and Vitamin E. It also contains valuable proteins and fat.

REDRAWN BY PERMISSION OF
OROWEAT BAKING COMPANY,
SAN FRANCISCO, CALIFORNIA.

Whenever possible, whole-grain cereals should be used, and 100 per cent whole-wheat bread or one of the highly fortified breads or cereals is a "must" in the diet; not only are they rich in vitamins but also in minerals (see the discussion of iron, page 470). Here again you should read the food label carefully; a hasty reading of it may be misleading. Certain cereal and bread labels boast that the product contains the daily requirements for the B complex, but they fail to note clearly that the entire box of cereal or the whole loaf must be eaten to meet the requirement.

In summary of this important group, the generous use of whole-grain cereals, legumes, green leafy vegetables, milk, and the recommended amount of meat, plus an additional supplement of wheat germ, will ensure the homemaker that her menus more than meet the recommended allowances for the essential vitamin B complex.

What Minerals Are Important on This Diet?

Only 4 per cent of your body's weight is composed of minerals; yet these minerals are in bones, teeth, soft tissue, muscle, blood and nerve cells and are involved in many vital body processes. Calcium, phosphorus, iron, chlorine, sodium,* sulfur, magnesium, fluorine and iodine are the principal minerals that man requires, and they need to be supplied daily.† In menu planning, particular emphasis should be placed on the minerals calcium and iron, since these are often deficient in the diet. If these minerals are supplied by natural and unrefined foods, the other minerals will also be automatically supplied, except possibly iodine and fluorine.‡

Calcium and Phosphorus

The skeletal system contains most of the body's calcium and phosphorus. Bone is constantly being synthesized and broken down chemically. Therefore it is extremely important that adequate amounts of these minerals be present all through a person's life to rebuild bone structure. Calcium and phosphorus are also present in the soft tissues and the body fluids, where they play essential roles.

Too often adults do not recognize that it is necessary to provide adequate calcium in their diet. To meet the RDA, the diet should provide 0.8 grams each of calcium and phosphorus, even for an octogenarian. Skim milk and skim milk products are excellent sources of these minerals. Three cups of skim milk meets the daily requirement for calcium and phosphorus.

* See "How to Restrict the Sodium on a Low Saturated Fat, Low Cholesterol Diet," Chapter XXVII.
† Other minerals, called trace elements, are found in minute amounts in the body; these trace elements are easily obtained from the diet without special consideration.
‡ The use of iodized salt and the fluoridation of water supplies these two minerals.

Calcium contents of one serving of the following foods are:

1 cup skim milk	0.29 grams calcium
1 cup yogurt	.29
½ cup skim milk cottage cheese	.1
1 slice bread	.01–.02
3 ounces lean meat	.01

The nonmilk drinker will find it extremely difficult to meet the RDA for calcium. A diet containing adequate protein and calcium will also contain enough phosphorus.

Iron

Iron is found in all body cells and is an important constituent of the blood. A deficiency of iron can cause anemia and lack of energy. Of all the nutrients, the RDA for iron is generally the most difficult to meet. In the low saturated fat, low cholesterol diet, the problem is increased, since excellent sources of iron such as egg yolk and liver are eliminated and red meat is restricted in quantity. It is therefore doubly important that other good sources of iron be included in considerable amount. They are: whole-grain cereals and bread (enriched, if possible), legumes, green leafy vegetables, dark molasses, wheat germ, and dried fruits, such as raisins, apricots, and prunes. The low calorie Daily Food Guides do not meet the RDA for men, and none of the Daily Food Guides for women meet the RDA, so an iron supplement may be necessary. Be sure to check with your physician.

Feed Plants with Egg Yolk

If you cannot use your surplus egg yolks in other cooking or for pets, perhaps you garden? Egg yolks are excellent plant food; they are especially convenient for potted plants because the smaller root space requires repeated applications of mild long-acting fertilizer. The ingredients of egg yolk are in about the right balance for growing plants as well as for chicks. The various chemical substances comprising value as plant food are all bound to the egg protein and hence have no harsh action on the tender roots; these substances are absorbed slowly as the protein is broken down by soil bacteria and the absorptive action of root hairs.

Suggested use: Blend 1 egg yolk in 1 quart of water. One quart of diluted yolk can be used to water plants in 10 6-inch pots (3 ounces per pot) or 20 4-inch pots (1½ ounces per pot). Be sure potted plants are well established. Applications of the blend twice a week during the growing season will give the plants approximately 2 grams of nitrogen per 6-inch pot, which is the seasonal requirement for vigorous plants. Large tubs and garden plants can be fed yolks also. Yolks contain approximately 0.56 grams of nitrogen per yolk. One cup of yolks is 100 grams and contains 23 grams of nitrogen, 0.6 grams of phosphorus, 0.14 grams of calcium, 0.01 grams of potassium, 5.5 milligrams of iron, and the trace elements and vitamins that are stimulating to plant growth.

FOOD AND NUTRITION BOARD, NATIONAL ACADEMY OF SCIENCES—NATIONAL RESEARCH COUNCIL
RECOMMENDED DAILY DIETARY ALLOWANCES,[a] Revised 1968

Designed for the maintenance of good nutrition of practically all healthy people in the U.S.A.

	Age[b] (years)	Weight (lbs)	Height (in.)	Protein (gm)	Fat-Soluble Vitamins Vitamin A Activity (IU)	Vitamin D (IU)	Vitamin E Activity (IU)	Water-Soluble Vitamins Ascorbic Acid (mg)	Folacin (mg)	Niacin (mg equiv)	Riboflavin (mg)	Thiamin (mg)	Vitamin B6 (mg)	Vitamin B12 (µg)	Minerals Calcium (g)	Phosphorus (g)	Iodine (µg)	Iron (mg)	Magnesium (mg)
MALES	10—12	77	55	45	2,500	4,500	400	20	40	0.4	17	1.3	1.3	1.4	5	1.2	1.2	125	10	300
	12—14	95	59	50	2,700	5,000	400	20	45	0.4	18	1.4	1.4	1.6	5	1.4	1.4	135	18	350
	14—18	130	67	60	3,000	5,000	400	25	55	0.4	20	1.5	1.5	1.8	5	1.4	1.4	150	18	400
	18—22	147	69	60	2,800	5,000	400	30	60	0.4	18	1.6	1.4	2.0	5	0.8	0.8	140	10	400
	22—35	154	69	65	2,800	5,000	—	30	60	0.4	18	1.7	1.4	2.0	5	0.8	0.8	140	10	350
	35—55	154	68	65	2,600	5,000	—	30	60	0.4	17	1.7	1.3	2.0	5	0.8	0.8	125	10	350
	55—75+	154	67	65	2,400	5,000	—	30	60	0.4	14	1.7	1.2	2.0	6	0.8	0.8	110	10	350
FEMALES	10—12	77	56	50	2,250	4,500	400	20	40	0.4	15	1.3	1.1	1.4	5	1.2	1.2	110	18	300
	12—14	97	61	50	2,300	5,000	400	20	45	0.4	15	1.4	1.2	1.6	5	1.3	1.3	115	18	350
	14—16	114	62	55	2,400	5,000	400	25	50	0.4	16	1.4	1.2	1.8	5	1.3	1.3	120	18	350
	16—18	119	63	55	2,300	5,000	400	25	50	0.4	15	1.5	1.2	2.0	5	1.3	1.3	115	18	350
	18—22	128	64	55	2,000	5,000	400	25	55	0.4	13	1.5	1.0	2.0	5	0.8	0.8	100	18	350
	22—35	128	64	55	2,000	5,000	—	25	55	0.4	13	1.5	1.0	2.0	5	0.8	0.8	100	18	350
	35—55	128	63	55	1,850	5,000	—	25	55	0.4	13	1.5	1.0	2.0	5	0.8	0.8	90	18	300
	55—75+	128	62	55	1,700	5,000	—	25	55	0.4	13	1.5	1.0	2.0	6	0.8	0.8	80	10	300

[a] The allowance levels are intended to cover individual variations among most normal persons as they live in the United States under unusual environmental stresses. The recommended allowances can be attained with a variety of common foods, providing other nutrients for which human requirements have been less well defined.

[b] Entries on lines for age range 22-35 years represent the reference man and woman at age 22. All other entries represent allowances for the midpoint of the specified age range.

CHAPTER XXXI

Low Saturated Fat,
Low Cholesterol Food Groups

(and their average servings)*

The "exchange lists" of the American Dietetic Association have been discussed in Chapter IV (see pages 26–27), where their use in planning menus is explained. This chapter tabulates some of the data.

A. Meat, Fish, and Poultry†

1 ounce very lean meat, fish, or poultry contains approximately:

2 grams total fat‡
21 milligrams cholesterol
8 grams protein
50 calories

3 ounces cooked meat is considered a serving. For accurate measurements use a small ounce scale.

---

* The data on equivalent food values other than meats and fats in this book are based primarily on material in "Meal Planning with Exchange Lists," prepared by a Joint Committee of the American Diabetes Association, Inc., and The American Dietetic Association, in co-operation with the Diabetes and Arthritis Control Program, National Center for Chronic Disease Control, Public Health Service, U. S. Department of Health, Education, and Welfare, 1950.

† Figures are "weighted" average composition of protein foods as given in Zukel, Marjorie: Revising Booklets on Fat-Controlled Meals, Journal of the American Dietetic Association, 54:22, 1969.

‡ "Weighted" figure for fat in 1 ounce meat is 2 grams, with 0.6 gram saturated fat and 0.1 gram of the fatty acid, linoleic acid. Zukel, ibid.

Beef, lamb, and pork (see Chapters VIII and IX)

These meats are limited to 4 servings per week.

Beef—very lean

    Ground round

    Roasts—pot roast, sirloin tip, tenderloin, rump, and cross-rib

    Steaks—flank, sirloin, rib, and round

    Soup meat—shank or shin

3 ounces (cooked weight) is approximately 2 slices roast beef, 3 by 3 by ¼ inches

Lamb—very lean and trimmed

    Roast—leg

    Chops—loin, rib

3 ounces (cooked weight) is approximately 2 to 3 small rib lamb chops (total raw weight, 6 ounces)

Pork—extremely lean and well trimmed

    Roast—sirloin and tenderloin

    Ham—center cuts, steaks, and butt and shank end

3 ounces (cooked weight) is approximately 2 slices center cut ham, 3 by 3 by ¼ inches

Poultry, fish, and veal

These meats may be used for 10 servings per week.

Poultry—(See Chapters VIII and XI)

    Chicken

    Turkey

    Cornish hen

    Duck

    Squab

    Pheasant

3 ounces (cooked weight) is approximately 1 leg and 1 thigh of a 2½- to 3-pound chicken

Fish—(See Chapters VIII and X)

    Use all kinds of fish except shellfish (see pages 79–80)

3 ounces (cooked weight) is approximately 4 ounces raw weight.

Veal—well-trimmed (See Chapters VIII and IX)

    Ground

    Roasts

    Steaks

    Chops

    Soup meats—shank or shin

3 ounces (cooked weight) is approximately 1 ground veal patty, 3 inches across and ½ inch thick.

Meat Substitutes

The following foods in the amounts listed contain approximately the same quantity of protein as does 1 ounce of meat (⅓ serving of meat). Because these foods contain negligible amounts of fat and cholesterol, they can be eaten in addition to or in place of your meat allowance on the low saturated fat, low cholesterol diet. These foods do differ from meat in caloric value; so remember not to exceed the total calories allowed in your individual Daily Food Guide. The following foods are excellent for enriching your menu with protein and calories without adding extra meat, fish, or poultry.

Food	Protein Equivalent of 1 ounce Meat	Approximate Calories
Skim milk cottage cheese	¼ cup	50
Egg whites	2	35
Egg white powder	4 teaspoons	35
Skim milk, liquid	1 cup	80
Skim milk, powder	5 tablespoons*	80
Skim milk yogurt	1 cup	85
Dried beans, lentils, etc., cooked	½ cup	115
Vegetable-protein main dish†	⅓ serving of recipe	varies

NOTE: It will take 3 times the amount of each food listed above to be equal in quantity of protein to 1 3-ounce serving of meat, fish, or poultry.

B. Fats and Oils

1 serving of oil‡ (1 teaspoon) contains approximately:
5 grams total fat
45 calories

* Depends on brand; read the label.
† See recipes for meatless main dishes, Chapter XIII. These recipes may contain some oil that must be figured as part of the oil allowance of the diet.
‡ One tablespoon of vegetable oil (an average of corn, cottonseed, safflower, and soybean oil) contains 14 grams of total fat. Of this total, 2 grams are saturated fat and 8 grams are linoleic acid.
One tablespoon of "special" margarine made with safflower oil contains 11 grams of total fat, of which 1.9 grams are saturated fat and 6.3 grams are linoleic acid.
One tablespoon of other "special" margarines contain 11 grams of total fat of which 2.5 grams are saturated and 3.7 grams are linoleic acid.
—From Zukel, Marjorie: Revising Booklets on Fat-Controlled Meals, Journal of the American Dietetic Association, 54:23, 1969.

Food	*Equivalent Amounts*
Corn oil	1 teaspoon
Cottonseed oil	1 teaspoon
Safflower oil	1 teaspoon
Sesame oil	1 teaspoon
Walnut oil	1 teaspoon
French Dressing★ (made with any of the above oils)	1½ teaspoons
Mayonnaise★ (made with any of the above oils)	1 teaspoon
"Special" margarine★	1 teaspoon
Walnuts	3 halves
Walnuts, chopped	1 tablespoon
Walnut Butter★	½ tablespoon

NOTE: The following foods may be exchanged for 1 teaspoon "special" margarine but not for oil in diets with 1800 calories or more.

Almonds	5 small
Almonds, chopped	1 tablespoon
Olives	5–6 small
Pecans	5 halves
Pecans, chopped	1 tablespoon

C. Skim Milk Group

1 serving of skim milk (1 cup) contains approximately:
Negligible fat
7 milligrams cholesterol
8 grams protein
12 grams carbohydrate
80 calories

Food	*Equivalent Amounts*
Skim milk, liquid	1 cup
Skim milk, dry powdered*	5 tablespoons
Skim milk, evaporated	½ cup not reconstituted
Skim milk buttermilk	1 cup
Skim milk yogurt	1 cup

* The amount of skim milk powder equivalent to 1 cup of skim milk depends on the brand used. Check the directions on the container.

D. Vegetable Group

Low Calorie Vegetables

These vegetables contain negligible carbohydrate, protein, and fat. You
may use as much as 1 cup at a time without counting the calories.
If 2 cups are used in one meal, count them as 1 cup of medium
calorie vegetable.

Asparagus	Mustard
Bamboo shoots	Spinach
Beans, string	Swiss chard
Bean sprouts	Turnip greens
Broccoli	Kohlrabi
Brussels sprouts	Lettuce
Cabbage	Mushrooms
Cauliflower	Okra
Celery	Peppers, green or red
Chicory	Radish
Cucumber	Sauerkraut
Eggplant	Squash
Escarole	Crookneck
Greens	Summer
Beet greens	Zucchini
Collard	Tomatoes
Dandelion	Tomato juice
Kale	Watercress

Medium Calorie Vegetables

1 serving (½ cup) contains approximately:
  Negligible fat
  2 grams protein
  7 grams carbohydrate
  35 calories

Artichoke (1 medium)	
Beets	Pumpkin
Carrots	Rutabaga
Onion	Squash, winter, acorn, Hubbard
Peas, green	Turnips

NOTE: High calorie and starchy vegetables are listed under Group F:
Bread, Cereals, Cereal Products, and Starchy Vegetables.

E. Fruit Group

1 serving of fresh, frozen, or canned fruit without sugar contains approximately:
Negligible fat
Negligible protein
10 grams carbohydrate
40 calories

Food	Amount for 1 Serving*
Apples	1 small, 2-inch diameter
Apple juice	½ cup
Applesauce	½ cup
Apricots, dried	4 halves
Apricots, fresh	2 medium
Apricot nectar	½ cup
Bananas	½ small
Blackberries	1 cup
Blueberries	⅔ cup
Boysenberries	1 cup
Cantaloupe	¼, 6-inch diameter
Cherries	10 large
Cranberry juice	⅓ cup
Dates	2
Figs, dried	1 small
Figs, fresh	1 large
Grapefruit	½ small
Grapefruit juice	½ cup
Grape juice	¼ cup
Grapes	12
Honeydew melon	⅛, 7-inch diameter
Mangos	½ small
Nectarines	1 medium
Oranges	1 small
Orange juice	½ cup
Papayas	⅓ medium
Peaches	1 medium
Peach nectar	½ cup
Pears	1 small
Persimmons	3 tablespoons
Pineapples	½ cup cubed
Pineapple juice	⅓ cup

* If the fruit has been frozen or canned in sugar, add 40 more calories per serving.

Plums	2 medium
Prunes, dried	2 medium
Raisins	2 tablespoons
Raspberries	1 cup
Strawberries	1 cup
Tangerines	1 medium
Watermelons	1 cup, diced

F. Bread, Cereals, Cereal Products, and Starchy Vegetables Group

1 serving contains approximately:
  Negligible fat
  2 grams protein
  15 grams carbohydrate
  70 calories

Food	Amount for 1 serving
Bread	1 slice
Biscuit, 2-inch diameter	1
Roll, 2-inch diameter	1
Muffin, 2-inch diameter	1
Corn bread, 1½-inch cube	1
Tortilla, 5½-inch diameter	
Cereal, cooked	½ cup
dry, flake, and puffed type	¾ cup
Flour	2½ tablespoons
Grits, cooked	½ cup
Macaroni, cooked	½ cup
Noodles, cooked	½ cup
Rice, cooked	½ cup
Spaghetti, cooked	½ cup
Vegetables, high calorie or starchy	
Beans and peas, dried, cooked (includes kidney, lima, and navy beans; black-eyed and split peas; cowpeas; etc.)	⅓ cup
Corn, fresh	⅓ cup or 1 small ear
Oyster plant	½ cup
Parsnips	⅔ cup
Popcorn	1 cup
Potatoes, white	1 small
Potatoes, mashed	½ cup
Potatoes, sweet	¼ cup or ½ small
Yams	¼ cup or ½ small

G. Dieter's Choice Group

Individual recipes in this book have the caloric value after each recipe.

Food	Approximate Calories*
Beverages†	
Beer, 8 ounces	115
Cocoa-Cola, 6 ounces	80
Fresca, 12 ounces	5
Ginger ale, 6 ounces	80
Diet 7-Up, 12 ounces	40
"Pop" (10–13% sugar), 6 ounces	80
Root beer	85
Skim milk, 1 cup	80
Skim milk buttermilk, 1 cup	80
Tab or Diet Pepsi, 12 ounces	70
Whiskey, 1½ ounces	115
Whiskey highball, 8-ounce glass with sweetened mixer	165
Wine, 3½ ounces	100
Bread, commercial, 1 slice	70
Candy	
Hard candy, 1 ounce	110
Gumdrops, 10 small	45
Marshmallows, 1 ounce	90
Cereals and Cereal Products	
Cooked cereal, ½ cup	70
Dry cereal, ¾ cup	70
Rice, macaroni, spaghetti, noodles, ½ cup (cooked)	70
Wheat germ, 1 tablespoon	15
Cheese	
Baker's, ¼ cup	50
Skim milk cottage cheese, ¼ cup	50
Desserts	
Angel food cake, ½₂ of 9-inch diameter cake	140
Commercial fruit-flavored gelatin, ½ cup	70
Honey, 1 tablespoon	60
Jam and jelly, 1 tablespoon	55
Syrup, 1 tablespoon	60
Sugar, 1 tablespoon	50

* Figures rounded to nearest 5.
† Low calorie beverages are cyclamate free

Egg white, 1 only	15
Fruit	
Fresh, frozen, canned without sugar, 1 serving	40
Canned with sugar, 1 serving	80–100
Fats and oils	
"Special" margarine, 1 teaspoon	45
Oil, 1 teaspoon	45
Mayonnaise★, 1 teaspoon	45
Nuts*	
Almonds, chopped, 1 tablespoon	45
Pecans, chopped, 1 tablespoon	45
Pecans, 5 halves	65
Walnuts, 4 halves	65
Walnuts, chopped, 1 tablespoon	45
Olives, 5–6 small*	45
Vegetables	
Low calorie, 1 cup	10–35
Medium calorie, ½ cup	35
Starchy or high calorie vegetables, ⅓ to ½ cup	70
Yogurt★, skim milk, 1 cup	80

H. Miscellaneous Group

These foods are allowed as desired, since they contain negligible calories.

Bouillon (fat free)	Rennet tablets
Clear broth	Saccharin
Coffee	Seasonings
Coffee substitutes	Spices
Gelatin, unsweetened	Tea
Lemon	Vinegar
Pickle, dill, unsweetened	

* These foods contain fat that must be calculated as part of your daily oil and fat allowance.

CHAPTER XXXII

Food Tables and Charts

THE tables and charts in this chapter present additional nutritional information about the foods in the low saturated fat, low cholesterol diet. These tables are included for your convenience in finding the approximate fat, protein, carbohydrate, cholesterol, and caloric content of foods. You may use these to calculate your daily menu or calculate your own recipes that you have modified to be acceptable for this diet. Included are the following:

1. MINI CHART OF APPROXIMATE NUTRIENT VALUES OF FOODS IN THE LOW SATURATED FAT, LOW CHOLESTEROL DIET

2. MINI CHART OF CHOLESTEROL VALUES

3. FAT CONTENT OF NUTS, SEEDS, AVOCADOS, AND OLIVES

4. FAT CONTENT OF COOKED MEAT

5. FATTY ACID CONTENT OF FATS AND OILS

The figures in the charts are adapted from:
United States Department of Agriculture Publications:

Composition of Foods, Handbook No. 8
Agricultural Research Service, 1963

Nutritive Value of Foods, Home and Garden Bulletin, No. 72
Agricultural Research Service, 1964

Revised Booklets on Fat-Controlled Meals, Marjorie C. Zukel
Journal of American Dietetic Association, January 1969, Vol. 54, No. 1

Composition of Loma Linda Foods, International Nutrition Research Foundation
Loma Linda Foods, Riverside, California

Additional cholesterol values are based on analyses by Dr. Ruth Okey, Professor Emeritus of Nutritional Science and Biochemistry, University of California, Berkeley.

For information on additional foods we suggest you consult the United States Department of Agriculture publications:

Handbook No. 8*
Food and Garden No. 72*

* For sale by the Superintendent of Documents, U. S. Government Printing Office, Washington, D.C. 20402 (Price: No. 8, 25 cents; No. 72, $1.50)

MINI CHART OF APPROXIMATE NUTRIENT VALUES OF FOODS IN THE LOW SATURATED-FAT, LOW CHOLESTEROL DIET*

Group	Food	Approximate Amount† Wt., gms.	Volume or number	Calories	Cholesterol mg.	Protein gm.	Carbo-hydrate gm.	Fat Total gm.	Fat Saturated Fatty Acid gm.	Fat Linoleic Acid gm.
A	Beef, Lamb, Pork, and Ham, *very lean*, cooked	30	1 oz.	65	21	9	—	3	1.3	—
	Fish, cooked	30	1 oz.	40	21	7	—	1.5	.3	.1
	Poultry, lean, cooked	30	1 oz.	50	18	8	—	2	.5	.3
	Veal, cooked	30	1 oz.	60	27	10	—	2	.8	trace
	Vegetable-burger	110	½ c.	125	—	21	5	3	.4	1.5
	Egg white	33	1	15	—	4	—	—	—	—
B	Oils									
	Corn	5	1 t.	45	—	—	—	5	.3	2.3
	Cottonseed	5	1 t.	45	—	—	—	5	1.3	2.3
	Safflower	5	1 t.	45	—	—	—	5	.3	3.3
	Soybean	5	1 t.	45	—	—	—	5	.6	2.3
	Safflower margarine	5	1 t.	35	—	—	—	4	.6	2.2
	Other "special" margarine	5	1 t.	35	—	—	—	4	.9	1.3
	Mayonnaise★	5	1 t.	45	—	—	—	5	.7	2.7
	Basic French Dressings★	15	1 T.	90	—	—	—	10	1	.5
	Walnuts, halves	50	½ c.	325	—	8	8	32	2	20
C	Skim milk, liquid	240	1 c.	80	7	8	10	neg.	—	—
	Skim milk powder	70	1 c.	250	21	25	36	neg.	—	—
	Skim milk cottage cheese	225	1 c.	200	16	38	6	neg.	—	—
	Skim milk yogurt	245	1 c.	80	7	8	12	neg.	—	—

D Vegetables, low calorie	100	½ c.	10	—	neg.	2	—	—	—
Vegetables, medium calorie	100	½ c.	35	—	2	7	—	—	—
E Fruit,‡ no added sweetening	100	½ c.	40	—	neg.	10	—	—	—
Fruit, canned in medium sirup	100	½ c.	80	—	neg.	20	—	—	—
F Bread	25	1 slice	70	—	2	15	—	—	—
Cereals and cereal products	100	½ c.	70	—	2	15	—	—	—
Vegetables, high calorie	100	¼–½ c.	70	—	2	15	—	—	—
Dried peas, beans, etc.	125	½ c.	115	—	8	20	neg.	figures not available	—
G Sugar	12	1 T.	50	—	—	12	—	—	—

* For a more complete list of foods, see Chapter XXXI, Groups A–G.
† Values are rounded off for convenience.
‡ For the fat content of avocados, olives, nuts, and seeds see page 487.

MINI CHART OF CHOLESTEROL VALUES*

	mg.
POULTRY (3 oz.)	54
BEEF, LAMB, PORK (3 oz.)	63
VEAL (3 oz.)	81
GLANDULAR MEATS (kidney, brain, etc.) (3 oz.)	375–2000
FISH (3 oz.)	63
SHELLFISH (shrimp, lobster, etc.) (3 oz.)	125–200
SKIM MILK (8-oz. glass)	7
WHOLE MILK (8-oz. glass)	27
BUTTER (1 oz.)	70
COTTAGE CHEESE WITHOUT CREAM (½ cup)	16
EGG WHITE	0
EGG YOLK (one)	275
OIL	0
VEGETABLES	0
FRUITS	0
NUTS	0
GRAINS (bread, cereals, etc.)	0
BROTH	0
GELATIN	0

* Figures are for average size portions: cooked meats, 3 oz.; milk, 8 oz.; cottage cheese, 4 oz. Values approximate.

FAT CONTENT OF NUTS, SEEDS, AVOCADOS, AND OLIVES

	Fat (total) per cent	Saturated per cent	Oleic Monounsaturated per cent	Linoleic Polyunsaturated per cent	Other unsaturated* per cent
FATTY ACIDS					
Shelled Nuts					
Almonds	54.2	4	36	11	3.2
Beechnuts	50.0	4	27	16	3
Brazil nuts	66.9	13	32	17	4.9
Cashews	45.7	8	32	3	2.7
Coconuts, dried	64.9	56	5	trace	3.9
fresh	35.3	30	2	trace	3.3
Filberts (hazelnuts)	62.4	3	34	10	15.4
Hickory nuts	68.7	6	47	12	3.7
Peanuts, roasted	48.7	11	21	14	2.7
raw	47.5	10	20	14	3.5
Pecans	71.2	5	45	14	7.2
Pistachios	53.7	5	35	10	3.7
Walnuts, black	59.3	4	21	28	6.3
English	64.0	4	10	40	10.0
Seeds					
Sesame, whole	49.1	7	19	21	2.1
Sunflower, hulled	47.3	6	9	30	2.3
Avocados	14.4	3	7	2	2.8
Olives	14.4	2	11	1	.4

* These fatty acids may be either mono- or polyunsaturated.

FAT CONTENT OF COOKED MEAT

The following chart compares the fat content of the *leanest* part of various cuts of lean cooked meat with each other and with the fat content of each *entire* meat cut (lean part plus marbled part) based on tests of meat from which the separable fat has been removed. You can see how your fat intake is reduced when you eat only the lean section rather than the lean plus the fat-marbled section of a cut of meat.

CUT OF MEAT*	LEANEST SECTION	ENTIRE CUT (*after separable fat has been removed*) (*Lean plus Marble*)
	Fat per cent	Fat per cent
BEEF		
Eye of round	No marbling; value same as for entire cut	6
Flank steak	7	10
Bottom round	8	10
Top round	5	7
Sirloin steak	6	11
Tenderloin steak	9	13
Sirloin tip roast	4	7
Arm pot roast	8	14
Heel of round pot roast	5	10
Rolled neck pot roast	6	13
Lean rump roast	8	11
Lean ground beef	Fat content depends on cut of meat used	
LAMB		
Leg	6	8
Loin chop	7	12
PORK		
Fresh ham, center cut	6	9
Sirloin roast	7	11
Tenderloin		12
Cured ham, butt end	5	11
Cured ham, shank end	6	14

VEAL

Loin chop)		7
Rib chop)		8
Arm steak)		5
Blade steak)	value same as for entire cut†	8
Cutlet, round)		4
Sirloin steak)		6
Rump roast	2	5
Sirloin roast	3	6
Lean ground veal	Fat content depends on cut of meat used	

LEAN POULTRY†

Light meat	value same as for entire cut†	3–4
Dark meat	value same as for entire cut†	6–8

FISH‡   value same as for entire cut‡   1–15§

* These are the leanest cuts of cooked meat from approximately fifty cuts tested. Figures are rounded out to nearest 1 per cent. Adapted from: Leverton, Ruth M., and Odell, George V., *The Nutritive Value of Cooked Meat*. Miscellaneous Publication, MP-49, Oklahoma State University, 1958.
† There is no marbling in lean cuts of veal, poultry, and fish and thus no "leanest section". The *entire* piece may be eaten after removing separable fat.
‡ Adapted from: *Handbook No. 8*, U. S. Department of Agriculture, 1963, and *Home and Garden Bulletin No. 72*, U. S. Department of Agriculture, 1964.
§ Fish vary a great deal in fat content. Fish fat is not as saturated as fat in other meats. See page 116 and footnote, page 77.

FATTY ACID CONTENTS OF FATS AND OILS*

Fat or Oil	Fatty Acids (per cent by weight)† *Saturated* per cent	*Oleic* (*monounsaturated*) per cent	*Linoleic* (*polyunsaturated*) per cent
Animal			
Beef tallow	48	50	2
Butter	46	27	2
Chicken fat	23	53	24
Fish oil‡		highly unsaturated	
Lard	38	46	10
Vegetable			
Cocoa butter	60	37	3
Coconut oil	90	8	2
Corn oil	10	28	53
Cottonseed oil	25	21	50
Margarine			
Hydrogenated§	60–68	18–24	9–22
Liquid oil§ ("special" margarines)	15–23	41–51	26–43
Olive oil	11	76	7
Palm oil	45	40	9
Peanut oil	18	47	29
Rice oil¶	18	48	34
Safflower oil	8	15	72
Sesame seed oil	14	38	42
Soybean oil	15	20	52
Sunflower seed oil	12	20	63
Walnut oil	7	18	75

* Adapted largely from U.S.D.A. Handbook No. 8.

† The total of fatty acids given does not always equal 100% because some unlisted fatty acids are also present.

‡ About 50% of the fat in many fish is composed of highly unsaturated fatty acids other than linoleic. Fish liver oils are high in cholesterol and must not be used in this diet.

§ First ingredient named in the list of ingredients on the label. Percentages of fatty acids vary a great deal depending on the margarine. Some margarines contain animal fat.

¶ Source: Kik, M. C., *Bulletin No. 416*, University of Arkansas Experiment Station, 1942.

Recipe Index

(Sugar-free means No-sugar or Low-sugar)

General Index

COOKING EQUIVALENTS

(approximate)

3 tablespoons dry cocoa plus 1 1/2 teaspoons
oil equals 1 square chocolate

1/2 pound cottage cheese or baker's cheese equals 1 cup

1 tablespoon cornstarch equals 2 tablespoons
flour (for thickening)

1 egg white equals 2 tablespoons (in volume)

8 to 11 egg whites equals 1 cup

4 cups all-purpose flour equals 1 pound

5 cups cake flour equals 1 pound

2 cups flaked fish equals 1 pound

1 large lemon equals 1/4 cup lemon juice

2 cups ground meat equals 1 pound

1 cup skim milk plus 2 teaspoons oil equals 1 cup whole milk

1 cup skim milk plus 1 teaspoon oil equals 1 cup low-fat milk

1/4 cup skim milk powder plus 1 cup water
equals 1 cup skim milk

1 cup less 1 tablespoon skim milk plus 1 tablespoon vinegar
equals 1 cup sour skim milk

1/3 cup vegetable oil equals 1/2 cup shortening or butter

2 cups granulated sugar equals 1 pound

2 2/3 cups light brown sugar equals 1 pound

1 tablespoon instant minced onion plus 2 tablespoons
water equals 1/4 cup
(4 tablespoons) finely minced fresh raw onion
or one medium-size onion